To our students

A Practical Guide for Writers

Diana Hacker
Betty Renshaw

With a section on research writing by Lloyd Shaw

A
PRACTICAL
GUIDE
FOR
WRITERS

Second Edition

Little, Brown and Company

Boston   Toronto

Library of Congress Cataloging in Publication Data

Hacker, Diana.
    A practical guide for writers.

    Includes bibliographical references and index.
    1. English language—Rhetoric. I. Renshaw,
Betty. II. Title.
PE1408.H27 1982   808'.042   81-12964
ISBN 0-316-336939   AACR2

Library of Congress Catalog Card No. 81-12964

ISBN 0-316-336939

9 8 7 6 5 4 3 2 1

RM

Published simultaneously in Canada
by Little, Brown & Company (Canada) Limited

Printed in the United States of America

Cover design by Susan Marsh
Interior design by Susan Marsh and Richard Maurer

The articles on pages 63–65 are reprinted with permission of The Washington Post.

Contents

Preface

A Practical Guide for Writers is a rhetoric and handbook for college students. Today's college students, whether they attend a four-year university or a community college, are a diverse group. They include grandmothers and sixteen-year-olds, dorm residents and commuters, disabled veterans and returning housewives. Many, but not all, read on the college level. A few are budding writers, but the writing goals of most are more modest. We have attempted to reach all of these students with a book that is readable but not simplistic, supportive but not patronizing.

Furthermore, we have attempted to make *A Practical Guide for Writers* adaptable to a variety of teaching styles. The rhetoric section can be used either with or without further elaboration; the supporting exercises suggest many different kinds of activities for both in and out of class; the handbook invites classroom discussion, if desired, or it can be used exclusively for reference.

Other features include:

- an emphasis throughout on writing as a process—often a chaotic process, but one that can be learned
- a focus on the writing situation, to encourage awareness of purpose and audience
- recognition of writing as a real-life pursuit
- a section on finding a writing voice and choosing appropriate language
- a step-by-step discussion of how to support a point in writing
- separate chapters on describing, narrating, and informing
- rhetorical principles illustrated by student writing
- a thorough discussion of research writing, with a sample paper
- more than a hundred writing topics that encourage students to write about what they know
- sample student papers, so that students can see what has worked for other students

- a variety of stimulating exercises
- a nonthreatening, thorough approach to problems in mechanics and usage
- an analysis of "dialect interference" problems, to help students become skillful readers of copy
- an informal, friendly style throughout
- avoidance of unnecessarily difficult vocabulary and syntax
- a careful attempt to avoid ethnic, class, and sexist bias.

The second edition of *A Practical Guide for Writers* is a better book than the first edition, we feel, because of these improvements:

- more student writing-in-progress
- an improved chapter on voice, emphasizing purpose, audience, and the writer's stance
- a new chapter on argument
- an expanded chapter on paragraphs, including methods of development
- more exercises that require writing
- sample student papers, now organized by modes
- an improved section on research writing
- new exercises in the handbook section
- writing topics refined to suggest a clearer sense of purpose and audience.

An instructor's manual is also available.

We continue to hope that *A Practical Guide for Writers* will reflect throughout our general approach to the whole process of writing: that learning about it is a human exchange between student and teacher, and that its results are a human exchange between writer and reader. To this end, we strive to be as sympathetic toward and supportive of the budding student writer as possible. We hope that by using this book, he or she can become more and more comfortable when confronted with that most complex and challenging of human activities—trying to communicate on paper with other human beings.

Acknowledgments

For their help with the second edition of A *Practical Guide for Writers*, we want to thank:

Our reviewers: Anna Y. Bradley, Mott Community College; Jean Brenkman, University of Wisconsin, Madison; George E. Gadda, University of California at Los Angeles; Gail Morrison, Midlands Technical College; Alice O'Melia, Essex Community College; Jeanne Sharp, Cazenovia College; and Tom Waldrep, University of South Carolina at Columbia.

Our colleagues at Prince George's Community College for their contributions and for their encouragement and support as we worked to make the second edition a better textbook than the original.

Our students whose writing appears in the second edition: Elizabeth Anderson, George Andrews, Louise Barr, Lisa Bennett, Henry Bertagnolli, Wesley Bickham, Emily Boyle, Joan Bradley, Yvonne Bridges, Michael Buongiorne, Judith Burgin, Marjorie Carson, Dorothy Carter, Frank Cohee, Gloria Connor, Jacqueline Cosey, Barbara Crossley, Mike DeGrandchamp, Robert Ducharme, Joan Easterling, Helen Eisenberg, Michael Elmore, Deborah Fletcher, Charles Ganley, Debra Harman, Thomas Insley, Robert Jeanotte, Brenda Jenkins, Beverly Johnson, Mary Kenny, Renee Klar, Catherine Knudsen, Martha Krause, Cathy Lawson, Bill Leith, Kathleen Lewis, Daniel MacFarland, H. C. McKenzie, Patricia Marquis, Kelly Meier, Pam Mitchell, Carlos Moncada, Anita Myers, Pat Napolitano, Karen Niswander, Ruth Parker, Doris Paugh, Nancy Powell, Nolan Presnell, Irene Rabun, Ethel Ramsey, Johnnie Randolf, Anne Reeves, Ruth Rezendes, Betty Ricketson, Marnita Riley, Irene Robb, Daryl Roe, Catherine Salsbury, Jenny Shelton, Jon Singleton, Margaret Smith, George Snellings, Cynthia Sofranko, Martina Solliday, Joyce Spring, Margaret Stack, Jefferson Stewart, Karen Sutton, Cynthia Syczepanski, Karen Thomas, Cleopatra Tyson, Marie Visosky, Tom Weitzel, Linda White, Andrew Woycitzky, and Sharon Wultich.

Our expert—and enduring—typist, Wanda Stewart.

All the people at Winthrop Publishers who saw the book through to completion: Denise Moderack, Roger Ratliff, Diane Ude, and freelancers

Susan Marsh and Pat Torelli. And of course and always, Paul O'Connell, sustainer of the book.

Note: We would welcome suggestions from other instructors for improving the book.

Diana Hacker
Betty Renshaw
Prince George's Community College
Largo, Maryland

A Practical Guide for Writers

PART ONE

The writing process

1 Getting started

If I start very early in the morning, with a fresh pot of coffee, sharp pencils, plenty of paper, a cat on my lap, and total silence, I might come up with something. A student

Some people think they should be able to sit down at a desk, take out a clean sheet of paper, pick up a pen or pencil, and begin to write. They feel that the writing should just come off the top of their heads, cold, unpremeditated. But the experience of just about everybody we know or have read about, including ourselves, says that is just not the way good writing happens. What has to happen first, often long before you sit down to write, is a less consciously directed, more random kind of thinking. You begin by musing, exploring, discovering—by letting your ideas go where they want to. You give yourself time for creative thinking.

Creative thinking

Creative thinking can occur almost anywhere, often while you are doing something else. Agatha Christie, creator of mystery stories that have delighted generations of readers, found that the best time for planning a book was while doing the dishes. American writer James Gould Cozzens says of his free-thinking time: "I meditate and put on a rubber tire with three bottles of beer. Most of the time I just sit picking my nose and thinking." Virginia Woolf, a British writer, planned much of her writing during long bubble baths. And one of our students says, "Many ideas come to mind before I fall asleep, when it's quiet and restful."

If you lead a busy life, you'll want to do your creative thinking while you are driving to work, cleaning house, taking a walk, or engaged in some other activity that does not require much concentration. Toni Morrison, a contemporary American author, tells us, "When I sit down to write I never brood. I have so many other things to do with my children and teaching that I can't afford it. I brood, think of ideas, in the automobile when I'm driving to work or in the subway or when I'm mowing the lawn. By the time I get to the paper something's there—I can produce."

Scribbling on scratch paper

While you are doing your creative thinking, make some random notes on whatever scratch paper is available at the moment. Don't worry about organizing your thoughts at this stage; just be sure to write down enough so you can decode it later.

Getting this much down on paper at once, as the thoughts are flowing, will help you when you finally sit down to write. Professional writers scribble ideas on the backs of envelopes, on recipe cards or paper bags or cocktail napkins or scraps of cardboard—whatever happens to be handy at the time. Anne Tyler, a writer and mother of two, remarks: "In the evenings, occasionally—between baths and other sorts of chaos—a sudden idea will flash into my mind . . . I write it down on an index card and take it to my study."

One of our students says: "I sometimes have to write on anything I can get my hands on when my thoughts are running quickly. I must write them down so I can return to them later." Another student comments: "Sometimes things pop into my head just before I go to sleep. Then I have to jump up and jot them down right away. I just scrawl, but if I don't do it then, I'll lose them."

Your scratch-paper scribblings don't need to be fancy, and only rarely will they resemble formal outlines. One of our students, for example, scrawled just these notes as she was generating ideas for a paper contrasting the glamorous image of flight attendants with the reality as she had experienced it:

How I was hooked
-- TV ad (Broadway Joe)
-- first-class flight to Dallas,
with champagne
-- good interview--I came off poised,
sophisticated, very much an adult
--excitement of being accepted

The reality
   *—six week course, with curfews and
   room searches, emphasis on beauty,
   pretended emphasis on safety
   —first trip: I was more a coffee
   and soda dispenser than a
   safety expert
   —lonely layovers, such as Christmas
   in Kansas City (of course I could
   always check my stack of
   businessmen's calling cards!)*

. . . .

When our student later sat down to write the paper, these notes
helped her get started. Within less than an hour she was able to draft a
rough version of the paper, which she later revised and polished into this
final draft:

Broadway Joe enters the cabin, smiles at the camera and says, "When
you've got it, flaunt it." Such an inducement was hard for a nineteen-year-old
to ignore, so I sent in my application for the position of airline stewardess.

All potential employees were flown to Dallas for their interviews. On the
day of my appointment there were two of us in first class. We received a great
deal of champagne and an equal amount of advice. It seemed to me that
Riley's life was rough when compared to that of a stew.

During the testing and interview, I remained unusually calm and poised. Of
course, I owed most of my relaxed demeanor to half a bottle of bubbly. When
the acceptance letter arrived ten days later, I was thrilled and so was my family.

The schooling was a six-week course consisting of early curfews, room
searches and weekly dismissals. In between these regimental restrictions, we
attended classes on makeup, on nail and hair care, on walking, talking, and
serving. The apex of the course was a week of training in first aid, federal
safety standards and evacuation procedures. During this week, we were
brainwashed into thinking the main reason for being on the plane was to fill
the role of safety expert. We were responsible for the lives of every passenger.
In case of emergency, this knowledge would be vital. The spirits of all the
students soared with the understanding of how important our jobs would be.

On my virgin trip, I soon learned that I functioned more as a coffee and soda dispenser than a safety expert. While we were refueling at the San Antonio airport, a woman in first class lighted a cigarette. I informed her that smoking was not allowed because of the fire hazard. "Go away, you silly girl," she replied. "I've been flying much longer than you. When you get a chance, bring me another martini." So much for safety expertise.

As for the excitement and glamour, I never saw it. When you first work in this job, you are on reserve. This means you fill in when a pattern-holder can't. By the time you have enough seniority to hold a monthly pattern, you've become so hardened that you either hide in the galley hoping no one will board or you quit. I chose the latter, but not before experiencing some very sad and lonely times.

The most lonely times were the "layovers," a normal part of the working trip. They involved spending the night in a motel room, eating cold sandwiches for dinner, and washing out a dirty uniform for the next day's flight. Sometimes I wasn't lucky enough to make it to a motel. I can remember spending my first Christmas eve away from my family sleeping on a bench in the Kansas City airport. Of course when I was really lonely, I could always refer to the stack of calling cards that were passed out by deplaning salesmen—"If you're ever in Chicago, give me a call and I'll show you around."

Flying did provide me the opportunity to visit places I might never have seen. I was also able to establish some close friendships and absorb some realities about people and life that have proved invaluable. But where was all the glamour behind those exotic places and beautiful faces? It existed in the Fifth Avenue ads and in the minds of those who had never been there.

Your writing environment

If any magic is connected with writing, it may come from your writing place. The more at home you are in the place where you write, the more free and easy you will feel. And there is likely to be a particular time of day or night when writing will come most easily for you. Carson McCullers did her writing "in a quiet room in the early morning hours." Van Wyck Brooks, on the other hand, believed that "as against having beautiful workshops, studies, etc., one writes best in a cellar on a rainy day." One of our students reports: "I write in the quiet of night, when the children are sound asleep." Another says he writes "whenever there's free time, wherever there's free space . . . and lots of coffee."

Certain items—coffee, cigarettes, coke, milk, a favorite pen, a legal pad, music—seem to be essential to some people as they write. We suggest you surround yourself with whatever you need to get started. Carson McCullers said that she took a thermos of tea to her quiet room. Ernest Hemingway wrote his more poetic descriptive passages with a pencil; he said he needed to hear the lead move on the paper. But he typed out his sharp-edged action sentences while standing at a chest-high desk. Thomas Wolfe did much of his writing while leaning on the top of a refrigerator; he was so tall that he was most comfortable in that position.

Another writer we know does all her first-draft writing seated in the corner of a worn sofa, with containers of both hot coffee and iced water at hand. She writes on a beat-up clipboard, with a large supply of freshly sharpened yellow No. 2 pencils close by. She cannot write very well anywhere else. Nor can she write at night. On the other hand, one of our students says she can write anywhere she can get comfortable: "in the tub, in bed, on the floor, in a semidark room, almost anywhere."

Tools of the trade

To do anything well, you need the right tools—and writing is no exception. Beyond plenty of paper and the writing instrument that feels best to you, you will need some items to help you be *flexible* as you write. With these you can cut and paste and rearrange what you write in numerous ways as you work toward your final draft. We recommend that you have handy sharp scissors, a stapler or transparent tape, and more paper, to attach your clipped pieces to as you cut and tape and rearrange your work.

Certain books will help you as you develop your writing skill. In addition to this book, we suggest that you have at your elbow at least two paperback reference books: a good, reasonably current dictionary, and a dictionary of synonyms and antonyms or a college thesaurus, which you will find an invaluable mine of words to enrich your writing. If you have serious spelling problems, an inexpensive dictionary that lists thousands of words (the words only, so you don't have to wade through definitions) will be a must for you.

Actually getting started

If you're like most writers, you'll do almost anything to avoid writing that first sentence. Suddenly your car needs washing, your refrigerator has to be defrosted, your closet demands a thorough cleaning. Even when you've all but chained yourself to your desk you find ways to avoid that blank sheet of paper. Your typewriter ribbon must be changed, the desk has to be cleaned, and your notes must be arranged in an elaborate, color-coded outline. Writer Jacques Barzun advises us at this point to "suspect all out-of-the-way or elaborate preparations. You don't have to sharpen your pencils and sort out paper clips before you begin."

Professional writers have discovered ways of forcing themselves to get started. Barzun, who assures us that "no writer has ever lived who did not at some time or other get stuck," begins by letting his first sentence "be as stupid as it wishes." Another author we know of types or scribbles gibberish, just to warm up his cold brain and get his fingers moving. Both these professionals assume that their first sentence will be thrown away; knowing this, they're not afraid to write it.

Flannery O'Connor, a Southern writer, had a method of getting started that you might consider. She set aside a regular time period for writing. As she told a group of students, "Every morning between nine and twelve, I go to my room and sit before a piece of paper. Many times I sit for three hours with no ideas coming to me. But I know one thing: if an idea does come between nine and twelve, I am there ready for it."

If you're attracted to Flannery O'Connor's method, try modifying it to fit your own writing needs. We would guess that you won't sit for hours without writing a thing. Sitting is too boring. And besides, you will have all those notes on scratch paper to help you get started.

. . . .

Exercise 1   For thought and discussion
. . . .

Professional writers have had a lot to say about "how I write." Mull over the following comments by professional writers to see what ideas you might pick up from them.

a. My working habits are simple: long periods of thinking, short periods of writing.
Anonymous

b. One takes a piece of paper, anything, the flat of a shingle, slate, cardboard and [writes] with anything handy . . . The blankness of the writing surface may cause the mind to shy . . . [but] Write, write anything . . . it is absolutely essential to the writing of anything worthwhile that the mind be fluid and release itself to the task.
William Carlos Williams, American poet

c. (on free writing, in a diary): . . . written rather faster than the fastest typewriting . . . the advantage of the method is that it sweeps up accidentally several stray matters which I should exclude if I hesitated, but which are the diamonds of the dustheap.
Virginia Woolf, British novelist and essayist

d. I just sit at my typewriter and curse a bit.
P. G. Wodehouse, British writer

e. When you start to write, you perceive many more relationships in your material than you were aware of at the start.
Albert D. Van Nostrand, professor of English

f. Get it down. Take chances. It may be bad, but it's the only way you can do anything really good.
William Faulkner, American author

g. I don't type [when I write] because . . . I often have the feeling that everything flows directly from my right hand.
Anne Tyler, American novelist

h. The more you write, the more you can write.
Anonymous

i. Writers kid themselves—about themselves and other people. Take the talk about writing methods. Writing is just work—there's no secret. If you dictate or use a pen or type or write with your toes—it is still just work.
Sinclair Lewis, American author

. . . .
Exercise 2 Written
. . . .

Our students have come up with some choice comments about the writing process as they experience it; some of these are quoted below. Try commenting on your writing process in a similar concise statement.

1. I just sit at my typewriter and talk to myself.

2. Quiet music makes my head spin. As it is spinning, the ink flows swiftly from my pen.

3. I write better under pressure of a deadline.

4. When writing about the forest, I go into the forest; when writing about the ocean, I go to the beach. Environment is everything.

5. I find a comfortable place to relax, fix something to drink, have my cigarettes handy and begin to put my thoughts together.

6. I swear a lot.

7. When I begin to write, that's exactly what I do—begin to write.

8. I must be alone, where there are no distractions.

9. I write either clothed or nude. Sometimes being nude allows me to be more open.

Exercise 3 For thought and discussion

Much has been written in recent years about the functions of the right and left hemispheres of the human brain. The theory is that the right brain is the seat of intuition, flexible thinking, and creativity generally, while the left brain controls our more systematic, analytical, rational thinking. One might say that the left brain is intellectual and the right brain intuitive. If this is true, then we need to be able to free up our right brains as much as possible during the initial, exploratory phase of the writing process, saving our left brains for later when we organize and clarify our thinking and writing. The following quotations might help you figure out how to open up your right brain and let it play around more freely.

a. There are few experiences quite so satisfactory as getting a good idea. You've had a problem, you've thought about it till you were tired, forgotten it and perhaps slept on it, and then flash! When you weren't thinking about it suddenly the answer has come to you, as a gift from the gods. You're pleased with it, and feel good. It may not be right, but at least you can try it out.
Lancelot Law Whyte, British philosopher and engineer

b. You can't think too much about these pictures that shimmer [in your mind]. You just lie low and let them develop. You stay quiet.
Joan Didion, American essayist and novelist

c. There may be fortunate writers with the ability to whip out a totally organized and coherent paper in as little time as it takes to write their thoughts down. I'm not one of those fortunate people. After I select my topic and before I start writing, I contemplate, by letting random thoughts about my idea just flow through my mind. This process helps me become better acquainted with the content of my paper and saves me the frustration of starting over and over.
A student

d. I could show how a passage originally shaped itself when [I was] in bed, how it became transformed upon arising, and again transformed at the moment of sitting down to record it.
Henry Miller, American author

e. I think about my topic and try to play it through my mind. If I like it, I write it down.
A student

f. You lose friends who can't understand why you never seem to recognize them in the supermarket. (Supermarkets are good places for letting your mind wander.)
Anne Tyler, American novelist

Observe yourself for several days and notice when your right brain seems to be most active: perhaps when you're driving, or sitting in the bathtub, or just before you go to sleep, or right when you wake up. Then think of something you might be interested in writing about and set your mind to thinking about that topic. Keep a pad of paper and pencil handy and jot down several pages of random notes as ideas come to you, to see how productive your right brain can be.

Exercise 4 Written

Browse through part VII of this book in search of a topic on which you might be able to write a good paper. Don't write the paper. Instead, scribble ideas informally on scratch paper. Make sure your scribblings are at least as extensive as those on pp. 5–6. Bring your scratch-paper notes to class, either to be handed in or to be discussed with other students in small groups.

Exercise 5 For thought and action

Virginia Woolf said that to write, you need a "room of your own." Do you have that kind of privacy for the writing you need to do? If you don't, think about what you might do to make your writing place more isolated and hence a better environment for the kind of concentration writing requires.

Exercise 6 For thought and action

How good are you at dealing with intrusions on your writing time? Let's say you are a parent of young children who is going to school at night, and one of your friends wants you to watch her children from nine till four, "since you're just sitting home all day." Or your boss wants you to work overtime three nights a week, although overtime work was not mentioned when you took the job. Or a friend, who knows you have a major paper due in sociology class tomorrow, calls up and pushes you to go out for a hamburger. Can you say "no" when you need to work on your writing?

. . . .
Exercise 7   For thought
. . . .

If you have a hard time remembering to jot down ideas for a piece of writing, try to imagine going into a large supermarket to buy a week's worth of groceries without a grocery list. There you are, in that huge world of the supermarket—and you don't know where to begin or where to go after that, you can't remember what you need, you're so confused you feel almost paralyzed; maybe you panic. Right in the middle of your fantasy, remember that all this can also happen to you when everything else important in your world is competing for your attention and you need to write. Those jottings you might have done would then help you out, in the same way a grocery list would help you out in the supermarket.

2 Writing and rewriting

I used to worry considerably about my writing. Yes, I used to fret, but that was out of fear. Now, though, I have enormous confidence because I know that I can always rewrite it.   Toni Morrison

Writing: sitting down to it

Let's get you into your writing place, at a good writing time, surrounded by whatever makes you feel at home. You have your supplies and reference books at hand. And before you is that blank sheet of paper. . . .

But you have something else, too, if you have been heeding our advice. Remember those scraps of paper on which you've been jotting down ideas? Now you can congratulate yourself for collecting them, for all those notes to yourself are about to become a content list for your paper. Pull your scattered ideas together on a sheet or two of paper, so you can think about them all at once. Don't worry about making a neat list; keep yourself free to play around. On page 15, for example, is one student's initial list.

Once this student had pulled his scattered ideas together, he was ready to begin to focus and organize his material. As he began to see the point he wanted to make, he scratched out items not related to that point and added any new related items he could think of. Then he rearranged the items by numbering. When he had finished, his list looked like the one on page 16. This kind of informal "thinking in ink" will give you control as you write your rough draft, and it will make that blank sheet of paper look a lot less threatening.

Sometimes you may not have a collection of scratch-paper items to work from. Then how will you get under way? One way is to plunge right in. If the idea you have for a paper has not been generating bits and pieces for you, try some free writing. Write down anything associated with your idea that comes to mind. You may be surprised at what happens once you get your pen or pencil *moving* on that piece of paper.

Causes of child abuse—unwanted births
frustration with
small children
poverty
alcohol
others—??

Kinds of CA—physical
emotional/psychological
sexual

Extent—all social classes
not ethnically determined
all economic levels
may vary according to socioeconomic
level

How prevent—preparent education
counseling of parents
improve social conditions.
generally

legal implications in
attempts at prevention
difficulty in getting preparents
and parents to cooperate

Use: example(s) from my ambulance runs to
emergency room of hospital—plus
stories I hear from my coworkers

(Physical)

Focus: *Child abuse: Causes and Methods of prevention*

① Causes of child abuse—unwanted births
                frustration with
                    small children ← *handle together*
                poverty
              [alcohol
              others—??
              emptiness of lives of some parents
              projection — anger from work
              gets displaced on children

Kinds of CA—(physical) ← *restrict to this*
           emotional/psychological   *use vivid examples as an opening device*
           sexual

Degrees—ranges from bruises (from beating) to broken limbs to cuts, third-degree burns, etc.

~~Extent = all social classes~~
      not ethnically determined
      all economic levels   — *off my focus*
      may vary according to socioeconomic
      level

② How prevent—preparent education *(a.)*
           counseling of parents *(b.)*
           improve social conditions
           generally *(d.)*

           ~~legal implications in~~   *would make my discussion too long*
             ~~attempts at prevention~~
          ~~difficulty in getting preparents~~
           ~~and parents to cooperate~~
      impose a fine on abusive parents — ? (c.)

Use: example(s) from my ambulance runs to
     emergency room of hospital—plus
     stories I hear from my coworkers

W. S. Merwin speaks in one of his poems of all that lies hidden and unknown in a pencil. You can find out what may be hiding in your pencil (or pen) through free writing. Such free-association writing may yield words and phrases from which you can build a content list. And thus you are well on your way to a whole paper, from a different kind of start.

Now you're ready to write—whether you started from a scratch-paper list or by free writing. At this point, treat your paper as a *rough draft* that will be improved later. Don't worry about neatness and spelling and precise word choice, or even about sentence structure and grammar. Go with the flow, roughing out the paper, leaving blanks when you get stuck, moving forward without stopping. You can always fill in the blanks later, after the paper has begun to take shape. The trick, says writer Gene Olson, "is to keep the words flowing, rolling, sliding onto the paper. You're *creating* at this stage, not being picky-picky. Go with the flow, then push it a little, just sort of nudge it along. Before your eyes, a few words turn into a sentence, a sentence into a paragraph and a paragraph into a composition . . . in the rough."

As you write your rough draft, it's a good idea to double space if you're typing or to write on every other line if you're writing longhand. That way you'll have room between the lines for small changes you may want to make later. And you should leave margins, again so you'll have space in which to experiment with improvements.

Getting distance

A first, rough draft is seldom an acceptable piece of writing. Even professional writers cannot control their rough drafts perfectly, so they take their writing through several drafts, or revisions. You will need to do so too.

But how do you decide what revisions your rough draft needs? Like most writers, once you have finished a rough draft you probably feel too close to it to view it objectively. So you'll need to get "distance" from your writing. You'll need, somehow, to begin to see your paper as if you hadn't written it—as if you were your reader.

One way to get distance is to allow your paper to cool off, preferably overnight, or even for a few days. After this cooling-off period, go back and read your paper as if it were someone else's. The hard-to-read parts will confuse even you; you'll begin to see what changes are needed.

Another way to get distance is to read your paper aloud, or better yet, have someone else read it to you. Problems with clarity and with sentence flow will show up vividly when your reader stumbles over a sentence or misreads it.

One of the best ways to distance yourself from your writing is to ask someone else—a friend, spouse, parent, or teacher—to serve as your reader. Choose someone whose judgment you trust, preferably someone who will level with you and who is not afraid of losing your friendship by responding honestly to your writing. Ask this person to be hard on you, to tell you where your paper is unclear or sounds awkward or is otherwise hard to read.

At this point, right before you begin rewriting your rough draft, you should probably ask yourself a tough question: "Is my paper *worth* rewriting?" Nothing is more depressing than trying to perfect a paper that you don't respect to begin with. If you feel sure you can't turn your rough draft into a paper that's worth reading, just throw it out and begin again. One professional writer claims that the most important piece of furniture in her office is a ten-gallon wastebasket. Her mistakes go into the wastebasket, sometimes with a dramatic hook shot. What doesn't go into the wastebasket is good enough to be rewritten.

Rewriting

Let's say that your paper is good enough to be rewritten. As you begin to rework the rough draft, make sure you have cutting and taping equipment close by, in case you need it: scissors and tape, or a stapler, and lots of clean paper. That way you won't have to waste time rewriting your rough draft over and over. You can cut up what you have and make a new rough draft by fastening the pieces to clean paper.

The first step in rewriting is easy and painless: Look over your paper in search of its strengths. Why is it worth rewriting? You will want to keep and perhaps embellish the strong parts.

Next decide whether you should delete anything. One of the hardest parts of rewriting is throwing out material that is repetitious, weak, or off the point. Train yourself to be merciless. As Sir Arthur Quiller-Couch puts it, be prepared to "murder your darlings." No matter how interesting a detail or an example or an idea may seem to you, if it does not clearly develop the main focus of your paper, then it must go.

Once you've scratched out any material that doesn't belong, check to see if the remaining sentences and paragraphs are ordered in the best possible way. If not, reach for your scissors and tape or stapler. Cut apart the pieces and reassemble them until you get the order you want. Then read over your cut-and-taped version in search of possible gaps—places where you may need to write new material—and get to work on that.

Let's see how the rewriting process worked for one student, whom we'll call Martha, as she wrote a paper encouraging parents to send their children to Sunday school. Martha's first draft, too preachy to convince many parents, found its proper home in the wastebasket. When she tackled the paper again a few days later, Martha produced a draft more carefully aimed at her readers. This time she decided that her paper was good enough to be rewritten. As you read her draft, which is printed below, consider its strengths and weaknesses. If you were Martha, what would you decide to keep, to delete, to add? Focus on large decisions rather than on the finer points of sentence structure and word choice.

Dear Parent,

I missed your child in my Sunday School class this past Sunday. I can not help remembering something you said when I visited your home a few weeks ago. You said, "I don't want to force my children to go to Sunday School, it may turn them against it. I leave the decision of going to church up to them."

This morning when I got up there was 6 inches of snow on the ground and I wondered how many parents leave the decision to the child as to whether to wear a coat, shoes, boots, mittens, etc., or did they say something like: "You are not going outside until you are properly dressed for this kind of weather." If they did, their child may not ever want to wear clothing again and they may find themselves selling their home and moving to a nudist colony.

How about the skateboard or bicycle that belongs to our neighbor's child and our child would like to keep it. Do we allow them to steal it or a candy bar or two when they go to the 7-11 store? If so, we may have hindered them on their way to becoming a well-known bank robber.

The course of least resistance is popular and just what it says, "of least resistance."

The government does not ask whether our children want to learn or go to school, nor does it say if it is raining outside today they can stay at home. Don't we make them go to bed early so that they can get up and go to school the next day? If we force our children to go to bed early, does that mean they may never want to sleep again? If we force them to go to school to learn to read and write when they grow up they may never want to read or write again?

How about other areas of our children's lives? Aren't we concerned that we buy and prepare the right kinds of food, and don't we try to give them a diet that includes the basic four food groups each day?

If we force our children to go to Sunday School they just might like all of the love and friendliness they find there. They might like Bible study and the good sermons they will hear about Jesus Christ who died for them and someone whom they can learn to pattern their lives; also the stories of men and women who were very human but had faith in God. They just might get enthused about the activities that are planned for them.

To take our children to Sunday School and church can be the most effective, enjoyable, and peaceful part of our week.

If we "force" our children to go to Sunday School by taking them with us on our way to church that word "force" seems to disappear. When we share in that love and friendliness of the church atmosphere, the children will want to be a part of it, too. When they see that Bible study and learning, singing, giving our tithes, and listening to a good sermon are important to us, and that this is part of worshipping God they will want to worship him, too.

Your child's Sunday School teacher,
Martha Krause

Martha put this draft aside for a few days, knowing that she was too close to it to view it objectively. When she returned to it later, she began by congratulating herself on the parts she had handled well. She was especially proud of her introduction, which addresses an imaginary reader, "Dear Parent," and then quotes the most common reason parents give when they fail to send their children to Sunday school. This introduction, Martha felt, would make direct contact with her readers. As she scanned the body of the paper, Martha admired her comparisons, though she suspected she was providing too many of them. When she looked again at her final paragraph, she liked its message but found it too flat for a conclusion. She hoped she would be able to come up with a livelier finish.

As she got to work deleting paragraphs and sentences that weren't carrying their weight, Martha was visited with new inspirations. A couple of fresh paragraphs flowed from her pen onto scratch paper. These she inserted into the paper by cutting her typed draft apart and taping the handwritten paragraphs in place.

As you read the new and improved draft printed below, notice that at this point Martha wasn't worrying about sentence structure and wording. She was focusing on major changes, knowing there would be time enough later for the fine points.

. . . .

Dear ~~Parent~~ *Mr. and Mrs. Hart*,

I missed Susan, *your daughter,* in my Sunday School class this past Sunday. I can not

help remembering something you said when I visited your home a few weeks

ago. You said, "I don't want to force my children to go to Sunday School, it may turn them against it. I leave the decision of going to church up to them."

This morning when I got up there was six inches of snow on the ground and I wondered how many parents leave the decision to the child as to whether to wear a coat, shoes, boots, mittens, etc., or did they say something like: "You are not going outside until you are properly dressed for this kind of weather." ~~If they did, their child may not ever want to wear clothing again and they may find themselves selling their home and moving to a nudist colony.~~

How about the skateboard or bicycle that belongs to our neighbor's child and our child would like to keep it. Do we allow them to steal it or a candy bar or two when they go to the 7-11 store? ~~If so, we may have hindered them on their way to becoming a well-known bank robber.~~

~~The course of least resistance is popular and just what it says, "of least resistance."~~

The government does not ask whether our children want to learn or go to school, nor does it say if it is raining outside today they can stay at home. ~~Don't we make them go to bed early so that they can get up and go to school the next day? If we force our children to go to bed early, does that mean they may never want to sleep again?~~ If we force them to go to school to learn to read and write *(does that mean that)* *want to* when they grow up they may never read or write again?

~~How about other areas of our children's lives. Aren't we concerned~~ ~~that we buy and prepare the right kinds of food and try to give them a diet~~ ~~that includes the basic four food groups each day.~~

If we force our children to go to Sunday School they just might like all of the love and friendliness they find there. They might like Bible study and the good sermons they will hear about Jesus Christ, ~~who died for them~~ ~~and~~ someone *after* whom they can learn to pattern their lives; also the stories of men and women who were very human but had faith in God. They just might get enthused about the activities that are planned for them.

There is just one catch—it might cost us something. We might have to get up just a little earlier on Sunday mornings. Ouch! The only morning that we have to sleep in. We would get up early to take them to catch a ride to go to King's Dominion, or to majorette practice, bowling, and go to see them perform at the ball game, wouldn't we?

Isn't it worth nurturing that part of them that will live beyond this earthly life?

To take our children to Sunday School and church can be the most

effective, enjoyable, and peaceful part of our week. ⟩

⟨ If we "force" our children to go to Sunday School by taking them
with us on our way to Church,
that word "force" seems to disappear. When we share in that love and friend-
∧

liness of the church atmosphere, the children will want to be a part of it,

too. When they see that Bible study and learning, singing, giving our tithes,

and listening to a good sermon are important to us, and that this is part of

worshipping God they will want to worship him, too.

*We would not let our children go out
into bad weather improperly dressed.
Should we let them walk out into life
spiritually undressed?*
                        Susan's Sunday School Teacher,
                          Martha Krause

. . . .

You can probably guess why Martha decided to delete certain sentences and paragraphs. She scratched out the last sentences in paragraphs
two and three because their humor didn't quite work. These sentences
were more distracting than entertaining. As for the fourth paragraph,
which consisted of a single sentence, it interrupted the reader's pattern of
thought. The paper flows better if the reader can move from one example
to the next without shifting his or her attention to abstract commentary.

Martha made cuts in paragraphs five and six because she decided she
was overloading the reader with comparisons. She cut the ones she
thought were weakest. In paragraph seven, the line "Jesus Christ who
died for them and someone whom they can learn to pattern their lives,"
aside from being awkward, was too preachy. So part of it had to go.

The handwritten additions, we hope you'll agree, are definite improvements. And you may have noticed another small but significant
improvement. "Dear Parent" has become "Dear Mr. and Mrs. Hart,"

and "your child" is now "Susan." This personalized touch makes Martha's appeal even more direct and even more difficult for her readers to ignore.

Rewriting, as we're defining it in this chapter, is the process you have just seen. First decide what is worth keeping, then delete the weak parts, and finally, write in whatever new parts seem needed. When rewriting, you don't need to pay much attention to wording and sentence structure. Such changes, which we call polishing, are dealt with in chapter 3. Martha later polished the draft of her paper which you have just read. You may be interested to know that the polished, final version appeared in *The Wesleyan Witness*, the newsletter of Martha's church.

Some final notes

Obviously, there is much more to writing and rewriting than we have covered in this chapter. All the rest of this book is intended to help you as you write and rewrite. As you learn more about focusing and organizing and paragraphing, you'll be better able to cut and tape your efforts into a workable rough draft that may need only polishing and proofreading. In the meantime, we suggest that even before you've read the rest of the book, you keep an imaginary reader looking over your shoulder whenever you write. That reader will help you decide what to delete, what to rearrange, and what to add.

We have tried to discuss the writing-rewriting process so that you can follow it step by step. But we know you won't always follow the steps in just the way we've presented them. Because writing is an act unique to each individual, there are as many different ways to go about putting a piece of writing together as there are writers. We like what Ezra Pound has to say here: "It doesn't matter which leg of your table you make first, so long as the table has four legs and will stand up solidly when you have finished it." You will discover which leg *you* find it easiest to make first as you write—and write. We say "as you write—and write" because you will soon realize that nothing reinforces good writing like writing.

. . . .
Exercise 1 Classroom activity
. . . .

As a class, select a topic from part VII and brainstorm about it on the blackboard. Call out everything you can think of about the topic, with no commenting on any items at this point. Once everyone's ideas are on the board, study the list and consider whether anything should be deleted. Consider also whether anything needs to be added to the list. Then discuss what order the items might take in a paper and number them accordingly. If some items should be used as minor details to develop major points, letter those items to show their relationship to the paper as a whole.

. . . .
Exercise 2   For thought and discussion
. . . .

If the idea of *re*writing—perhaps even several drafts—sounds like just too much trouble to you, maybe the following comments by both professional writers and successful student writers will help to convince you. Think about the comments and be ready to talk about them in class.

a. What is written without effort is in general read without pleasure.
Samuel Johnson, British writer and critic

b. The best reason for putting anything down on paper is that one may then change it.
Bernard De Voto, American writer

c. There is no such thing as good writing, only good rewriting.
Louis Brandeis, Supreme Court justice

d. I read my paper over and over. I think about it a lot. I use a great deal of paper. I rewrite and rewrite until it says what I want it to say.
A student

e. I have never thought of myself as a good writer. . . . But I'm one of the world's great rewriters.
James Michener, American writer

f. Easy writing makes hard reading.
Ernest Hemingway, American novelist

g. My goal in everything I write is simplicity. I'm a demon on the subject of revision. I revise, revise, revise, until every word is the one I want.
Ben Lucien Berman, American author

h. I can't write five words but that I change seven.
Dorothy Parker, American writer

i. I keep rereading what I have written, making changes where needed. I do this about six or seven times until I feel it is right.
A student

j. Writing and rewriting are a constant search for what it is one is saying.
John Updike, American novelist

k. He would scratch and then put in a word and scratch and work and then paste

on another piece of paper and the whole thing would be new. And then when the typed script would come he was still working on it.
Raphael Hamilton, about J.R.R. Tolkien

. . . .
Exercise 3 For discussion and action
. . . .

Professional writers tell us that rewriting is an essential part of the writing process. But in spite of all the talk about the importance of rewriting, most writers—especially beginning writers—are tempted not to rewrite. If you find yourself tempted to skip the rewriting stage, try to discover *why*. When urged to be honest in an anonymous poll, our students came up with this list of reasons. Are any of these *your* reasons?

1. I wait until the last minute, so there's no time to rewrite.

2. My first draft is the best I can do. I can't improve it.

3. I don't know whether my first draft is any good or not, so how can I improve it?

4. I don't know where to begin, and I wouldn't know when to stop.

5. Well, frankly, I'm lazy.

6 When I tinker with my sentences, they just turn out worse.

7. I don't really care about what I'm writing, so I just want to get it over with.

8. Rewriting is too messy. I like to work with clean-looking pages.

9. I'm such a bad writer I hate to read my own writing.

10. Rewriting is my instructor's responsibility.

11. Rewriting is painful. I can't stand the agony.

12. If I can't get it right the first time, I must be stupid.

What can you do to overcome the temptation not to rewrite?

. . . .
Exercise 4 For class discussion
. . . .

A friend has just written his first draft of a review of the Pines Steak House, and he has asked you to help him get distance from the paper. Begin by saying something positive. Why is the paper good enough to be rewritten? Then suggest possible improvements, focusing on large-scale changes, not on fine points such as sentence structure and wording.

> The Pines Steak House is a nationally known, underclassed chain of restaurants. Its main entrée, of course, is steak and potatoes.

I think that the Pines, as it is often called, is underclassed because people usually compare it with fast-food restaurants such as McDonalds and Hardees. If these people would just take a good look at the advantages of the Pines, however, they would surely stop comparing it with fast-food joints.

One good factor of the Pines is the prices that they charge for their dinners. The dinners are quite inexpensive when compared to other restaurants that specialize in steak. Consider the meat used by the Pines. It is fresh, tasty, and prepared to order. The meat used by some fast-food restaurants is probably not even 100 percent pure beef.

When you visit the Pines you will do well to select the baked potato instead of the french fried potatoes because a baked potato not only tastes better, but is also better for you. McDonalds prepare their french fries by using grease. If you select a baked potato, I suggest using butter, salt, and pepper to enhance its taste.

The Pines' drinks are cold and thirst-quenching; their hot rolls are fresh and soaked with butter.

For vegetarians the salad bar is ideal. The bar is stocked with fresh lettuce, juicy tomatoes, crisp onions, beans, pickles, peppers, and several types of dressing that go with salads. The purchase of a dinner entitles a diner to all the salad he or she can eat.

The seven or eight dinner choices range from chopped steak on a roll to a belt-tightening and satisfying T-bone special. A diner at the Pines also has plenty of choices for dessert: strawberry cheesecake, chocolate pudding, jello, cake, and pie.

When you go to the Pines and there is a long line of people waiting to order dinner, do not be discouraged; just wait the few minutes it takes to get a great dinner. You definitely will not be disappointed.

Take your steak dinner to the beautiful dining area and take your time eating so you can savor every bite.

. . . .

Exercise 5 Written

. . . .

Browse through part VII of this book in search of a topic on which you might be able to write a good paper. Give yourself time for creative thinking and doodling on scratch paper. Then, when you are ready, write your rough draft fairly quickly, in the manner suggested in this chapter. Don't worry too much about sentence structure, spelling, and so on.

If your draft is really bad—and don't be surprised if it is—throw it out and try again, perhaps on a different topic. Once you have a draft that is good enough to be rewritten, bring it to class, even though it is not yet perfect. In class either your instructor or your fellow students will help you to get distance from the draft.

. . . .
Exercise 6   Written
. . . .

The next time you hand in a paper, attach a list of your own concerns about it for your instructor to respond to during his or her evaluation. Making such a list can help you to get distance from your paper. Handing in this page of questions and comments can be helpful to both you and your instructor, as it establishes a sort of mini-dialogue about the paper.

. . . .
Exercise 7   Just for fun
. . . .

> I've always tried out my material on my dogs first. You know, with Angel, he sits there and listens and I get the feeling that he understands everything. But with Charley, I always felt that he was just waiting to get a word in edgewise.
> *John Steinbeck, American novelist*

3 Finishing up

Blot out, correct, insert, refine,
Enlarge, diminish, interline;
Be mindful, when invention fails,
To scratch your head, and bite your nails.   Jonathan Swift

Polishing

When your reworked paper says pretty much what you want it to say, you are ready to think about some finer points—ready to "polish" your writing. We suggest you work on polishing only after dealing with the larger problems we discuss under writing and rewriting in chapter 2; if you try to do your polishing too early, you will probably neglect something really important in your first, major revisions.

Polishing consists of a variety of improvements in sentence structure and wording. Here, for example, are two rough-draft paragraphs from our first chapter as they appeared after they were polished:

While you are doing your creative thinking,
While ~~your content is playing around in your head during any of these~~ ~~you are thinking creatively~~

random   whatever
~~times, you will find it useful to~~ make some ~~little~~ notes on ~~bits and pieces of~~

scratch paper or is
~~whatever writing surface is~~ available at the moment, ~~so keep something~~

at this stage;
~~available~~. Don't worry ~~here~~ about organizing your thoughts; just be sure to

write down enough so ~~that~~ you can decode it ~~when you need it~~ later. ~~Most~~

~~of us forget quickly.~~

this much   as the thoughts are flowing,
will help you later
Getting ~~something~~ down on paper at once, ~~may prove invaluable to~~

~~you~~ when you finally sit down to write. Professional writers ~~know this, so~~

~~they~~ scribble ideas on the backs of envelopes*ₓ on recipe cards or paper bags*ₓ
or cocktail napkins

or scraps of cardboard—on whatever happens to be ~~around~~ *handy* at the time.

Anne Tyler, a writer and mother of two, ~~says:~~ *remarks:* "In the evenings occasion-

ally—between baths and other sorts of chaos—a sudden idea will flash into

my mind . . . I write it down and take it to my study."

. . . .

An important part of polishing is deleting excess words. In our sample rough-draft paragraphs, for example, this word-heavy sentence appeared:

> While your content is playing around in your head during any of these times, you will find it useful to make some little notes on bits and pieces of whatever writing surface is available at the moment, so keep something available.

Without losing an ounce of meaning, we cut the sentence in half:

> While you are doing your creative thinking, make some random notes on whatever scratch paper is available at the moment.

This shorter sentence, relieved of the clutter of excess words, is easier to read. It is also more pleasing to the ear.

Following are several student sentences that have been revised for wordiness:

. . . .

The bus driver had already made the blacks ~~get up and give~~ *relinquish* their

seats to whites. I took one look at the weary old black woman and ~~asked~~ *offered*

her ~~to take~~ my seat.

Through the years I have come to enjoy several ~~different kinds~~

~~of~~ sports~~, or exercise type activities.~~

Was the water ~~really~~ colored in the "COLORED ONLY" fountain or did it taste ~~entirely~~ different?

My first time at bat I struck out, and every time after that, *because* ~~This was probably due to the fact that~~ I would swing at anything that came my way.

....

As you work to delete excess words, you'll probably notice words that need changing for one reason or another. Maybe you used the word *attire* when the more ordinary word *clothing* would have sounded better; or perhaps you wrote *friend* when *benefactor* would have been more precise. You may have any number of reasons for deciding to change words, as you can see from the examples below.

....

1. Already the gale-force winds ~~came~~ *roared* through the walls. (more vivid verb)

2. Until recently, ~~those individuals fortunate enough to further their knowledge with a college education~~ *college graduates* were always in demand. (less pretentious language—and fewer words, too)

3. The ~~loud~~ *raucous* cry of the seagulls greeted us as we neared the shore. (more precise adjective)

4. The doctors all had very ~~expensive~~ *lucrative* practices. (correct word to replace word improperly used)

5. If you think these strangely named sandwiches will ~~cost you an arm and a leg~~ *empty your wallet,* don't worry. (more vivid image to replace cliché)

6. The ~~pecking~~ *rat-a-tat-tat* of a woodpecker woke me early the first morning of our

camping trip. (livelier word to replace awkward repetition of "peck")

7. The ghost of this captain did not stop appearing on flights until all parts

of his wrecked plane ~~was~~ *were* retrieved. (plural verb to match plural subject,

"parts")

8. ~~Emotion~~ *Tension* began to build as the union committee debated the wage-and-

inflation spiral. (more specific word for exact emotion felt)

. . . .

Just as you may have different reasons for changing words, you may have a variety of reasons for deciding to restructure sentences. A restructured sentence might be clearer, or more forceful, or more emphatic, or more rhythmic than the original. It might connect more smoothly with the sentences that come before, or point more clearly to the sentences that come after. To give you a feel for the variety of reasons you might have for changing sentences, we print the following polished sentences from students' rough drafts.

. . . .

1. We agreed ~~to the idea that it~~ *that the arrival and departure of the Concorde* must have been an impressive sight. ~~to have seen the Concorde arrive and depart~~. (more forceful, more rhythmic—and less

wordy)

2. Slowly ~~the realization had taken place~~ *I realized* that this was something I could

not control. (more direct)

3. The officers told us that someone *in our seating section had been* ~~was throwing particles of ice from the~~

~~vicinity of our seats,~~ pelting the innocent fans ~~down~~ below. *with pieces of ice.* (more straight-

forward, less pretentious)

4. The exhausted merrymakers drag themselves home, thinking about what

character or w*they will portray*hose band they will play in next year. (clearer because now

more complete)

5. This is the first day of Carnival in Trinidad, West Indies*, a*~~This~~ celebration

that occurs two days prior to Ash Wednesday each year. (more emphatic, more

fluid)

6. After replacing the carburetor and air filter, the idle *you should set* ~~should be set~~ at about

1500 RPM. (more direct—and corrects the impression that the idle was doing

the replacing)

7. ~~The thunderous roar of~~ the waves ~~can be heard as they~~ crash into the stone

breakers *with a thunderous roar.* (more vigorous and emphatic)

8. The spinner bait is a V-shaped object with two metal spoons at one end /

and ~~At the other end is~~ a hook ~~with~~ *camouflaged by* a skirt ~~which is camouflaging it.~~ (more

at the other. balanced and smoother)

. . . .

With polishing done, you are ready to type or handwrite your final draft. Then only one task remains before your paper is finished. It is a very important, if not a very exciting, task—proofreading.

Proofreading

Proofreading is a slow and careful reading in search of errors that you overlooked when you were struggling with more important matters. As you proofread, you will look for mispunctuation, spelling mistakes, words left out, word endings left off, capital letters misused, and such problems as subject-verb disagreement, faulty pronoun references, misplaced modifiers, and so on.

Many students have difficulty proofreading. Several times a semester we hear comments like this one, from a frustrated student: "I've tried proofreading, but I just don't see my own errors. When they're pointed out, the problems seem so obvious—so stupid. Why can't *I* catch them?"

One answer is that proofreading requires special skills. Your tendency when reading is to scan individual words quickly in search of the meaning of a whole passage. To proofread, you need to fight your ordinary reading habits. Since the purpose of proofreading is not to grasp meaning but to spot errors, you need to pay more attention to surfaces than to content. This special kind of reading is difficult, because your usual habits keep pulling your attention away from the errors you are trying to spot. Professional proofreaders become skilled only through practice, and with practice you too can improve.

The best way to proofread is to read your paper out loud, making yourself say aloud *exactly* what is on the page—not just what you intended to write there. If you read this way, slowly and deliberately, word by word, your ear will often tell you that you've added an unnecessary comma, dropped a letter from a word, or left out an entire word. When you read silently, these errors can slip right past you.

When you're proofreading, it helps if you know what you're looking for. If you make a great many mechanical and grammatical errors, you may have trouble proofreading because you have to look for too many things at once and because you're probably not sure when you've made an error. If this is your problem, talk to your instructor about it. The two of you working together can identify your most common errors and invent a style of proofreading that will work for you. You may decide, for example, to proofread several times, perhaps once for spelling, once for punctuation, and once for omitted words or word endings.

The handbook section of this book will serve as a reference book to help you as you proofread. There you will find a more detailed explanation of how to proofread for punctuation and for spelling, as well as a great deal of information about correcting other kinds of mechanical and grammatical errors. We suggest that you scan the handbook now so that you will know what you can find there when you need help.

As we mentioned earlier, proofreading is not the most exciting part of the writing process, but it is nevertheless important, not so much because errors confuse readers—often they don't—but because they're distracting and annoying. They suggest too much haste and too little care. Such errors say to a reader, "Apparently the writer did not have much respect for this piece of writing, so why should I?"

We know that the writing process may not occur quite as systematically as we have suggested in these three chapters. We have deliberately divided the procedure into definable steps, so that we can talk about everything that might need attention as you rework your early drafts. But certainly you may spot a misspelled word at the same time that you are considering reorganization. So much the better. But we would caution you against consciously trying to deal with all the big questions and all the little errors at once. That can get to be overwhelming and counter-productive.

Letting it go

After so much serious talk about reworking your paper, we want to warn you against perfectionism. It is possible to worry a paper to death: Are my sentences varied enough? Shall I use this word or that one here? A comma or not there? A writer needs to know when to quit—when to release his or her writing to the world, to let it go.

Perhaps there is a fine line between not caring enough about your writing and caring too much. We don't know how to help you draw that line. But it is only fair to warn you that if you are a perfectionist in other areas of your life, you may tend to be the same way toward your writing. Our best advice here: Remember that there is no such thing as a perfect piece of writing; there will always be alternative ways to handle every part of it. Just try to make your writing clear, readable, and at least somewhat interesting—a piece of work you yourself can reasonably respect. Then let it go.

. . . .
Exercise 1 Classroom activity
. . . .

Interview someone you know who does quite a lot of writing, either on the job or in college. Find out from this person in as much detail as possible how he or she approaches writing tasks. In conducting your interview, you might use the following questions as guides:

1. Do you type rough drafts, write them in longhand, or dictate them to a secretary or into a machine?

2. Are you addicted to any sort of paper and pen?

3. How do you organize your ideas—in your head or on paper? Do you use outlines, and if so, how formal are they?

4. How do you go about rewriting, if you do rewrite? Do you use scissors and paste?

5. Do you have someone read what you have written, get advice, and then rewrite? Or do you handle it all on your own?

6. How do you go about editing your writing? Or do you do this at all?

7. Do you use a dictionary, a book of synonyms, a thesaurus, a grammar handbook, or any other kind of writer's reference book?

Bring the results of your interview to class and be prepared to share them with the group. If possible, also bring a page or two of rough copy from the person you interviewed, so other members of the class can get some sense of what your writer's in-process writing looks like. Be prepared to tell why—for what exact purpose—your writer writes.

Exercise 2 Classroom activity

Bring the rough draft of a paper you are working on to class. Then, working with one other student, read each other's rough drafts aloud and try to spot sentences in need of polishing, either for clarity or for smoothness. As your partner reads your paper aloud, mark any problem sentences. Then go off by yourself to polish those sentences. Ask your partner to read your new version to check on its clarity and smoothness.

Exercise 3 For class discussion

Below are a number of rough-draft sentences that have been polished. Why do you suppose the writers made these changes?

a. I flopped down on my belly and slid about fifteen feet until my skis ~~hit~~ *grabbed*

a tree.

b. Sister *Charity* got her kicks from passing out writing punishments: translate the

Ten Commandments into Latin, type a ~~hundred~~ thousand-word essay on

good manners, write the New Testament with a quill pen.

c. My husband, fearing his head might be snapped off, was ~~apprehensive~~ *afraid* to

approach me.

d. For the first time in a long ~~time,~~ *while* I ~~put~~ my $300 Raleigh ~~on my shoulder~~ *shouldered*

and brought it up from the basement.

e. We learned to listen to a lecture and take notes ^ *well-organized* ~~in a much better organized~~

~~train of thought.~~

f. The odor of burnt grease permeated the room and a thick, gray cloud of

smoke hung low, ~~over the vicinity.~~

g. Where else could you get an entire steak dinner for about ~~two dollars and~~ *three dollars?*

~~ninety four cents?~~

h. The nurse is our ~~middleman.~~ *link with the doctors.*

i. The plainclothes officers ~~reinstated~~ *restated* their demand that we leave with them.

j. ~~We had just~~ *as we* pulled ~~into~~ *up to* the entrance gate, ~~when~~ a man ~~approached my car~~ *put out his hand*
demanded
and ~~asked for~~ three dollars.

. . . .

Exercise 4   For class discussion

. . . .

Below are three paired paragraphs. One in each pair is a rough draft, and
the other is the writer's polished revision. Which one do you think is the
new and improved version, and how is it better? (*Note:* Each paragraph
is taken from a whole paper. The first is from the middle of a paper, the
second is an introduction, and the third is a conclusion.)

1a. The receptionist at the counter tells the owner to have a seat until the doctor is ready. To the client the room is cheerful, with its plants, bright red floor, and picture window. The dog, hiding under a glass top table, thinks of plans of escape. The counter is too high to jump over and the window is too risky. A cat across the room hisses and he loses control. The owner is embarrassed and cleans up the puddle on the floor.

1b. The receptionist at the counter tells the owner to have a seat until the doctor is ready. "My, what a cheerful little room," thinks Mrs. Williams as she notices the plants, bright red floor, and picture window. Pootchie, hiding under a glass-topped table, is thinking of escape routes. But the counter is too high to jump over and the window is too risky. A cat across the room hisses and poor Pootchie loses control. Embarrassed, Mrs. Williams cleans up the puddle on the floor.

2a. On our wedding day some nineteen years ago, I did not know just how much "to love and to cherish" would mean to that man in my life. He is such a lover—of football, baseball, basketball, tennis, golf, boxing, and horse racing.

2b. On that very important day some nineteen years ago, I did not realize just what "to love and to cherish" was going to entail. He is such a lover of football, baseball, basketball, tennis, golf, boxing, horse racing, and (if there are others) many more.

3a. As I was entering my apartment I heard the noise coming again, and I was furious. Upon reaching the door of the offender, I noticed something was on there. What was it? It looked like a doorbell. Why would she have a doorbell in an apartment? I decided to push the button, and in a few seconds the door opened. Standing there was this lady. In a boisterous voice I said this noise has to stop. I worked hard today and I want some peace and quiet. She put a finger up as if to say just a minute and closed the door. Boy, she is weird. The door opened and she handed me a piece of paper as if she wanted me to write down my problem. This puzzled me, but I wrote my complaint in plain English. She then responded with a note of her own: "Sorry for the noise. I did not know the children were disturbing you. I'll try to do my best to keep it down. I cannot hear or talk. Thank you, Mrs. Johnson."

3b. As I was entering my apartment, I heard the thumping again, and I was furious. When I reached the door of the offender I noticed a doorbell, which seemed odd since no one else in the building had one. I decided to push the button, and in a few seconds the door opened. Standing there was an attractive young woman. In a loud voice I proclaimed, "This noise has to stop. I worked hard today and I want some peace and quiet." She put her finger up as if to say "just a minute," then closed the door. "Boy, is she weird," I thought. When the door opened, she handed me a piece of paper as if she wanted me to write down my problem. This puzzled me, but I wrote down my complaint in plain English. She then responded with a note of her own: "Sorry for the noise. I did not know the children were disturbing you. I'll do my best to control them. I cannot hear or talk. Thank you, Mrs. Johnson."

. . . .
Exercise 5 Written
. . . .

Below is a paper that needs to be polished. Read it through carefully, looking for wordiness, inappropriate choice of words, weak sentences, and other such problems. On a separate sheet write your polished version of the paper to bring to class.

One of the places in our community where you can find a good evening's entertainment is the Hayloft Dinner Theater. Too few people seem to be aware of this local cultural attraction on Route 450. As its name suggests, the Hayloft offers you not only a great evening of enjoyment but also includes in the price of an $11.00 ticket your evening meal.

The Hayloft is open Tuesday, Wednesday, Thursday, Friday, Saturday, and Sunday nights. Dinner is served buffet style, with a waiter coming to your table to take drink orders and menu preferences; this begins at 5:30. There is a salad bar to which everybody is invited to go, featuring many chopped vegetables, cottage cheese, bacon bits, and lots of kinds of salad dressings. You can almost stack up a meal at the salad bar itself.

When my father, mother, brother, sisters and I ventured out to the Hayloft recently, we ordered several different main dishes. A list of these is chicken kiev, ham supreme with pineapple, crab imperial, stuffed veal, lasagna, and egg rolls with fried rice; the variety of food at the Hayloft is very varied. Each serving was really enormous and everything tasted good. I could have left the Hayloft truly full and happy after that fantastic meal.

But of course we stayed for whatever else was to come. That night the Hayloft Hayseeds had planned to perform "Fiddler on the Roof." The Hayseeds are especially well-known around these parts for the musicals they put on—and they certainly did a good job when they acted in "Fiddler." Everyone seemed to get into the spirit of the evening, and by the time we all stood up to give the cast a big hand of standing applause, it was hard to believe that it was nearly 11:00. Just then someone shouted, "Chef! chef!" so that we were able to express our appreciation of the food as well as the play.

So gather your family or friends and head for the Hayloft. I assure you that you will find there a night of cheap fun.

Note: You will find an exercise on proofreading following "Revising Problem Sentences" in the handbook.

PART TWO

The writer's voice

4 Finding a voice

The personality I am expressing in this written sentence is not the same as the one I orally express to my three-year-old who at this moment is bent on climbing onto my typewriter. For each of these two situations, I choose a different "voice," a different mask, in order to accomplish what I want accomplished. Walker Gibson

"False starts in writing," says writing teacher Gerald Levin, "are often failures to discover the right voice." The right voice will be one you're comfortable with, one that suits your personality. But more than that, it will be a voice appropriate to your *purpose* in writing and to the particular *audience* you have in mind. As Walker Gibson says, a writing voice is the mask you put on to accomplish what you want to accomplish.

Purpose and audience

Often you will know exactly what you hope to accomplish in a piece of writing. Consider on-the-job writing, for example. Usually your audience will be quite clear: perhaps your supervisor, a client, a board of directors, or your coworkers. And you will nearly always know why you are writing: maybe to inform your supervisor about a workshop he or she did not attend, to ask a client to pay an outstanding bill, to present next year's budget request to the board of directors, or to encourage coworkers to cooperate with you in implementing a training program.

In such writing situations, which have a given purpose and audience, common sense often tells you which writing voice to adopt. You might decide to sound businesslike in the memo to your supervisor, diplomatic but firm in the letter to the client, impersonal and objective in the budget request, and personable and persuasive in the letter to your coworkers.

In college English, unlike many other writing situations, you are not automatically supplied with a purpose and an audience. You may seem to have a specific audience—your instructor—and a clear purpose—to impress him or her with your writing ability. But if you write papers merely to impress your instructor, the result is almost certain to be voiceless "assignment prose," a kind of writing that in fact impresses few teachers of writing.

Consider, for example, the following student paper, written at the very beginning of the semester:

> *Psycho,* directed by Alfred Hitchcock, is an excellent movie. This contemporary classic is seen occasionally on television and is released to movie theaters quite often. Probably the most well-known scene from *Psycho* is the one in which Janet Leigh is murdered. In this scene and throughout the entire film, Hitchcock combines suspense, symbolism, and an ingenious plot.
>
> It is advisable to see *Psycho* more than once. Many seemingly obscure details will become important after the second viewing. Hitchcock's twists and turns make *Psycho* a truly exciting movie.

The voice in this paper does not speak to readers because the writer hasn't decided who they are. Did the student write for an audience interested in hearing about an exciting, suspense-filled movie? Is she trying to get these readers so excited about the film that they'll rush out to see it? Or is she writing for another group of readers, perhaps those interested in the film's artistic merits? Is she analyzing *Psycho* for them, the way one might analyze a poem by Emily Dickinson or a play by George Bernard Shaw?

Most likely the writer had neither group of readers clearly in mind. Since she wasn't sure who she was writing to, or for what purpose, our student couldn't decide what to say. She mentions that *Psycho* is an excellent movie; a classic; an artistic film with suspense, symbolism, and an ingenious plot; a film so complex it requires several viewings; and an exciting movie. But notice that none of these messages has been developed. Readers truly interested in hearing about the film's complexity, or those who would like a vivid description of the "well-known scene in which Janet Leigh is murdered," are disappointed. The paper mentions these points and others, then drops them all.

You may feel that we're being too hard on this student writer. After all, her vocabulary is impressive, her sentence structure is sophisticated, and she hasn't made a single grammatical mistake. True enough. But we nevertheless persuaded her to toss this paper out and try again, perhaps on another topic. We weren't sorry, and neither was the student. A week later she wrote a paper not in "assignment prose," but in a voice that speaks to readers. Here is her final draft:

The Therapeutic Parachute

Troubles of the mind have continued to perplex doctors, nurses, and patients alike. Now, as a student nurse I've been told that a parachute is going to unlock the minds of some of these troubled patients. The whole idea is insane—or is it?

I was handed a folded army surplus parachute and told to accompany ten uptight psychiatric patients and a movement therapist to the gym. My first impression: the gym's a convenient place to rid the psychiatric ward of these patients, thus relieving the nurses. The movement therapist is a surrogate nurse hired to play games with the disturbed.

"Everyone take your shoes off. Hard soles have been known to mar the surface of the floor," shouted the therapist. Reluctantly everyone did as instructed. With the removal of our shoes, formality was banished.

Barefooted, we all hurried onto the floor to help unfold this khaki-colored bundle of cloth. This was a job in itself and it took all available hands to unfold it. With mission accomplished, we awaited our next step. What on earth could this wacky therapist have planned for us and this monstrous-looking mass of cloth?

Again we were hustled into activity. "Take hold of the parachute and shake it. Shake it hard. That's good . . . now less forcefully."

Just then I looked up into the faces of my patients. Faces that were once expressionless, angered, frightened, or sad were undergoing change right before my very eyes.

Myra, who had been without expression and in an almost catatonic state, had the look of belonging. Gary, my favorite, a fifteen-year-old who was filled with anger and hostility, seemed tranquil. This sudden release of energy without reprimand or repercussion had freed him of plenty.

I believe the most rewarding transformation came over Lee. Lee, husband and father of two, was a deeply depressed man. He had tried to take his life just days before. As we were shaking the parachute it created a breeze that felt to me like a wind from a mild autumn day. The gentle surge of air made me feel so warm and relaxed. As I looked into Lee's face I could see that I was not the only one experiencing this warmth and relaxation. It looked as if the weight of the world had been momentarily lifted from his shoulders.

Next we spread the parachute out flat on the floor. Each person was encouraged to lie on it while the rest of us took hold of the chute and tried to create different sensations for the rider. Most of us preferred the slow walk of the group, which created a rocking-chair effect. When I took my turn in the center of the chute, with eyes closed, the wavelike motions enveloped me in a serenity that I had not experienced in years.

As we left the gym that day, we did so united. We no longer felt alone, at least for the time being. If this hunk of army surplus can lighten the load of a troubled mind, if only momentarily, it is indeed of great value for the well-being of a psychiatric patient.

Here our writer has a clear sense of who her readers are. They are people who are skeptical, as the writer once was, about using a parachute for psychiatric therapy. Her purpose is to convince those readers that a "hunk of army surplus" can indeed "lighten the load of a troubled mind."

Probably the most important advice we can give you this semester is to write for readers you can envision, as this student did. If you're writing about the junk food in the vending machines at your child's school, don't tell your instructor about it. Aim your paper at other parents and write with a purpose—to get the parents to help you take action. Or if you're contrasting the merits of the Suzuki and the Harley-Davidson, write to readers who are interested in buying motorcycles; help them decide how to spend their money. When giving advice on the care of hanging ferns, imagine readers who don't know how to care for them but want to learn. Or if you think you have the secret to success in tennis, imagine readers eager to improve their game. Don't worry if your instructor is not a plant lover or a tennis nut. Your instructor is interested in your ability to communicate purposefully, not in your ability to figure out what he or she is interested in.

Writer and readers

As we mentioned in chapter 1, the early stages of the writing process are creative, mysterious, hard to pin down. This is true partly because writing involves people, and because only one of them happens to be present: you, the writer. As you mull over ideas while weeding petunias or repairing your bicycle, as you jot down notes late at night, or as you sharpen pencils and pour yourself another cup of coffee, you're becoming acquainted with your future readers. They aren't there, of course, but you're thinking about them, sometimes even inventing a role for them. And at the same time you're beginning to discover your own role as writer, or to invent it.

For example, one young woman, who wrote about a strange plant that she had recently discovered, began to see her readers as gardeners desperate for an easy-care houseplant that wouldn't die on them. Once she had envisioned these readers, she understood her own role as writer. She would be the self-confident expert with the perfect answer to their problem: the air fern, a plant that couldn't die on them because it was already dead.

Having settled on one role for herself as writer (the expert) and another for her readers (desperate gardeners willing to try anything), this student was able to find just the right voice for her paper, as you can see from her first paragraph:

> Do you love plants, yet they always seem to die on you? You can't decorate your indoors with greenery because the little devils shrivel up to an ugly brown? If you weren't born with a green thumb, I have the perfect plant for you. It's the poriferan, more commonly known as the air fern.

Even if you don't happen to be in search of the perfect houseplant, you are probably willing, as you read on, to play the role of the desperate gardener. Sensing from the opening paragraph that this is the role the writer has created for you, you are willing to cooperate with her, and to enjoy her tongue-in-cheek humor along the way.

> The air fern is a gorgeous, delicate little plant that really isn't a plant at all. It's dead. Aside from its dainty appearance, being deceased is its greatest asset. It needs no tender loving care to sustain its life, because it has already passed on.
>
> Under no circumstances will you have to prune, weed, repot, or fertilize your air fern. This is one plant you'll never have to sing to or talk to or play classical music for. Now you won't have to hide your plants in the other room when you're having a loud party. Play any type of music *you* want to hear—it doesn't care.
>
> Are you worried about where to put your new houseplant? Well, your worries are over. Put it anywhere—in a corner, on a table, on a shelf, or even in a closet. Air ferns can survive anywhere.
>
> No need to fuss about getting a neighbor to water your air fern while you are on vacation; in fact, no need to water the beauty at all. Which of course eliminates the problem of measuring water, counting days between watering, and misting. Never, never water the air fern.
>
> Cost? An attractive vase of air fern will cost approximately two dollars. To make it thrive, you'll need no expensive food or plant lights. And you'll never need to replace it, because it can't die on you like the more costly, temperamental plants.
>
> Follow the simple instruction "Leave your air fern alone" and you will be the green thumb of your neighborhood. When your friends compliment you on your healthy ferns, just smile, relax, and enjoy the fact that they are dead.

The writer's stance

As you're deciding on roles for yourself and your readers, you'll need to choose a stance or a point of view from which to deliver your message. Will you address readers from the first-person point of view (*I* or *we*), putting yourself into the paper? Will you write from the second-person point of view (*you*), pitching your message directly to readers? Or will you choose the more distant third-person point of view (*he/she, one,* or *they*)?

You may have to experiment awhile before discovering a comfortable stance. In the following rough-draft introduction, for example, the writer is having trouble finding his footing:

> Psychology is a course which will arouse one's curiosity about such subjects as mental illness, suicide, dreams, forgetfulness, and your everyday routine. After learning about these and other subjects, you will begin to understand yourself and others a little better.

Notice that the writer begins in the distant third-person point of view ("*one's* curiosity"), then shifts to the second person ("*your* everyday routine . . . *you* will begin"). This wavering commitment to a point of view plagued the writer's entire rough draft. Some of the later paragraphs addressed readers in the third person: "Dreams are another subject that proves interesting to many *students* of psychology." Other paragraphs spoke more directly, in the second person: "Do *you* have a fear of high places (acrophobia), open spaces (agoraphobia), or darkness (nyctaphobia)"?

As the writer reread his rough draft, he realized that he would have to settle on one stance or the other. After thinking about his purpose—to convince fellow students to sign up for a psychology course—he decided on the direct approach. He rewrote the paragraph that began "Dreams are another subject that proves interesting to many *students* of psychology," this time from the second-person point of view: "Have *you* ever dreamed that you were falling from a cliff, running from wild animals, or choking on ashes?" He aligned the openings of all of the other paragraphs in the body of the paper with this one, and rewrote the introductory paragraph as follows:

> Psychology is a course that will get *you* interested in mental illness, suicide, dreams, forgetfulness, and even your everyday routine. After learning about these and other subjects *you* will begin to understand yourself and others a little better.

But, you may be wondering, what ever happened to the prohibition against using the word *you*? Shouldn't the writer have stuck to the impersonal third-person point of view throughout?

We don't think so. Some instructors might argue, with reason, that students need practice writing in the third-person point of view, but few would claim that the use of *you* is never effective. Our student writer decided, quite intelligently, that given his purpose and audience, addressing his readers as "you" was more effective than writing about "psychology students" in general.

Consider another well-known prohibition: the rule against using the word *I*. It's true that sometimes this little pronoun can sound intrusive. Sometimes it puts too much emphasis on the writer, too little on the subject. But once again, the choice depends on what the writer is trying to accomplish. For certain purposes the "I" point of view is the best.

For example, the former flight attendant whose paper is printed in chapter 1 first drafted her paper from the third-person point of view, carefully removing herself from her subject, the supposed glamour of her former profession. But nearly everything she wanted to put into the paper came from personal experience. So she decided, halfway into the paper, to redraft the whole essay from the first-person point of view. She found it simply too artificial to remove herself from the subject, so she gave up the attempt, with good results. Here is the rough draft of her opening paragraph, written from the distant third-person point of view:

> On the surface the life of an airline stewardess seems ideal. Advertisements on television portray the stewardess as a beautiful girl with a fascinating and exciting job. Upon closer scrutiny, however, this occupation is not as glamorous as it may seem.

Not bad, really, but the revised version, drafted from the "I" point of view, is better:

> Broadway Joe enters the cabin, smiles at the camera and says, "When you've got it, flaunt it." Such an inducement was hard for a nineteen-year-old to ignore, so I sent in my application for the position of airline stewardess.

Once she had shifted her stance, this writer improved her voice just as dramatically later in the paper. Consider, for example, this paragraph from her original draft, written from the third-person point of view:

> A social life can be difficult to arrange when one is on short layovers or working different shifts. The stewardess may fly to exotic places; however, very often the plane must make the return trip immediately. So, if she is on a "run" to Paris, she may never see it! Nor is she likely to get to know many Parisians.

Again, this is not bad writing. But it's uninspired, because in avoiding the use of the word *I*, the writer has put an unnatural restriction on herself. Once she decided to tell us what her own social life was like, instead of writing about stewardesses' social lives in general, she wrote a much more powerful paragraph:

> The most lonely times were the "layovers," a normal part of the working

trip. They involved spending the night in a motel room, eating cold sandwiches for dinner, and washing out a dirty uniform for the next day's flight. Sometimes I wasn't lucky enough to make it to a motel. I can remember spending my first Christmas eve away from my family sleeping on a bench in the Kansas City airport. Of course when I was really lonely, I could always refer to the stack of calling cards that were passed out by deplaning salesmen—"If you're ever in Chicago, give me a call and I'll show you around."

Writers often attempt the third-person point of view when the "I" or "you" stance would be more appropriate. But there are situations, of course, in which the third person is the appropriate choice. Business writing, technical writing, and much college writing is often best composed from the impersonal third-person point of view.

The third-person stance puts both writer and reader behind the scenes, where they frequently belong. In the following introductory paragraph, for example, the writer decided to put his subject up front, without injecting himself or his readers into the discussion:

Although the sixties saw blacks struggling to attain civil rights, they are still a long way from the equality they need. However, for a group that has been oppressed in this country for two-hundred-odd years, the black population has been socially significant. Blacks have influenced the white middle class by their modes of dress, language, music, and dance.

Here the third-person stance was an appropriate choice. If the writer had mentioned his own identity as a black or a white, or if he had assumed certain racial attitudes on the part of his readers, he would have distracted us from his message: that the black culture has had a significant impact on the life-styles of white Americans.

Like the students we have quoted in this chapter, you'll be able to find the right voice for a paper once you've experimented awhile. But don't expect to sound like the same person every time you write. You might be an experienced mountain climber in one paper, an outraged victim of discrimination in another, the devoted parent of a retarded child in still another. Writers are something like actors. As Walker Gibson puts it, "Somehow the writer has to evoke, out of mere ink marks on the paper, a character whose language the reader will trust, enjoy, profit from."

. . . .
Exercise 1 For thought and discussion
. . . .

Writers often speak of the importance of the human voice behind a piece of writing. Here is what some have said. Think about their observations in relation both to writing you have read and to your own writing.

a. Somehow the writer has to evoke, out of mere ink marks on paper, a character whose language the reader will trust, enjoy, profit from.
Walker Gibson, writing teacher

b. Style usually means some form of fancy writing—when people say, oh yes, so and so is such a "wonderful stylist." But if one means by style the voice, the irreducible and always recognizable and alive thing, then of course style is everything.
Mary McCarthy, American author

c. The audience fails to understand the writer because the writer has failed to understand the audience.
Anonymous

d. The ideal reader of my novels is a lapsed Catholic and failed musician, short-sighted, colorblind, auditorily biased, who has read the books that I have read. He should also be about my age.
Anthony Burgess, British writer

e. Who touches this book touches a human being.
Walt Whitman, first page of Leaves of Grass

f. I've enjoyed writing in a course where I've been encouraged to experiment with my own voice. I didn't think I would because I never did enjoy English. I found out that I can do some things in writing that I never thought before I could.
A student

g. Writing, when properly managed (as you may be sure I think mine is), is but a different name for conversation.
Laurence Sterne, English novelist

. . . .
Exercise 2   For class discussion
. . . .

Following part III, "Writing to Support a Point," you will find ten sample student essays, each written in support of a point; and at the ends of the three chapters in part IV, "Writing to Describe, Narrate, and Inform," you will find seven descriptive, seven narrative, and six informative essays. Though these student papers appear at four different places in this book, we have numbered them consecutively throughout for easy reference. Several exercises in the text refer you to these sample essays. This is the first such exercise.

Read the student essays listed below and consider the purpose and audience of each. What relationship with his or her audience does the writer assume? What is the writer's purpose in writing for this audience?

. . . .

Exercise 3 For class discussion
. . . .

Discuss the writer's stance in each of these introductory paragraphs. Does the choice of first-, second-, or third-person point of view seem appropriate, considering the writer's apparent purpose and audience? If not, what would you suggest instead?

a. Every afternoon that I am home and not otherwise occupied, I sneak down into the basement at one-thirty and hide there in the semidarkness until three o'clock doing something that I really don't like to talk about. I have been doing this for more years than I care to say, and, I am forced to admit, there is no end in sight. I am a "closet viewer" of television soap operas.

b. Looking for a late-night snack, but everything is closed? Well, my friend, there's always the Shrimp Boat. It's open twenty-four hours a day, seven days a week. As a matter of fact, the only time it ever closes is when someone from the Health Department stops in.

c. As I sit at a table with my friends, I invite you to join me at an African party. Although it is half past twelve o'clock, the party is just beginning. Drain the glass that has been set before you, clean your plate, and be prepared to dance 'til your legs fall off. Welcome to Moses' and Sylvia's wedding reception.

d. Most people learning to shoot want to learn as a sport. No one wants to get hurt, but accidents can happen through negligence and oversight. Novice shooters need to learn the correct and safe methods of operating a firearm. Some of the basics are discussed in this paper.

e. When I was a teenager, I used to feel sorry for pregnant women. I thought that they felt fat and ugly and sloppy and embarrassed. I even felt embarrassed when I saw them. No one ever corrected this impression, so I was in for a few surprises when I finally became pregnant.

f. Grab your most comfortable jeans and your tennis shoes. Pack a bag lunch and bring a deck of cards. You'll be waiting a long time. Where are we going? Why, we are going to see the King Tutankhamen exhibition at the National Gallery of Art.

g. When my mother became ill three years ago with a heart condition, she was put on a low-salt, low-calorie diet. Today we are convinced that a good nutritional diet may prevent and even cure some illnesses. It worked for our family, and it can work for yours.

. . . .
Exercise 4 For thought
. . . .

Unless you choose writing topics that will work for *you*, you'll have a hard time finding your voice. Wayne C. Booth, an English professor, tells a story that makes this point very well:

> Last fall I had an advanced graduate student, bright, energetic, well-informed, whose papers were almost unreadable. He managed to be pretentious, dull, and disorganized in his paper on *Emma,* and pretentious, dull, and disorganized on *Madame Bovary.* On *The Golden Bowl* he was all these and obscure as well. Then one day, toward the end of the term, he cornered me after class and said, "You know, I think you were all wrong about Robbe-Grillet's *Jealousy* today." We didn't have time to discuss it, so I suggested that he write me a note about it. Five hours later I found in my faculty box a four-page polemic, unpretentious, stimulating, organized, convincing. Here was a man who had taught freshman composition for several years and who was incapable of committing any of the more obvious errors that we think of as characteristic of bad writing. Yet he could not write a decent sentence, paragraph, or paper until . . . he had found a definition of his audience, his argument, and his own proper tone of voice.

When this graduate student finally discovered something he wanted to say—to someone who wanted to hear it—he found his voice.

"How am I to know," the despairing writer asks, "which the right word is?" The reply must be . . . "The wanted word is the one most nearly true. True to what? Your vision and your purpose."   Elizabeth Bowen

As a speaker, you command several varieties of English. When applying for a job or speaking to the congregation at church, you speak formally; but when you relax with friends on Saturday night, you relax your language as well. When explaining your latest modification of a VW engine to your little brother, who knows nothing about the inner workings of automobiles, you use easy-to-understand, nontechnical English. But explain the same thing to your best friend, who has just modified his Corvette, and your language is suddenly filled with cams and crankshafts and cc's.

Among strangers you keep your language distant, but with your in-group—people of your age, your social class, or your ethnic or geographic background—you use language common to that group. If you're from Appalachia, you might talk one way to people from your part of the country and a slightly different way to outsiders. If you're an Afro-American or a Puerto Rican–American or a Mexican-American, you may have the ability to shift, depending on the situation, between an ethnic language and a more neutral language common to all.

Perhaps you come from a highly educated family around whom your grammar is perfect. If so, you probably tone down that perfect grammar when hanging out with friends from a different background. Or maybe you're a middle-aged veteran who has returned to college. On campus you make friends with a crowd of younger vets, and before long you find yourself picking up all their latest slang. When you get together socially with people your own age, you may throw in just enough of the new slang to be interesting, but not so much that you'll look like you're showing off.

In speaking, then, you have an amazing ability to choose, on the spot, from a number of language varieties. It's as if you were computerized to judge every complex social situation in which you speak. Your computer gives you the answer immediately: it tells you how formal, how technical, how slangy, how ethnic, how intimate, how youthful, how class-conscious, how personal, how regional you should be. Sometimes you may make mistakes; for example, you may speak too informally for the situation, or you may choose language too technical for your listeners. But on the whole your instincts—and those of almost all native speakers of our language—are remarkably accurate.

Writing, like speaking, requires you to choose from among a number of language varieties. Often the same instinct that guides you as you speak will help you as you write—but not always, because writing and speaking are not quite the same.

When you write, your judgment may trip you up more often than when you speak. You are more likely to adopt a formal tone when an informal one would be more suitable, to use slang or jargon in situations where they're not appropriate, or to mix styles in odd ways. The question to ask yourself as you write is, "What language is *appropriate* to the situation in which I am writing?" This chapter offers guidelines to help you answer that question for many writing situations in which you may find yourself.

Formal or informal?

You will choose a relatively formal voice when applying for a job, explaining your aesthetic beliefs in a philosophy paper, or arguing in a letter to the editor that a traffic light should be installed at a dangerous intersection. In such writing situations an informal voice would be inappropriate.

But there are also situations in which a formal voice would be inappropriate. In a letter to a friend or in a memo to a coworker, a formal voice might sound too distant or too unfriendly. Similarly, if you were describing your first blind date, the absurdities of a soap opera, or the recent pranks of your six-year-old, a formal voice might sound pretentious.

You may be tempted more often to assume a formal voice when an informal one would be better than to write informally when formality is needed. We want to show you a paper written in a formal voice when an informal voice would have carried the writer's message more clearly and more convincingly.

I had a very high level of response to that fine work of fiction by Mrs. Kate Chopin, "The Storm." This phenomenon happened because the masterpiece evoked significant memories of my early years in New Orleans, where I lived between the ages of nine and twelve. My brain still records the uniqueness of a rainstorm in that grand old city, where rain fell on one side of the street while the sun shone on the other. At times the rain precipitated so violently that it appeared to be descending sideways. Then suddenly that miracle of nature would occur: a rainbow.

The paper continued with a reference to "magnificent" chinaberry trees on whose berries the birds "became inebriated." Further on, our writer referred to a sentence of Cajun dialect she had memorized as "the patois of the inhabitants of antique New Orleans."

Some consultation on this paper helped its writer to see that her message had been obscured by a too-formal style. She decided to rewrite the paper in a more informal voice. Then it sounded like this:

> The short story "The Storm" by Kate Chopin brought back pleasant memories of my childhood in New Orleans, where I lived when I was nine to twelve. I remember rain falling on one side of the street and the sun shining on the other side; I always thought there was magic involved, especially when the rainbow came out. We would run in and out of the rain, one minute wet and the next dry. Sometimes the rain fell so hard it seemed to be coming down sideways.
>
> Chopin's reference to a chinaberry tree also took me back to my childhood, reminding me of two large chinaberry trees in our front yard. My dad had told me birds would get drunk from eating chinaberries, so I spent hours waiting to see whether they would fall off the limbs, drunk. Our Creole friends in New Orleans made chinaberry wine, so maybe what he said was true.
>
> Chopin's use of dialect also appealed to me; in it I could hear the sing-song of Cajun speech. My brothers and I thought we could speak Cajun because someone taught us the sentence: "Youseemycowdowntheroadyoupush'im-home'eh?" If you repeated that very rapidly, you were speaking Cajun.

We think you will agree that the new version sounds more like pleasant memories of childhood.

Writers who usually assume an appropriate voice sometimes slip temporarily out of voice while writing. That happened to a student while he was writing a paper about the benefits of long winter walks:

> Sometimes I wake up early in the morning in the wintertime. I get dressed, start the coffee, bring in the paper, and begin my day with a winter walk. With the rest of the family still under their quilts, a lengthy walk helps to purify some of the confusion and tension inhibiting my mind. Breathing in country air, watching the sunrise, listening to the birds, glimpsing an occasional deer running across the pathway—all this outdoor activity helps to banish whatever worries may be on my mind.

When our writer's attention was called to "a lengthy walk helps to purify some of the confusion and tension inhibiting my mind," he realized immediately that he needed to rewrite that portion of his sentence. It tended to jar with the informality of the rest of his paragraph. He changed it to read: "a long walk helps to clear my head." With this revision, the paragraph flowed smoothly throughout.

A similar jarring effect can occur if you lapse into a too-informal voice in an otherwise formal paper. Here is a paragraph from a student's paper about the trip he dreams of taking to the British Isles:

> I want to see for myself all the historical sites I have seen only through the eyes of others in books I have read. I would like to see whatever remains of Charles Dickens's world. And I would surely pay a call at the large old homes that figure so prominently in Agatha Christie's mystery stories. Nor would I miss Buckingham Palace, where I would hope to arrive in time for the changing of the guard. I remember reading about that as a child in A. A. Milne's Pooh books; it must be a bang-up affair every time it occurs. Next I would travel north to the Yorkshire dales James Herriot wrote about in *All Creatures Great and Small*. There I would tackle the moors on foot, as Emily Brontë used to do, and then I would hit the coal-mining country I have heard about through D. H. Lawrence. And all the time I would feel close to the authors whose books had lured me to the British Isles.

When our writer reread his paragraph, some words jumped out at him: *bang-up affair, tackle, hit.* These words were too informal in tone to go with the rest of the paragraph. He decided to change "bang-up affair" to "spectacular event," "tackle the moors on foot" to "wander across the moors," and "hit" to "view." If you read his revisions into the paragraph, we think you will see why he was pleased with his changes.

When you write, then, you'll want to adjust your writing voice to fit your writing situation. Sometimes you will choose a formal voice, sometimes an informal one. And once you've chosen your voice, you'll want to maintain it.

"In-group" or standard?

Years ago students were taught to avoid all "in-group" language in their writing. "Never use slang," preached English teachers, "and never write in an ethnic or a regional dialect. Always use standard English." But today most English instructors agree that in-group language is sometimes appropriate, even though in most writing situations it is not.

When are slang and dialect likely to be appropriate? They are clearly acceptable when you are quoting the words of people who actually speak in slang or dialect. If you are quoting Sojourner Truth's famous "And Ain't I a Woman?" speech, you wouldn't "correct" Truth's dialect as some misguided English teachers once did. You would let ex-slave Sojourner Truth speak with the ringing authority of her own voice:

> That man over there. He says women need to be helped into carriages and lifted over ditches and to have the best everywhere. Nobody ever helps me into carriages, over mud puddles, or gets me any best place.
>
> *Ain't I a woman?* Look at me! Look at my arm. I have ploughed. And I have planted. And I have gathered into barns. And no man could head me. *And ain't I a woman?*
>
> I could work as much, and eat as much as any man—when I could get it—and bear the lash as well. *And ain't I a woman?* I have borne thirteen children and seen them sold into slavery, and when I cried out with a mother's grief, none but Jesus heard me. *And ain't I a woman?*

It is appropriate, then, to quote the special language of others. No one is likely to disagree with this. But when is it appropriate for you to put your own slang or dialect into your writing? Here we are on more dangerous ground; any guidelines are likely to be controversial.

In general, dialect and slang are more appropriate in creative, "expressive" writing than in practical or intellectual writing. If your purpose in writing is to express your personality or your ethnic or regional identity, then it may be appropriate to write in your own speaking voice, as this student did:

> Look, white brother, ya got no soul. No brother, I am not referring to your heart. I mean real down-to-earth soul. Nah man, I am not talking about soul food, like chittlings, hamhocks or pigs feet. I am talking 'bout soul, ya know? Rockin', grindin', windin', bindin', bumpin' soul. No, Lester, I do not mean to exercise. Brother, I am talking about something hip, mean, bad, out-a-sight. Lester, I did not say anything about a hippopotamus who can not see. Lester, you must be some type of nut. Lester, you are impossible. For heaven's sake, let's forget the whole thing.

As black poet Imamu Amiri Baraka (LeRoi Jones) points out, the spoken dialect carries an expressive meaning that can't be translated:

> I heard an old Negro street singer last week, Reverend Pearly Brown, singing, "God don't never change!" This is a precise thing he is singing. He does not mean "God does not ever change!" He means "God don't never change."

Slang and dialect, since they are spoken by in-groups, can be very effective when you're appealing to an in-group audience. The common language is a way of expressing your solidarity with the group. A union leader, for example, might write campaign literature in the language of the steelworkers who will be voting in the election. Or a Chicano community leader will write to his or her constituents in the language they all share. Here, for example, are the words of José Ángel Gutiérrez, addressed to fellow Chicanos:

> You've got a handful of gringos controlling the lives of *muchos mexicanos.* And it's been that way for a long time. . . . In 1960 there were twenty-six Texas counties in which Chicanos were a majority, yet not one of those counties was in the control of Chicanos. If you want to take that you can. You can be perfectly content just like your father and your grandfather were, *con el sombrero en la mano.*

In-group language is often appropriate for informal writing. For example, here are some sentences from a student paper about the after-hours pranks of a cross-country track team:

> Tires could be heard squealing in the night as my car pulled away, with the town-and-country wagon following. I turned off the main drag down a side street, with a pair of headlights still trailing some distance behind. While I was concentrating all my efforts on controlling my swaying mobile, my backseat buddies thought it would be fun to lob a firecracker at our trailing team members. Simultaneous with the firecracker's disposal came the word "Cop!"

Sometimes, then, in-group language is appropriate in writing. You'll find, however, that most writing situations require you to tone down your natural speaking voice and write in standard English. Slang and dialect attract a reader's attention to the writer's *way* of speaking, and in most situations this is distracting. If you want readers to focus on *what* you're saying, you won't make them too conscious of *how* you're saying it. Also, in most writing situations slang or dialect is simply out of place, as a matter of courtesy. It's bad manners to assert your uniqueness too strongly in a business letter or a college term paper, especially when your readers don't share your in-group language. So unless you have a special reason for choosing an in-group language, you should write in standard English.

Technical or plain English?

Sometimes you'll need to choose between technical English, understandable only to specialists, and plain English that everyone can understand. Usually your audience will determine your choice. A lawyer, for example, will use legal language when writing a brief to other lawyers, but he or she will shift to nontechnical English when summarizing that same brief for a client. Someone we know who supervises computer technologists finds that she must write technically accurate directives for her staff and simplified memos in plain English for her own supervisors. If she writes the directives in ordinary English, her staff will make mistakes. If she writes technical memos for her supervisors, who are not specialists, they won't understand her—and they'll be annoyed with her for wasting their time.

A sociologist will use a great deal of technical language when writing for other specialists, but will shift to ordinary language when writing a textbook for beginners. He or she may introduce technical terminology in the book but be careful not to overwhelm the beginner with too much of it, even at the risk of sacrificing complete accuracy. Of course, we have all been victims at one time or another of a textbook writer who forgot his or her audience. But the really good textbook writers are those who suit their language to their audience. They write in plain English, so their readers can understand them.

Writers often use technical English when nontechnical would be more appropriate. Doctors, lawyers, scholars, and government or military officials are sometimes so impressed with themselves for having mastered a technical vocabulary that they use it whenever they get a chance—even when it's clearly inappropriate. For example, a scholar once asked a farmer if he was "excavating a subterranean channel." The farmer replied, "No, sir, I am only digging a ditch."

Supreme Court Justice Oliver Wendell Holmes, himself a highly educated man, once complained about such misuse of technical language. Said Holmes, "I know there are professors in this country who 'ligate' arteries. Other surgeons only tie them, and it stops bleeding just as well." Like Holmes, we think it's best to avoid technical language when ordinary English will do as well. Don't write "This semiautomatic, small-caliber, shoulder-fired weapon, because of mechanical derangement, ceased to function." Just tell your readers that the rifle jammed.

Let's conclude with a useful guideline. In general, choose plain English. Use technical English only when 1) you are knowledgeable enough to use it correctly; 2) your readers are knowledgeable enough to understand it; and 3) your purpose in writing truly requires it.

Nonsexist language

Sexist language is fast becoming acknowledged as inappropriate in our society because it demeans women and girls simply by not recognizing them. Such language emphasizes maleness as the human norm, with the inevitable consequence that femaleness becomes less than quite human.

Think of how often you encounter such expressions as *mankind, the brotherhood of man, man and his universe, All men are created equal, The Norsemen settled along the coast of . . .* , and *Anthropology is the study of man*. None of these common expressions recognizes that at least one-half of the human beings in the world are female.

You might argue, of course, "Oh, everybody knows those uses of *man* mean *all* people." But even if that were absolutely true, there is a wide gap between possible inclusion and clear, equal recognition. Because women remain invisible in such "man-words," there is at least a fifty-fifty chance that they will not be equally recognized in the consciousness of the writer—or the reader. You can be sure that your reader will know you mean everybody when you substitute for these man-words such words as *human, humanity, person, people,* and *individuals*. Some of these substitutions may feel awkward to you at first, but every expression in our language was new and awkward at some time.

Just as *mankind* does not clearly include everybody, neither do the pronouns *he, his,* and *him* when used in a general sense. A sentence like the following one would seldom recognize everyone in a class: "The student who hands in his final paper even an hour late will risk a grade of 'incomplete' for the course." Restricting yourself to the masculine pronoun can indeed lead to some strange sentences—like this one uttered by a New York state legislator: "When we get abortion law repeal, everyone will be able to decide for himself whether or not to have an abortion."

The two most common singular pronoun forms now used to indicate everybody are *he and she* (sometimes *he or she*) and *he/she*. These can become *his and her* or *his/her,* and *him and her* or *him/her,* as needed. Using either of these, you could write: "The student who hands in his or her (his/her) final paper even an hour late will risk a grade of 'incomplete' for the course."

You may find yourself puzzling over how to eliminate the sexism in sentences containing pronouns such as *each, one, none, either, neither, any, every, somebody,* and *whoever*. No doubt you have been taught the rule that all such pronouns must be singular: "Everyone wore his oldest jeans to the senior hayride." Actually, everyday usage—language evolving on its own, as it so often does despite our made-up rules—is not waiting for us to decide to change this rule. Everyday usage is moving toward *they, their,* and *them* to follow such singular pronouns. For example: "Every student in turn added their books to the growing pile as they rushed out to the game, taking their flags and their cheering cards with them."

Or you may want to recast your singular sentences into the plural to include everybody: "Students who hand in their final papers even an hour late will risk a grade of 'incomplete' for the course"; "All the students in turn added their books to the growing pile as they rushed out to the game, taking their flags and their cheering cards with them." You will find more examples of sentences that resolve the gender-linked pronoun problem under "Match Your Nouns and Pronouns" in "Revising Problem Sentences" in the handbook section.

Another way to remove sexism from your language is to avoid sex-linked occupational and organizational terms. As more careers attract both men and women, our former occupational terms are gradually becoming false designations. You will be more accurate if you say *worker* instead of *workman,* *flight attendant* instead of *stewardess,* *firefighter* instead of *fireman,* and so on. And if you listen, you will notice that in many organizations *chairperson* is replacing *chairman.*

When we first wrote this chapter, in 1978, sexist language was becoming inappropriate in our society. Now, in 1981, we can report that it *is* inappropriate. You have probably noticed this yourself. Newspapers refer to *police officers,* not to *policemen,* and few writers today would risk the term *police lady.* Government offices routinely edit sexist language from their publications. *He* has become *he or she, congressman* has become *member of Congress,* and words such as *mankind* are taboo. Writers and speakers everywhere are learning to recast their sentences in the plural so that the issue of sexist pronouns doesn't even arise.

Why, you may ask, are people going to all this trouble? The answer is simple, really. More and more readers, both men and women, are finding sexist language offensive. And most writers, no matter what their personal feelings on the issue might be, don't want to offend their readers. Nonsexist English is a matter of courtesy—of respect for and sensitivity to the feelings of others.

. . . .

Exercise 1 Written

. . . .

The student writer of a paper about ways to relieve the monotony of dull jobs had some trouble maintaining his writing voice. Read the following paragraph from his paper to decide whether a formal or an informal voice is more appropriate. Then revise the paragraph so that it is all in the voice you choose.

At my job, whenever the tedious routine begins to get to me, I rely on Butch to come up with something to break the monotony. One such instance immediately comes to mind. While I was busy working one day, I noticed Butch waving for me to "come over here." Noting the level of his enthusiasm, I promptly moved toward him. As I drew near, he revealed to me a frog, which he had just found. "So what?" I commented. With a gleam in his eye, Butch said, "Let's put it in the new guy's lunch pail!" A smile immediately materialized on my face. Butch recognized my approval, and we made our way toward the truck. As the lunch hour approached, we compared expectations as we anxiously anticipated what we imagined would occur. Eagerly the new guy opened his lunch pail—and out popped the frog, landing right under his nose. By that time, Butch and I were laughing so hard we were about to explode.

. . . .
Exercise 2 For class discussion
. . . .

What kind of language would you choose for each of the following writing situations? Would you write formally or informally? Would you use technical language in any instances? Where would you consciously avoid technical language and take care to write in plain English? Would in-group slang or jargon be appropriate in any case? As you think about how you would handle each of these writing situations, you might begin to make notes on some of the topics that interest you, to use in developing papers later.

1. Your cousin in a distant city is planning to move to your area and wants to apply to your workplace for a job similar to yours. Write to him or her about your job.

2. Write an enthusiastic review of a ballet, a symphony concert, or a dinner-theater production to encourage some of your friends to enjoy such an evening's entertainment.

3. Write an article for your church newsletter encouraging all members of the congregation to create items for the spring fair that funds summer activities for the children of the church.

4. If you are dissatisfied with one of your professors and talking with him or her has not helped, write a letter of complaint to the head of the department in which the professor teaches. (no names, please)

5. Write some publicity for a Halloween hayride several teenagers you know are sponsoring. Proceeds from the event will help pay for a weekend celebration at the beach following high-school graduation.

6. Write a paper in which you encourage a friend to take up a particular sport, such as tennis, golf, biking, or swimming.

7. In *On Death and Dying,* Elisabeth Kübler-Ross describes the five stages of dying. Read that portion of the book and write about it in a letter to a friend who is seeing someone through those stages.

8. Write a paper in which you try to convince a friend to take a course you have enjoyed taking.

9. Write a letter to your brother or sister, who was on your high school's basketball team, about the recent victory of this year's team in the big game of the year.

10. Write an article for publication in the monthly bulletin of a large agency with many employees, in which you argue for child-care facilities at the work site.

11. If you know about a diet prescribed for a particular physical condition, encourage someone you feel it would help to use it by explaining the diet and its benefits in a paper.

12. Write a description of what you do at work to be included in a directory of local occupations being compiled by career counselors at your college.

13. Write a character sketch of one of your children.

14. If you know anything about play production, try to involve your classmates in a college play by writing a paper about set building, stage lighting, costume designing, and so on.

15. Describe the solar heating or some other energy-saving device in your home to your brother-in-law, who wants to install a similar device in his home in another town.

16. Write a letter to your public library requesting it to purchase three children's books that you find particularly delightful.

. . . .
Exercise 3 For thought and discussion
. . . .

To illustrate some of the differences between a formal and an informal voice, we would like to share with you two items that appeared in the *Washington Post* just after Smokey Bear died at the National Zoo. First, read this excerpt from an informal article entitled "Smokey's Enduring Appeal."

> Like many greats, Smokey Bear had to pass on to get the attention he lacked in the declining years of his life.
>
> Now, nothing is too good for the only animal in America with his own private zip code (20232). He was jetted out to Albuquerque yesterday in a

specially made box painted forest green with handles on both sides, and a boulder in Smokey Bear Historical State Park will commemorate his passing. . . .

Even his wife, Goldie, was reconciled to him at the end. They had a pro forma marriage that even Ann Landers couldn't have saved, but Goldie alone was with him at the end. "She didn't want to leave, she had to be coaxed out," a zoo spokeswoman said. "It was very heartbreaking. . . . "

He [Smokey] was discovered in June, 1950, a 5-pound cub clinging to a burnt tree in New Mexico's Capitan Mountains. A forest ranger's daughter nursed him back to health, fed him pablum, and catered to his penchant for sleeping in washing machines. As soon as he was healthy, he was flown to Washington in a plane with his picture painted on the fuselage and slotted to be the living symbol of a cartoon character a California agency had dreamed up five years earlier.

Smokey's popularity has been phenomenal. . . . His mail ran as high as 13,000 letters per week, enough to keep three people working full time dashing off answers over his pawprint.

Now read Smokey's obituary, written in the formal voice considered appropriate for an obituary and headed "S. Bear, Fire Fighter."

Smokey Bear, an employee of the National Park Service from shortly after his birth until retirement last year, died in his sleep Monday night at his home in the National Zoo. He was 26.

"It was just old age," a Park Service spokeswoman said simply of Mr. Bear's demise. "When they went to check him this morning, they found he had died."

Mr. Bear was the zoo's best known resident, and was familiar to millions of Americans as the symbol of the national campaign to prevent forest fires. His deep but kindly bass voice was often heard over radio and television as he declaimed, "Remember, only you can prevent forest fires!" [He] was perhaps better known to Americans than any personality other than the president. A 1968 survey revealed that nine out of 10 citizens knew who Smokey Bear was.

A native of New Mexico, he was himself intimately familiar with the horrors of blazes in the woodlands of the nation. He was less than a year old when a park ranger found him in the smoking ruins of what had been a forest in New Mexico, and rescued Mr. Bear, who was suffering from a burned paw. Mr. Bear was flown to Santa Fe, New Mexico, and from there to Washington where he took up residence at the National Zoo.

Although he had no formal schooling, Mr. Bear was accepted into the Park Service shortly after his arrival in Washington, and remained with that agency until his retirement a year ago this month. . . . When he retired Mr. Bear was made a member of the National Association of Retired Federal Employees and was given a membership card by that organization. . . .

Mr. Bear was married in 1962 to the former Goldie Bear, who was not a blood relation, despite the similarity of last names. In 1971 the still childless couple adopted a youngster from New Mexico, whom they named Young Smokey. Last April, Young Smokey, who is now about 6 years old, took over for his father following Mr. Bear's retirement.

Mr. Bear is survived by his wife of the home in Washington; and the son, Young Smokey, also of the city.

Mr. Bear's body is being flown to New Mexico for burial.

Read the two excerpts again. This time think about how word choice and sentence structure help to make one sound informal and the other formal. Come to class prepared to discuss how formal and informal voices have been achieved in these two pieces of writing.

. . . .

Exercise 4   For discussion
. . . .

Look at the following student papers and comment on how either formal or informal language contributes to the effect of each paper. Is the language appropriately chosen?

"Irish vs. American Education" (#1, p. 173.)
"Escaped Prisoner" (#22, p. 223.)
"Water-skiing to Signals" (#27, p. 243.)
"Growing Orchids" (#28, p. 244.)

. . . .

Exercise 5   For reading and listening
. . . .

For at least a week, look and listen for examples of sexism in language in your day-to-day life—at work, at school, in advertisements, at home, in stores, on radio and television, at social events, wherever you go. Try to be alert to all the sexist language problems pointed out in this section: man-words, pronouns, occupational and organizational terms, and so on. Perhaps you can even find some absurdities, like this one from a children's book: "Man, like the other mammals, breast-feeds his young." Bring your five choicest items to class.

. . . .

Exercise 6   Classroom activity
. . . .

Remove the sexism from the sexist language collected for exercise 5.

···

Exercise 7 Just for fun

···

One of our students wrote the following poem about language:

Nostalgia
(or, Getting with It)

I remember
 when a chick was the offspring of a hen,
 when a dude was a ranch vacationer,
 when a greaser was a garage mechanic,
 when a square was a geometric figure,
 when a freak was a side-show performer,
 when a sucker was a lollypop,
 when a shrink was a dry-clean-only dress,
 when a pig was a farm animal,
 when cool was the opposite of warm,
 when making out was being successful (at anything),
 when flipping out was missing the mat in tumbling,
 when to dig had to do with ditches,
 when a hangup was Monday's wash on the line,
 when my bag was the grocery sack,
 when a bug was an insect,
 when pintos, mustangs, and cougars had legs,
 when uptight was how a corset was laced,
 when grass was something you mowed,
 when tea was something you drank,
 when pot described grandpa's belly,
 when a weed was a nuisance (to anyone),
 when high was the sky,
 when a joint was a hangout,
 when hash was mashed corned beef,
 when upper referred to the department store level,
 when a trip involved packing a suitcase,
 when rock had to do with geology,
 when acid had to do with chemistry,
 when a bust was part of the anatomy,
 when bread was something to butter,
 when a head-shop was a beauty parlor,
 when long-haired described classical music,
 when a turn-on involved a light switch,
 when a ripoff meant getting out the sewing basket,
 when a pad was something you wore, periodically.

PART THREE

Writing to support a point

*Have something to say, and say it as clearly as you
can.* Matthew Arnold

Try this reading test. Read the paragraph *once* only.

> Suppose an elevator starts at the first floor with six passengers, and stops
> at the next floor where four people get out and two get on; it continues
> upward to the next floor where three get on and no one gets off, but at the
> following floor two get off; at the next floor two get on and three get off.

Now answer the question: How many times did the elevator stop?

Chances are you did not "pass" this reading test, even if you are a
very good reader, because the test was rigged against you from the start.
Most readers think they're supposed to be watching for the number of
people on the elevator, so they focus their attention on the people getting
on and off the elevator, not on the elevator stops.

If you "flunked" this test, it was the writer's fault, not yours. Suppose
for a moment that you were the writer giving the test. If you really
wanted your readers to watch for the number of times the elevator
stopped, you would probably ask the question *before* the test. Being a
sensible person, you would let your readers know in one way or another
what the point was.

As you write papers this semester, what can you do to make sure
readers won't miss your point? The answer is surprisingly simple. State
your main point clearly and concisely, preferably in one sentence, and put
that sentence early in your paper—either at the beginning or at the end of
an introductory paragraph. The one-sentence declaration of the main
point of a paper is called a *thesis statement*. This thesis statement is the
most important sentence in your entire paper. It tells readers the point of
the paper so that they can spot the most important ideas as they read on.
In essence, your thesis statement maps out the territory into which you
are taking your readers.

Let us show you a few examples, so you can see how a thesis

statement focuses the reader's attention on the main point of a paper. This student writer has placed his thesis statement at the end of his introductory paragraph:

> During my childhood I had to pass the city jail to get to town. The barred windows of the jail were easily visible from the street. Of the many times I passed that jail I recall seeing only black faces behind those bars. It was many years later before I knew why that was so. *The primary reason for the disproportionate number of blacks in our jails and prisons is their low economic status.*

The thesis statement (italicized) clearly announces the writer's main point: that blacks populate our jails and prisons in disproportionate numbers because they are poor. Readers know what to expect in the rest of the paper; as they read they will look for evidence that poverty is the main reason so many blacks are behind bars.

Another student writer begins his introductory paragraph with a thesis:

> *Supermarkets are not designed for the quantity family buyer.* To see what I mean, come with me on a typical weekly grocery-buying trip for my family of eight. We will shop at an average supermarket, my neighborhood A & P.

Readers learn the point immediately: that supermarkets are not set up for customers who buy in quantity. The rest of this student's paper will show readers just how true this statement is.

Here is one last example, written by the mother of a first-grader. She places her thesis at the end of her opening paragraph:

> Without a doubt my daughter Nicole suffered academically from not entering Forestville at the beginning of her kindergarten year. Instead she was computerized, zoned, and bused to Brookline Elementary. *Though by all outward appearances our community's two elementary schools are comparable, Forestville is academically superior to Brookline.*

The thesis prepares readers for a paper that contrasts the merits of Forestville with the shortcomings of Brookline. Readers know exactly what the writer intends to show them: that Forestville is academically superior to Brookline.

Writing a thesis

Now that you have seen some thesis statements in context, let us take a closer look at these important sentences. A thesis statement, as we said before, is *a one-sentence declaration of the main point of a piece of writing.* A successful thesis statement has three characteristics.

First, a thesis statement must be a *generalization;* it cannot be merely a fact. A flat statement of fact, such as "Edgar Allan Poe was born in 1809," doesn't communicate a main point, so it just won't do as a thesis. It takes a generalization to state a main point. "Edgar Allan Poe's life was filled with bitter disappointments"—a general statement requiring specific development later in the paper—would make a good thesis. So would "According to his biographers, Poe had difficulty relating to women sexually." That's a generalization about Poe's life, not just a fact about it. You could develop it into a paper filled with facts about Poe's relationships with women.

Your thesis must communicate a generalization that you can develop in the rest of the paper. Let's say you want to share with readers your enthusiasm for Professor Baldwin's History 157. You wouldn't choose as your thesis statement "History 157, taught by Professor Baldwin, is offered at 10:00 on Tuesdays and Thursdays." You might include that fact in your paper, to be sure, but you wouldn't use it as your thesis. You would choose a generalization, perhaps one like this: "Whoever said that history is nothing but polishing tombstones must have missed History 157, because in Professor Baldwin's class history is very much alive." That's an idea that you could develop further. It's a good focal point for a whole paper.

Or imagine that you want to write a paper showing the dangers of the "55," a helicopter in which you nearly died. You are tempted to use " I nearly crashed to my death in a '55' helicopter" as your thesis, until you notice that it is too factual. So you choose a generalization instead, one that sums up your main point: "Though it looks innocent enough, the '55' is an extremely dangerous helicopter."

One last example: If you wanted to show readers that golf is an expensive sport, you wouldn't use "A good set of golf clubs costs at least $150" as your thesis. That's too factual. You would state your main point in a generalization, maybe one like this: "If you've never played golf before but are thinking of trying it, I'd advise against it—unless you have the funds to support this expensive hobby."

So a thesis statement is a generalization. But—and this brings us to the second characteristic of a successful thesis—it should not be *too* general. It should be a *limited* generalization, one that can be developed within your word limit. If your generalization is too broad, you're promising readers too much, unless you happen to be writing a book. In freshman English you will normally be writing papers of 300 to 1000 words, so you'll need to be especially careful to limit your thesis statements. You should not choose a thesis like "Marriages are breaking up at an accelerating rate for a variety of complex reasons," because you can't develop this statement convincingly in a short paper. You would be better off limiting the generalization radically, perhaps to "My first

marriage ended in divorce because I married for the wrong reasons."
This you could probably develop in a 500- to 1000-word paper—unless,
of course, you got carried away.

It takes common sense to decide when a thesis statement is too broad.
If you love Italian food, you might be tempted to work with a thesis like
"San Francisco has more first-rate Italian restaurants than any other
major American city." But common sense warns you against such a
thesis, which is much too broad to develop in a short paper. Common
sense leads you to a more limited generalization, such as: "At the top of
my list for good food, good service, and a charming atmosphere is a little
Italian restaurant called Luigi's."

Or imagine you want to show parents how to provide outlets for their
children's aggression. You begin with the thesis "There are many ways to
provide your children with outlets for their aggressive feelings," but then
you realize you can't do justice to such a statement in one short paper. So
you limit your thesis: "A number of toys on the market provide safe and
effective outlets for your child's aggressive feelings."

So far we have said that a successful thesis is 1) *a generalization,* and
2) *a limited generalization.* The third characteristic of a successful thesis
statement is that it is *sharply focused.* It is not too vague. A thesis like
"Edgar Allan Poe is an interesting writer," for example, is too vague. You
could write about Poe's life, about his theory of poetry, about his horror
stories, about almost anything connected with Poe, and still be more or
less sticking to your thesis that Poe is an "interesting writer." So the
thesis is poorly focused.

A vague thesis is not quite the same as an overly broad one, though a
vague one may also be too broad. Consider "Most P.E. instructors are
incompetent," for example. The first problem with this thesis is that it is
too broad. "Most P.E. instructors" includes those from Bogotá, from
Chicago, from Kyoto, from London, from anywhere. It would take a
very long book to prove that P.E. instructors all over the world are
incompetent. Obviously, the thesis needs limiting. It might be limited, for
example, to "The majority of P.E. instructors at City College are incompetent."

This limited thesis is much better, but it is still too vague. The key
word, *incompetent,* could mean too many different things. Do the instructors skip classes or show up drunk, are they so overweight they can't
participate in sports, are they unskilled, are they poor teachers, or what?
The thesis needs a more precise focus. We might sharpen its focus like
this: "The P.E. department at City College is more interested in promot-
ing winning teams than in teaching lifetime sports to average students."
That's a thesis a writer could probably work with. It is limited, and it is
sharply focused.

Usually the vagueness of a thesis can be traced to a word that could mean too many different things—a word such as *interesting* or *enjoyable* or *lousy*. Where precisely is a paper going when it promises to show us that Poe's life is "interesting" or that swimming is "enjoyable" or that *Citizen Kane* is a "lousy" movie? Your guess is as good as ours.

As you scribble on scratch paper in search of a thesis, you commonly begin with one that's too vague, because your ideas may not yet be clearly focused. Sharpening a too-vague thesis is part of the process of discovering what you really want to say. Each of these students, for example, began with a blurred focus and ended with a sharp one:

Too vague	*Sharpened focus*
Alimony is a rip-off.	Alimony is an injustice to men and an insult to the dignity of women.
The Parkdale Community College cafeteria serves bad food.	At the Parkdale Community College cafeteria you will search in vain for a nutritious meal.
Conquering a weight problem can be rewarding.	After trying every diet that's been popularized in the past five years, I finally found one that worked: old-fashioned calorie counting.
The Moto-guzzi is a better bike than the BMW.	The Moto-guzzi is a better all-round touring bike than the BMW.

A more precise thesis, though it may be harder to write than a vague one, gives you control over the rest of your paper. So it is worth the extra effort.

To sum up, a thesis statement is a one-sentence declaration of the main point of your paper. A good thesis statement has three characteristics: it is a generalization, not a specific fact; it is limited, not too broad; and it is sharply focused, not too vague.

We have devoted much of this chapter to just one sentence in your introduction because it is so important. But now we would like to consider your introductory paragraph as a whole.

Writing an introductory paragraph

Your introductory paragraph should *introduce* readers to your paper. Remember that readers come to your paper cold, not knowing what to expect. They have no idea what your point is. So your job, in your very first paragraph, is to announce the main point of your paper.

Your thesis statement—the one sentence that most clearly announces your main point—should nearly always appear either at the beginning or at the end of your introductory paragraph. Whether you place it at the beginning or the end depends on the effect you want to achieve. For a slow-paced effect, put the thesis at the end; for a blunter, more straight-forward effect, put it at the beginning.

For a slow-paced effect, you begin a few steps back from your thesis, orienting readers and giving them a feel for the subject area into which you are taking them. Then you zoom in on your thesis, the last sentence of the paragraph. If you think of a zoom-lens movie camera, you'll have some notion of how this kind of paragraph works. With a zoom lens you can film a broad panorama as background for your actual subject, then zoom quickly to the subject itself. Here is an example of what we might call a zoom paragraph:

> Little League sports were developed many years ago as amateur sports for young people. Little League's primary purpose was physical development, sportsmanship, and the advancement of peace and good will through athletic competition. However, if our local organization is a good example, Little League sports have strayed far from these goals. *The Palmer Park Little League is clearly run for the benefit of the adult coaches and parents.*

The writer begins broadly, speaking of Little League sports in general, and then zooms in on the message of his paper: that one specific Little League organization (the one the writer is familiar with) is run for the benefit of adults, not children.

Here is another zoom paragraph:

> During my junior year of high school my family moved from a suburban American community to a small village in rural Ireland. The change was a very pleasant one once we got over the initial cultural shock; and we learned a great deal from the visit. My biggest discoveries came from being enrolled in the local convent, a school that was very different from my old high school. *The difference lay not in the subjects that were taught, but rather in the way they were taught and the surroundings they were taught in.*

The first three sentences of this introductory paragraph are designed to orient readers. They let readers in the door, gradually making them feel at home. If the writer had hit her readers with her thesis right away, they would have felt she was pushing them into her paper too quickly, without giving them a chance to catch their breath.

The zoom paragraph allows you to chat awhile with readers before getting to your main point. The effect is polite and friendly, as if you were inviting readers into your paper. Notice, for example, how smoothly this student writer eases us into her paper on the violence in Grimms' fairy tales:

> The Brothers Grimm have always seemed a friend to parents at bedtime. They have helped get the kids into bed without too much trouble, and they've sent them quickly off to dreamland. But little do parents realize, when they leave the room and turn out the lights, that their children dream of wicked witches in gingerbread houses, trolls under bridges, and poisonous apples. *In their own way, the Brothers Grimm have been teaching children that life is no fairy tale.*

As you have seen, the zoom paragraph builds toward the thesis. For much of the writing that you will do this semester, the zoom paragraph will serve very well. Sometimes, though, you may decide to get to your point faster—with what we'll call a pointed paragraph. A pointed paragraph begins with the thesis:

> *Fresh foods are more economical than commercially prepared frozen foods or prepared mixes.* Let's do some comparison shopping to see just how true this is.

Pointed paragraphs are often appropriate in practical writing situations, when readers expect you to get right to the point. This kind of introductory paragraph can be short, sometimes as short as the thesis statement alone. Though it often lacks the graceful flow of the zoom paragraph, the pointed paragraph has the advantage of being straightforward. Notice, for example, how quickly this writer gets to her point:

> *Tippy's Taco House, on Route 1 in College Park, is a good place to stop when you are craving Mexican food.* Both the food and the service are better than you can usually expect from a small, inexpensive fast-food restaurant.

The effect is straightforward, almost blunt, but quite appropriate for a paper with an obviously practical purpose: to entice lovers of Mexican food to Tippy's Taco House.

Whether you begin with a zoom or a pointed paragraph, your readers should understand immediately, without even consciously thinking about it, that your introduction is an introduction. And they should understand, again without effort, just what your thesis is. When you're writing to support a point, the primary function of your introduction is to let readers know your point. It's as simple as that.

Rewriting your introduction

Don't be surprised if you go through several false starts before coming up with an introductory paragraph that's workable. It would be helpful if you always knew before putting pen to paper (or fingers to typewriter) just what your main idea would be. Then, as you wrote your opening paragraph, you could confidently introduce readers to your paper— before you had even written it. But you won't always have that kind of control over your material right from the start.

Often you'll need to write your introductory paragraph not to reveal your focus, but to discover it. And discovery is not a neat and tidy process; it almost always involves false starts. Here, for example, is one student writer's false start:

> The women's liberation movement which started its big push in the United States back in the 1960s is a well-intentioned movement. And I agree with its basic goals. *At the same time I do have some disagreements with its goals.*

Not bad for a false start, but the focus is pretty foggy. The student's next try was better:

> I agree with the economic goals of the women's liberation movement, such as equal pay for equal work and the right to credit. *However, the women's movement goes too far in challenging two traditional roles for women: the role of wife, and the role of mother.*

It's a good idea to experiment awhile, as this student did, before settling on an introductory paragraph. Keep writing introductory paragraphs until you think you've got the focus you want, then turn to the business of writing the paper. Don't worry too much at this point about how your introduction sounds. Why not? Because you may need to rewrite the introduction later, after you've written the paper.

Papers have a way of changing as they are being written, and this is not necessarily a bad thing, as long as you are aware of the changes—and as long as you are prepared to rewrite your introduction later. Sometimes a paper becomes more clearly focused as you write it. Other times the focus changes as you discover, through writing, what you really want to say.

For example, once he began drafting the body of his paper, the student who wrote the introductory paragraph criticizing the women's movement discovered that he couldn't write a convincing argument in support of his main point. He had said that he was in favor of the economic goals of the women's movement but that he did not support its challenges to the roles of wife and mother. Once into the paper, he realized that the roles of wife and mother were more tied to economics than he had thought, because in a society where divorce is common, these traditional unpaid roles leave women economically vulnerable. As soon as our writer saw this problem, he scanned his rough draft in search of a main point that he would be able to develop convincingly.

As it turned out, the strongest section of this student's rough draft was a description of his wife's job as mother of their six children. At the time the paper was written, the women's movement seemed to be saying that women such as his wife weren't leading meaningful lives. It didn't give full-time mothers the recognition this student felt they deserved. So he revised the paper, focusing on his new point: that motherhood, though unpaid, can be a full-time job that deserves our respect. Here is the student's revised introductory paragraph. Notice how much his introduction has changed since his first effort.

> The women's movement should be applauded for helping women make economic gains. But the movement should be careful, in its push for economic goals, not to lessen our respect for women's traditional unpaid roles— particularly the role of mother. *If you think motherhood is not as challenging, meaningful, and rewarding as other full-time jobs, let me show you a day in the life of my wife, Lurleen, mother of six.*

You may be surprised to hear that a student writer spent so much effort rewriting his introduction. But successful student writers, like professionals, often spend more time on the introduction than on any other section of the paper—and for good reasons. The introduction establishes the focus of the whole paper, and it's not always easy to settle on a good focus. Also, the introduction must be logically related to the body of the paper, and in a rough draft the body of the paper doesn't always support the introduction as well as it might. Sometimes, when the body and the introduction don't fit together properly, you'll choose to rewrite the body. But more often you'll probably decide to rewrite the introduction, because that is easier to do. And, finally, your introduction needs more work than the rest of the paper simply because it is so important. It determines how readers will approach the paper. If you head them in the wrong direction, their reading of the whole paper will be confused or distorted. So introductions are important enough to deserve your special attention. One professional writer claims he puts 85 percent of his effort into his introductory paragraph. That's pretty extreme, but not as extreme as you may be tempted to think.

....
Exercise 1   For class discussion
....

Let's say you are an experienced mountain climber. Because you know quite a bit about this subject, you decide to write a 500- to 1000-word paper on it for your freshman English course. You scribble on scratch paper awhile, trying to come up with a good thesis. Which of these thesis statements would you reject as too factual, too broad, or too vague? Which ones do you think might work as your thesis statement?

1. Of the many unsuccessful attempts to climb Mt. Everest, each one failed for a variety of reasons.

2. Mountain climbing, as dangerous as it may seem, is actually a very safe sport.

3. Mountain climbing is an extremely dangerous sport, regardless of the climber's ability.

4. On the last attempt to conquer Mt. Everest, two climbers lost toes to frostbite.

5. Mountain climbing is an exciting sport.

6. As hard as it is to believe, the sport of mountain climbing depends less on physical preparedness than on mental discipline.

7. Planning an expedition to climb Mt. McKinley takes years.

8. For me climbing is an ego trip.

9. A mountain climber must be able to put his or her life in other people's hands.

10. Many mountain-climbing expeditions fail not because of the mountain, but because the climbers' personalities keep getting in the way.

11. Being able to give entirely of oneself is the most important part of being a successful mountain climber.

12. Tying knots is an important skill in mountain climbing.

· ·
Exercise 2 Written
· ·

Look through the topics in part VII. Choose three on which you think you could write papers in support of a point, then scribble on scratch paper awhile to try to come up with a good thesis statement for each of your three topics. Circle your best thesis for each topic, then bring your thesis statements—still on scratch paper—to class.

Working in small groups, ask your classmates to evaluate each of your thesis statements, using these questions as guidelines: 1) Is it a generalization, not a specific fact? 2) Is it limited, not too broad? and 3) Is it precisely focused, not too vague?

If the thesis statements of some of your group's members are weak, help each other out. Make sure each member of the group ends up with at least one successful thesis statement that could lead to a paper the other group members would be interested in reading.

Exercise 3   For class discussion

How well does each of the following introductory paragraphs serve to orient you, then focus your attention on the writer's main point?

1. When you bought your home or leased your apartment, you signed a contract. Did you read it before you signed it? Did you understand it? If you've taken Business Law 105, the answer to these questions will be "yes." Business Law 105 is the most informative and useful course I have taken at City Community College.

2. Child abuse is physical or emotional harm to children by parents or guardians. Physical abuse includes intentionally inflicted bruises, fractures, burns or other wounds, attempts to drown, and so forth. Emotional abuse is battering with words that reject or ignore a child.

3. Traditional Japanese architecture and furnishings are so different from those of the West that it is virtually impossible to reproduce the style of a formal Japanese dinner party outside Japan. Nevertheless, I would like to venture a simple account of the basic essentials which a Western hostess can adapt.

4. Today people are more conscious than ever of health, and exercise seems to have become the most important ingredient for good health. Never before has one seen so many joggers and bicyclists out on our streets. For the over-thirty gang who are overweight, out of shape, nonathletic, but healthy, I recommend rope jumping as a convenient form of exercise.

5. So often we make the mistake of thinking of jails as prisons. They need to be distinguished. I had the misfortune of spending several months incarcerated in both of these dreadful institutions.

6. Catholic grammar schools have their place in society. They offer an alternative education and a religious atmosphere. However, the liabilities of such a school may outnumber the assets. Catholic schools force their values on you, divorce you from reality, and limit your curriculum.

7. After spending about a month in the hospital I believe that it is safe for me to say that the hospital is not a very nice place to be. When I was injured I weighed about one hundred and sixty pounds and was in very good condition. But by the time I was released I was down to about one hundred and thirty pounds, I had a bad case of jittery nerves, and I had broken out in pimples again. Most of the weight was lost because the first week I was on a liquid diet. Then when I was able to eat, I found the food was so bad that I didn't want to eat. Then there were the damn holes in the roof. There were millions of them and after staring at them for a short time I would look away and everything would have holes in it.

8. Most kids can hardly wait for Saturday morning so they can turn on their television sets. They look forward to the superheroes such as Superman, Wonderwoman, Spiderman, and Shazzan. Television is the highlight of their morning.

9. Karate teaches a philosophy of respect, self-discipline, and nonviolence. I learned this a few years ago when I was looking for the answer to a problem my son was having.

10. Sports heroes come and go. Some dominate their particular sport for a few years, then fade away, later to become answers to trivia questions. A handful obtain a level of greatness and are inducted into a hall of fame. Still fewer surpass all others before them, yet strive to improve their game. In the world of golf, one man stands above all others. His name is Jack Nicklaus.

. . . .
Exercise 4   Written
. . . .

Turn to the topics in part VII and scan them until you find three topics on which you think you might be able to write papers. Write an introductory paragraph for a paper on each topic, but don't write the papers. Bring your introductory paragraphs to class to test them out on sample readers.

Working in small groups with other students, test each introduction on your sample readers. Does each introduction orient them, make them feel at home? Does it let them know the main idea in a clear thesis statement? Does it get them interested in reading further?

As you work in class, be on the lookout for your classmates' successful efforts. You can learn much about writing by seeing what works for others.

. . . .
Exercise 5   For class discussion
. . . .

Below are several paired introductory paragraphs. One in each pair is a rough draft, and the other is the writer's revision. Which paragraphs do you think are the new and improved versions, and in what ways are they better?

1a. I belong to a baby-sitting club. One of the greatest assets of belonging to the club is that you're almost guaranteed to find a sitter whenever you need one. The club's bylaws give detailed information as to what is expected of its members.

1b. I belong to a baby-sitting club. Because I am a member of this club, it has never taken me more than fifteen minutes to find a sitter. And my sitters have always been mature, reliable, and free. Let me tell you how you can start such a club in your own neighborhood.

2a. I do not think prayer should be allowed in the schools. During most of my school years, the Lord's Prayer was part of our opening exercises. I never thought about it one way or another. I never heard anyone complain about it. When prayer in the schools became an issue in the courts, I was surprised. I never thought of the Lord's Prayer as being a threat to individual rights or as a breakdown in the division between church and state.

2b. During most of my school years, the Lord's Prayer was a part of our opening exercises. I never gave it a second thought, and I never heard anyone complain about it. So when prayer in the schools became an issue in the courts, I was surprised to hear that anyone viewed it as a threat to individual rights or as a violation of the division between church and state. But now that I've thought about it, I would not like to see the practice of prayer in the schools reinstituted.

3a. After reading many self-improvement books, finally I got up enough gumption to fulfill an ever-returning dream of enrolling in college. Since the psychological theories I had been reading about were all so positive, I signed up for a psychology class. I was convinced that a psychology professor, having majored in such a humanistic subject, would be sensitive to students' feelings. However, by the end of the evening of my first class with Dr. Crumb, I was not so sure.

3b. After being out of school for fifteen years, I finally got up enough gumption to enroll in college. This in itself was a feat. In the past years, I had felt intimidated by most authority figures and most college graduates. Last year I experienced a family crisis and sought counseling to get through a difficult time. I read many self-improvement books and decided psychology would be a very interesting subject.

4a. Beauty is in the eye of the beholder, but glamour is for anyone who can afford it. Head-to-toe miracles are performed on both sexes, young and old alike. Nature no longer binds people to their bodies; if they desire to add to or subtract from their frames to create a new image, the change agent may be as close as the nearest drugstore or as advanced as the tip of a plastic surgeon's scalpel.

4b. Nature no longer binds people to their bodies. If they desire to create a new image, the change may be as close as the nearest drugstore or as advanced as the tip of a plastic surgeon's scalpel. Beauty is in the eye of the beholder, but glamour is for anyone who can afford it.

7 Supporting your point

It is easy to write a check if you have enough money in the bank, and writing comes more easily if you have something to say.   Sholem Asch

You can think of your introduction, particularly your thesis statement, as a contract between you and your readers. You are contracting with readers for a bit of their time. In return, you promise to show to the reader's satisfaction that what you claim is true. Readers who don't care whether the thesis is true probably won't read past the introduction unless they have to. But readers who do care will expect solid, respectable evidence in return for their investment of time. So your thesis statement is a commitment, a promise. Once you have stated your thesis, your job as a writer is to meet your commitment, to honor your promise.

Think for a moment about the writing that will be required of you after this course is over, in other college courses and on the job. Most of you are already familiar enough with school writing to know that professors are impressed with fact-filled presentations. You know very well that an essay exam filled with unsupported generalizations gets a lower grade than one packed with relevant details and solid information in support of a point. And work-related writing requires as much substance as school writing, sometimes even more. Most supervisors are busy people who do not appreciate having their time wasted, so they request substantive writing—writing filled with relevant and necessary information.

In your other college courses and in on-the-job writing, you probably won't have too much trouble coming up with appropriate material with which to support your points. Usually the material is almost given to you, or you know where to find it. For example, let's say you are writing a paper for Ancient History 103. Your instructor has asked you to compare two cultural heroes, Gilgamesh and Job, to show the difference between Babylonian and Hebrew values. Because your material comes from the reading you have done in the course, you won't have much trouble filling out your paper; as a matter of fact, you'll have trouble trimming down such a wealth of material. The same is true of on-the-job writing. If your writing task, for example, is to summarize for your supervisor the important decisions made in a meeting that he or she was unable to attend, you'll have no problem coming up with material for your summary. Your problem will be deciding what is important enough to mention and what to highlight. You'll have more information than you need.

But freshman English may present you with a unique writing situation. It is a course in *how* to write, so it doesn't necessarily provide you with material to write about. So, while you have material almost given to you in other college courses and in on-the-job writing, in freshman English you may have to come up with material on your own. And let's face it, this is not always easy.

Choosing a thesis you can support

In writing for freshman English, be careful to choose a thesis you will be able to support. Unless you are writing a research paper (in which case you will get your supporting material from written sources), we advise you to write about what you already know. To help you discover how much you already know, we have printed approximately two hundred writing topics in part VII in the back of this book. These topics cover a wide range of subjects: sports, religion, race, men and women, violence, and so on. At least some of them will touch on your areas of expertise.

You may be a police officer, a government worker, a basketball player, an amateur actress, a mountain climber, a vegetarian, a nurse's aide, a sports-car enthusiast. Such people have special knowledge worth sharing with readers. If you think you know nothing worth sharing, we believe that you, like the students we have taught, will find that you have a great deal to say once you look through our topics.

To illustrate how you can use your own knowledge to support a thesis, here is a list describing other students' successes.

1. Trained as a helicopter pilot at Ft. Walter, Bob experienced firsthand the dangers of helicopter school. He was especially aware of the dangers of the "55," a helicopter in which he nearly died. He had more than enough knowledge to write a convincing essay on the dangers of the "55."

2. Brenda, a mother concerned about the quality of her neighborhood high schools, had done some investigating. She had talked to school officials, to teachers and counselors, to other parents, and to students. Finding that the schools were just barely adequate to prepare a student

for college, she wanted to share her discovery—and her alarm—with other residents of her community.

3. Sue, a lover of art galleries, took her readers on an appetite-whetting tour of her favorite gallery, the Phillips, in Washington, D.C. She visited the gallery again right before writing the paper, so the details would be fresh in her mind.

4. An avid ice-hockey fan, Lloyd was disturbed by the violence of the game—not because he was squeamish, but because the violence was making the skills of the players almost beside the point. He wrote a paper arguing that if the violence were reduced, the players would be better able to display the true skills of the game.

5. Steve had gone to most of the Italian restaurants in town in search of the perfect pizza. Having finally discovered it at Geppetto's, he shared his discovery with fellow pizza-lovers in a glowing review of the restaurant.

6. Tom had been hearing a number of arguments against allowing girls into Little League baseball, and he was struck by the absurdity of the arguments. So he wrote a paper which simply displayed these arguments in all of their absurdity, leaving his readers to conclude that girls should be allowed to participate in Little League.

7. Lurleen, a young woman whose father had recently died of cancer, was bothered because everyone, herself included, had pretended to her father that he wasn't dying. She had read a book, *On Death and Dying*, which made her wish even more that she had spoken honestly with her father. So she wrote a paper, based primarily on her own experience, to share her insights with readers.

8. Ken, a career Air Force person, had spent several years in Japan. He was fascinated by Japanese sports, especially Sumo wrestling. Because most westerners know very little about this unusual sport, he put his readers on the scene with ringside seats in an action-packed essay.

Getting close to your subject

But, some of you may be thinking, I haven't gone to helicopter school or to Japan or even to local art galleries; I have not discovered the perfect pizza, never attended ice hockey games, and couldn't care less about my neighborhood schools. *I* don't have anything to write about.

We doubt that is true, but if you think it is, here's some practical advice. If you are having trouble developing your papers because you lack material with which to fill them out, you can always choose a topic that requires you to look for material. Select topics that ask you to seek out material in the world you live in. Some of our topics in part VII encourage you to do just that. Here are a few examples:

1. Write an article advertising a natural-foods store in your community.

2. Be alert to how people about sixty or older are portrayed on television. Does stereotyping occur? Watch enough situation comedies and similar programs to be able to describe two or three stereotypes.

3. If one of your instructors gave a lecture this week, summarize it for a friend who missed class.

4. Find out about family life in another culture, preferably by talking to someone who has experienced it firsthand. Report on your findings in an interesting, readable style.

5. Interview someone who does work that is interesting. Describe the job to readers who might want to consider that line of work.

6. Take your reader on a tour of an art museum you have visited. Write the paper to encourage a visit by your reader.

7. What picture of American Indians, black Americans, Italian-Americans, Southern whites, Chinese, or another minority group is presented in movies or television dramas? Limit this topic radically, perhaps by discussing the image of one of these groups as presented in one film or one TV series.

8. If you have seen a violent movie recently, describe it in a way that emphasizes the violence and shows how ridiculous—or how sordid or painful—it is.

9. Contrast your expectations of a concert with the reality of it.

To do a good job with any of these topics, you would need to get close to your subject. Then the necessary details, the material for your writing, would be right there in front of you. Literally getting close to your subject is a good method for writing, even if you already know something about your subject. As Stuart Chase put it, "It is much easier to sit at a desk and read plans for a billion gallons of water a day, and look at maps and photographs; but you will write a better article if you heave yourself out of a comfortable chair and go down in tunnel 3 and get soaked."

Your instructor may have his or her own way of helping you get close to a subject. Some instructors, for example, use a collection of essays to provide material for writing. Others ask students to write about literature or "great books." When you write about a particular essay, story, or book, your material is right at hand. If you read carefully, you'll be close enough to your subject to write a paper filled with detail. Here are a few of our topics from part VII, based on such reading:

1. Read Hermann Hesse's *Siddhartha,* a short novel about a young Indian searching for spiritual understanding. Write a character study of Siddhartha.

2. Write a humorous essay in which you show that certain fairy tales (or some other stories intended for children) are perversely violent.

3. Read the first seven chapters of Elisabeth Kübler-Ross's well-known book *On Death and Dying.* Summarize what she says for someone who has not read the book.

4. Read about "situation ethics" (see, for example, books on the subject by Thomas Fletcher and James Pike) and make a statement about how this approach to "living religiously" strikes you for your own life.

5. *The Coming of Age,* a book by Simone de Beauvoir, contains an interesting chapter on "old age in historical societies." Read this chapter and summarize it for someone who doesn't have the time to read it.

Brainstorming on scratch paper

Let's say you have selected a thesis you think you can support, and you have written a first-draft introductory paragraph that either begins or ends with a thesis statement. Your next step is to decide just how you will support your point. What you're really deciding, of course, is how to write the rest of the paper.

Unless you have a very clear idea of how to support your point, it's a good idea to stop and brainstorm on scratch paper. Put your thesis statement at the top of the sheet, then jot down as many details, facts, or examples as you can think of to back it up or support it.

One student brainstormed this list before writing a paper showing the difficulties of enduring a five-day Navy "survival" school.

Thesis: If you think it's easy to survive off the land, let me set you straight. Here's how I managed to get through a five-day Navy "survival" school.

found 50 crabs—for 105 hungry men
captured a dozen limpets (tasted like art gum erasers)
followed a recipe for grass soup—tasted like weeds!
chased a tiny ground squirrel, not really enough to serve one person—and didn't catch it anyway
discovered the yucca plant, very tasty—but had the effect of a bushel of dried prunes
raunchy-looking grubs and lizards—not so bad when you're desperate

With this list as a guide, the student wrote a fact-filled paper showing readers just how hard it is to survive off the land.

If you think it's easy to survive off the land, let me set you straight. Here's how I managed to get through a five-day Navy "survival" school.

The first evening the instructors dumped 105 of us onto a deserted beach. All we had were eight parachutes to use for tents, some string, and instructions on how to make nets and crab traps. In about three hours we had managed to trap about 50 crabs. Do you know how far 50 crabs go among 105 hungry men? Later that evening, after wandering along the beach, I found about a dozen limpets, which I had been told were edible raw. I was so hungry at that point I would try anything once. But eating raw limpets, I found out, is like trying to eat art gum erasers. After chewing on about half of them, I decided I wasn't really as hungry as I'd thought.

The next morning the instructors took us up to Warner Springs, where we were to survive four days in the mountains. The days were spent looking for food and the evenings were spent preparing it and feeling sorry for ourselves. On days two and three we ate a lot of soup made from the grass that we were able to gather. We had been told that it was healthy and good. It tasted like weeds. The fourth day, while scavenging for food, a group of us stumbled upon a ground squirrel. Five grown men chased that squirrel for three hours, though even if we had caught it it wouldn't have been enough to feed one. Well, we didn't catch it, so we headed back to camp with a few handfuls of weeds for the community pot.

On the fifth day we discovered the yucca plant, which grows abundantly in the mountains. The stalks of the plants are similar to sugar cane. They were sweet and so much better than the weeds we had been eating, so we gorged ourselves. An hour later we learned that yucca has the same effect as a bushel of dried prunes. Well, after losing my bout with Montezuma's revenge, I was ready to eat just about anything. One of the group brought back a load of grubs and some small lizards. Realizing how hungry I was, I decided they wouldn't kill me. Actually, as raunchy as grubs and lizards look, they weren't really all that bad. Roasted lizard tastes a little like beef jerky.

That night I dreamed of the steak dinner that I felt sure would be waiting for us back at base. As we helicoptered out of Warner Springs the next day, all talk was of food: sirloins and filet mignon, pork chops and ribs, baked potatoes with sour cream, dumplings with gravy, and beer, beer, beer. After landing, we raced to the mess hall for the Navy's reward to its 105 heroic survivors. But the hall was closed, and a notice was pinned to the door: "All personnel report to the command post for evasion course. You have three hours to get from one side of the course to the other, a distance of about two miles, without getting captured. If you are not captured, you will be rewarded with a piece of fruit and a sandwich."

The main purpose of brainstorming is to get enough details down on paper, as this student did, so you won't have to stop to think them up as you're writing. But brainstorming sometimes has a side benefit. Occasionally it will show you before you even attempt to write a paper that you don't have enough evidence to support your thesis. For example, one student began with the thesis, "Single people are often discriminated against in job interviews." Once he began brainstorming on scratch paper, it became clear that he had too little evidence to support his point. As it turned out, his only evidence was that he suspected he had once been discriminated against in a job interview because he was single. Since this one example was not enough to prove his point, and since this student saw no way to get the evidence he needed in the time available, he decided to give up on the topic. He found another thesis instead, one he could support more convincingly.

Revising your supporting material

As a paper is being written, it can begin to have a life of its own. You probably know from experience what we mean. Maybe you once wrote a thesis in favor of capital punishment, but found that your paper slanted in the opposite direction. Or perhaps you intended to show that the Ten Commandments are important rules for twentieth-century Americans to live by, yet were unable to justify more than six of them. Or maybe you just went off on a tangent as you were writing. For one reason or another, then, your rough draft won't always turn out the way you have planned. So once you've finished a rough draft, it's a good idea to read it over with a critical eye. Ask yourself: Does the body of this paper adequately support its thesis statement?

A good technique is to read the rough draft as if you were someone who *disagreed* with your thesis. If you find it impossible to pretend that you disagree, find a test reader, preferably one who *does* disagree with your thesis. Or ask your instructor or someone else who is likely to be objective to read the paper.

Though a test reader will help you spot flaws in your supporting material, your own common sense will take you a long way. Just ask yourself some tough questions. If you're trying to show that fresh foods are less expensive than canned, frozen, or ready-mix foods, ask yourself: Does my paper contain enough facts to convince even skeptical readers? Or if your point is that suicide is immoral, ask yourself: Is my paper persuasive enough to change the minds of readers who believe the opposite?

If your answer is *yes*, fine. If it's *no*, you have some more work to do. You'll need to strengthen your supporting material so that readers who do not already agree with your thesis will at least be forced to take it seriously, even if they do not end up completely in agreement with you.

....
Exercise 1 For class discussion
....

Consider what evidence a writer could use to support each of these thesis statements, which were mentioned in chapter 6.

1. Supermarkets are not designed for the quantity family buyer.

2. Though by all outward appearances our community's two elementary schools are comparable, Forestville is academically superior to Brookline.

3. Poe, according to his biographers, had difficulty relating to women sexually.

4. Whoever said that history is nothing but polishing tombstones must have missed History 157, because in Professor Baldwin's class history is very much alive.

5. Though it looks innocent enough, the "55" is an extremely dangerous helicopter.

6. If you've never played golf before but are thinking of trying it, I'd advise against it—unless you have the funds to support this expensive hobby.

7. At the top of my list for good food, good service, and a charming atmosphere is a little Italian restaurant called Luigi's.

8. A number of toys on the market provide a safe and effective outlet for your child's aggressive feelings.

9. The Palmer Park Little League is clearly run for the benefit of the adult coaches and parents.

....
Exercise 2 For class discussion
....

Discuss how the writer has supported his or her point in each of the following student papers.

"Irish vs. American Education" (#1, p. 173.)
"Borrowings from Black Culture" (#3, p. 175.)
"Learning to Decide" (#6, p. 179.)
"Euthanasia for Animals" (#7, p. 181.)

....
Exercise 3 For class discussion
....

Comment freely on the following quotations.

a. There is no need for the writer to eat a whole sheep to be able to tell what mutton tastes like. It is enough if he eats a cutlet. But he should do that.
W. Somerset Maugham, British writer

b. If I had sat down to read everything that had been written—I'm a slow reader—I would never have written anything.
E. B. White, American essayist

c. Do not be grand. Try to get the ordinary into your writing—breakfast tables rather than the solar system; Middletown today, not Mankind through the ages.
Darcy O'Brien

d. To tell about a drunken muzhik's beating his wife is incomparably harder than to compose a whole tract about the "woman question."
Ivan Turgenev, Russian novelist

e. An abstract style is always bad. Your sentences should be full of stones, metals, chairs, tables, animals, men, and women.
Alain, French philosopher

f. I'm a bit like a sponge. When I'm not writing I absorb life like water. When I write I squeeze the sponge a little—and out it comes, not water but ink.
Georges Simenon, French mystery writer

g. A writer who does not speak out of a full experience uses torpid words, wooden or lifeless words, such words as "humanitary," which have a paralysis in their tails.
Henry David Thoreau, American writer

h. Writers get ideas . . . from real life. It's OK to lock yourself in the broom closet to write, if you have spent 95% of your time involved in life.
A student

. . . .
Exercise 4 For thought
. . . .

In recent years there has been a trend in the Western world to pay more attention to the wisdom of the East. Could the following Zen story help you in any way in your search for material for your writing?

> Daiju visited the master Basō in China. Basō asked: "What do you seek?"
> "Enlightenment," replied Daiju.
> "You have your own treasure house. Why do you search outside?" Basō asked.
> Daiju inquired: "Where is my treasure house?"
> Basō answered: "What you are asking is your treasure house."
> Daiju was enlightened. Ever after he urged his friends: "Open your own treasure house and use those treasures."

. . . .
Exercise 5   Just for fun
. . . .

I always start writing with a clean sheet of paper and a dirty mind.
Patrick Dennis, creator of Auntie Mame

8 Arguing your point

We never fully grasp the import of any true statement until we have a clear notion of what the opposite untrue statement would be.
William James

When writing to support a point, imagine that you're arguing with readers. If you have asserted that your favorite baseball team, the Chicago Cubs, is finally headed for a pennant victory, aim your paper at Yankee fans who think the Cubs don't stand a chance. Or if you have claimed that alimony should not be awarded except in rare, isolated cases, pitch your argument to readers who believe just the opposite.

Imagining a tough, skeptical audience—readers from Missouri who say, "Show me"—will help you decide what kind of evidence and how much evidence you need to prove your point. This is especially true when you are writing on clearly argumentative topics such as capital punishment, the peacetime draft, or abortion. But it is also true when you are writing on less obviously argumentative topics that require you to support a point. The student who wrote about the Navy's survival school, for example, imagined a hard-to-convince group of readers, as you can see from his opening paragraph:

> If you think it's easy to survive off the land, let me set you straight. Here's how I managed to get through a five-day Navy "survival" school.

With a skeptical group of readers in mind, the writer knew he would have to present plenty of evidence to prove his point. And his paper is the better for it, even for readers who aren't quite so hard to convince.

Setting ground rules

Arguments, like games, proceed better if certain ground rules are set up, so the participants know what counts as fair play. As a writer you have a certain advantage: Since you're the only participant present, you get to make the rules.

If you're planning to argue in favor of the Supreme Court decision outlawing prayer in public schools, for example, you get to decide on the precise issues to address and on the type of evidence that will count in the argument. Usually you will make your ground rules clear in your opening paragraph, and especially in your thesis, as this student has done:

> Although the Supreme Court has ruled against prayer in public schools on First Amendment grounds, many people still feel that prayers should be allowed. These people, most of whom hold strong religious beliefs, are well-intentioned. What they fail to realize is that the Supreme Court decision, although it was made on legal grounds, makes good sense on religious grounds as well. Prayer is too important to be trusted to our public schools.

Notice that as the student has drawn it, the issue has little to do with the legal decision of the Supreme Court. Arguments over the wisdom of the Court's decision are put firmly outside the scope of this paper. Notice also that arguments concerning the value of prayer are swept outside the scope of the paper. The writer assumes that both he and his audience consider prayer important. Once these issues have been eliminated, we are left with the student's chosen issue, as stated in his thesis: *Prayer is too important to be trusted to our public schools.* The paper will argue this point alone, and the only evidence that the writer will allow into the discussion will be that which bears on this point.

Selecting evidence

Once you've set the ground rules, you're ready to decide what kinds of proof are admissible in your argument. The student who wrote about school prayer decided that the following kinds of evidence would help him prove his point even to skeptical readers:

1. Evidence showing that public school teachers are often unqualified to lead students in prayer, and that ministers, priests, rabbis, and concerned parents are more qualified.

2. Evidence showing that school is a poor environment for prayer (the writer remembered from his childhood, for example, that students had thrown spitwads and fights had broken out during school prayers), and that churches, homes, and quiet, solitary places such as forests or lakesides are much more appropriate environments.

3. Evidence showing that school prayers are often so homogenized to avoid offending anyone that they are really not prayers at all.

In deciding on this evidence, the writer thought seriously about the *opposite* of his thesis: Prayer is too important to *leave out of our public schools*. The people who believe this, he surmised, must feel that (1) public school teachers are qualified to lead students in prayer; (2) school is an appropriate environment for prayer; and (3) school prayers are meaningful enough to deserve the label "prayer." The writer's job, then, was to show these readers that they were mistaken on all three counts. If he could do this, the writer felt, his readers would change their minds on the subject.

Changing people's minds on controversial subjects is not easy. As philosopher George Santayana put it, "People are usually more firmly convinced that their opinions are precious than that they are true." And as one novelist confided, in a moment of truthfulness, "I'll not listen to reason. . . . Reason always means what someone else has got to say." Thus, to get readers to give up their precious opinions is quite an accomplishment. If you don't at least try to look at your issue through the eyes of skeptical readers, you're not very likely to convince them.

Considering the other side

Let readers know you've looked at both sides of your issue, but in considering the other side, be careful not to allow opposing arguments to persuade your readers. Instead of just presenting these arguments, do your best to disprove them. One student writer, for example, as he argued in favor of girls' participation in Little League baseball, confronted the opposing arguments directly:

> Along comes the traditionalist who announces that such athletic competition will cause unnatural muscular development in girls. This belief is unfounded. Girls have been playing softball in physical education classes for a long time, and they have always looked pretty good to me. Little League baseball provides girls with an excellent opportunity to develop strong, healthy, attractive bodies.
>
> One of the loudest arguments against boys and girls playing ball is risk of injury. But girls are no more susceptible to injury than boys. Moreover, baseball is essentially a noncontact sport. You must remember that we are talking about baseball, not football or field hockey.
>
> Recently I heard the most absurd argument of them all. A father stated during a news interview that he didn't want his daughter playing organized sports with boys for fear of having his little girl groped. Either the man is sick or he has never played any sport. In the heat of competition, the last thing on anybody's mind is a free feel. How would that look at second base?

These paragraphs leave most readers feeling that the traditionalists' arguments are misdirected, even absurd. Though we have been exposed to them, we are not convinced by them.

Another student, writing the first draft of an argumentative paper, was not quite so skillful. As you read her opening paragraphs, notice how dangerously close she has come in the second paragraph to persuading her readers of the opposite of her thesis.

> Abortion has always been a controversial issue in our society. The Catholic Church takes a firm stand against abortion because it sees it as murder. As a Catholic, I have to disagree with the Church. I feel that abortion should continue to be legalized—for the sake of the unborn child.
>
> Opponents of abortion have shown that by the time most abortions are performed, the fetus has the exact physical appearance of an infant. Therefore, destroying the fetus is the same as murdering a child. This is a good point to make. It would convince most people against abortion if it was the only thing considered. However, a more important aspect to consider is the kind of life the child would live if it were born rather than aborted.

The writer seems to be agreeing with those who believe abortion is murder, since she calls this view "a good point to make." But if she agrees with this point, how then can she argue in favor of abortion?

In fact, the writer does not believe that abortion is murder. She simply presented this argument in an effort to be fair. Once she realized that her paragraph swayed readers in the wrong direction, she had to make a decision. Either she had to argue that abortion is not murder, or she had to sweep that issue outside the scope of her argument. As it turned out, she chose the latter approach, since the point she really wanted to make was that unwanted children are often neglected and abused. (The writer worked in an emergency room and saw all too many examples of child abuse.) The murder issue, she felt, was so complicated that it would take most of her paper to deal with it, thus pulling the reader's attention away from the point she actually wanted to press. In putting this issue outside the scope of her argument, the writer was of course giving up on the attempt to change the minds of those who truly believe that abortion is murder. Instead, she was directing her paper at readers she felt might be brought to her point of view.

Avoiding fallacies

Whenever you argue a point, you will want to try to avoid the trap of fallacies. It is easy for an unconscious fallacy to trip up the reasoning of any writer. Sometimes writers use fallacies deliberately, in an attempt to load an argument unfairly. You'll want to avoid using them by mistake, though, for they can undermine your argument.

There are several kinds of fallacies. We would like to alert you to some that might cause trouble in your writing.

Arguing in a Circle. This fallacy occurs when a writer merely restates in the second half of a sentence what he or she has already said in the first half. The statement reads as if the second half is proof of the first half, when actually the statement simply circles back on itself.

For example, let's assume you have found a nursery school you want to recommend to other mothers and fathers who need care for their children while they attend classes. You write: "The days at Derry Dale Nursery School are pleasant for the children because they have a good time from the moment they arrive until they are picked up." But then you notice that the second half of your sentence does not really expand upon the first half; it merely repeats it. To avoid arguing in a circle, you'll need some specific details to support your point that "the days at Derry Dale Nursery School are pleasant for the children." Such details might include, for example, the high level of individual attention the school provides, the variety of stimulating board games and puzzles, the challenging but safe outdoor play equipment, and the well-balanced lunches that include a special treat every day.

Faulty Cause-and-Effect Reasoning. The fact that two events occur in sequence does not necessarily indicate that the second results from the first. Let's say that I work in a hospital emergency room, where I see many children with concussions, broken limbs, and deep burns. Since it is well known that some of these "accidents" are actually cases of child abuse, I decide to write a paper arguing for more careful investigation of suspected child abuse.

I know that in one week my emergency room treats an average of ten accidents involving children from the inner city, where unemployment is high and much borderline poverty exists, and only two from the more affluent suburbs to the northwest. However, I cannot automatically assume that unemployment and poverty create more child abuse. I cannot use those two factors alone to argue that the most intensive investigation should be conducted in the inner city. I must take into account other possible factors. Perhaps most of the abused children in the suburbs are taken to other hospitals; perhaps the level of child abuse inflicted on suburban children does not as often reach emergency proportions; perhaps most of the cases reported as accidents in the inner city really *were* accidents, the inner city being a more dangerous place to live. I must consider all possible contributing factors before I try to analyze the causes of a particular effect—in this instance, child abuse.

Hasty Generalization. A hasty generalization, as the name suggests, is a claim made too hastily, on the basis of too little evidence. For example, the statement "Eleanor Roosevelt was our greatest first lady" is a claim you might be tempted to use as a thesis statement. But to support that statement, you would have to compare and contrast Eleanor Roosevelt with all the other outstanding first ladies in American history. A better thesis would be "Eleanor Roosevelt was one of our greatest first ladies," since you could prove that by discussing several of Mrs. Roosevelt's accomplishments.

To avoid hasty generalizations, be especially alert to unqualified statements. Such statements often contain words such as *always, never, all,* and *everyone.* Sentences with these words in them are quite likely to be untrue because there are exceptions to almost every possible situation. For instance, the following sentence appeared in one student's paper about her plans for her children's education: "Since we all love our families so much, I am of course saving for college for Sue and Bob." But it is simply not true that "we all love our families so much"; there is too much evidence in the world to the contrary.

We want to call a few other fallacies to your attention:

1. *Using loaded words and labels:* "The federal government should not fund attempts to rehabilitate street drunks. Those bums are repulsive, filthy characters who should be put away for good instead of being allowed back out on the street following some kind of treatment." Labeling all public victims of alcoholism "street drunks" and "bums" and describing them as "repulsive, filthy characters" is more likely to alienate readers than to win them over.

2. *Name-calling, or arguing against the person instead of arguing the point:* "Don't listen to Amy Stein when she supports Planned Parenthood. She doesn't have any children, and besides, she's been divorced twice." This argument implies that Amy Stein's childlessness and two divorces automatically disqualify her as a supporter of Planned Parenthood. She may in fact be a thoughtful advocate of careful family planning.

3. *Appealing for sympathy:* "Columbia Hospital should hire more floor aides from the surrounding neighborhood. The hospital needs more staff, and the poverty-stricken unemployed who live nearby are logical candidates for those jobs." Here the writer of the argument ignores whether those "poverty-stricken unemployed" can qualify to care for the ill.

Fallacies, then, don't actually support an argument—and sometimes they may damage it. If you assume that your readers will be looking for substantial evidence in support of arguments, you won't want to disappoint them with fallacies.

· ·
Exercise 1   For writing and class discussion
· ·

Assume that you are going to write an argument in support of at least three of the following statements. Make a list of the points you would use to support each statement you select. Bring your lists to class for a blackboard brainstorming session.

1. Because our society is coming to depend more and more on computers, no one can be considered educated today without basic computer literacy.

2. A week of camping in close quarters with at least two other people is a good way to test one's adaptability.

3. Even in a country that stands for freedom of expression, as does the United States, violent scenes should not be allowed on television during the family viewing hours.

4. Because a sensible diet is basic to good health—both physical and mental—one should plan his or her life so as to be able to eat well every day.

5. There are times when a person should be allowed to die—times, indeed, when one should be helped to die.

6. A fine arts course—in art, music, or theater, for example—is an important part of anyone's higher education and should be required in all curricula.

7. Working parents cannot adequately attend to the needs of their children; unless basic survival depends on both parents' holding jobs, one or the other should remain at home to be available to the children.

8. A job lifeguarding for a community pool is not as pleasant a way to spend a summer as some people may think.

9. Human beings need the kind of belief system and sense of community they can find in organized religion; therefore people need to belong to an established church or synagogue.

10. Although our college's program of developmental activities for handicapped children serves a limited population, the county should be fully funding the program. The parents of these children should not have to assume the added burden of paying for this special training.

· ·
Exercise 2   For class discussion
· ·

Each item below contains one of the following fallacies: (a) arguing in a circle, (b) faulty cause-and-effect reasoning, (c) hasty generalization,

(d) using loaded words and labels, (e) name-calling, or (f) appealing for sympathy. Mark each item with a letter from this list to identify the fallacy, and come to class prepared to discuss the flaws in the items.

1. The law requiring motorcyclists to wear helmets should be reinstated, despite the arguments of cyclists for freedom of choice. Last year fifty riders died following accidents.

2. That ore is ancient because it is carbon-dated 1200 B.C.

3. Jane Robertson should be elected to the city council of Boonesville because there are no handicapped persons on the council.

4. The reason ferns are not easy to grow is that they are difficult to care for.

5. Marriage is essential for raising healthy children.

6. Welfare mothers should be sterilized as soon as they have borne two children. I don't want my tax money used to support careless breeding by such loose women.

7. Unless the preparation of secondary-school teachers improves radically, nationwide test scores on the verbal skills of high-school students will continue to decline.

8. The public library should not charge overdue fines to children from poor homes. For most of these children, the library is the only source of books to read for pleasure.

9. If you are an American citizen sixty-five or over, retirement holds little promise of pleasure for you unless you can afford to live in a retirement colony in Florida.

10. Those baby-killers just don't appreciate the sweet joys of motherhood.

11. The chemicals buried by the government at Brown's Corner, Texas, have caused a wave of cancer in that town: among fifteen families on one street, six women have had breast cancer, and two other people are suffering from bladder and throat cancer.

12. Too many young people begin to drink and use drugs while still in elementary school. Actually the candy and other inviting snacks found in many school vending machines are a blessing in disguise, for if children cannot find goodies on the school grounds, they will leave in search of them and will then succumb to other temptations such as alcohol and drugs.

13. Don't let Georgianna Sullivan serve on the county mental health board; she hasn't contributed to the local Heart Fund drive in three years.

14. Everybody should exercise fairly vigorously each day.

15. Luther Wayne should not be allowed to coach the Little League because he drinks more than he should at political fund-raisers.

16. In these days of energy consciousness, no one should drive a large car.

17. I hope you will give me at least a B in this course; otherwise I cannot transfer into the professional degree program I want to pursue.

9 Shaping your paper

Writing is not the dainty arranging of superficialities, it is the solid construction of thoughts. Donald Murray

A paper will probably start to take shape in your head; its shape will become clearer as you scribble on scratch paper and perhaps sketch an outline; then, after you have written the rough draft, you may find yourself reshaping it with numbers and arrows or even with scissors and tape.

It's safest to plan a paper before you begin your rough draft. If you just plunge in, hoping to get your bearings as you write, you may write a well-organized paper, but the odds are against it. So plan the shape of your paper, at least sketchily, *before* you begin to write.

Organize before you write. This sounds like simple enough advice to follow, but you probably know from experience how tempting it is *not* to do so—particularly if you haven't had much practice organizing in your head, or on scratch paper, or with outlines. Maybe you've tried organizing in your head, but found that one thought led to another which led to another and so on, leaving you with a string of loosely related ideas. Or maybe you've turned to formal outlining in hopes of pinning down your ideas but found it more trouble than it seems to be worth. When students are required to submit formal outlines with their college papers, many of them write the outline after they've written the paper. Some of these students are probably just lazy, but we think many of them believe that formal outlining won't help them write a better paper.

Scribbling on scratch paper

Organizing in your head and formal outlining are two ways of shaping a paper before you write, but they are not the only ways. Somewhere between the extremes of "just thinking" and Roman-numeraled outlining is a middle ground: scribbling on scratch paper. As you become a practiced writer, you'll discover that thinking informally on scratch paper has advantages over both the extremes.

Scribbling on scratch paper is a better way to organize a paper than just thinking, because it helps you pin down your ideas. It gets them out where you can see them, so you can have some control over them. But unlike formal outlining, which can pin down your ideas too soon, scribbling doesn't commit you prematurely. If your scribbling doesn't lead you to a good idea for organizing your paper, you can always throw it out and then scribble some more until you do hit on a bright idea.

Let us show you how several students organized their thoughts on scratch paper. As you will see, in each case the jottings on scratch paper grew out of the writer's purpose. For example, one student's purpose was to convince readers to try a local Italian restaurant. He decided that readers would be tempted by the restaurant's atmosphere, its menu selection, the quality of its food, its friendly service, and its low prices. This list of items, jotted down beneath a stripped-down version of his thesis, became the blueprint for his paper.

. . . .

Luigi's is a first-rate Italian restaurant
charming atmosphere
wide menu selection
excellent food and wine
efficient, friendly service
moderate prices

. . . .

Once this much was jotted down, the writer might have decided to arrange these items in a different order, perhaps stressing the prices first and the atmosphere last, or he might have decided to delete one or two of the items. But with this simple list he was able to control the shape of his paper.

Another student wanted to show readers that divorce rulings often treat men unfairly. Although this student wasn't well enough informed to give an accurate summary of the ways in which his state's divorce laws treated men unfairly, he did have three friends whom he felt had been treated unfairly by divorce rulings. Because his friends' experiences were the only material the student had to work with, he decided to organize his paper around these real-life examples. His scribblings on scratch paper were very simple:

Divorce rulings often treat men unfairly.
   Fred -- unfair allotment of
              finances
   Joe -- lost custody of
              children, unfairly
   Larry -- financial losses and
              the loss of his only
              child

As it turned out, these were the only jottings on scratch paper that this student needed. He was able to organize each of the three sections of the paper in his head. But if he had had any trouble organizing the material within a section of the paper, he could have turned once again to scratch paper. These new jottings might have looked like this:

Joe -- lost custody unfairly

Joe's wife is barely competent as a mother.
-- yells at the kids
-- beats them
-- lets them stay out late, eat junk food, watch whatever they want on TV

Joe is a devoted father.
-- reasons with the children, rarely resorting to physical punishment
-- sets limits on the children

-- shows no
interest in
doing things
with the
children

-- takes them to
ball games
and on
camping trips,
helps with
homework, goes
to PTA meetings

Our third student, who had recently visited her city's art museum, planned to show readers what a wealth of art was hiding in a converted townhouse in an out-of-the-way neighborhood. To whet her readers' appetite for this museum, the writer decided to take readers along with her on a visit. She took them down the street, in the door, and through the various rooms, pointing out the noteworthy paintings as she went along. The shape of the museum almost shaped her paper for her. These few notes were the blueprint for her paper:

describe where the gallery is--
in a once-elegant neighborhood

the old wing
of the building

- Van Gogh
- Degas
- Cézanne
- Renoir

the new wing

- Picasso
- Braque
- Rothko

A last example: One student, a police officer who regularly watched two police programs on television, intended to show that TV has glamorized the police profession. Here is a scratch-paper sketch of the paper:

. . . .

"*Police Story*" -- Contrast the
exciting events in one
episode with the *dull*
routine of one evening
on the job.

"*The Rookies*" -- Contrast the
illegal procedures of
the rookies with the
strict rules police
officers must be
careful to follow.

. . . .

As you can see, he organized his paper around two TV programs he knew something about, "Police Story" and "The Rookies." For each program he contrasted the televised fantasy with the reality he had experienced as a police officer.

There are any number of ways to sketch the shape of your paper on scratch paper, and your own jottings, which need be understandable only to you, are likely to look messier than the examples we've shown you. You might write lists in random order, then number the items; you might scatter ideas all over a page, then draw lines between related ideas; you might use circles or boxes or arrows or even a second color of ink. Do whatever helps you visualize the shape of the paper you are about to write.

Outlining

Sometimes, especially when you're writing long papers, you'll find that outlining gives you greater control over your rough draft than informal scribbling on scratch paper does. You might doodle a bit on scratch paper first, since that keeps you flexible as your ideas are taking shape. But once your ideas have begun to take shape, you may want to write a sentence outline.

A sentence outline with the thesis statement placed at the top pictures the logical relationships among your ideas. The thesis statement is the "point" you are going to support in your paper. The rest of the sentences in the outline are layered to picture their relationship to the thesis.

Thesis Statement: _____.
- **A.** _____.
  - **1.** _____.
  - **2.** _____.
  - **3.** _____.
- **B.** _____.
  - **1.** _____.
  - **2.** _____.
- **C.** _____.
  - **1.** _____.
  - **2.** _____.
  - **3.** _____.
  - **4.** _____.

First-layer supports (the A's and B's and C's) are direct proofs of the thesis statement. They are indented and listed under the thesis statement to show that they support it. You think of them as propping up your thesis, which would collapse without them. Second-layer supports (the 1's and 2's and 3's) prove the first-layer supports. Again, each one is indented and listed under the statement it supports, to picture that support relationship. You could of course have third- and fourth-layer supports, but unless you are writing very long papers, your outline should not be so detailed. Your outline is merely an overall picture of your paper. You fill in the details as you write the rough draft.

Your main purpose in writing a sentence outline is to picture the relation between your thesis statement and the major sections of your paper. To picture that relation as clearly as possible, you should keep your outline simple. An outline for a 500- to 1000-word paper can and probably should be as simple as this student's was:

Thesis Statement: Concentration is the key to becoming a consistent winner in tennis.

A. Chris Evert wins consistently because she is a master of the art of concentration.

B. Ilie Nastase improved his game after he learned to concentrate.

C. Jimmy Connors plays erratically because he has not yet learned to concentrate.

Notice that the most important word in the thesis—concentration—is echoed in each of the supports. This keeps the focus on the main point of the paper. Notice also that the three supporting sentences are structured very similarly: "Chris Evert wins consistently . . ."; "Ilie Nastase improved his game . . ."; "Jimmy Connors plays erratically. . . ." Each of the three sections of the paper will support the thesis in exactly the same way, through an example, and this parallel sentence structure helps to picture that similarity.

When you are outlining, don't be afraid to repeat words and sentence structures, even to the point of monotony, as this student has done:

> *Thesis Statement:* Scientists tell us that our nuclear weapons testing, supersonic aircraft, and aerosol sprays are gradually destroying the protective ozone layer that surrounds our planet.
>
> **A.** Nuclear weapons testing is destroying the ozone layer.
> **B.** Supersonic aircraft are destroying the ozone layer.
> **C.** Aerosol sprays are destroying the ozone layer.

This very simple sentence outline helped its writer to keep focused on her main point as she wrote her rough draft. It helped her remember just *exactly* what she was trying to show her readers. As a matter of fact, as she got into her rough draft, she was tempted to discuss the politics connected with nuclear weapons testing and the controversies surrounding the supersonic Concorde airplane. But her outline showed her that she would be straying from her points: that nuclear weapons testing *is destroying* the ozone layer; that supersonic aircraft *are destroying* the ozone layer. Her outline told her to stick to scientific evidence of this destruction.

A complicated outline might sound better than a streamlined one, but it won't be nearly as useful. When you write your rough draft, you'll probably want to vary your wording and sentence structures to avoid monotony. But while outlining, don't let yourself get too fancy.

If you feel the need to write a two-layer outline, we suggest that you work on it a layer at a time. First block out the overall structure of the paper with a simple, one-layer outline. Then go back and work on the second layer. This way you won't get too bogged down in the details of the outline while you're still struggling with your paper's overall design.

We have learned through our own experience and the experiences of our students that complex outlines can paralyze writers. They force the writer to decide too much too soon. Simpler outlines will keep you flexible for the creative process of writing a rough draft. Because they are just sketches of the overall design of your paper, simple outlines leave room for new insights that may occur to you as you write.

Cutting and taping

Even though it's safest to organize before you write, we're aware that writers—both students and professionals—don't always choose this method. A writer sometimes begins with just a hint of a plan, then writes awhile in hopes that the paper will take shape as it is being written. This is a perfectly acceptable, if risky, way to organize a paper. Your rough draft may turn out so tangled that your only hope is to begin all over again. But if the rough draft at least begins to take shape as you're writing it, you will probably be able to cut and tape it into shape later. Even when you begin with a clear blueprint, sometimes your rough draft won't turn out quite the way you planned. Then, too, cutting and taping is your answer.

In chapter 2 you will find a general discussion of the cutting and taping process. This process includes deleting unnecessary material, possibly moving paragraphs and sentences about, and writing any new material that seems needed. For an example of cutting and taping, you can turn back to chapter 2.

In this chapter we will focus on cutting and taping to improve the organization of a paper. Let's begin by looking at such organization from the point of view of a reader.

Reading expert Mortimer J. Adler tells us that good readers X-ray their reading material. They make every effort to see the skeleton that lies beneath what they are reading. The skeleton shows them how the parts of the paper are connected to each other and how they contribute to the main point of the whole paper. "The reader tries to *uncover* the skeleton," say Adler, and "the author starts with the skeleton and tries *to cover it up* . . . to put flesh on the bare bones."

Readers will look for the bones of your paper in certain *key sentences,* and in general you should make sure you've put these sentences in places where readers will be looking for them. The thesis statement is of course the key sentence for the whole paper, and readers tend to look for it in the first or last sentence of the opening paragraph. Within a paper readers will look for other key sentences that help them see how the parts of the paper are related to each other and to the whole. These sentences are most often found at the beginnings of paragraphs, and that's where readers tend to expect them. As you probably know, these key sentences are known as *topic sentences.*

As a general rule, your thesis statement and topic sentences should interlock. Just by reading them, readers should be able to see the shape of the paper. Let us give you a couple of examples to show you what we mean.

The young woman whose outline for a paper on tennis you saw

earlier began her paper with this paragraph, opening with her thesis statement:

> *Concentration is the key to becoming a consistent winner in tennis.* And to achieve concentration you must learn to control your emotions. A look at three professional tennis players will make this point clear.

Here are the topic sentences of the student's next three paragraphs. Notice that each one clearly connects with the writer's thesis:

> Few women players today can even compare with Chris Evert, for she is a master of the art of concentration.
>
> Ilie Nastase, better known as "Nasty," probably the rudest player ever to come on the tour, improved his game once he learned to concentrate.
>
> Jimmy Connors is an erratic player because he has not yet learned to concentrate.

These topic sentences have been lifted straight out of the student's paper, and if they resemble an outline when they are connected with the thesis, that's no accident. Take the key sentences out of a well-organized paper and you have a sentence outline.

Here is the skeleton of another student paper. The thesis appears at the end of the introductory paragraph:

> Locating an ideal campsite requires a great deal more than a desire to nestle down by a campfire near a quiet stream. The place which offers the greatest eye-appeal can quickly lose its charm when night comes, the fog rolls in and the mosquitoes infest your camp. So resist choosing your campsite just for its beauty. *Instead, look for natural protection, the right soil conditions, and easy access to running water.*

The topic sentences interlock with this thesis; we've italicized the part of each topic sentence that most clearly points back to the thesis:

> Nature provides many *natural sources of protection* against the elements if you are resourceful enough to use them.
>
> The *soil condition* is of vital importance no matter where you are camping.
>
> Although water-logged soil can turn out to be a real source of trouble, your camp should be located *close to a spring of running water.*

As you can see, the skeleton of this student's paper resembles an outline. Just by reading the key sentences of the paper, readers can see how the parts all add up to the whole.

When you are trying to improve the organization of a rough draft, begin with the skeleton of the paper. Can a reader, just by scanning your thesis and topic sentences, tell how your paper is organized? If not, strengthen that skeleton.

As you work to strengthen the skeleton, you may find yourself making other changes—deleting material, moving sentences or paragraphs about, even adding new material. With the help of scissors and tape you can take apart and reassemble your paper, experimenting with new arrangements of your material. Don't worry if your pages start looking messy—this is your rough draft, after all.

If you're having a hard time deciding whether a rough draft needs reorganizing or if you can't think of a way to reorganize it, ask someone for help. A friend, instructor, or parent—anyone with a fresh perspective—may have ideas that will lead you in the right direction.

Sometimes just talking about the shape of your rough draft or trying to draw a picture of its shape on scratch paper will lead you to a new insight. Keep yourself flexible, experiment with different possibilities, and sooner or later you will discover the right shape for your paper.

In this chapter we have given you three practical strategies for organizing a paper: scribbling on scratch paper, outlining, and reorganizing with scissors and tape. If you're not in the habit of using these techniques—and many students aren't—give them all a try this semester. See for yourself the difference they can make.

. . . .
Exercise 1   For class discussion
. . . .

To outline or not to outline is often a question for novice writers. And whether to require an outline is a question for composition instructors. Some discussion in class of both the advantages and disadvantages of outlines could well be worthwhile. Here are some professional writers' observations that might help get such a discussion going.

a. [Outlining] too often becomes an artificial framework that a student has to justify. If writing is a learning process, then you will discover better ways of doing things as you go along.
Cyril H. Knoblauch

b. How can you tell what your house will look like or keep up with the building of it if you don't start with a blueprint?
Anonymous

c. If you are used to starting every writing job with an outline, don't. Wait until you have felt the click. Before that, any outline will tie you down.
Rudolf Flesch

d. [The] writer may create a formal "Harvard" outline in which each point is in a complete sentence. It is more likely, however, that he doesn't follow the rules of Roman numerals and Arabic numbers, of capital letters and small letters, but draws what he has to say in a circle or a square, develops it in chart form, or

scribbles it very informally, putting ideas down in random patterns and then drawing lines between ideas.
Donald M. Murray

e. If you are the kind of person who loves card files, try dropping all your cards on the floor some time. It will do you no end of good.
Rudolf Flesch

f. Complicated outlines tempt you to think too much about the fine points of organization, at a time when you should be blocking out the overall structure.
Anonymous

- -
Exercise 2 Written
- -

We know one woman who can take almost any subject and break it into three logical parts. How did she pick up this skill? Well, she's the daughter of a Southern Baptist preacher whose sermons were always divided, quite logically, into three parts. As a child our friend was forced to sit through her father's sermons twice every Sunday, so she learned how to organize almost without effort.

You too can increase your organizing skills by paying attention to the structures of sermons, classroom lectures, television documentaries, and sometimes even politicians' speeches. Sometime this week while you are listening to a sermon or a classroom lecture or a chalk-talk at the office, jot down notes that outline the structure of what you have heard.

- -
Exercise 3 Written
- -

Write a scratch-paper sketch or a sentence outline for a paper you are thinking about writing. Bring your sketch or outline to class and be prepared to discuss it with other students or with your instructor.

- -
Exercise 4 For class discussion
- -

Analyze the skeletons of the following student papers:

"Borrowings from Black Culture" (#3, p. 175.)
"Hollywood Trucking" (#5, p. 178.)
"Soap Operas" (#8, p. 182.)
"Alternative Sources of Fuel" (#9, p. 183.)
"Living vs. Waiting to Die" (#10, p. 184.)

10 Building paragraphs

The paragraph [is] a mini-essay; it is also a maxi-sentence.   Donald Hall

If paragraphing hadn't been invented, just how easily could we do without it? What would it be like, for example, to read a 300-page book that was not divided up into paragraphs? Probably you wouldn't even try to read such a book; but if you did, you would find yourself reading at a slow pace, with less comprehension than usual.

Paragraphs help readers in several ways. First of all, they ease the reader's eye by breaking up black print with restful touches of white. They assure the reader that there will be stopping points along the way. We like what writer Donald Hall has to say about this: "Paragraphs rest the eye as well as the brain. . . . Those little indentations are hand- and footholds in the cliff face of the essay." Paragraphs help readers in another important way. They help readers visualize the shape of what they are reading. Just by looking at the way the paragraphs are blocked out, readers begin to understand how the whole has been divided into parts and how the parts add up to the whole. Finally, paragraphs show readers how sentences are related to each other. Just by seeing a group of sentences clustered together in a paragraph, readers immediately understand that they belong together in some way. The topic sentence of the paragraph tells them just how the sentences belong together, how they all add up.

When we talk about paragraphs in this chapter, we will limit ourselves to "body paragraphs," those used to develop the main idea of a paper. We will not be considering paragraphs with special functions: introductory, concluding, and transitional paragraphs. These special-function paragraphs are discussed in other chapters.

Focusing with a topic sentence

The topic sentence of a paragraph is a mini-thesis statement. It announces the main point of the paragraph, preparing readers for the sentences to come. Notice, for example, how well this student writer has focused our attention with a topic sentence:

> *The teacher had complete control over the class.* When she was in the room, everyone was quiet and worked in an orderly manner. When she left the room, noise would naturally pick up, but as soon as she reappeared, order resumed. If you had a question or knew an answer, you raised your hand. You were not allowed to speak unless you were acknowledged. When your class left the room, you walked in an orderly line with your group, and talking was not permitted when passing other rooms.

This student's topic sentence has all of the characteristics of a good thesis statement: it is a generalization that needs to be supported by more detailed information; it is limited (not too broad); and it is precisely focused (not too vague).

Here is another well-focused topic sentence, as it appeared in a paragraph taken from a paper describing the adoption of a Vietnamese orphan by the writer's parents:

> *Because Tiet was an orphan in a country at war, my parents spent a lot of time cutting red tape and bargaining in the customary Vietnamese fashion— with monetary bribes.* The nuns of the orphanage, in a subtle way of course, let my parents know that if money wasn't sent for a new well and milking machine then the Lord never meant for Tiet to be adopted. Money had to be sent to village heads and Saigon officials as a gesture of respect. Even the President of Vietnam, who must sign all citations of adoption, was sent a token of esteem—namely, one thousand dollars.

Notice how clearly the topic sentence prepared you for the examples that followed.

Like the student writers we have quoted, you should generally put your topic sentence at the beginning of a paragraph rather than in the middle or at the end. The topic sentence is designed to focus the reader's attention on the main point of the paragraph and to direct his or her attention to the supporting material that follows; it should therefore come first. It makes no sense to prepare readers for a paragraph they have just finished. Another reason for putting your topic sentence first is that readers tend to look for it at the beginning of a paragraph. So when you put your topic sentence first, you are fulfilling your readers' expectations, going along with their natural reading habits.

Occasionally you will have a good reason for violating your readers' expectations. You may decide, for example, to delay your topic sentence until the end of the paragraph because you want to surprise your readers, or even sneak up on them. We recall one student paragraph that ended with a topic sentence calling for increased taxes. The student felt, quite rightly, that if he had hit his readers right off with the main point they would be reluctant to read on. So he gave his arguments first, because he thought he could get readers to go along with them, and saved his unpopular topic sentence for the end.

The writer of the following paragraph also had a good reason for delaying her topic sentence. Recognizing that her examples were more vivid than her topic sentence, she decided to dazzle her readers first, with a vivid opener, then let them know the point later, at the end of the paragraph. She judged that her readers would know from the context what the examples were supposed to illustrate, so by putting the topic sentence last she didn't risk confusing them.

> Our impressionable tykes read about homicidal old ladies offering poisoned apples long before they discover SWAT. They cope with Alice's encounter with madness and Red Riding Hood's mugging without tension or discomfort. No red-blooded American child would wince during Peter Pan's battle with the pirates or Dorothy's gruesome attack by winged monkeys. *These worldly little people are not likely to faint because of television crimes: more likely they will be disappointed by the quality of the violence.*

Rarely will you have a good reason for putting your topic sentence in the middle of a paragraph, but often you will have reason to delay it a bit. Sometimes, as you move from one paragraph to another in your paper, you'll find that you need a transitional or "bridge" sentence before your topic sentence. The purpose of a transitional sentence is to show readers the connection between what went before and what is about to come. Here is an example of a student paragraph that opens with a transitional sentence followed by the topic sentence:

> Aside from sexual incompatibility, there was another problem. *Although David was a good and decent man, he lacked initiative.* All decision-making, regardless of importance, was relegated to me. "You decide" was his answer. Home and car repairs went untended until I either insisted he make repairs or saw to them myself. If the roof leaked, it continued leaking until I had it mended. If the furnace went out, I negotiated for repair or arranged for purchase of a new one. All of our financial affairs were left for me to handle.

As a general rule, then, put your topic sentence at the opening of the paragraph unless you have a good reason for putting it elsewhere. Sometimes you may even want to echo your topic sentence at the end of a paragraph in a "clincher" sentence. The topic sentence orients, prepares, and points ahead; the clincher sentence concludes, emphasizes, and points back. Clincher sentences work well for stressing a point, as the following student paragraph demonstrates.

> *It is true that I have had a few warning signals that I'm not as young as I used to be.* I do notice a slight shortness of breath after climbing several flights of stairs. Looking in the mirror, I see facial lines that weren't there before. The grocery boy at the store used to call me "Babe." Now his respectful reply is "Yes, Ma'am." As I sit here with aching feet and dead tiredness after a day at work, it hits me. *All of a sudden I'm over thirty.*

Filling out paragraphs

Paragraphs, like whole papers, should be developed fully enough to satisfy a reader. Once you have focused on a topic sentence, ask yourself how much evidence and what kind of evidence your readers need to hear. There are many possible ways to prove a topic sentence, and in this section we would like to discuss some of the most common: examples, illustrations, details, reasons, and comparisons and contrasts.

Examples

A few well-chosen examples will often satisfy readers as to the truth of a topic sentence. Three vivid examples are enough to convince us in the paragraph below:

> *Throughout history, women have resorted to many extremes in order to attain the standard of beauty popular at the time.* In China women's feet were bound to keep them small, because men admired tiny feet. A tribe in Africa measured the affluence of the husband by the wife's weight, so women put on so much weight they could not move. In our own country we don't have to look too far back to a time when women were prone to fainting spells because they had cinched their twenty-five-inch waists down to a fashionable eighteen.

"Yes," we think as we finish this paragraph, "women have been driven to some pretty bizarre extremes to reach their culture's standards of beauty."

The quality of a writer's examples is at least as important as their number. The mother who wrote this next paragraph could have given us many more examples of her daughter's "peculiar reactions to ordinary experiences," but she wisely chose to limit herself to a few of the most memorable.

> *When Julie was about two, I realized that she had peculiar reactions to*

ordinary experiences, but I did not know why. She would see a toy across the room, crawl over to it, and then ignore it. She was afraid to sit on the edge of a chair. When I held up a favorite doll and cuddled it to me, she would laugh and seem to want it. When I offered it to her, the closer it got, the more afraid she became of it. You may have already figured out her problem. And I admit, it does seem simple with all those clues to think about at once. Yes, vision. Julie had a severe vision problem.

Though often just a few examples will do to fill out a paragraph, occasionally your purpose will require more. One student, while working in a day-care center, had discovered a number of toys that allowed children to blow off steam without hurting each other. Since the purpose of her paragraph was to acquaint parents with those toys, she decided to mention as many as she could remember. Her readers will leave the paper with quite a few practical examples.

A number of toys on the market provide safe and effective outlets for your child's aggressive feelings. For example, you can buy a small punching bag for a small bully. In the case of fighting brothers and sisters, soccer boppers are quite effective. Soccer boppers are a primitive form of boxing gloves that protect the children from actually hurting each other, but allow them to keep on fighting until they feel better. When you have a child who likes to throw things, the "Nerf" airplanes and animals are your answer. With these toys not too much can get broken, because they are made of foam rubber. In the case of the child who enjoys biting, a rubber hand might be appropriate. You can always find these around Halloween. When you have a child with an uncontrollable amount of aggression, one solution is a padded room. However, these are not yet on the market for home use.

Had this paragraph been much longer, the writer would have split it at a natural pause between examples. A topic sentence sometimes introduces the material in more than one paragraph.

Illustrations

When an example is extended and told in the form of a story, it is called an illustration. Because readers enjoy stories perhaps more than any other form of writing, illustrations, when appropriate, can be a powerful way of proving a point.

Hospital workers know that at any moment they can be faced with a crisis. For example, while I was running an EEG (electroencephalogram) one day, the pens started clacking and throwing ink around the room. I knew then that I was in trouble. My patient was having a seizure. Pressing the alarm button, I ran to the patient to immobilize her. Poor little thing, she was only four years old. Within seconds, three other members of my clinic rushed into the room.

The physician started giving instructions and technicians rushed about, while the patient lay there helpless. As I drew the medication, the physician prepared her arm for the injection. When he gave the medication, a soft hush fell over the room. Slowly the pens stopped swaying and clacking. The patient's movements calmed. I knew then that everything would be all right for this child, this time—but that there would be other patients in my life just like her.

Notice that the writer carefully limited his topic sentence so that a single illustration would be enough to prove it: "Hospital workers know that *at any moment they can be faced with a crisis*." If the writer had wanted to show us that such crises are commonplace, a single illustration wouldn't have been enough. To prove this broader point, he would have needed several illustrations; or, since several illustrations might have become too long, he could have resorted to short examples instead.

Details

To prove some topic sentences, you'll decide to sketch in relevant details. These might be statistics, facts, items, parts, facets, or other particulars. The best details are specific, as in the following student paragraph:

> *In our one-room schoolhouse in Green's Harbour, final exams were taken seriously.* These exams were written the third week of June after school closed for the summer. They were mailed from the Department of Education to the chairman of the school-board, who had to be present during the entire three-day exam period. We could not bring anything into the exam room except for pens, pencils, erasers, rulers, and a mathematical set. One of our parents had to be present to pick up anything we might drop because we could not bend over to pick it up. Our seats were spaced three feet apart in all directions, and there was a time limit for each exam. At the end of each day's work, the completed exams were placed in envelopes, sealed, stamped, and then delivered to the post office—by three people. The results of the tests were mailed to the chairman of the school board in August, at which time we learned of our success or failure.

We are left with few doubts as to the truth of this writer's point: At his school in Green's Harbour, Newfoundland, final exams were taken very seriously indeed.

To decide how many details to include in a paragraph, simply consider your purpose and audience. One student writer, for instance, hoped to convince readers that the form letters sent out from her desk were the best she could manage under the circumstances. Several statistics, she felt, would make this clear.

> *Those who complain about receiving form letters from our office should consider themselves lucky to receive any acknowledgement of their application at all.* On the average we receive about 500 applications a month from

every out-of-work attorney on this side of the hemisphere. During peak periods, our office (which consists of three people, only one of whom can type) answers nearly 2000 applications in two or three weeks. I do not advise anyone to call or visit during this time, as tempers run extremely short. Too many of these 2000 nameless faces feel that their submission makes us the best of buddies, so they phone, usually early on Mondays, to chat. The conversations often conclude with appeals to our "friendship": "Can't you pull some strings and find me a job?"

Reasons

Reasons are a fourth way of filling out paragraphs. They are appropriate when a topic sentence begs for an answer to the question "Why?" If a paragraph recommends that we install a wood stove or vote Republican or send our kids to camp, we want to know why. The writer's job, then, is to tell us why—to give some reasons.

In a paper on the pros and cons of the open-space classroom, one writer included a paragraph explaining why such a classroom can be disastrous for students like her son, David.

Though the open-space classroom works for many children, it is not practical for my son, David, for several reasons. First, David is hyperactive. When he was placed in an open-space classroom, he became confused and frustrated. There were so many distractions because of the large number of children in one area that he was tempted to watch the movement going on around him instead of concentrating on his own work. Second, David has a tendency to transpose letters and numbers, a tendency that can be overcome only by individual attention from the instructor. In the open classroom he was moved from teacher to teacher, with each one responsible for a different subject at a different level. No single teacher worked with David long enough to diagnose his problem, let alone help him with it. Finally, David is not a highly motivated learner. In the open classroom he was graded "at his own level," not by criteria for a certain grade. He was in Area I, not in second grade. He could receive a "B" in reading and still be a grade level behind, because he was doing satisfactory work "at his own level."

Notice that our writer has supplied readers with clear transition words—*first, second,* and *finally*—to help them see where one reason ends and the next begins. Without such help many readers would have lost the thread that ties the paragraph together.

Comparisons and contrasts

To compare is to call attention to similarities; to contrast is to point out differences. If you're arguing that the $15,000 sports car your friend is thinking of buying is nothing more than a slickly packaged version of a much cheaper model, you'll use comparisons. You may mention a few differences, including the prices, but you will focus on similarities. If on the other hand your purpose is to help your friend decide between a Corvette and a 280Z, you'll focus almost entirely on differences.

Whether you need to compare or to contrast, you can use one of two basic ways to fill out your paragraph. You can discuss your two items point by point, or you can deal with them one at a time. Here is a paragraph of comparison developed by the point-by-point method:

> *Both Karen and I had strict parents.* We weren't allowed to date, talk to boys on the phone, or even use the phone after nine o'clock; we couldn't spend a weekend over at a girl friend's house or go roller-skating without a chaperone. Karen and I were the only girls in our group who couldn't wear make-up or go to school dances until we were in the eighth grade. We used to joke with each other that we lived in jails.

Clearly the point-by-point method was a good choice here, to avoid running through the list of restrictions twice.

The point-by-point method is often effective for paragraphs of contrast, such as this one:

> *Strangly enough, instead of being academically inferior to my American high school, the Irish convent was superior.* In my class at home *Love Story* was considered pretty heavy reading, so imagine my surprise at finding Irish students who could recite passages from *War and Peace*. In high school we complained about having to study "Romeo and Juliet" in one semester, whereas in Ireland we simultaneously studied "Macbeth" and Dickens's *Hard Times,* in addition to writing a composition a day in English class. In high school I didn't even begin algebra until the ninth grade, while at the convent seventh graders (or their Irish equivalent) were doing calculus and trigonometry.

Here the point-by-point method sharpens the contrast: *Love Story* vs. *War and Peace;* "Romeo and Juliet" vs. "Macbeth," *Hard Times,* and a composition a day; elementary arithmetic vs. calculus and trigonometry. The writer could have dealt with the academic requirements of the American high school and then of the convent, but she decided that the point-by-point method highlighted her contrast more dramatically.

Sometimes your material won't lend itself to the zigzag structure of the point-by-point method. Then you'll deal with your two items one at a time. For instance, in a paper contrasting small-town and urban life, one student writer decided to put us on the scene, first in a small town.

> Let's go on a routine grocery trip in small-town America. First you get a cart and begin to make your selections. As you shop, people nod, agree that

prices are outrageous, and they may even tell you, for instance, why they are buying green grapes today. As you pass the meat counter, you are told "hello," usually by name. The meat man knows just what type of meat you like and usually buy. Often he has put a special cut in the back because he thought you would like it, and he tells you to wait while he gets it to show it to you. You are not particularly flattered, because this is what you are used to.

After you have finished shopping, you push your cart up to the line at the cash register. While you wait in line, everyone smiles and talks to each other. You may be told what nice apples you picked out. The weather, inflation, and even the latest hemlines are often discussed. When it is your turn, a bag boy takes your groceries out of the cart and places them on the counter. While the cashier adds up your total and chats with you, the bag boy is bagging your groceries. By the time you pay, your groceries are in a cart ready to go out as you do. Now you really get personalized service. The bag boy walks out with you, pushing your groceries to your car. He opens the trunk and loads them for you. As he leaves, he says with a smile, "Thank you, Mrs. Ricketson. Have a nice day."

Now that we have experienced small-town America, our writer takes us to the city.

Let's shop now at the same grocery chain, but this time in the suburbs of a large city. From the start you are on your own. No one will talk to you or even look at you. The meat man has no idea who you are or what you might like, even if you shop there twice a week. When you finish shopping and get in line, no one will speak to you. If you are brave and say to the couple next to you, "Hi. Nice day, isn't it?" they will look at you as though you just threatened them. Maybe they will give you a quick reply, but there will be no conversation. When it is your turn, *you* take your groceries out of the cart and place them on the counter. The cashier adds them up, silently. If you write a check and hand it to the cashier, even if you have been through her line many times, she will look you straight in the face and say, "Do you have a card on file?" When this happened to me last week, I couldn't resist the temptation. I looked right back at her and said: "No, I have never been here before." I thought she would laugh, but she didn't. She looked kind of strange and said, "Oh."

Usually you help bag your groceries and put them into a cart. Then you push them outside, go get your car, and drive up to the curb, and wait in line to reach your groceries. If you are lucky, a bag boy will be on duty to put them into your car. And when he is finished, you will finally get a borrowed bit of small-town gentility, because he will say, mechanically and without smiling, "Have a nice day."

These paragraphs echo the ones that came before. In the city suburb, as in the small town, we enter the store, pass the meat counter, stand in line, get checked out, walk to the parking lot, and leave with a word from the bag boy. Because so much is the same, the contrast is all the more vivid.

In this chapter we have surveyed some of the most common ways of filling out paragraphs: examples, illustrations, details, reasons, and comparisons and contrasts. Don't expect every paragraph you write to fit one of these models, for you'll often use a combination of methods and you'll sometimes invent others. Just consider your topic sentence, your purpose, and your audience, and then give readers the kind of evidence you think they need to hear.

How long should a paragraph be?

How long should your paragraphs be? Our general advice is to be flexible, because there is no one consideration that outweighs all others. Using a few rules of thumb, you will need to make decisions for yourself.

Often you can tell whether a paragraph is too long or too short just by noticing how it looks on the page. Remember that one major function of a paragraph is to rest the reader's eye, so if you have a 500-word paragraph (two pages typed, double-spaced), you can be pretty sure your reader will get tired. You'll need to break up the 500 words into two or three, maybe even four paragraphs for your reader. By the same token, if you have broken 500 words up into ten paragraphs, you can be fairly certain that your readers will get too much "rest." It's like taking them on a ten-mile hike and insisting that they rest every mile; you break their momentum and wear them out from too much starting and stopping.

Thus, you need to notice how long your paragraphs look on the page. And that, of course, depends on what kind of page we're talking about. As you write papers in college, your paragraph length will be determined to some extent by your decision to type or to write longhand. Typed paragraphs generally can be a bit longer than handwritten ones.

Earlier in this chapter we made the point that paragraphs help readers understand the shape of what they are reading. This is a very important consideration in determining the lengths of your paragraphs. If at all possible, let your paragraphs reflect the shape of your ideas. If, for example, you are writing a 500-word paper in which you give the reader three examples to illustrate your main point, you'll probably decide on five paragraphs: a paragraph of introduction, three body paragraphs (one for each example), and a short concluding paragraph. If one of your examples is much longer than the other two—so long that it will tire your reader's eye—you'll probably want to split it at some convenient point. The more closely your paragraphs reflect the shape of your ideas, the clearer your paper is likely to be.

One final word about paragraph length: How consistent should you be in the lengths of your paragraphs? Should you try to make them all about the same length, or should you vary them, playing off long ones against short ones? These questions are hard to answer. Paragraph lengths, like sentence lengths, give a paper a kind of rhythm that readers can feel but that is hard to talk about. A very short paragraph can be just the right kind of pause following a long and complex paragraph. Or a series of paragraphs of about the same length can give the reader a very satisfying feeling of balance and proportion. But let us say no more about this; you'll have to follow your own ear.

. . . .

Exercise 1 For class discussion

. . . .

Identify the topic sentence of each of the following student paragraphs. If the writer chose not to place the topic sentence at the very beginning of the paragraph, do you see a good reason for its being elsewhere?

1. Now for those prepared mixes. I know that the Duncan Hines Cake Mix looks very tempting, but have you ever considered what you actually get for your seventy-nine cents? Let's take a look. For seventy-nine cents you get items that are usually already in your kitchen cabinets—flour, sugar, shortening and leavening. In addition, you get certain undesirable preservatives. After getting the mix home, you find that you must add your own eggs and in some cases butter for a better-tasting cake. Since the ingredients for a cake are usually in your cabinets, why not make your own mix and save your seventy-nine cents?

2. Soap opera characters are far from being realistic. They are all upper-class people, living in the finest of homes and wearing the latest fashions. You never see any poor people on these shows or anyone who has an ordinary job. No, these character are all doctors or lawyers. The cities in which these soap operas take place must have to ship people in to do the less prestigious work.

3. Another example of research aimed at preventing sexual child abuse is under way at California State Hospital. Operating under the theory that most child molesters have led highly inadequate social and sexual lives, psychologists teach offenders how to talk to and relate to adults. The California State Hospital program is so sophisticated that it even has volunteer counselors from local gay organizations coming in to teach homosexual offenders how to pick up adult partners.

4. Today the two oldest are out of college with well-paying jobs. The oldest one went into dentistry and then into the Navy. He is stationed in South Carolina, and has his own office to work in. The second child passed through college with high honors and now is a certified public accountant, working for the second largest firm in the United States, making $18,000 yearly and awaiting a $5000-dollar raise. The youngest is still in college, planning to go into business.

5. The atmosphere of the Berwyn Cafe was easygoing, unhurried. Some of the customers who had finished their meals were washing their own dishes, talking and sharing vegetarian recipes with the cooks. As they left, people paid for their meals by dropping their money into a large wooden bowl, retrieving the change themselves.

6. The dream of every cyclist is to own a Cinelli. A Cinelli is the highest-quality, most expensive bicycle made. Each part on a Cinelli is machined individually by hand. The wheels are laced and trued to the millimeter, by hand—a process which can take forty hours for just two wheels. The special lightweight tubing on the frame is thickened at the joints and thinned in the middle, a design known as double butting. A Cinelli could be all yours for just $1300. At least that's how much I saw it advertised for on one of the rare occasions a Cinelli was ever advertised.

Exercise 2   Small-group activity

Working in small groups of three or four people, help the writers of the following skimpy paragraphs come up with more ideas for expanding the paragraphs. Have one member of the group jot down the ideas on scratch paper. Your instructor may then ask the groups to pool their ideas.

1. Almost anything that will hold water can be used as a plant container. Try painting empty coffee cans or hollowing out old pieces of wood. Just use your imagination.

2. People who want to save energy should start in their own homes. They should change their life-styles so that they consume less. Lights and televisions should not be kept on in unoccupied rooms. Junk mail should be sent back because it is only a waste of paper. These examples are only a few things that can be done in the home.

Exercise 3   For class discussion

Following are a number of paragraphs developed according to the methods discussed in this chapter: examples, illustrations, details, reasons, and comparisons and contrasts. Identify the method that has been used in each paragraph. Does the method seem appropriate, considering the writer's topic sentence? Has the writer given readers enough development to prove or at least strongly to suggest the truth of the topic sentence?

1. *On the inside your worst fate was to be discovered as an informer or a "snitch."* One evening during our recreation period, when the cells were open, making it possible to go to the ground floor to play cards, watch TV, or just talk, I saw how snitches were dealt with on Cell Block One. This area, like all the cells, is separated from the guards by grill and screen. While I was playing cards with Hink, a small scuffle disturbed our game. Looking up, we saw two men, labeled as snitches, ritually getting their throats cut. The guards on the other side of the grill would not enter to offer any assistance until everyone had returned to their cells to lock in. In the meantime, the two men bled to death.

2. *The ambulance is well equipped.* There are neck braces in case of whiplash, eye pads for particles in the eye, sanitary napkins for extensive bleeding, air masks to help breathing, burn sheets for burn victims, restraining straps in case of seizures, a suction unit for getting blood out of the throat, and a complete first-aid kit. The kit includes all possible shapes and sizes of gauze bandages for cuts and scrapes and lacerations. The ambulance is also equipped with a radio which enables the medics to talk directly with the hospital to which they are en route, and a computer for monitoring vital signs.

3. *The Irish convent had almost none of the educational facilities or equipment believed necessary in America.* There was no cafeteria or food service. There were no science labs (although my biology teacher *did* bring a dead frog once and dissect it for us). The home economics department consisted of one stove and seven sinks. There was no library, really, just a box of paperback books that the English teacher let us borrow from. There was one record player for the entire school and a tape recorder that dated from World War II.

4. *Not that the Irish were completely superior in educational standards.* Many of the students at the convent had never even heard of chemistry, much less sex education. They knew by heart the exploits of Cuchulain (a legendary Irish warrior), but knew nothing of Freud or Marx or of any religion but their own. The average Irish student seemed to have a firm knowledge of the classics but was out of touch with the world of today.

5. *For the over-thirty gang who are overweight, out of shape, but healthy, I recommend rope-jumping as a most convenient form of exercise.* First of all, the equipment is simple and can usually be found in the home. All you need is a rope. A piece of clothesline will do, but if you want to feel a little more professional about it, go to a sports store and buy a leather rope weighted with ball bearings. A second convenience is that no special setting is needed. You can jump anywhere at any time to suit your schedule. You can jump outside—on the patio, the driveway, or the lawn—or inside—in the basement, attic, or even the living room. If you are traveling, you can jump rope in your hotel room. If you forgot your rope, just hook several belts together. Finally, since rope-jumping is a private exercise, you won't need to buy expensive sports attire. You may wear anything that's comfortable and won't get in your way.

6. *Hospitals are concerned with keeping the heart beating, not with the dignity of life.* The eighty-three-year-old father of a friend of mine, who had a slow-growing cancer of the prostate and whose veins were collapsing due to old age, was treated by the hospital staff as a collection of symptoms, not as a person. The nurses insisted on checking his blood pressure often, even though he found this very painful. In addition, they took blood tests every day, in spite of the fact that they had difficulty finding his veins. Before he died, he also had to endure the torture of being X-rayed to check the progress of the cancer. Mercifully, he died after being in the hospital only a few weeks. Unfortunately, an eighty-nine-year-old aunt of mine suffered for seven months in the hospital before she died. She went in and out of comas, had pneumonia a couple of times, and was pulled back to life to suffer more. She was a shrunken, senile old lady begging for death when she died.

7. *Since children learn a good deal by imitation and often have trouble distinguishing between fantasy and reality, parents should be cautious about what they expose their children to on television.* My older son's addiction to "Kung Fu" reruns, for instance, cost me a trip to the hospital last summer. During a particularly heated argument, he Kung Fu-ed his little brother on the head. As for "Batman," we've had a few jammed knees and wrists from jumping off picnic tables and porches with a towel pinned on as a cape. And once a bottle of perfume was emptied as "bat spray." Within the past year NBC featured an early evening film, "Born Innocent," which showed the sexual attack of a young girl with a broom handle by female inmates of a juvenile detention home. A mother has sued the station, charging that the show inspired a similar attack on her nine-year-old daughter.

8. *Buying and maintaining their equipment requires quite an expenditure for the musicians.* Hundreds of dollars are spent just for an instrument. Each instrument (except drums) then needs an amplifier and a head, to produce the precise volume and sound needed for nightclubs. Amplifiers and heads also run hundreds of dollars apiece. Other necessary equipment—microphones for the vocalists, a PA board (the broadcast transmitter), and speaker cabinets—can total over a thousand dollars.

Since this heavy equipment is transported from club to club and receives excessive use, blown tubes and fuses and wornout cords must be replaced frequently. A piano needs to be kept in tune. For this, the pianist either pays thirty to forty dollars per tuning or buys a $400 strobotuner and learns how to tune.

9. *Now that I'm over thirty, I'm not as naive as I was in my twenties.* I know how to resist a car salesman, how to handle an obscene phone call, what precautions to take when I'm out alone. I know how to handle a bank account, plan a week's menu, run a household, and raise a child. I know how to dress for an interview, how to find my way around a strange city, and how to vote. All of this I have learned through experience, by trial and error.

. . . .
Exercise 4 Written
. . . .

Browse through the topics in part VII in search of a subject that would work for a paragraph of 150 to 250 words. (Feel free to narrow any of the topics radically.) Jot down a list of ideas which you would use if you were going to write the paragraph, but don't actually write it.

. . . .
Exercise 5 Written
. . . .

Select a topic from part VII that could be developed in a paragraph of 150 to 250 words. Before you write the paragraph, jot down a list of ideas on scratch paper. If your list shows little promise, throw it out and start another one, maybe on another topic. Once you have a workable list on scratch paper, write the paragraph. (Don't worry if the paragraph doesn't exactly fit the list—the list is there to give you control, not to straitjacket you.) Hand in your paragraph and your scratch-paper list.

11 Holding it all together

Word carpentry is like any other kind of carpentry: you must join your sentences [and paragraphs] smoothly.   Anatole France

We come now to what may at first strike you as a minor detail: the coherence of your writing, or how it all hangs together. Although coherence is one of the finer points of writing, it is nonetheless a very important one. If your paper does not flow along so that readers can easily follow it, they will feel confused, even lost. Readers have a right to expect your writing to flow, to move so naturally that they are not even aware of the movement. You will need to make it easy for them to stay with you, both within paragraphs and while moving between paragraphs.

We might define the verb *to cohere,* from which *coherence* comes, in three ways: 1) to be connected logically; 2) to be consistent; and 3) to stick together. Let's talk first about attending to the logical connections within a piece of writing.

Logical connections

One way to achieve coherence is to establish logical connections by careful organization. Once the introduction has established the promise of a paper, the shape of the rest of the writing should echo that promise, which can often be traced through the topic sentences of the remaining paragraphs.

As a general rule, as we mentioned in chapter 9, your thesis statement and topic sentences should interlock. Just by reading these key sentences, readers should be able to see how the parts of the paper are related to each other. In the following paper, for example, the writer connects his topic sentences to his thesis statement so carefully that a reader can't possibly get lost. His thesis statement and his topic sentences are italicized.

A favorite pastime of mine is observing people, and my favorite place to observe is at the horse races. *After about fifteen encounters with the racing crowd, I discovered that there are four distinct groups of people that appear at the track: the once-a-year group, the professionals, the clubhouse bunch, and the welfare and unemployed group.*

The largest group at the track are the ones that show up once a year. They know little about horses or betting. They rely strictly on racetrack gimmick sheets and newspaper predictions for selecting possible winners. If that doesn't work they use intuition, favorite numbers, colors, or appealing names. They bet larger amounts as the day goes along, gambling on every race, including the long-shot bets on exactas and daily doubles. Of course, the vast majority go home broke and frustrated.

A more subtle and quiet group are the professionals. They follow the horses from track to track and live in campers and motor homes. Many are married couples, some are retired, and all are easily spotted with their lunch sacks, thermos jugs, and binoculars. Since most are familiar with one another, they section themselves off in a particular area of the stadium. All rely on the racing form and on personal knowledge of each horse, jockey, and track in making the proper bet. They bet only on the smart races, and rarely on the favorites. Never do they bet on exactas or daily doubles. More often than not they either break even or go home winners.

In addition, there exists the clubhouse group. They can be found either at the cocktail lounge or in the restaurant, usually involved in business transactions. They rarely see a race in person and do their betting via the waiter. It's difficult to tell whether they go home sad, happy, or in between. They are just there.

The most interesting members of the racetrack population are the unemployed and welfare group. They won't be found in the clubhouse, but right down at the rail next to the finish line. It is here one can discover the real emotion of the racetrack—the screaming, the cursing, and the pushing. They are not sportsmen. Betting at the races is not a game for them, but a battle for survival. If they lose they must borrow enough money to carry them until the next check comes in, and then, of course, they head right back to the track. This particular group arrives at the track beaten and leaves beaten.

I have probably lost more money than I have won at the track, but observing these four interesting groups of people makes it all worthwhile.

As you may have noticed, this writer even bothered to echo the sentence that concludes the first body paragraph. Those in the once-a-year group "go home broke and frustrated"; the professionals "either break even or go home winners"; the clubhouse bunch are so remote it's hard to know how they go home; and the welfare group "arrives at the track beaten and leaves beaten." These clincher sentences, along with the topic sentences and the thesis statement, pull the various parts of the paper together. And because the parts are so clearly connected, the paper is extremely easy to follow.

Consistency in perspective

To keep your reader with you throughout your paper, you will need to be consistent. A sudden awkward shift in the perspective from which you are writing will make your reader puzzle, "What happened here? I don't understand what's going on." Consistency in perspective will help to keep your writing clear for your reader.

You might make a sudden awkward shift in several ways. To help you understand the importance of consistency, let's look at a paragraph that makes some awkward shifts. Reading the paragraph aloud will help you hear them.

> Isaac Asimov's short story "The Ugly Little Boy" shows how much a human being needs to be loved and needed. The nurse becomes very attached to the little boy as she cared for his physical needs and taught him to speak. He is so loved by her that she risks her own life. People will do that if someone or something means enough to them. She knows that she may die if she stays with him. I thought that was too big a price to pay for being loved and needed, but by the end of the story you know her choice is worth the risk to her.

Did the second sentence sound awkward as you read it aloud? That sentence contains a shift in verb tense: the writer begins in the present tense (*becomes*), then shifts to the past tense (*cared* and *taught*). As you moved from the second sentence to the third, did you hear the shift from active to passive voice? Sentence 2 begins "The nurse becomes . . . ," while sentence 3 begins "The boy is so loved by her . . . ." Would the sentences read more smoothly together this way: "The nurse becomes . . ." followed by "She loves him so much . . ."?

Did the fourth sentence of the paragraph suddenly take you away from the nurse and the little boy? Such a general-observation sentence, which reads as if it has been dropped into a paragraph, is called an aside. Does this sentence belong in the paragraph at all? Finally, did you feel a jolt in the last sentence when the writer abruptly shifted from *I* to *you*?

All shifts in perspective startle and confuse a reader. It's fairly common for shifts to slip into a rough draft; just be on the lookout to correct them as you polish a paper. And you will need to take care not to shift your perspective as you begin new paragraphs, as well as within paragraphs. For more about shifts, see "The Writer's Stance" in chapter 4 and section 25 in the handbook.

Clear organization and consistency in perspective, then, serve to keep an entire paper connected naturally, so that it flows. In addition, you can use some specific devices to help your writing to cohere, or to "stick together," as our third definition puts it.

The echo effect: repetition and parallelism

One device that helps your writing stick together is the repetition of key words or phrases or ideas, which produces a sort of echo effect. Such repetition keeps reminding readers of the main point within a paragraph and focuses their attention on major ideas throughout a paper. In the paper printed below, the writer echoes whole sentences. "The husbands comfort their wives" is echoed in the beginning of paragraph 2 and at the end of paragraph 3. In addition, the question "Who is to comfort the husbands?" creates an echo effect to open paragraph 4.

> The first thing I saw when I opened my newspaper this morning was a photograph of two sets of parents at the graveside of their young daughters, brutally murdered recently. The caption beneath the photograph, in which the mothers were clearly grieving, ended with the sentence "The husbands comfort their wives." Those last five words leave an important question unanswered: Who is to comfort the husbands?
>
> "The husbands comfort their wives." I believe that the women in the picture are indeed receiving comfort from their men. But I believe they are getting more comfort in the open release of their emotions. Such open release allows twofold benefits. First, the women's display of emotion elicits a sympathetic reaction from others, who rush to comfort the grieving. Second, and I believe most important, their open grieving allows for a release of tensions that would otherwise build up inside. Such public display of emotion is therapeutic, and it is acceptable behavior for women.
>
> I look more closely at one of the husbands. He sits there with his "stiff upper lip," surrounding his wife with his comfort-giving arms. I look closely at his eyes and the circles under them. In even such a poor-quality photograph I can see the grief in his eyes longing for release. But that release cannot come, not in public, for he is "strong"; he is a "man." He is expected to give comfort to the "weaker" female. And so this husband comforts his wife.
>
> But who is to comfort the husband? He is expected to "take it like a man." And he will. He will hold his grief and allow the tensions to build, until an acceptable time and place for release. Meanwhile, he acts "like a man"—in a display that is not very healthy, but that is acceptable behavior for men.

Another way to achieve the echo effect is to use synonyms, a device that also helps to avoid the monotony of simple repetition. The following paragraph uses synonyms for the word *marijuana* in this way.

The effects of *marijuana* are hotly debated. And whether the *drug* will be decriminalized largely depends on the outcome of the controversy now under way. Whether the pleasurable results from smoking *grass* should be considered worth the possible risks of its use is a real question in a free society. What are the long-term effects of the substance affectionately known among its advocates as *Mary Jane*—and how much should its detractors be listened to? Let us try to take an objective look at *marijuana*.

You can also create an echo effect by using parallel structure, in which parallel elements of a sentence or a paragraph are expressed in the same way. In the following paragraph, for example, five successive sentences begin with a verb that invites an art museum visitor to enjoy a painting in various ways.

Suddenly, in the midst of your musings, you find yourself in a room ablaze with light, color, and life. There on the wall is Renoir's "Luncheon of the Boating Party." Take a seat and treat yourself to a longer look. Settle back and feel the joy and warmth of the painting. Smell the early summer breeze off the Seine. Hear the rustle of the leaves and the hum of the conversation. Stay as long as you like, but remember, there is more.

Here are the sentences listed so that you can more readily recognize the parallel structure:

Take a seat and treat yourself to a longer look.
Settle back and feel the joy and warmth of the painting.
Smell the early summer breeze off the Seine.
Hear the rustle of the leaves and the hum of the conversation.
Stay as long as you like, but remember, there is more.

In our next example, parallel structure has been combined with repetition to produce an echo effect.

You come up on the desert of the White Sands from the cultured East or the deep South or the industrial North and suddenly you breathe. The sand beneath you is white and the sky above you is blue and there is no need even to define the colors, for the white is the whitest you have ever seen and the blue is the bluest. There is nothing else. You take off your shoes and slide your feet quietly onto the whiteness and walk. You address the blue sky and walk. You breathe.

Parallel structure can also be used to carry along an entire piece of writing. In a paper by Jo Goodwin Parker entitled "What Is Poverty?"

eight of the fifteen paragraphs begin "Poverty is . . . ." Here are the topic sentences of Parker's opening paragraph, and several of her other paragraphs:

> You ask me what is poverty?
> Poverty is being tired.
> Poverty is dirt.
> Poverty is staying up all night on cold nights to watch the fire, knowing one spark on the newspaper covering the walls means your sleeping child dies in flames.
> Poverty is looking into a black future.
> Poverty is an acid that drips on pride until all pride is worn away.

Transitional bridges

The final coherence device we want to tell you about is one of the simplest, and also one of the easiest to learn how to use. It is providing bridges to carry your reader from one part of your paper to the next. You can use these bridge words or phrases, sometimes called transitions, to move your reader from sentence to sentence or from one paragraph into the next.

Below is a chart of some bridge words and phrases. You can train yourself to use these bridges by asking yourself certain questions as you write: Does the next thing I am going to say simply make an *addition* to something I've just said? Or does the content of my next sentence set up a *comparison* or a *contrast* with what is in my last sentence? Am I involved in a *cause-and-effect* discussion? Am I about to illustrate my point by using an *example*? You can ask yourself the same questions as you begin a new paragraph, of course.

. . . .

Transition to indicate:	*Bridge words and phrases:*		
1. Addition	furthermore	or	third
	also	nor	next
	in addition	moreover	last
	further	again	finally
	besides	first	
	and	second	

Example: For the fruit-testing project we tasted sour green apples; furthermore, some of us consented to try very green bananas.

Transition to indicate:	Bridge words and phrases:		
2. Time	while	immediately	never
	after	later	always
	when	soon	whenever
	meanwhile	in the meantime	sometimes
	during	afterwards	now
	next	following	once
	then	at length	simultaneously

Example: For the fruit-testing project we tasted sour green apples. Soon several of us developed stomach cramps.

3. Place	here	beyond	adjacent to
	there	wherever	neighboring on
	nearby	opposite to	

Example: For the fruit-testing project we tasted sour green apples; nearby another group of volunteers was trying very green bananas.

4. Exemplification or Illustration	for example	for instance
	as an illustration	to illustrate
	to demonstrate	e.g. (means
	specifically	"for example")

Example: For the fruit-testing project, volunteers were expected to taste a variety of samples; our group, for instance, tried very green bananas.

5. Comparison	in the same way	in like manner
	by the same token	likewise
	similarly	in similar fashion

Example: For the fruit-testing project we tasted sour green apples; in similar fashion, some of us tried very green bananas.

6. Contrast	on the contrary	yet
	in contrast	and yet
	nevertheless	notwithstanding
	but	otherwise
	at the same time	however
	although that may be true	after all
	nonetheless	though
	on the other hand	instead
		rather

Example: For the fruit-testing project we tasted sour green apples; however, most of us refused to try very green bananas.

Transition to indicate:	Bridge words and phrases:	

7. Clarification

that is to say	to clarify
in other words	to rephrase
to put it another way	i.e. (means
to explain	"in other words")

Example: For the fruit-testing project we tasted sour green apples. In other words, we experimented with the possible effects of green fruit on our health.

8. Cause

owing to	since
because	for that reason

Example: Since we were afraid they would make us sick, several of us refused to try very green bananas during the fruit-testing project.

9. Effect

therefore	thus
consequently	hence
as a result	accordingly

Example: For the fruit-testing project we ate sour green apples; consequently, we were all in bed the next day with stomachaches.

10. Purpose

in order to	to that end
for this purpose	so that

Example: For the fruit-testing project we tasted sour green apples. In order to earn full pay for volunteering, some of us tried very green bananas.

11. Qualification

almost	perhaps
nearly	maybe
probably	although

Example: For the fruit-testing project we ate sour green apples. Perhaps I shall never feel more uncomfortable than I felt following that experiment.

12. Intensification

indeed	undoubtedly	doubtlessly
to repeat	in fact	certainly
by all means	without doubt	surely
even more so		of course

Example: For the fruit-testing project we ate sour green apples; without doubt, that was one of my most unpleasant sensory experiences.

*Transition
to indicate:*   *Bridge words and phrases:*

13. Summary   to summarize   in short   in brief
                   in sum   to sum up   in summary

Example: We ate green apples for the fruit-testing project. Then we were handed very green bananas to try. Next came pears almost as hard as rocks. In brief, we were provided a steady diet of green fruit throughout the afternoon.

14. Conclusion   in conclusion   to conclude   finally

Example: To conclude my report on tasting green fruits, I would simply advise my readers to find another way to contribute to the health studies of the nation.

Here is the rough draft of a student paragraph before the writer attended to his transitions. Notice how his pile-up of unconnected short sentences makes the paragraph jerk along when you read it aloud.

> Kid porno is highly immoral. I don't care for adult pornography because it is violent. That does not seem as wrong to me as child pornography. Adult pornography uses adults. They know they are being used and they consent. Children don't understand how kid porno exploits them. It uses them to sell products. It can encourage promiscuous sexual activity. They are too young to realize what they're doing. Kid porno can promote such sexual behavior among other children. Kid porno is highly immoral. It is more immoral than adult pornography.

Rewriting, this student built in transitional bridges he needed to weave those jerky sentences together. His new version read more smoothly, as you can see. The added bridges are in italics.

> Kid porno is highly immoral. I'm not interested in adult pornography because it is violent, *but* that does not seem as wrong to me as child pornography. Adult pornography uses adults. They know they are being used and they consent. Children, *on the other hand,* don't understand how kid porno exploits them; *for example,* it uses them to sell products. *Furthermore,* it can encourage them toward promiscuous sexual activity *while* they are too young to realize what they're doing. Kid porno can *also* promote such sexual behavior among other children. *Therefore,* kid porno is highly immoral—*even more so* than adult pornography.

You will want to take care not to overuse transitional words and phrases. If you do, your writing may begin to sound mechanical, almost as if it had been written by a computer instead of a human being. Can you hear such a mechanical effect as you read the following paragraph aloud?

> Watching football on television is my favorite way to relax. First, I put on my grungies in order not to be worried about wrinkling my business clothes. Second, I turn off the telephone; therefore, my game won't be interrupted. Third, I chase everybody else from the room so I can be alone with my game. Fourth, I have a bowl of popcorn and a jug of root beer close by; consequently, I don't have to get up for refreshments. Finally, I become totally involved in the action on the screen, with the result that I totally escape from my real life. In conclusion, this is how I relax in my favorite way—with football on television.

Did you hear any bridges you as reader did not need? Or any necessary ones that stuck out as mechanical? Would some other bridge sound better in those places? Remember, you don't need to overconnect your writing; just build in the bridges without which your reader can't get along.

Transitions are not always merely single words or phrases. Sometimes whole sentences or even paragraphs work as bridges to smooth the way for your reader. Here is a student paper that uses a transitional paragraph:

> This paper is a salute to black women all over our nation who have suffered almost unendurable hardships trying to keep their families together in the face of relentless day-to-day oppression. American history and American literature are slowly beginning to show us some of these strong black women, their struggles, their heartaches—and, always, their pride.
>
> I can think of no better example of these proud, tenacious women than Phoenix, in Eudora Welty's short story "A Worn Path."
>
> Old Phoenix was a product of the cruel institution of slavery. She had been freed by the Emancipation Proclamation, and had had no formal education. However, she was able to survive in a country hostile to freed slaves. . . .

The second paragraph, one sentence long, is transitional. Transitional paragraphs can be composed of one, two, or perhaps even three sentences, but they are unlikely to be very long.

Tying it all together: conclusions

The conclusion of your paper ties it all together. Just as your introduction introduced your main point, your conclusion drives it home. As we pointed out in an earlier chapter, your introductory paragraph should either begin or end with your thesis statement. The same is true for your concluding paragraph. Either begin or end it with a sentence that echoes your thesis.

If you decide to echo your thesis in the first sentence of your conclusion, use the remaining sentences of the paragraph to drive the point home. That's what this student has done, for example, to end a paper arguing for the rights of nonsmokers:

> Though I recognize the right of others to smoke privately, public smoking infringes on the rights of nonsmokers. It is more plausible for the smoker to curtail smoking than for the nonsmoker to curtail breathing.

The first sentence echoes the main point of the paper, that public smoking infringes on the rights of nonsmokers. The final sentence drives home that point with a witty remark: "It is more plausible for the smoker to curtail smoking than for the nonsmoker to curtail breathing."

Another student, whose paper showed how much the life-style of some homosexuals has changed over the past fifteen years, ended her paper like this:

> As you can see, the life-style of some homosexuals has changed tremendously in the past fifteen years. Homosexuals have had a long, hard struggle, but the end result has been worth it. As my friend Rhoda put it, "We feel like birds just released from our cage. We're just beginning to spread our wings and prove that we can fly."

Like the first student, this writer uses the first sentence of her conclusion to echo her main point. The other sentences, especially the quotation at the very end, drive home that point by showing what it means to one human being.

Here is one more example of a concluding paragraph that echoes the main point in the first sentence. This one concludes a paper showing readers that the Phillips art gallery is worth a visit.

> In any event, go to see the Phillips Collection. If you are an art lover, you can't miss at the Phillips. If you are not an art lover, you just might become one.

With her main point restated in her first sentence, our writer then uses a pair of pleasingly balanced parallel sentences in one last effort to entice readers to the gallery.

Sometimes you may decide to end rather than begin your concluding paragraph with an echo of your thesis. In that case, the earlier sentences of the paragraph will build toward the restatement of your main point. Here, for example, is how one student writer constructed a final statement of her main point:

The mother-at-home situation may produce secure, well-adjusted children. But not necessarily. It may result in a happy home. But not necessarily. The question of whether mothers of small children should work has no single answer. Since family situations are different, the answer to the question must be tailored to meet the needs of every family member—wife, husband, and children.

Another concluding paragraph that builds toward the echoed thesis is taken from a paper on the advantages of having twins:

There have been many times when I've asked myself, "Why me?" But, when I stop to think that I have not one but two beautiful, healthy six-year-old daughters, I know I'm a lucky person.

One last example. This paragraph concludes a paper on the difficulties involved in becoming a pro golfer.

Some have become millionaires playing golf. Others have made millions through advertising, writing, and investing. But when you think of the obstacles that must be overcome to make it big in the world of golf, you begin to realize that there are easier ways to make a living.

Whether you choose to echo your main point at the beginning or at the end of your final paragraph, remember that this is your last chance to drive home that point. So don't settle for a dull restatement of your thesis. Try to put some life into your concluding words, so readers will leave your paper with a strong final impression.

This is not always easy to do, as you probably know. Strong conclusions sometimes seem to be a matter of instinct. Occasionally, as you near the end of a rough draft, just the right finish will come to you in a flash of inspiration. More often, though, you'll probably find yourself dully restating your thesis instead of forcefully driving it home. If that happens, try to get away from your paper awhile, even for a few minutes. Then reread the paper, getting into its spirit, and try again. Hemingway claimed that he rewrote one ending thirty-nine times before he was satisfied. When an interviewer asked what the problem was, Hemingway paused for a moment, then gave his answer: "Getting the words right." You too may have to try more than once before getting those final words right.

. . . .
Exercise 1   For class discussion
. . . .

Turn to these two student papers: "Time Out" (#2, p. 174) and " It Was Halloween Night" (#18, p. 219). The writers of both papers skillfully used the techniques this chapter suggests for achieving coherence. Read each paper aloud so you can hear its smooth flow. Then discuss the techniques each writer used to make this happen.

. . . .

Exercise 2 Written
. . . .

Improve the paragraph in this chapter about watching football on television. You may want to delete some transitions altogether and change some others. As you do so, you may need to restructure sentences slightly; take care not to lose any of their essential content. Refer to the chart of transitional words and phrases for variety in new transitions.

. . . .

Exercise 3 Written
. . . .

Read the following paragraph aloud to hear how repetition of the word *just* and of words made from it becomes dull. Improve the paragraph by substituting synonyms. You need not change every *just;* some repetition of it will help to reinforce the point of the paragraph.

> The question of justice for all in our courts is of great concern to me. It seems only just that all should be treated equally when being tried under our system of justice. But surely that does not happen. Too often, affluent, well-educated, white-collar individuals in our society are treated more justly than the poor, who are often less-educated minority persons. Since that is true, can our court system really be called just?

. . . .

Exercise 4 For class discussion
. . . .

If unrelated sentences are included in a paragraph, or if sentences are not arranged in logical order, the coherence of the paragraph will suffer. Analyze the following paragraph for such problems and then improve it. The first sentence is the topic sentence.

> The sculpture of Louise Nevelson relies on her placing unlikely pieces of wood together to create interesting surfaces that emphasize light and shadow. Nevelson's appearance is striking, almost bizarre; she wears unusual clothes combinations and many chains and beads. Her studio is in New York City. Nevelson collects bedposts, two-by-fours, mantels, spools, dowels, and other shaped wood and then begins to experiment with these shapes in various arrangements. One summer her work was being shown in three different galleries at the same time. Sometimes Nevelson paints the finished sculpture—gold, silver, flat black, perhaps white; sometimes she leaves the

piece in its natural state. Once arranged, the protruding pieces of wood stand out as if highlighted and create shadows on the recessed areas. She nearly always ends up with an exciting collection of wood that distinguishes her as a sculptor.

. . . .

Exercise 5 Written
. . . .

Read the following paragraphs aloud for problems in coherence. Each one needs to be improved by establishing consistency, creating parallel structure, or adding bridges. You may have to restructure some sentences if you add bridges. Improve the paragraphs.

1. One summer I worked as a camp counselor. Each counselor was in charge of a cabin of ten boys. The nine-year-olds were in my cabin, Tahoe. All my campers were white except one. He was a black youngster named Jonathan. The rest of the campers ignored Jonathan in the beginning. Sometimes they outright excluded him from their activities. The camp master had told the counselors that each cabin should function as a unit. I worked hard to create a unit of those nine-year-olds. I succeeded. My most treasured object from that summer is a photograph of Jonathan hoisted on the shoulders of three new friends with six more nine-year-olds crowded around—all of them Jonathan's cabinmates from Tahoe.

2. The Chuckling Oyster at Land's End serves delicious seafood. It is known that their specialties are crab imperial, oyster stew, fried clams, salmon steak, and stuffed flounder. The last time we were at the Chuckling Oyster, I ordered salmon steak and my wife ordered crab imperial. Most salmon steak comes from the Pacific Northwest, but it tastes fresh at the Chuckling Oyster on the East Coast. First, our waiter brought us a large salad with house dressing and salty rye bread. We were served the next course—corn on the cob with plenty of butter—by another waiter. After that, a waitress delivers lime sherbet "to cleanse the palate for the specialty." By then you are almost too full to eat your main course. When we finally finished, I left the Chuckling Oyster convinced that it must be one of the best seafood restaurants in the United States.

3. Have you ever known a hermit? A hermit named Mr. Joe was a special part of my childhood. Mr. Joe knew about everything, or so it seemed to us children: how to catch minnows by hand, cracking walnuts so the meat came out whole, the sun as a record of time. Mr. Joe lived way back in the woods in a log cabin he had built himself. The hammock in his yard had been hand-tied by him. He dug his trout-breeding pond himself. All the flowers around his cabin had been dug up in the woods and transplanted by him. But the best thing about Mr. Joe was that, even being a hermit, he loved us kids and always carried treats for us—sweet, juicy oranges; shiny, crunchy apples; lollipops that were sometimes stale but were candy nonetheless; and, always, fresh, forbidden Juicy Fruit chewing gum.

Exercise 6   Classroom activity

Bring your most recent rough draft to class with you. Working in pairs, check your writing for coherence by having your partner read your paper out loud to you. Listen for rough, bumpy-sounding spots in your writing. Then, with your partner's help, try to discover the source of each problem. Is there a failure in logical connections, a lack of consistency in perspective, an absence of transitions, a need for the echo effect? By the end of your work session you should be ready to revise your paper for coherence.

Exercise 7   For class discussion

Discuss how the conclusion drives home the paper's main point in each of the following papers.

"Time Out" (#2, p. 174.)
"So He's Driving You Crazy" (#4, p. 176.)
"Learning to Decide" (#6, p. 179.)
"Living vs. Waiting to Die" (#10, p. 184.)

12 Constructing sentences

A sentence should read as if its author, had he held a plough instead of a pen, could have drawn a furrow deep and straight to the end.
Henry David Thoreau

If you're like most writers, your success with sentences varies. Sometimes your sentences flow onto the page smoothly, with grace and clarity. Other times they sound as if they were cranked out by a rusty machine. Listen to these sentences, for example, written by a student on a bad day. Listen out loud:

> *Prostitution* for centuries has been a word that was seldom mentioned in society, and when it was mentioned, it was in a negative manner. However, now for many reasons I feel that we as citizens of the United States of America need to take another look and to re-evaluate the positives of prostitution. The legalization of prostitution would drastically cut down the number of rape cases reported each year which is one of the worst violations that could occur to a woman's body; not to mention the psychological effect. Not only are women affected by this kind of experience, but children as well.

Pretty bad, we hope you agree. But if you're tempted to dismiss this student as a poor writer, listen to some sentences she wrote the week before:

> On a day that was of no particular significance to the country or the state of North Carolina—it was not a holiday—on May 31, 1935, I was born, the fifth of seven children. I am reasonably certain that there was nothing exciting about my birth except for the fact that Mother no longer had to "look ugly with her belly sticking out." Mother often said that she never wanted more than four children. Throughout my childhood, she let me know it.

Yes, that really is the same student writer. Here she is clearly in command of her sentences. But a week later, when she wrote the paper on prostitution, she seemed to have lost her touch. How is it that a writer's command over sentences can vary so dramatically?

When we talked with the writer of these paragraphs, she told us that she had not felt at home with the topic of prostitution. When she began to write, she had only a vague sense of where the paper was headed and wasn't sure she had enough material to develop her thesis. So as she wrote, every sentence was burdened with decisions: "What am I going to say next, how does it connect with my thesis, where are my facts going to come from," and so on. Each new sentence was a problem—a number of problems, really. She had to do so much stopping and starting as she wrote, it's no wonder her sentences sound jerky.

This student's smooth sentences appeared in a paper she obviously wanted to write, one showing the effects on a child of a mother's rejection. She knew exactly what she wanted to share with readers, and she knew where her material was going to come from—her own experience—so every sentence wasn't laden with decisions. Her writing could flow.

The more comfortable you feel about your writing, the more your sentences are likely to flow. One way to make yourself comfortable is to sit with stacks of scratch paper, close to a wastebasket. Beginning writers often forget that wastebasket. Apparently feeling that they have only one chance to write a sentence, they stiffen up. If they would move closer to a wastebasket, they might relax a bit. Good sentences are more likely to flow from a relaxed writer, one who is willing to take chances, secure in the knowledge that bad sentences can always be thrown out or rewritten.

As you write a rough draft, you can't afford to worry too much about sentence structure. You should of course try to write in English sentences, but don't fuss over them. You can do that later, as you revise the paper. When you read over your rough draft—especially if you read it aloud—your ear will often tell you which sentences need revising. You'll hear that you need to weave together the too-short sentences, trim down the wordy ones, and straighten out the crooked ones.

Your ear will take you far in making sentence decisions, particularly with practice. But in this chapter we would like to supplement your good ear with an understanding of basic sentence structure. If you understand the basic architecture of sentences, you'll be able to make more intelligent choices as you revise them.

Sentence cores and modifiers

Let's begin by looking at sentences in the simplest possible way. A sentence is primarily composed of a *core,* where its message is centered, and *modifiers* that give readers additional information about the core.

Simplified sentence diagrams will help you visualize the relationship between the core and its modifiers. The core appears on the top line; the modifiers, which expand the core with further information, appear on the lines below. Study these simplified diagrams of two sentences to get a feel for this very basic relationship between the sentence core and its modifiers.

Uncle Will's favorite instrument was a six-string dulcimer made out of cherry.

instrument	was	dulcimer
Uncle Will's favorite		a six-string
		made out of cherry.

During most of his working life, my father held two jobs, since one usually did not pay enough.

father	held	jobs
my		two
	During most of his working life	
	since one usually did not pay enough.	

Modifiers add to the meaning of the sentence core. You can think of them as answering questions about it. For the first sentence diagramed, you might ask, "Which instrument?" The modifier is the answer: "Uncle Will's favorite." And you might ask, "What kind of dulcimer?" Your answer is "a six-string" one "made out of cherry." For the second diagramed sentence, the modifier *my* tells you whose father; *two* tells you how many jobs. The other modifiers answer two questions: "When did he hold two jobs?"—"During most of his working life" and "Why did he hold two jobs?"—"Since one usually did not pay enough."

You probably already have a feel for this basic structure of sentences. You may not know how to label all the parts of a particular sentence, but you have a radar that detects sentence cores as you read. As you are reading these words right now, your RADAR DETECTS our SENTENCE CORE, because you know that the sentence's message is carried in its core.

Skilled readers pay more attention to the cores of sentences than to modifiers. They read modifiers quickly, understanding that they contain less important information. The function of a modifier, after all, is to expand the core with further information. Modifiers are subordinate to the sentence core; they depend upon it.

You may be wondering why we are telling you all this. Well, it's not just a grammar lesson. If you can improve your sentence radar, you'll be better able to revise weak sentences. When you write a rough draft, you may not take full advantage of the strength of sentence cores. You may put important information in the modifiers and lesser details in the sentence core. When you do this, you draw your readers' attention to the wrong part of the sentence. The following sentence will help you see what we mean:

> At 10:00 on the night of December 14, a Chinese HOME on Chien Ying WAS ENTERED by eleven Japanese soldiers who raped four Chinese women.

The sentence core is HOME WAS ENTERED, so those are the words the readers' attention is drawn to. But let's hope the writer of the sentence didn't think this was the sentence's most significant content. The sentence should be revised to emphasize its most important information:

> At 10:00 on the night of December 14, eleven Japanese SOLDIERS RAPED four Chinese WOMEN after breaking into a home on Chien Ying.

This revision puts SOLDIERS RAPED WOMEN into the sentence core, so that the sentence emphasizes its most important content.

As you revise the sentences in your rough draft, watch for weak sentence cores. One student, for example, discovered, as she read over her rough draft describing a recent visit to a prison, that she could strengthen a number of sentences with more forceful sentence cores. Some of her sentences carried unimportant information in the sentence core, then buried important content in modifiers. For example, at one point she wrote:

> The VISITING PERIOD WAS NEARLY OVER when the guard tapped me on the shoulder.

The sentence core tells us that the visiting period was nearly over, but this was not the information the writer wanted to draw her readers' attention to. To stress the point she wanted readers to notice, she revised the sentence like this:

> Shortly before the visiting period was over, a GUARD TAPPED ME on the shoulder.

At another point in this paper, the writer wanted to emphasize how impersonal her visit with the prisoner had been. Her first-draft sentence read like this:

> I SAT in a chair, viewing the prisoner through the glass as we talked on the visitor's telephone.

When the writer reread this sentence, she noticed that it pulled her readers' attention to the fact that she was sitting in a chair. The information about viewing the prisoner through the glass and talking to him over the phone—the facts she really wanted to emphasize—were buried in modifiers. To improve the sentence, the writer revised it to:

> Sitting in a chair opposite the prisoner, I VIEWED HIM through a glass wall and SPOKE TO HIM over the prison telephone.

Here the important information appears in the sentence core, and the lesser information about sitting in the chair has been turned into a modifier.

When you check over your rough drafts, make sure your sentences are working with you, not against you. If you want to stress your close call with death, don't write "The ROTOR HIT, gouging a hole about an eighth of an inch deep in my helmet." Write "When the rotor hit, IT GOUGED a HOLE about an eighth of an inch deep in my helmet." Or if you want to emphasize your shock upon meeting a monstrous snake at eye level, don't write "I YANKED OPEN the DOOR, whereupon I saw a 48-inch blackish-grey snake resting at eye level on the ledge of our storm door." Write instead: "When I yanked the door open, at eye level on the ledge of our storm door LAY a 48-inch blackish-grey SNAKE."

Compound sentences

Whether you're conscious of it or not, the structure of a sentence—content aside—sends its own messages. Take compound sentences, for example. A compound sentence is made up of two separate statements hooked together with a connector word (such as *and, but, or*) or a semicolon.

	, and	
[Statement]	, but	[Statement]
	, or	
	;	

This structure sends certain messages to readers, no matter how you fill in the blanks. First, it tells readers that they are reading about two important ideas, each one deserving its own statement. Second, it tells readers that these two ideas are approximately equal in importance, since they are balanced as a pair. And third, it alerts readers to the relationship between the two ideas, depending on the connector. *And* suggests that the two ideas are being added together, *but* tells us they are being contrasted, and *or* lets us know that they are alternatives. A semicolon suggests balance between two similar or two sharply contrasting statements.

Thus, the structure of a compound sentence sends certain messages. Don't let the structure of a sentence shout one message while the content shouts another. Listen to the clashing messages in this sentence, for example:

> Once Betty was driving to our house, and her daughter accidentally fell out of the car window.

The compound structure of this sentence tells us that we are dealing with two ideas of about equal importance. The content, however, suggests the opposite: the daughter's falling out of the car window is surely more important than the fact that Betty was driving to someone's house. Moreover, the connector *and* suggests that the relation between the two parts of the sentence is one of addition. But is this really accurate? Isn't the relationship more clearly expressed as follows?

> Once when Betty was driving to our house, her daughter accidentally fell out of the car window.

With this simple revision, we have a sentence designed to carry its message. "Once when Betty was driving to our house" is a modifier appropriate for carrying the information of lesser importance. And the time-word *when,* placed as it is, serves much better than *and* to convey the relation between the two ideas in the sentence.

Unfortunately it is easy to misuse as well as to overuse compound sentences in your rough drafts. As you compose sentences for the first time, your ideas sometimes come haltingly. To keep them going, you may string them together with *and*s. Some of these compound sentences will turn out to be perfectly in tune with their content, but others will need to be revised.

Here are a number of ineffective compound sentences discovered by students in their rough drafts. In each case, the student's revision is printed following the original.

1a. I told her that this might be my last meal and I wanted to enjoy it.

1b. I told her that since this might be my last meal, I wanted to enjoy it.

2a. I entered high school, and I had a male teacher for the first time.

2b. When I entered high school, I had a male teacher for the first time.

3a. Working directly with children is an important part of my job, and that is why I enjoy it so much.

3b. I enjoy my job a great deal because it allows me to work directly with children.

4a. Nutritious foods can be easily prepared and they can give the body the basic carbohydrates, fats, minerals, and proteins.

4b. Nutritious foods, which give the body the basic carbohydrates, fats, minerals, and proteins, can be easily prepared.

You'll need to revise compound sentences that are sending wrong messages to readers. But don't be too hasty about getting rid of your compound sentences. When properly used, so that the structure is working with the content, these sentences can be strong. For example:

1. Uncle Will's dulcimers disappeared as soon as he put them up for sale, but he always kept one for himself.

2. Sometimes we would end up at a big red brick teacher's college across town, and sometimes we would just follow the railroad tracks.

3. The children at the Goddard Day Care Center "brown bag it" for lunch, or they meet their parents in the cafeteria.

4. A man was respected for his money, power, or intelligence; a woman had to rely on her looks.

In each of these compound sentences the content fits naturally within the structure. Two important ideas, about equal in significance, are balanced together. And they are joined with a connector that reveals the relationship between them—*and, but, or,* or a semicolon.

Simple sentences

The structure of a simple sentence—one statement that stands alone—also sends messages to readers. It tells them that the content is fairly important, deserving a statement all to itself. The simple sentence also suggests to readers that its content does not closely depend on that of sentences close by. So a simple sentence should contain fairly important material that doesn't beg to be pulled into any neighboring sentences.

It's common to overuse simple sentences in a rough draft. Look at these sentences, for example, taken from a student's paragraph describing the chests in a museum exhibit:

> The last chest is the most impressive. It is carved from ivory. There is a painting in the lid showing King Tut and his queen. This painting is bordered with engraved flowers and animals.

Your ear tells you that some of those simple sentences ought to be woven together. But which ones? The answer is easy. Just decide which sentences carry important ideas and let them stand. Then find the sentences that contain less important supporting information, and hook that content into the sentences you're allowing to stand. If you followed this advice, you might pull the first two sentences together like this:

> The last chest, carved from ivory, is the most impressive.

And the next two together like this:

> On its lid, within a border of engraved flowers and animals, is a painting of King Tut and his queen.

In each of our suggested revisions we have woven supporting information into the sentence that it seemed to support naturally.

Simple sentences, like compound ones, can be effective when the content works well with the structure. Here, for example, are some strong simple sentences (those italicized) to draw the reader's attention to important content.

> *The ultimate test, in my child mind, for finding out the difference between black and white occurred one day in a bus station in Alabama.* While waiting with my parents at the station, I studied the two water fountains against the far wall. *Side by side they stood. A big sign above one read "whites only." The sign above the other fountain read "colored only."* I decided that once and for all I would satisfy my curiosity about the water fountains which always carried the signs above them. Was the water colored in the "colored only" one, or did it taste different? Since no one was watching me, I slipped over and quickly took a sip of the water in the "colored only" fountain. When I found it was every bit the same as the water in the "whites only" fountain, I ran back to my parents and shouted, "Dad, I just drank some water from the 'colored' fountain and it tasted just the same as the other." *My father's answer was a quick, hard slap. That day I learned not to question the difference between black and white.*

Each simple sentence in this paragraph carries information important enough to deserve a whole statement all to itself. The cores of these sentences draw the reader's attention to important content, as you can hear by reading the sentences aloud:

> **1.** The ultimate TEST, in my child mind, for finding out the difference between black and white OCCURRED one day in a bus station in Alabama.

2. Side by side THEY STOOD.

3. A big SIGN above one READ "WHITES ONLY."

4. The SIGN above the other fountain READ "COLORED ONLY."

5. My father's ANSWER WAS a quick, hard SLAP.

6. That day I LEARNED NOT TO QUESTION the difference between black and white.

Simple sentences, especially short ones, draw attention to themselves, particularly when they follow longer, more complex sentences. Probably the most emphatic simple sentence in the paragraph we've been discussing is "My father's answer was a quick, hard slap." This relatively short sentence follows several longer sentences, so it has a blunt impact on readers. The sentence core—ANSWER WAS SLAP—overpowers everything else you've been reading.

Parallel structure

When you want to stress the similarity of your content, you can put it into equal grammatical structures. Notice how similarly, for example, the first two sentences of this paragraph read:

> On March 14, 1978, Karen Riley was admitted to Suburban General Hospital with three broken ribs and a punctured lung. On July 8, 1978, Denise Porter was admitted with a broken arm and severe facial lacerations. These women were not victims of terrible automobile accidents, nor were they attacked as they walked down a dark city street. Both were products of an age-old phenomenon called wife-beating.

Here are the two sentences printed so you can see how very similarly they are structured:

On March 14, 1978,	On July 8, 1978,
Karen Riley was admitted to SGH	Denise Porter was admitted
with three broken ribs and	with a broken arm and
a punctured lung.	severe facial lacerations.

The writer of the paragraph wanted to stress the similarity of the two cases, so he structured the sentences almost identically. He deliberately used parallel sentence structure to reinforce parallel content.

Sometimes, as you are writing your rough draft, you'll think of using parallel structure to draw a reader's attention to similar content. But occasionally you may not have used parallelism to the best effect in your rough draft. Then, as you revise, you can improve those sentences by presenting parallel ideas in parallel structure. For example, one of our students found this sentence in her rough draft:

> *Roots* is the story of a black boy stolen from his native land, chained and treated as though an animal, to be brought by ship here to America to be a slave.

As she read over her rough draft, the writer noticed that this sentence reports that the black boy was stolen, chained, treated like an animal, and brought to America. Since these items were similar—all brutal events that happened to the boy—she saw that she could strengthen the sentence with parallel structure, like this:

> *Roots* is the story of a black boy stolen from his native land, chained like an animal, stowed on a ship like cargo, transported to America, and enslaved.

A much stronger sentence. The parallel structure underscores the inhumanity of the treatment of the young black boy. Let's print the sentence so you can see the parallel structure more clearly. Read the sentence aloud so you can hear its strength.

> *Roots* is the story of a black boy stolen from his native land,
> chained like an animal,
> stowed on a ship like cargo,
> transported to America,
> and enslaved.

Another student's rough draft read as follows:

> The Japanese barber doesn't just cut your hair. He gives you a shampoo and a shave, and he cleans your ears and cuts the hair in your nose and ears. He even places a hot towel on your face and massages your scalp and shoulders.

Using parallel structure, the student revised the sentence like this, pulling all of the details into one long sentence. The revised sentence is printed so that you can see the parallel structure.

> Besides cutting your hair, the Japanese barber will
> shave your face,
> clean your ears,
> give you a shampoo,
> cut the hair in your nose and ears,
> place a hot towel on your face,
> and massage your scalp and shoulders.

Here parallel details are presented in parallel form to reinforce the sentence's point: that the Japanese barber's services seem almost limitless.

Sentence variety

When you read through your rough draft, particularly if you read it aloud, your ear will probably pick up sentence monotony. Sentences will begin to sound monotonous when they are nearly the same length or when they repeat the same structures over and over.

If you revise your sentences as we suggested earlier in this chapter, the problem of sentence monotony may take care of itself. As you put important content in sentence cores and lesser information in modifiers, as you restructure misused compound sentences, and as you weave unnecessary simple sentences into the sentences they modify, your sentences will probably turn out to be varied in both length and structure.

Let's look at a student paper in early draft, before the writer considered sentence variety. This student decided to write her paper about the advantages of jogging in the form of a letter to her sister:

Dear Mary Jane,

As you know, I have taken up jogging. It has helped me a great deal. I hardly know how to tell you how much. I'd like to convince you to join me. Maybe I can, by telling you what jogging means to joggers all over the country.

Millions of other Americans are jogging too, you know. They frequently battle a variety of odds to do so. They field attacks from sidewalk hecklers and unfriendly dogs. Their own fatigue and even the elements sometimes get in their way. Why do they keep on jogging?

Perhaps they continue to jog because jogging is one of the best promoters of overall fitness known. That's why I go out to run every day. This activity can promote weight loss and increase your energy supply. It can decrease nervous tension and eliminate the need for tranquilizers. Substantial improvement of your figure, digestion, complexion and circulation are other benefits of jogging. It can help you give up smoking. It can also reduce the chances of hardening of the arteries.

Jogging is free. It's convenient. Safety is not a problem, so long as you choose your route and your running time wisely. You need good running shoes. It doesn't require any other special equipment or any special skills. It has specific benefits for the "over-thirty" and the "well-over-thirty" groups. These people may no longer regularly exercise. Through jogging they can regain physical fitness. They might think they had lost that forever.

Jogging is different from most other popular physical fitness programs. Weight-lifting, isometric exercises, and calisthenics emphasize muscle-building. Jogging improves the heart, lungs, and circulatory system. Other body muscles are exercised as well. The most important benefit comes from improving the way the heart and lungs work. Bulging biceps and pleasing pectorals may boost the ego. When you're past thirty, as we are, life and health may depend upon the fitness of the heart and lungs.

So won't you join me in jogging? Put on some good running shoes—and come on out. If we both persist, we can wave as we meet each other running across the United States someday!

When our writer read this draft of her paper aloud, she was not satisfied with how it sounded. Realizing that her sentences needed to be combined and rearranged in various ways, she set to work.

Dear Mary Jane,

As you know, I have taken up jogging. I can hardly tell you how much it has helped me, and I'd like to convince you to join me. Maybe I can, by telling you what jogging means to joggers all over the country.

Millions of other Americans are jogging too, you know, frequently battling a variety of odds in order to run. They field attacks from sidewalk hecklers and unfriendly dogs; in addition, their own fatigue and even the elements sometimes get in their way. Why do they keep on running?

Perhaps they continue to jog—as do I—because jogging is one of the best promoters of overall fitness known. Jogging can promote weight loss and increase your energy supply; decrease nervous tension and eliminate the need for tranquilizers; substantially improve your figure, digestion, complexion and circulation; help you give up smoking, and reduce the chances of hardening of the arteries.

Jogging is free. It is convenient. It is safe, so long as you select your route and your running time wisely. Except for appropriate running shoes, it requires no special equipment or skills. And jogging has specific benefits for the "over-thirty" and the "well-over-thirty" groups, people who may no longer regularly exercise. Through jogging they can recapture a level of physical fitness they may have thought they had lost forever.

Jogging is different from most other popular physical fitness programs. Unlike weight-lifting, isometric exercises, and calisthenics, which emphasize muscle-building, jogging improves the heart, lungs, and circulatory system. Although other body muscles are exercised as well, the most important benefit comes from improving the way the heart and lungs work. Bulging biceps and pleasing pectorals may boost the ego. But when you're past thirty, as we are, life and health may depend upon the fitness of the heart and lungs.

So, Mary Jane, won't you join me in jogging? Put on some good running shoes—and come on out. If we both persist, we can wave as we meet each other running across the United States someday!

This later draft flows more smoothly than the earlier one because the sentences are more varied, in both length and structure. And because the letter has become more pleasing to read, so that its form no longer detracts from its content, it is more likely to convince Mary Jane that she too should jog.

. . . .
Exercise 1   Written
. . . .

Try your hand at revising the following rough draft so that the sentences all emphasize the writer's main point, as summed up in the topic sentence. Put important ideas in sentence cores and lesser content in modifiers.

> A typical hot lunch at City College has little nutritional value. For example, one day's menu might be zippy pot roast, mashed potatoes, creamy green beans, an ice cream sandwich, and milk. The zippy pot roast contains more fat than lean meat. The mashed potatoes are instant flakes mixed with water, causing them to turn out dry and thick. They contain a low amount of protein and vitamins. The creamy green beans are usually cold, watered down, and faded in color, which causes them to lose vitamins. The frozen ice cream sandwiches consist of artificial flavoring, instant milk, and nitrochloric acids. The last item on the menu is milk, which has the most nutrition. The milk is whole milk consisting of iron, certain vitamins, and calcium. So the hot lunch at City College does not provide much of nutritional value, except for milk.

. . . .
Exercise 2   Written
. . . .

Assume that the sentences below are from the rough draft of a paper describing your mandolin-playing career. As you look back over the rough draft, you notice that you have written quite a few compound sentences. Which ones do you decide to keep because their content fits well into a compound sentence? Which ones need revising? Try rewriting at least five of the compound sentences that you think are ineffective.

1. Owen had an antique mandolin from Italy, and it had a round back and beautiful wood inlaid on the front.

2. Owen's mandolin intrigued me, so I borrowed it in hopes of figuring out how to play it.

3. Later that weeekend Owen left for England, and he took his old mandolin with him.

4. My mandolin career might have ended there, but I found a used instrument listed in the classified ads for ten dollars.

5. The mandolin had been in someone's shed for almost thirty years without a case, but the price was right.

6. The mandolin player for "The Seldom Scene" had made his own instrument, and we spent most of an afternoon in the shade of his camper pickin' bluegrass music.

7. My new mandolin was a Gibson "A" model from 1911, and it sounded, and played, like solid gold.

8. By the time I had played with "Kinfolk" for a month, I felt like a professional; after two months, I was a professional.

9. Playing at the Berwyn Coffeehouse was rewarding, and the people there loved us.

10. As my music got better my grades in school got worse, so I decided to leave my regular gig to study full time.

· ·

Exercise 3 Written

· ·

The following paragraphs by a student contain some ineffective compound sentences. Revise the sentences that need improvement.

> I've known Sugar Ray for four years now, and he was always determined to succeed as a fighter. Each morning at about six o'clock you could find Ray jogging and training very hard. After his workout each morning he would go home, clean up and leave for school. Then, after school, each evening Ray could be found down at the community recreation center training.
>
> Sugar Ray's training paid off, and he became one of the best young fighters in the country, and he was chosen to represent the United States in the Olympics. Ray attended the 1976 Olympics and he brought the gold medal back home with him. A few months after the Olympics were over, Ray received an offer to turn professional. Ray accepted the offer and turned pro.

· ·

Exercise 4 Written

· ·

Below are some passages from student papers containing too many short, choppy sentences. Rework each passage by pulling subordinate information into the sentence it seems to support naturally.

1. My father works for the Washington Trucking Company. Right now he is district manager for several different terminals. I believe he has twelve different terminals, all of which are located in the mid-eastern region of the country. Traveling is very important in his work. He travels about three times a month.

2. I had an appointment with one of my physicians. It was on a hot, humid September day. My appointment was at four o'clock in the afternoon.

3. The jewelry found in King Tut's tomb is perhaps the most exquisite of all the relics. There are gold necklaces, beaded bracelets, gold rings, and earrings. Many of the above are decorated with colored glass. This glass was usually shaped as a scarab, the symbol of the sun god. The most magnificent of all of the jewelry is the necklace that had been placed on King Tut's mummy. It is in the form of a vulture goddess with spread wings. Different shades of red and blue glass are used to decorate the necklace. This ornament was supposed to provide magical protection.

4. Have you ever wanted to find the perfect Mexican restaurant? I found the perfect restaurant for me. It is located on Riverdale Road in Riverdale, Maryland. The place is called the Alamo.

. . . .

Exercise 5 For class discussion
. . . .

Eldridge Cleaver wrote *Soul on Ice* while serving time in California's Folsom State Prison. In this spiritual autobiography Cleaver expresses himself powerfully, often using parallel sentences. Here are four such sentences, with discussion questions for each. We have printed the sentences so that you can see the parallel structure. As you discuss the sentences, be sure to read them aloud:

> I'm perfectly aware
> > that I'm in prison,
> > that I'm a Negro,
> > that I've been a rapist,
> and that I have a Higher Uneducation.

This sentence, which appears early in the book, has a powerful effect on readers. Can you account for its power? What do you suppose Cleaver means by "Higher Uneducation," and why does he put this item last? Why is Cleaver putting all these facts about himself in one parallel-structured sentence?

Our next sentence from *Soul on Ice* describes the night-time longings of a man behind bars:

> Because we were locked up in our cells before darkness fell, I used to lie awake at night racked by painful craving
> > to take a leisurely stroll under the stars, or
> > to go to the beach,
> > to drive a car on a freeway,

to grow a beard,
or to make love to a woman.

What impact does this sentence have on you as a reader? How does
the sentence's parallel structure contribute to this impact? Why does
Cleaver order his "cravings" as he does?

The following sentence was not written by Eldridge Cleaver. Cleaver
quotes it, from Malcolm X, to explain his own one-time hostility toward
white people:

How can I love the man who raped my mother,
      killed my father,
      enslaved my ancestors,
      dropped atomic bombs on Japan,
      killed off the Indians
    and keeps me cooped up in the slums?

What does Malcolm X mean by "the man"? How do you interpret
"raped my mother" and "killed my father"? Why has Malcolm X included the Japanese and the Indians as recipients of "the man's"
atrocities? Why has he ordered the atrocities in just this way, and why does
he end with "keeps me cooped up in the slums"? To which words in the
sentence does the parallel structure draw your attention, and how does
this contribute to the sentence's power?

For the next sentence, you need some background information. While
Cleaver was in Folsom, he was impressed by the Christ-like quality of a
philosophy professor who taught at the prison. Cleaver wrote this one-
sentence paragraph about this man, whom he called "the Christ" as a
mark of respect:

The Christ could weep
   over a line of poetry,
   over a single image in a poem,
   over the beauty of a poem's music,
   over the fact that man can talk,
         read,
         write,
         walk,
         reproduce,
         die,
         eat,
         eliminate,—
  over the fact that a chicken can lay an egg.

This sentence should be read aloud more than once, as you discuss it;

its power will grow on you. What kind of man is Cleaver describing? Why does Cleaver order the sentence as he does? Why end with "over the fact that a chicken can lay an egg"? Why begin with three lines about poetry? Why put that long list of human activities just where it is in the sentence? Why does Cleaver use *eliminate* instead of a synonym?

. . . .
Exercise 6   For class discussion
. . . .

Read aloud the two drafts of the student paper printed at the end of this chapter. In the later draft, listen for the effects of sentence variety. Then discuss how the writer's use of varied sentence lengths and structures achieves those effects.

. . . .
Exercise 7   For thought
. . . .

In an article entitled "Why I Write," Joan Didion compares sentence structures with camera angles:

> To shift the structure of a sentence alters the meaning of that sentence, as definitely and inflexibly as the position of a camera alters the meaning of the object photographed. Many people know about camera angles now, but not so many know about sentences. The arrangement of the words matters, and the arrangement you want can be found in the picture in your mind. The picture dictates the arrangement. The picture dictates whether this will be a sentence with or without clauses, a sentence that ends hard or a dying-fall sentence, long or short, active or passive. The picture tells you how to arrange the words.

13 Choosing words

The difference between the right word and almost the right word is the difference between lightning and the lightning bug. Mark Twain

One of the secrets to building strong sentences is careful, conscious choice of words. Choosing your words carefully will make your writing clearer and more vivid.

We have placed "Choosing Words" near the end of this section of the book because we feel that writing will be easier for you if you do not worry too much about single words until late in the writing process. Stopping to think about every word when you first begin a paper will slow down your writing. When that happens, you risk sacrificing your flow; you may even get stuck and have a hard time getting started again. So we advise you to attend first to focusing and shaping your material into paragraphs made up of strong sentences, and only then to concentrate on your words.

Deleting excess words

When you are ready to think about words, we suggest that you first look for those you can delete. Deleting the excess baggage—the wordiness—from your writing is essential to building forceful sentences. Sentences full of "deadwood" drag along, blurring your meaning and boring your reader. Listen to these sentences read aloud, for example:

1. The roses that grow in my largest rosebed are flame orange and pale yellow in color.

2. There were two women who ran for senator in the state of Virginia last year.

3. To our great disappointment, the circus did not get to town on time. This was because one of the elephants decided to go AWOL during the long march from the train station.

4. Judith wanted to move away from living with her parents and move to Chicago, where she wanted to go to the university and specialize in the field of law.

5. The popcorn was vacuumed up by Bruce, the chairs were stacked by Donna, and the house was aired by Lou, before the party was declared over for the night.

6. It was known for a fact by their families that John and David had left San Francisco to surf in Hawaii without enough money to live on in Hawaii.

Simply removing the deadwood from these sentences immediately livens them up. Suddenly they are clearer, easier to read.

1. The roses in my largest rosebed are flame orange and pale yellow.

2. Two women ran for senator in Virginia last year.

3. To our great disappointment, the circus did not get to town on time, because one of the elephants decided to go AWOL during the long march from the train station.

4. Judith wanted to leave her parents' home and move to Chicago to specialize in law at a university.

5. Bruce vacuumed up the popcorn, Donna stacked the chairs, and Lou aired the house before they declared the party over.

6. Their families knew that John and David had left San Francisco to surf in Hawaii without enough money.

George Orwell, one of the most effective writers in the English language, has suggested a sort of ground rule about wordiness: "If it is possible to cut a word out, always cut it out." Listen to the difference between the following loose, wordy student paragraph and its revision:

. . . .

~~This summer~~ *(this summer, the kindness and friendliness)* While I was vacationing in Switzerland, ~~the one thing that~~ *of the Swiss impressed me more than anything* ~~impressed me most was how kind and friendly the people were.~~ *else.* The people ~~who worked in~~ ~~T~~he hotel *staff* ~~where we stayed were extremely nice. They~~ went out of their way to make our stay ~~an even more enjoyable one.~~ *pleasant.* The maids and bellboys greeted us with ~~a~~ smile; the women behind the desk always

asked how we were, and ~~the people in the hotel~~ restaurant *the* ~~always went out~~ *personnel gave*

~~of their way to give~~ us excellent service. Although ~~there was~~ a language

barrier *existed,* everyone we ~~would~~ talk to was very patient while we tried to com-

municate ~~and get our point across~~ with the few ~~words of~~ German and French *words*

we knew. *Indeed,* ~~The friendly people of Switzerland~~ *Swiss* added to ~~a wonderful trip to~~ *the pleasure of our visit to Switzerland.*

~~their beautiful country.~~

. . . .

You have probably noticed that the revisions make the paragraph considerably shorter than the original. But nothing important has been lost. When you write, don't let yourself be tempted into leaving in the deadwood just for the sake of quantity. Your rough drafts may often be too wordy, especially if you make yourself keep writing steadily to maintain your flow. Writing for flow is not a bad idea; just don't forget to trim out the deadwood when you revise.

On the other hand, we would caution you against worrying so much about wordiness that you sacrifice essential content. Leaving out needed material is not the same thing as deleting wordiness. One has to do with content—what you have to say; the other, with form—how you go about saying it.

The idea, then, is to make your writing as concise, and hence as direct and clear, as possible, while including what needs to be included. Every word you choose should be working to make your writing strong and interesting and alive. As the poet Wallace Stevens said, "Life is the elimination of what is dead."

Saying it simply

Writers sometimes become wordy, and their writing lifeless, because they overwrite; that is, they try to impress their potential readers with "fine writing." What usually happens instead is that these writers end up sounding pompous, and their writing is stilted and artificial.

Such overdone writing has been called "doublespeak," because it generally makes little sense by the time a reader has managed to get through it. Doublespeak is sometimes used deliberately to obscure meaning, when writers do not want to assume responsibility for their words; it often emerges from the government, the military, the educational system, and other such institutions. We bring it up here because you are so surrounded by it every day that we want to warn you against letting it influence your own writing.

For example, here is a quotation from a release by the Bureau of Land Management (BLM) of the United States Department of the Interior:

> Because the heavy mistletoe infestation in the Kringle Creek area has rendered the residual timber useless for timber production, the ultimate goal is to establish a healthy new stand of Douglas Fir.

The BLM release apparently means to say:

> Because mistletoe has taken over the timber in the Kringle Creek area, we need to plant a new stand of Douglas Fir.

OSHA, the Occupational Safety and Health Administration, wrote this thirty-nine-word definition of *exit:*

> That portion of a means of egress which is separated from all other spaces of the building or structure by construction or equipment as required in this subpart to provide a protected way of travel to the exit discharge.

But government is not the only source of doublespeak. Representatives of our other institutions use it, too. The following sentence was in a letter to the editor from a doctor: "If home births are an indictment of impersonal and dehumanized health care in our hospitals' obstetrical units, then attempts should be directed toward increasing the human factor in our health-delivery systems."

Doublespeak also often plagues college textbooks. Beware of it; it could find its way into your own writing almost by osmosis. This student writer, for example, may have been unduly influenced by a textbook for a speech course:

> Effective listening requires the senses of hearing and seeing, working in harmony, to correctly interpret incoming communications. Now, more than ever before, body language—that nonverbal part of a communication—contributes significantly to the intent of a transmission and how it is received.

The student who wrote the following paragraph had spent years in the military and had gone from there into a career in business:

> As a supervisor I am charged with the responsibility of insuring maximum production through utilization of all resources, both manpower and machines. However, the increasing level of the younger employee and the state of the art in business has created a problem for supervisors in trying to find new techniques to use in motivating subordinates. This group of individuals expects

rapid growth and promotion and wants to take an active role in the decision-making process.

Getting rid of doublespeak was the most difficult part of freshman composition for this writer. However, he learned to simplify his writing enough so that the above paragraph became:

As a supervisor I am responsible for seeing that all our resources—both personnel and machines—are as productive as possible. One of my challenges is how to motivate those persons working under me. Younger employees, especially, expect to advance rapidly, and they also want to be involved in decision-making.

Doublespeak often uses euphemisms. A euphemism (pronounced *you-fuh-miz-em*) occurs when less direct and less vivid phrasing is substituted for words that might be considered offensive. Euphemisms, then, diminish the strength and the honesty of language. Journalist Meg Greenfield refers to them as "verbal chloroform." Some euphemisms, substituted for reality, are downright dangerous, as you will recognize as you read the list below. Here the euphemisms have been "translated" into "real" language.

Euphemism	*Real language*
selected out	fired
over-aggressive self-initiative	anger
attitude adjustment hour	cocktail hour
Society for Investigation of Human Ecology	CIA's cover organization for experiments in brainwashing and behavior control
therapeutic misadventure	medical malpractice
energetic disassembly	nuclear power plant explosion
plutonium has taken up residence	plutonium contamination following nuclear explosion
radiation enhancement weapon	Pentagon's designation for the neutron bomb, which destroys only people

Whenever you write, you need to be constantly aware of that other human being, your reader. Doublespeak ignores the reader's need for simplicity and clarity. It sacrifices both clarity and meaning to an attempt at eloquence. We like a piece of advice attributed to "a wise old woman": "Keep away from fancy words because you never can tell what they mean." Or as John O'Hayre, who tried to eliminate doublespeak from the Bureau of Land Management, suggests, "To kill this big word bug, stop [writing] like a mechanical nobleman who has been stuffed to overflowing with impressive, exotic words, and start [writing] like the genuine, natural human being you are."

Saying it vividly

If doublespeak words are too fancy, too big and heavy, there are other words you will want to avoid because they are weak. Some of these words began their existence as slang. All of them have become "tired words"; they have been used until they are exhausted. When such words slip into our conversation, we tend not to pay much attention to them. But when someone else is reading what we have written, instead of listening to us speak, he or she can stop to question the actual content of such words. In writing, their emptiness becomes apparent; they do not say much, for the life has gone out of them.

Here is a list of such words:

amazing	fantastic	incredible	really
awful	fascinating	interesting	stupendous
bad	funny	lovely	terrible
beautiful	glorious	magnificent	terrific
big	good	marvelous	thing
colossal	gorgeous	neat	tremendous
enjoyable	great	nice	very
exciting	horrible	outstanding	wonderful
fabulous	huge	pretty	

You will probably be able to think of some more tired words.

Using these words occasionally is of course all right; attempting to avoid such everyday words completely could make your writing sound awkward and unnatural. However, if you discover that your writing is dotted with weak words, you can liven it up with substitutes from a dictionary of synonyms or a college thesaurus.

The paragraphs below are from an early draft of a paper about Seattle. The weak words are italicized.

Seattle is a *beautiful* city, full of *wonderful* sights and *interesting things* to do. It is surrounded by *big* bodies of water that the sun dances off of in *marvelous* fashion. More water greets visitors to Seattle as they discover the city's several *fabulous* fountains. Furthermore, the city has many hills, providing *really glorious* views. One of these views is of Mount Rainier, with its *gorgeous* snow-covered peak. In addition, Seattle has some *magnificent* buildings—its public library and the IBM building, to name two. There are *interesting things* to do in Seattle, too, at its playhouse, its opera hall, and its science center. And I must not forget to mention a visit to the *incredible* Space Needle, that features an *amazing* revolving restaurant at its top.

The weather varies greatly in Seattle, it is true, and some people say that all those rainy days in a row must be *awful*. But, believe me, one *nice* day of *glorious* sunshine on those fountains and mountain peaks and buildings makes one forget weeks of rain. Surely Seattle must be one of the *neatest* cities in the United States.

When the writer of these paragraphs read them over, she realized they would not make readers see Seattle vividly. She knew those weak words would not convey to a reader what it is actually like to be in Seattle. As she rewrote, she kept her dictionary of synonyms close by. Here is the beginning of the new version of her paper:

Seattle is a splendid city that offers breathtaking scenery, striking build-ings and varied activities. The sun dancing off the water that surrounds Seattle makes the whole city seem to sparkle. More water greets visitors to Seattle as they discover the city's several fountains. Some of these fountains, like the one by the City Library, are constructed of sculptured metal. However, the most unusual fountain in Seattle is one in which the rise and fall of the water is synchronized with both music and varicolored lights. In Seattle, mountain-views exist side by side with water-views. One such view is of the glistening snow-covered peak of Mount Rainier.

Now readers will come closer to experiencing Seattle with our writer.

We do have some suggestions about how to use your synonyms book. Once you have located the synonym list for your weak word, be sure to read all the way through the list before choosing your substitute word; the one you most need may not be among the first two or three listed. Try, too, to find a word that will read smoothly in your sentence. If you are not sure about the exact meaning of a particular synonym, turn to your regular dictionary and look it up to be sure that you finally use the most appropriate word.

You will also want to be alert to clichés that may slip into your writing. A cliché (pronounced *klee-shay;* a term borrowed from French) is a worn-out phrase, an expression that you have heard so often that it is empty of meaning. You will probably recognize some clichés in the following paragraph:

The mechanic rescued us, cold and miserable, from beside the road and towed our car in. He saw that we were safe and sound, and then, as the hours wore on, he looked after us above and beyond the call of duty. We found it hard to believe, in this day and age, that someone would be so kind to total strangers who had appeared in his life out of nowhere. It was indeed a moving experience.

Did you pick up the clichés? They are included in the list below:

above and beyond the call of duty	in this day and age
all walks of life	ladder of success
appeared in his life	last but not least
at this point in time	moving experience
believe it or not	on a silver platter
beyond a shadow of a doubt	out of nowhere
brought back to reality	pride and joy
cold and miserable	rude awakening
easier said than done	safe and sound
facts of life	sink or swim
first and foremost	straight and narrow
hours wore on	total stranger
	tried and true

Don't let clichés weaken your own writing. Either delete such phrases entirely, or rephrase flat, cliché-ridden sentences to make them more vivid and lively.

Choosing just the right word

The more you read and write, the more aware you are likely to become that words with the same *meaning* can carry widely differing *feelings*. Words with essentially the same *denotation* can have varying *connotations*. They can be emotionally loaded, either positively or negatively. For instance, different expressions connected with growing old, though they all denote old age, carry different connotations. They affect us differently when we hear them. Consider the image and the accompanying feelings the following phrases create. To which do you react positively? To which negatively? Are any of the expressions relatively neutral?

the elderly	the aged
senior citizenship	the golden years
the declining years	old age
old man (or old woman)	old folks
growing older and wiser	older person

Here are some other sets of words with essentially the same meaning but with varying connotations. As you read a set, observe how each word affects you, what it "says" to you:

run	alternate life-style	stubborn
bolt	homosexuality	persistent
dash	sexual deviancy	resolute
flee	sexual preference	persevering
rush	the gay life	hardheaded
scamper	perversion	tenacious
dart		determined

Use this emotional loading of words when you write. For example, if you want your readers to visit a space museum you have just discovered, appeal to them by describing its display area as *vast* or *expansive,* instead of using *cavernous,* which sounds more threatening. Or if you are recommending an instructor whose only flaw is a soft voice, say that his or her delivery is *low-keyed* rather than *inaudible.* On the other hand, if you are writing a letter to your local newspaper about a popular child's toy that worries you, referring to the toy as *hazardous* will be more effective than merely saying it is *unsafe.* Use your dictionary of synonyms or your thesaurus to locate the best word for the connotation you want.

There is one more matter of word choice you will want to be sure to attend to: accuracy. The clarity of your writing depends heavily on its accuracy. If your writing is flawed by careless word choice, its entire effect may be lost, because your reader may not understand what you are talking about.

Sometimes inaccurate word choice produces hilarious sentences. Just for fun, here are a few such sentences by professional writers:

1. A study is underfoot.

2. Bulldozers have left the earth baron.

3. We hope that all employees can remain relapsed and calm.

4. He has worked in several places. Most recently, he put in a stench at HUD.

5. They treated him as if he had Blue Bonnet plague.

6. The Barbie and Ken dolls are so realistic that the Ken doll even has a full set of Gentiles.

7. Let's wait and see whether there is any follow-out from the incident.

8. Do you think she was speaking thumb-in-cheek?

Can you find the misused words?

No doubt you can appreciate how the misused words in these sentences could stop a reader. And as soon as readers have to stop to puzzle out what you are talking about, they lose the continuity of your writing. If you sometimes confuse words, ask a friend to read over your writing to help you find any such confusions.

Collecting words

We want to remind you here that increasing your supply of words, by whatever means, is absolutely basic to becoming a good writer. A writer needs to be on the lookout for new words all the time: while listening to TV or the radio, during conversation, while reading, during lectures and class discussions, even eavesdropping while traveling—wherever he or she encounters words, written or spoken. If you truly want to develop a rich vocabulary, this kind of word awareness is one of the easiest and most pleasant ways to achieve one.

You can train yourself to be aware of words in exactly the same way you train yourself to concentrate on anything else, whether it's basketball, singing, cooking, or karate. The payoff for taking the trouble to build up a rich vocabulary is that you will be a better writer—because a more precise one—for the rest of your life. It doesn't have to cost you any extra money, and you can start right away. Turn to the editorial page of your newspaper, or leaf through *Time* or *Newsweek*, to see if you can find words you don't ordinarily use. Use some of them, as you talk and as you write, as often as possible during the next two weeks. They will soon belong to you.

. . . .

Exercise 1   For thought and discussion
. . . .

E. B. White said it succinctly: "Omit needless words." After mulling over the following quotations, discuss why this is an important principle of good writing.

a. In composing, as a general rule, run a pen through every other word you have written; you have no idea what vigor it will give your style.
Sidney Smith

b. I apologize for this long letter; I didn't have time to shorten it.
Pliny

c. Clutter is the disease of American writing. We are a society strangling in unnecessary words, circular constructions, pompous frills, and meaningless jargon.
William Zinsser

d. I once said his prose is dipped in chicken fat.
Oscar Levant, referring to David Susskind

e. To write simply is as difficult as to be good.
Somerset Maugham

f. He can compress the most words into the smallest ideas of any man I ever met.
Abraham Lincoln, speaking of a fellow lawyer

g. If you give me an article that runs to eight pages and I tell you to cut it to four, you'll howl and say it can't be done. Then you will go home and do it, and it will be infinitely better. After that comes the hard part: cutting it to three.
William Zinsser

. . . .

Exercise 2 Written

. . . .

Remove the deadwood from the following sentences, taking care not to change the meaning of the originals. Bring your revised sentences to class for discussion.

1. In this age of fierce competition for a limited number of well-paying jobs, I have found that in order to be successful at a career I need to put all of my available time and resources toward my education.

2. The atheist, who did not believe in God, avoided church regularly each Sunday.

3. In "Raisin in the Sun," a black family decides to buy a house which is in an all-white neighborhood where no blacks have been allowed to buy in the past.

4. During our tour of New England in the hot summer month of August, cool glasses of iced coffee were served every afternoon.

5. The student answered the question that Mr. Battle asked with a negative answer of no.

6. The principal finally located the injured child's parent by means of the telephone after 3:00 P.M. in the afternoon.

7. There are problems that confront an educated black person who applies for a job that may not affect a white person of exactly the same level of education.

8. The food that is included in an actual Chinese meal is quite a bit different from what you find on the menu in many Chinese restaurants.

9. Sociologists claim that in the case of hardened criminals rehabilitation is rarely achieved.

10. The image of the American Indian through the eyes of the TV media is, to put it mildly, an insult to American Indians.

....
Exercise 3   Written
....

Look over the list of weak words in this chapter and choose five that you feel you use too often. Develop a list of synonyms for each word. Write down all the synonyms you can think of on your own *before* you go to a synonyms dictionary or a thesaurus, so that you can see how many substitute words you already have. Then expand your lists by using a book of synonyms. Share your lists with the class.

....
Exercise 4   Written
....

Make a list of all the words you can think of that mean the same thing as any five of the words below. Work first without your dictionary of synonyms or thesaurus, then go to that source to complete your list.

1. advise	**7.** fat	**13.** serene
2. agree	**8.** fix	**14.** straightforward
3. ask	**9.** get	**15.** thin
4. conscious	**10.** inactive	**16.** walk
5. disagree	**11.** sensitive	
6. evaluate	**12.** sentimental	

Bring your sets of words to class for a discussion of connotation.

....
Exercise 5   Written
....

Connotation can be used to slant a piece of writing. Write on one of the following topics in two ways. In one paper, attempt to prejudice your reading audience *for* the idea; in the other paper, attempt to prejudice your audience *against* the idea. Deliberately choose words with either positive or negative connotations to strengthen your position.

1. A mother of a two-year-old wants to go to work. The income she would make is not required for the family to live. In one paper, support her going to work; in the other, argue against her taking a job.

2. Introductory psychology is being considered as a required course for all first-semester freshmen in a community college. Argue in one paper in support of the requirement; in another, attempt to defeat the requirement.

3. A university establishes a coed dormitory in which unmarried couples can live together. Write papers (perhaps letters) from two sets of parents with students enrolled; one set supports the idea, the other rejects it.

Exercise 6   Classroom activity

Try to translate the following euphemisms. Listen for others to bring to class to challenge your classmates. Advertising, political statements, work memoranda, and hospital language are some likely sources for euphemisms.

1. adult entertainment
2. correctional facility
3. down-sized car
4. encore telecast
5. Egyptological pornoglyphic sarcophagi
6. engage the enemy on all sides
7. expired, passed away, left us
8. for motion discomfort
9. grief therapist
10. inner city
11. nervous wetness
12. powder room
13. preowned automobile
14. protective reaction strike
15. twilight years

Translations of the euphemisms will be found in the appendix.

Exercise 7   Just for fun

My husband had lost his temper at the church ballgame on Saturday, resulting in an embarrassing scene, so I decided to pay an impromptu visit at the pastor's house and apologize for his temper.

The pastor and I chatted briefly; then, intending to emphasize my husband's good qualities, I blurted out, "I sure wish Allen could learn to control his temper. He is good in so many ways. He's thoughtful. Kindhearted. Very generous. But *most* of all, he is so passionate!"

Unaware of the inevitable phone call, I returned home feeling satisfied that my mission had been accomplished. Opening the front door I called out, "Hon, I'm home."

There he stood in the kitchen with arms folded and a Cheshire grin to greet me. With a chuckle he said, "Hi, hon. By the way, the word is *compassionate!*"

Sample student papers: supporting a point

1. Irish vs. American Education

During my junior year of high school my family moved from a suburban American community to a small village in rural Ireland. The change was a very pleasant one once we got over the initial cultural shock, and we learned a great deal from the visit. My biggest discoveries came from being enrolled in the local convent, a school that was very different from my old high school. The difference lay not in the subjects that were taught, but rather in the way they were taught and the surroundings and atmosphere they were taught in.

In contrast to my ordinary brick high school, the convent was a Gothic mansion with tall, narrow windows and doors, vaulted ceilings, and endless, winding corridors. Included in the school uniforms were soft slippers that wouldn't mar the marble floors or teak staircases. Not only were our steps hushed, but the gloomy, ancient decor intimidated us into speaking in whispers when walking along passageways. To run or yell in a hallway was unthinkable.

Unlike its American counterpart, the convent was badly heated and had almost none of the educational facilities or equipment believed necessary in America. There was no cafeteria or food service. There were no science labs (although my biology teacher *did* bring a dead frog one day and dissected it for us). The home economics department consisted of one stove and seven sinks. There was no library, really, just a box of paperback books that the English teacher let us borrow from. There was one record player for the entire school and a tape recorder that dated from World War II.

Strangely enough, instead of being academically inferior to my American high school, the Irish convent was superior. In my class at home *Love Story* was considered pretty heavy reading, so imagine my surprise at finding Irish students who could recite passages from *War and Peace*. In high school we complained about having to study "Romeo and Juliet" in one semester, whereas in Ireland we simultaneously studied "Macbeth" and Dickens's *Hard Times,* in addition to writing a composition a day in English class. In high school I didn't even begin algebra until the ninth grade, while at the convent seventh graders (or their Irish equivalent) were doing calculus and trigonometry.

Not that the Irish were completely superior in educational standards. Many of the students at the convent had never even heard of chemistry, much less sex education. They knew by heart the exploits of Cuchulain (a legendary Irish warrior) but knew nothing of Freud or Marx or any religion but their own. The average Irish student seemed to have a firm knowledge of the classics but was out of touch with the world of today.

The main reason for this contrast may be the way the classes were taught. In America the teacher is usually approachable and his or her teaching style is informal. The students feel relaxed and very often daily life is discussed, ranging anywhere from politics to personal problems. Unfortunately, some people take advantage of this and waste hours and hours of class time to the detriment of other students.

At the convent there was no disruption, no disorder, no wasted time. Classes ran smoothly and on a tight schedule. Unfortunately, this made for dull, regimented classes where tension ran very high. We stood when asked questions and fired off the answer as quickly as possible, never asking questions for fear of being singled out and drilled for lacking knowledge.

After experiencing these two systems of teaching, I am not sure which is the better one. Perhaps a combination of the two would be the best way—a system in which there is order and discipline but without suppression and fear.

2. Time Out

Howard Cosell is not the only offender. Most television sports announcers set my teeth on edge. I enjoy televised professional sports, especially football, but I cannot understand the low quality of sports broadcasting provided by the networks. I could forgive the numerous technical errors and the consistently mispronounced names, if the persistent running commentary was tolerable. Every Sunday during football season, overstatements abound, clichés cascade, and "touching" anecdotes turn this viewer's stomach.

Each rookie who displays any talent is proclaimed a future Hall of Fame nominee. Each participating team becomes the "toughest, meanest, and most interesting to watch." Any pass completion is "fantastic," and every call by an official is "controversial." A second stringer having a good day is said to be the "most underrated player in the league."

The local fans each week are dubbed "the most loyal in the world" and "the best to be found in any stadium." The head coach always seems to be "the most respected man around" and has always "done a great job with the boys." According to the exaggerations of our announcers, there are no adequate athletes performing well, only superb superstars gaining glory.

During the pre-game chit-chat, the weather is described as "picture perfect" or "unbearably miserable." Even the elements are not allowed to remain ho-hum in television land.

Quarterbacks are "men of great courage" and specialty teams are "suicide squads." Every person on the field is "a real man" with "a lot of heart." If a team is losing by twenty-eight points in the fourth quarter, we are instructed not to "count this team out" because these "tough competitors" have been known to "turn it around."

Even more offensive than the overstatements and clichés are the maudlin personal stories that sportscasters force upon us. When they deplete their supply of handy statistics, they turn to pathos. The viewer is informed that a certain hulking linebacker was a sissy in second grade. Another bought "dear old mom" her dream house with his first playoff bonus. We hear vivid descriptions of previous injuries, and suffer through some poor guy's "excruciatingly painful" experience with a pulled groin muscle. Billy Kilmer, who was not expected to walk after his car accident, has a daughter with cerebral palsy for whom he "plays his heart out" weekly. O. J. Simpson is enduring a period of great stress. He wants to be near his family in California, but is forced by his contract to earn millions in Buffalo.

If players are aware of these gushy interludes, they must find them embarrassing. All this "True Confession" trivia is being broadcast to a national audience who tuned in to hear football action, not soap opera. "Dear old mom" might be watching, and might not want her neighbors to realize that she doesn't make her own mortgage payments.

I would prefer objective, impersonal announcing. I'd like valid appraisals of athletic ability and relevant statistics. Descriptions should contain honest adjectives and fewer trite phrases. Why not allow the reality of a well-played game to project its own excitement, and let the tension of the competition provide the color? It doesn't seem like an unreasonable request. I wonder if Howard and friends could stop chattering long enough to consider it?

3. Borrowings from Black Culture

Although the sixties saw blacks struggling to attain civil rights, they are still a long way from the equality they need. However, for a group that has been oppressed in this country for two-hundred-odd years, the black population has been socially significant. Blacks have influenced the white middle class by their modes of dress, language, music, and dance.

There was a time when the African look was threatening to whites. But times changed. In the sixties love beads became a unique means of expression for blacks and whites alike. Whether made of elephants' ivory tusks or plain old plastic, beads were commonplace. Dashikis also started a style of their own, along with bandeaux and shawls. And the Afro hairstyle has become popular with Caucasian men as well as women.

The English language has picked up so many words from "Black English"—as it is sometimes referred to—that even Henry Higgins would find decoding difficult these days. How can anyone accurately explain the meaning of *soul food,* or *boogie,* or *funky,* yet these words are frequently heard. Nouns which originated in Black English and slipped into our everyday conversation include *dude* (male), *bama* (someone who doesn't dress well), *brother* (friend), *blood* (fellow black), and *honky* (white person). Some adjectives that many of us are familiar with are *solid* (good), *bad* (great), *phat* (well built), *cool* (no problems, all right), *hip* (up to date), and *uptight* (nervous). Verbs which have achieved considerable acceptability are *jam* (improvise), *rap* (converse), *jive* (exaggerate), and *hassle* (badger). Phrases also abound: *dig it, strung out, old lady,* and *out of sight* are all mainstays.

Black music has also been a trend setter. Starting with rhythm and blues, this music developed into a rage yet to die down—rock and roll. Black musicians who helped create rock include Muddy Waters, Chuck Berry, and Little Richard. Later came black vocal groups which helped develop the sound known as "soul music": the Temptations, the Supremes, the Miracles, and the Four Tops. Recently we have been introduced to disco, as interpreted by Van McCoy, Natalie Cole, and the Tramps. Other forms of music developed by black artists which have come to appeal to white ears include jazz, reggae, acid rock, and funk.

One of the stereotypes of blacks is that they all have rhythm and can dance. This, of course, is a fallacy. But they must be credited with introducing many new steps. The Twist, the Funky Chicken, and the Locomotion are black dances from some years back. More recently have come the Robot, the Hustle, and many variations of disco. These steps have been adapted, improved, and literally sold to whites.

Clearly black culture has had much influence on the mainstream culture in our country. Blacks have given as well as received customs to help develop the style that is known as American.

4. So He's Driving You Crazy

So he's driving you crazy? That soft, rosy bundle of joy you welcomed into your life just a short time ago has, seemingly overnight, become an iron-willed perpetual motion machine. He has the curiosity of a cat, the agility of a mountain goat, and more energy than most power plants are capable of producing. He's faster than a speeding bullet, more powerful than a locomotive, and today he learned to climb the shiny new fence that just set you back $800. Take heart, dear friend. Do not despair. Save your strength, because things are definitely going to get worse. The "terrible twos" can't hold a candle to the traumatic teens.

This is not to say that the care and feeding of young children is not a difficult, time-consuming task. Your aching back and weary step are living proof of that. But, after all, how much trouble can a three-year-old really get into? How far from home can he get? By the time he is fourteen, there will be hours on end when you really have no idea where he is. No matter how good your lines of communication may be, all you really know about a teenager's whereabouts is what he tells you when he leaves the house.

Of course your child would not lie to you. He really does plan to go to Tommy's house. Indeed, he does. But therein lies the rub! He and Tommy, finding things dull there, go on to Jim's, and then to the drugstore, the ballfield, Charlie's, the library, back to the drugstore and, finally, hours later, home—where you, his innocent parent, greet him and ask if he had a nice time at Tommy's.

All of this is, of course, compounded when, at the magic age of sixteen, the State decides he is mature and responsible enough to drive a car. The State, however, does not know him as well as you do. He is also not driving the State's car. He is driving yours. And who do you think will be up calling the hospitals when he is an hour late getting home? Not the good old Department of Motor Vehicles, that's for sure!

What all this really means is that now when he leaves home to go to Tommy's, he will drive. And when he and Tommy get bored, they will seek adventure at (you hope) speeds up to 55 mph. The wonderful world of the Capital Beltway will open to your Precious Baby, and the wonderful world of Lady Clairol will open to you as you discover at least ten new gray hairs every morning.

One of the biggest traumas of the toddler years is toilet-training. I have seen strong women—and stronger men—reduced to quivering heaps while trying to coax their Little Darling into the bathroom. Years later, these same people will spend an equal number of hours pleading with them to come out.

While the rest of the family lines up in the hall with soap, towels, shampoo, etc., the Crown Prince is using the last drop of hot water for his shower and will be at least another twenty minutes blow-drying his hair. One parent I know read *War and Peace* waiting to take a shower while her offspring lounged in the tub shrinking his jeans; and while cold showers are certainly invigorating, too many too often are not conducive to pleasant intrafamily relations.

"But," you protest, "at least teenagers eat. My toddler will surely come down with malnutrition, beri-beri, or bubonic plague if I don't convince him to eat something!" Relax. By the time he is fifteen, he will be eating everything in sight that isn't either nailed down or still moving. In ten years your grocery bill is bound to make you see those times when you finally got him to eat two green beans and a bite of roast beef as the good old days they really were. I predict that at some time during your child's teen years you will seriously consider the purchase of (a) a cow; (b) a peanut farm; (c) stock in the McDonald Corporation; or (d) all of the above.

Of course, while he is doing all this eating, he is growing at a fantastic rate. Right out the clothes you paid $100 for last week. It is not enough that his clothes keep him warm and dry. They must be "in." Unfortunately, what is "in" is usually expensive. There is no point in buying what is "in" when it is on sale, because by that time it is most assuredly "out," and will remain unworn in the closet until you donate it to Goodwill.

I do hope that the foregoing has not been too discouraging for you. Do press on in the marvelous adventure of parenthood. You have not yet begun to fight. While coping with teenagers can be an exercise in frustration, the rewards are many and varied. A team of scientists at Harvard is working under a federal grant conducting research to determine just what those rewards are—and when they find out they have promised I'll be the first to know.

5. Hollywood Trucking

As the beautiful new tractor and trailer rig comes barreling up the highway, with heat waves shimmering on the road, a small red convertible is in the way. The horn blares, the girl smiles, the movie begins. We enter the glamorous world of Hollywood trucking, a world that's a far cry from the dull reality.

Perhaps Hollywood's greatest misconception surrounding the trucker concerns the CB radio—that magic box that warns the drivers where the bears are hiding. Using the CB, Burt Reynolds and Jerry Reed avoided Sheriff Jackie Gleason throughout the movie "Smokey and the Bandit." The Rubber Duck was able to hold together one thousand trucks which toured the country in song and movie, recklessly breaking tollgates and speed limits.

However, in reality the CB is used constructively more than it's used to avoid the law. CB's are used to find parts, equipment, food, lodging, and whatever else a driver may need. Channel 9 is reserved for emergency transmissions only, and is monitored by REACT, a national organization. Many times a trucker has been the first to respond to an emergency call. But is this service shown in the movies?

Nor is the misconception about the use of the CB the only distortion of trucking by the film industry. Did you ever notice the type of tractor and trailer rigs the stars drive? Brand-new trucks, complete with every chrome ornament available—chrome gas tanks, chrome exhaust stacks, even chrome wheel lugs. The paint is clean, bright, and unscratched. And all new trailers, too. Not a hint of road dirt on the mudflaps. A spotless rig—no dust on the windshield, no bugs on the grill, not even exhaust deposits on the trailer. And who owns these new rigs? Why, the driver, of course.

However, the silver screen is not life. Most rigs are company-owned or leased. The trucks are often dirty, with dull paint and bent bumpers, and chrome is practically nonexistent. The few privately owned rigs actually belong to banks. In a movie, if a tractor breaks down, a tow truck is called and a genuine mechanic works on it. In real life, nine times out of ten the driver is also the mechanic.

Perhaps the greatest distortion on screen is the image of the drivers. Many people believe, thanks to Hollywood, that a truck driver is a young, free-wheeling, single guy, good-looking enough to pick up a beauty queen within minutes of hitting the asphalt. But most drivers are actually middle-aged and attached to a family. If he's lucky enough to own his rig, a driver usually also owns a house, a station wagon, and a dog.

Trucking is a vital form of commercial transportation. But it's dull. To make it sell, producers had to create an appealing image, dispelling the loneliness of the long haul. So the screen trucker was born. Although the image is attractive, it's distorted.

6. Learning to Decide

To some extent, we are all affected by our environment. And one of the most powerful influences upon us is the personalities of the significant people in our lives. These influential people can either nurture and promote our growth and development as individuals, or they can inhibit it. Having been raised in the home of my father and mother and now living in my own home with my husband, I am acutely aware of the value of supportive personalities.

In our home, my father was the indisputable authority. Male supremacy was both assumed by my father and accepted by my mother. He considered it to be his prerogative to govern every facet of life for anyone who resided in his domain. My mother was not even permitted to select a new piece of furniture or carpet. If he liked a particular chair but she thought the fabric or color was inappropriate for our large family, he bought it and she tried to keep it clean.

With my mother having virtually no voice in most subjects, it followed that we, as children, had even less. This was inhibiting to all of us, but it was worse for my sister and me than for my brothers. Naturally my father did not share our interests, so he proclaimed them frivolous and unnecessary. On the other hand, since my brothers shared many of his interests, they had the opportunity to participate in activities they enjoyed. Dad insisted that we all spend our leisure time together.

He liked boating and fishing, so we all went boating and fishing. And my being subject to motion sickness was completely irrelevant. Therefore I spent countless Saturdays and Sundays with clenched teeth and a queasy stomach. Although there were four children in our family, we never went to the zoo or to an amusement park. Only once did we ever go to a movie. But we never missed the annual boat and auto shows. We were expected to enjoy Dad's interests and given little opportunity to enjoy normal childhood activities.

What little individuality Dad did not crush, Mom discouraged. An "A" in algebra-trig was trivial, because she managed a house and family with a knowledge of only basic mathematics. But a disinterest in home economics was unforgivable. She totally rejected the idea that I might be anything other than a wife and mother. Any mention of a career was met with murmurs concerning the immoralities of unmarried women and her opinion that a mother's place was with her children.

Between the two of them, they tried to mold us into duplicates of themselves, complete with their hobbies, professions, and opinions.

After marrying, I found it confusing to be expected to have my own point of view. My new husband insisted upon knowing my preference before purchasing any household items. At first, this was extremely difficult for me, because I discovered that I usually did not have a preference. Whenever that occurred, Bill would assume that I needed more time to decide, so he would suggest that we wait until I had made my decision. After a week of stumbling around in our dark apartment, I selected some lamps.

Eventually, forming my own opinions and making decisions became easier. Vacations, activities, and purchases were mutually planned. I truly realized how much progress I had made when we started to build our house.

We had decided, for economic reasons, to use a precut or package-style house. After obtaining floor plans and brochures from several companies, we found ourselves overwhelmed by the task of selecting the right house. Finally I sorted through the plans and eliminated those that did not meet our minimum requirements or that were too large. Next I considered which ones either included the extras we wanted or could be altered to include them. I was left with three plans, one of which I felt was the best house for us.

When I showed Bill the plans and explained my method of selection and ideas for alterations, he immediately agreed that my first choice was the house for us. It was built, complete with the alterations I had suggested. Five years before, I could barely choose a lamp, but now I felt confident enough to select a house.

As a child, I was expected to accept the opinions and obey the decisions of others without question. Now I am encouraged to think, to reach, and to achieve whatever is within my capabilities. For the first time in my life, I am expected to be me, with my own interests, hobbies, opinions, and dreams.

7. Euthanasia for Animals

Euthanasia, the process of helping an animal die by administering certain drugs, is legal and accepted in the veterinary profession. But it is still the hardest part of my job as a technician in an animal hospital. Sometimes it is justifiable to put an animal to sleep because the creature is suffering and needs to be put out of its misery, but at other times euthanasia is a waste of an animal's life.

An animal brought to the hospital to be put to sleep is called an "E and D" patient. "E and D" means euthanasia and disposal. Euthanasia is accomplished by injecting the drug T-61 into the animal, usually directly into the vein. The animal's foreleg is tied off above the elbow with a tourniquet. The fur is wetted down with a moist cotton ball and the needle is inserted. As the tourniquet is loosened, the drug is injected. Cats and small dogs have very small veins which are hard to find, so T-61 is injected directly into the chest cavity. This is easier for the technician but harder for the animal because it takes the drug longer to take effect. I was surprised to learn that animals do not close their eyes and look peacefully asleep when they die. I often wonder what the animal feels; sometimes I have nightmares of a burning sensation going throughout my body, with animals all around me asking, "why?"

Animals are put to sleep for many different reasons, some justifiable, some not. A good example of justifiable euthanasia is the case of Trixie, a 13-year-old fox terrier who began to feel her age, which would have been the equivalent of 91 in a human. Her owners wanted to do all that was possible to keep her alive, but each day she became weaker. Soon she gave up eating and drinking and waited painfully for her time to come. There was nothing anyone could do for Trixie. Instead of watching his beloved pet suffer, the owner brought her to the hospital for euthanasia.

Another example was the litter of three puppies that a cruel person had abandoned in a burlap sack on a roadside. A passerby found the puppies and brought them to the hospital after the sack had been struck by a car. One puppy was in shock, one had a broken pelvis, and the third had serious internal injuries. They were going through much pain and suffering, so each puppy was euthanized. These animals were better off being put to sleep than being allowed to suffer.

Many times, though, I am asked to perform unnecessary euthanasia. For example, Ms. Wilson brought two beautiful cats to the hospital to be euthanized. One was an adult blue point Siamese that someone had given her, and the other was a young healthy black beauty. When asked why she wanted them put to sleep, she replied, "I've just bought a new beige carpet for my living room and these cats are constantly shedding their hair." Another woman, Ms. Ford, wanted her beagle put to sleep because she was moving and couldn't find a suitable home for it. By coincidence a man came in at the same time who just happened to be looking for a beagle to train as a hunting dog. When I tried to arrange for him to take the dog, the woman refused, saying that she didn't want her dog to be trained to hunt. Because of her feelings about hunting, she deprived her pet of life.

Whenever I must euthanize, I tell myself that it is part of my job and that I must do it, no matter what the reason. I certainly can't save all of the animals or give them homes. I harden myself just like the doctors and other technicians do, pretending not to think about it and making jokes. I try to forget it. But the look in an animal's unclosed eyes and the unpleasant dreams are hard to forget.

8. Soap Operas

Every afternoon that I am at home and not otherwise occupied, I sneak down into the basement at one-thirty and hide there in the semidarkness until three o'clock doing something that I really don't like to talk about. I have been doing this for more years than I care to say, and I am forced to admit there is no end in sight. I am what I once saw referred to in an article as a "closet viewer" of television soap operas.

It has been said that there are only three indigenous American art forms—jazz, musical comedy, and soap opera. The first two are universally acceptable forms of entertainment, but mention that you watch soap opera and you are immediately typed as an empty-headed housewife with her hair in curlers and a sink full of dirty dishes. This is not necessarily the case. Sammy Davis, Jr., Andy Warhol, and Justice Thurgood Marshall are all admitted viewers. I don't know why they watch, but I will attempt to explain why I sit there mesmerized for an hour and a half each day.

First of all, the soaps are virtually the only live drama left on television. Occasionally they are taped, but for the most part they are being performed as they are telecast. There is a certain air of excitement to any live performance. No matter how well-rehearsed the cast may be—and many characters in the soaps are Broadway actors with excellent credentials—there is always the chance that someone will forget a line, or trip over a rug and fall flat on his face.

Second, the soap opera world is total fantasy. Everyone is beautiful and successful. The characters spend their days in beautifully decorated, spotlessly clean homes, which no one has to dust or scrub. Everyone is always beautifully coiffed and dressed, even first thing in the morning. Nothing is ever broken or dirty or messed up. Nobody's children catch cold or fight with the neighbor's kids. Nobody's car ever breaks down. Nobody ever wonders how they are going to keep up with the tax increases on those beautiful homes or pay the department store bills for all those designer clothes. They are too busy solving the dilemma of the latest illegitimate pregnancy in the family, or how to face up to the current fatal illness.

Finally, the soaps are an excuse to relax. For a little while every day, I can sit in a comfortable chair, enjoy a cup of coffee, and watch all those refined, attractive people air their dirty linen on coast-to-coast TV. I can even fold the laundry or do some mending at the same time, and sometimes I do. Other days, I am on the curlers-and-dirty-dishes side of the ledger. But I am in front of the set regardless.

So there you are. After all these years, I have publicly admitted my weakness for soap operas. I have come out of the closet, you might say. Just don't ask me about them ever again, because Thurgood Marshall notwithstanding, I am going right back into the closet.

9. Alternative Sources of Fuel

Faced with today's high energy costs and tremendous consumer demand, our country needs to find alternative energy forms for fuel oil. During the past five years, consumers have tried conservation as a means of defense against high gasoline and home heating oil prices. They purchased smaller, more gas-efficient cars and insulated their homes with storm windows and doors. While these conservation measures improved the efficiency of oil consumption, they had no effect on continually increasing oil prices. Since conservation alone is not the answer, what alternatives are available now?

One readily accessible substitute energy form is solar energy, produced by the sun. Solar collectors—made of insulation, serpentine tubing filled with water, and glass—absorb the heat from the sun and distribute it to radiators or baseboard heaters. Hot water for bathing is available through this same process.

Gasohol is another alternate fuel. Gasohol is a mixture of ten percent alcohol and ninety percent gasoline. Cars travel more efficiently on this fuel due to its high octane content. In fact, Henry Ford designed the Model-T Ford to run on pure alcohol. Gasohol should be carefully considered as an alternate fuel, because the alcohol needed is easily derived from just about anything, such as corn, wood, or organic garbage.

We could also look to our natural resource the wind. Some experimentation is being conducted in the Midwest using windmills to generate electricity. As a matter of fact, one major catalog store sells windmills around the country.

Coal and wood should also be considered as substitute fuels. People heated their homes with wood stoves and coal furnaces long before oil was available as a home heating fuel. My own home is now heated with a wood- and coal-burning stove, eliminating any need for fuel oil.

Although there are no easy or comfortable ways to get around our energy problems, comfort has to be placed after our real need, which is to find substitutes for fuel oil. Replacement energy forms are available to fill that need.

10. Living vs. Waiting to Die

The quality of old age is determined by one's attitude and personality. This was made apparent to me by the difference in how my two grandmothers managed the later years of their lives.

My maternal grandmother is still alive at the age of eighty-four, but she essentially stopped living many years ago. While in her mid-sixties, she ceased to venture out of her house and to mingle with people. The travel trailer they had purchased when Grandpa retired was put up for sale. Their only company, other than family, was neighbors who Grandpa invited. Toward the end of his life, Grandma even refused to accompany him to the grocery.

After Grandpa died, she would not allow her neighbors in the house, and had my uncle install one lock after another. Soon she would not even open a window or permit some of her own children and grandchildren to enter the house. Deprived of social contact, my maternal grandmother, Grandmother Wendell, has drifted into a fantasy world of her own that has resulted in confusion and chaos.

My paternal grandmother, who was widowed at the age of sixty-five, has remained in the real world. After a very brief interval following her husband's death, and in spite of the objections of her children, she obtained a position as housekeeper for a professional couple with three children. Since both husband and wife were busy obstetricians, managing the household and governing the children were left in Grandma's capable hands. In this bustling environment, she thrived for almost a decade, until she retired.

However, it was following her retirement that she truly exhibited her independence. Grandma traveled. She never learned to drive a car, but if a plane, train, or bus went there, so did Grandma.

After crossing the continent twice, she settled into an annual routine similar to that of a Canadian goose. She flew to Newfoundland, her birthplace, in the late spring to visit her twin sister and two of her brothers. Before the first Canadian snowfall, she would return to New York where she had other family and friends. Later she'd spend some time with us in Maryland, a friend in Washington, and a daughter in Virginia. Then she was off to Florida for the winter. In the spring the migration was reversed.

With Grandma traipsing about in this fashion, it soon became standard procedure to ask her where she was whenever she called. During one call, Dad assumed she was in New York, quickly asked if she were well, assured her we were fine, and in an effort to keep the cost of the call minimal, hastily concluded the conversation and hung up. About half an hour later, we answered the door, and there Grandma stood with her suitcases. She had been calling from the bus stop about a mile away.

Although Grandma had three heart attacks before the fatal one at the age of eighty-one, she never ceased her gallivanting. It was while visiting a niece and discussing both her previous visit with her cousin and her future visit with her brother that Grandma had her final heart attack. She died while having a cup of tea with a favorite niece.

Grandmother David lived until the end. She had an active life filled with family and friends. But Grandmother Wendell has spent the last eight years virtually alone, just waiting to die.

PART FOUR

Writing to describe, narrate, and inform

14 Describing

It is a good deal easier for most people to state an abstract idea than to describe and thus re-create some object they actually see.
Flannery O'Connor

Let's say your uncle gave you for graduation a thirty-day bus pass to travel around the United States, and you want to thank him by sending him your impressions of the Grand Canyon, a part of the country you know he especially likes. Or say the department for which you work is to be renovated, and all employees are being asked to describe in writing their ideal new working quarters. Or your daughter has just moved into a new home, and you want to tell her grandmother, who is not well enough to visit, all about the house.

Perhaps your history professor has assigned a project in local history, for which you are to write about some building at least one hundred years old. Or the editor of the weekly family section of your local newspaper has called to ask if you would like to send in a feature article about your family's recent reunion. Or your father's friend who owns an inn needs some paragraphs for an ad about his menu specialties and has offered to pay you to do the job. Or a friend who has applied to serve on a local commission on human rights has asked you to write a personal recommendation for her.

In each of these situations, you will be doing descriptive writing. How will you go about it?

Observing and selecting details

When you get ready to write a description, you need first to be sure you are familiar enough with what you are describing. You need to have *observed* carefully enough to be able to convey an exact picture to someone else—your reader. In her statement at the beginning of this chapter, writer Flannery O'Connor recognizes that this kind of "re-creating" by describing is not easy. But careful observation—"actually seeing," as O'Connor puts it—is the key here.

You will need a *focus* around which to collect details, to help you decide which details you should actually use to write your description. For instance, if you wanted to share with your uncle the awesomeness of the Grand Canyon as a spectacle of nature, you would focus on details of size and perhaps the overwhelming variety of texture and color the canyon presents. However, if you were most interested in emphasizing the canyon as a geological phenomenon, you would highlight details of its rock formations, the variation in color created by different minerals in the rock, and the way in which water continues to carve away the rock bed. Your focus tells you which details to delete as well as which to include. And having your focus clearly in mind as you observe details will help you to keep your paper unified when you finally sit down to write.

Let's watch a student as she observes and selects details and then shapes them into a descriptive paper. At the beginning of one fall semester, students in a science course were assigned to take a botany walk where flowers grew wild and to identify as many flowers as possible. The students were to report the identifications, with brief descriptions of each flower, in a paper. One student walked around several blocks in an overgrown area near her apartment complex. She repeated the walk to look more closely at the flowers she had identified and to see whether she could spot any others. As soon as she got home, she made a list of what she had seen while the walk was still fresh in her mind:

thistles / heads turning white
goldenrod / gives me hayfever
large yellow-black spider, spinning remarkable web
trumpet vine / flaming
sumac—leaves turning / maroon berry cones
two white flowers I didn't know
white honeysuckle all over everywhere

When she was ready to write up her botany walk, our student checked her assignment one more time. She realized immediately that her list included some details she could not use. She was to report on flowers she could identify and briefly describe each. So she wrote at the top of her list:

FOCUS: TO IDENTIFY AND BRIEFLY DESCRIBE FLOWERS SEEN ON A BOTANY WALK

That focus told her right away that she could not use that large spider in the remarkable web, even though it was one of the most interesting things she had seen. Nor should she talk about goldenrod causing hayfever. And she would not mention that she had seen two white flowers she didn't know; she was only to write about flowers she could identify, so a mention of unidentified ones would hardly impress the botany professor. The student marked through all the unrelated details on her list.

As you can see, our student writer deleted the details that were outside her focus *before* she began to write. That way she did not waste time writing a paper that wandered around, and her botany walk report ended up unified and in focus:

> On a botany walk in my neighborhood I saw several flowers I could name. First, standing high above the undergrowth, were spiny purple thistles, going to seed in white puffs. Nearby I spotted goldenrod, which deserves both halves of its name; it's gold like rich butter and it grows in a proud, upright rod. The trumpet vine I saw next boasted flaming red-orange blossoms shaped like the trumpet mouth they are called after. Sumac bushes further down the block were reaching their height in color, with bright green leaves turning ruby-red and maroon-colored cones of berries. White honeysuckle, with tiny blossoms but bold vines, tried to take over everything else I saw. I finished my botany walk glad that I grew up with a grandfather who taught me the names of some flowers.

Developing your details

Because well-done description plays on a reader's five senses, you will want to take particular care to get as much sensory detail as possible into your descriptive writing. When readers encounter strong descriptive writing, they find themselves experiencing what is being described with the writer; they identify with the situation through sight, smell, sound, touch, taste, or some combination of these.

For example, this student writer manages to appeal to four of our five senses (all but touch):

> I shall always remember those Sunday morning breakfasts I used to have as a child. At seven in the morning the smell of fresh-perked coffee would snake its way down the long hall which led to my room and fill it with an indescribable aroma, awaking me to tell me breakfast was ready and waiting. And what a breakfast it was! I first see a tall frosty glass of just-made orange juice filled with orange pulp. Steaming hot coffee is being poured into a small mug with sugar and country cream already in the bottom. Pancakes cooked to a golden brown are stacked almost a foot high, with butter oozing down the sides. Warm maple syrup covers the cakes with a soft glaze and slowly drips down to form a small pool in my plate. In a side dish are oven-baked apples sprinkled

with cinnamon, nutmeg, vanilla, and raisins and served hot with the cooking juices still bubbling. Thick-sliced country bacon rounds off the meal. Whose mouth would not water, just thinking about this kind of breakfast served on a cold wintry morning—an "old fashioned breakfast"?

We would guess that your mouth did indeed water when you read the paragraph, especially if you were hungry. And that is exactly what the writer intended. He wanted to involve you, to take you back with him to the Sunday morning breakfasts of his childhood.

The breakfast paragraph illustrates the heightened sense of detail that characterizes effective description. One of the ways in which you can involve a reader in your descriptive writing is by piling detail on detail, so that the description is packed and its effect intensified. Furthermore, each detail should be as precise and as vivid as you can make it. For example, the breakfast paragraph refers to the smell of coffee "snaking its way down the long hall," to a "tall frosty glass" of juice, and to baked apples with their "cooking juices bubbling." A useful rule of thumb to follow in descriptive writing is "Show your readers, don't just tell them." The breakfast paragraph does that, through its specific sensory details.

We do want to warn you against overdoing the pile-up of detail that we have just advised. Overdone description tends to become so lush that you risk overwhelming your reader; there is simply too much to digest. The following sentence about the cliffs around a lake in Oregon is an example: "The shores are lined with searing, blood-red clay cliffs that produce a staggering display of fluorescence and kaleidoscopic colors at sunset." A reader could feel overpowered by that sentence. Such expression is sometimes referred to as "overheated diction." You can almost feel the writer trying too hard.

Here is an overheated paragraph:

> On a summer morning Eagle Rock Camp is the most captivating and blissful place in the world. The camp, located high in the mountains of upper New York State, is tucked away in the midst of mighty oak trees that seem to be reaching out elegantly in a creative dance movement. The exquisitely sweet summer breeze floats softly through the air, bending the slim blades of grass and kissing the golden buttercups.

However, even overdone description is better than abstract, "floating off" description that lacks concrete sensory details with which a reader can identify. You nead to keep a description externalized to keep your readers with you. If you allow the writing to float off into a kind of abstract philosophizing inside your own head, your readers will become confused; they cannot follow you there. So keep your descriptive writing sensory by using concrete sensory details. Concrete description might be said to be grounded, so that a reader can get hold of it, while abstract description floats off into vagueness.

This paragraph by a student who started out to describe a walk on the beach is an example of such vague, "floating off" writing:

> When I take a walk on the beach I am a king surveying his kingdom. Gulls soar ahead to herald my approach and the waves bow at my feet. The sea belongs to me as far as I can see. And yet I am lonely, as lonely as a man lost on an empty desert. The seagulls have become hawks circling above their prey. The waves are mirages that retreat as I move toward them. And the expanse of the sea merely intensifies my loneliness. I realize my intense aloneness, my place as an almost nonexistent speck in the universe. I am a king no more.

Too much of this takes place internally, inside the writer's head; he leaves the physicality of the beach, and with it the kind of details a reader could identify with: the gleam of sun on water; the feel of sand and pebbles underfoot; the plaintive sound of a bell buoy.

Creating word pictures

In descriptive writing, you can often use word pictures to good effect. Word pictures give your reader a concrete image on the page with which to identify. You can use three major devices to produce word pictures: the simile, the metaphor, and personification.

A *simile* creates a word picture by comparing what is being described with something else, using *like* or *as* to express the comparison. In his novel about migrant workers, *The Plum Plum Pickers*, Raymond Barrio uses a simile to describe apricot harvesting: "The plump orange balls plopped pitter patter like heavy drops of golden rain into his swaying, sweaty canvas buckets." Annie Dillard, in *Pilgrim at Tinker Creek*, finds two similes to describe the translucent entrails of a rotifer (a water creature): "Something orange and powerful is surging up and down like a piston, and something small and round is spinning in place like a flywheel."

In a *metaphor*, the thing described in a sense becomes the object with which it is being compared. In a passage from Frank Walters's novel *The Man Who Killed the Deer,* a sacred lake becomes an eye as an American Indian describes it: "We wanted the mountains, our mother, between whose breasts lies the little blue eye of faith. The deep turquoise lake of life." In a student paragraph about Washington in midspring, a cloud formation becomes "little sheep flocks" of cloud and the Washington Monument is "a sharp, clean sword." Here is one more especially effective metaphor: "A burning silver sword slit through the heavy cloud's fat stomach and it bellowed in rage . . . and then cried like a child." Do you recognize the image?

Personification makes descriptive writing more vivid by giving life to inanimate objects. Sappho, a poet of ancient Greece, made dawn perform a human act in these lines: "Standing by my bed in gold sandals/Dawn that very moment woke me." A student writer gives life to the sun as she describes an afternoon on the beach: "The sun takes an afternoon break while the clouds bluff a storm. Now the sun returns to work, laughing at his naive victims below." Playful images like this one are often especially appealing to a reader.

You can increase your skill at creating word pictures if you consciously try to do so. First you concentrate on what it is you want to describe—an object you see while driving, an aroma you pick up during a walk, the sensation you experience when sand runs through your fingers. Then you set your mind to work trying to think of different ways you could compare the object or the aroma or the sensation with something else. Your skill will increase with practice, and you will develop a store of images to draw on when you need them.

We should caution you against getting caught up in creating a word picture. This one, for example, may be overdone: "Morning comes over the bay like a young woman gowned in palest blue chiffon trimmed with billowing white lace, as cloud puffs drift across the sky." Your reader may get lost in trying to follow your image all the way through if you overdo it.

It is also possible to create an *absurd image,* a word picture that doesn't quite make sense. Here are some illogical or nonsensical images: "You can hear the ruffling of lifeless leaves as the trees embrace you"; "She accepted her husband's death with open arms"; "The insurance agent stepped over our heads and signed a renewal contract without our permission."

Mixed images don't make sense either—images like "At this point in my life I sit in a stew that smacks of irony" (a stew cannot "smack"); "The talk I had with my grandmother helped to dissolve the generation gap between us" (a gap is bridged, not "dissolved"); "Gales of the late November wind glide around you" (gales would not "glide").

The wrong word, or words, might also find their way into your images: "My going to school has put some fire on the skillet"; "When I told my husband I was taking this course, he told me right off the back not to discuss anything I had learned with him"; "My being away from home and in the college library so much was one of the main flaws in the ointment." Can you see how an image has become confused in each of these sentences?

Finally, let us warn you again to beware of tired images or clichés in your writing. "White as a sheet," "cool as a cucumber," "pretty as a picture," "hungry as a bear," "hot as hell," "tired as a dog," and "cold as a clam" are only a few of the many clichéd images you will want to avoid. One way to test for clichés in your writing is to consider whether you can automatically supply the second half of a comparison when you hear the first half.

Naming as a descriptive device

In addition to creating word pictures, you can use the device of naming to involve your reader in a description. If you are writing about a person or an animal—any animate being—your reader will become involved with your subject much more quickly if you name him or her.

A student decided to describe her grandmother to support the point that older people can be good company. The first version of her description referred to her grandmother throughout as "my grandmother." As she worked on the description, she realized that she did not think of her grandmother as a grandmother at all, nor did she particularly want her readers to do so. She decided to use her grandmother's nickname, CG; that made her grandmother seem more lively—which reinforced the point of her paper. Here is the paragraph about CG from the finished paper:

> My sixty-three-year-old grandmother, Cathy Gaither—whom we call "CG" for short—has always amazed me with her youthfulness. I can remember one time when we went to visit CG and she had her arm in a cast. She had had an accident on her motorcycle. Besides riding her motorcycle solo, CG engages in risky activities with the rest of us. We all go camping in the mountains together, with few or no provisions, ice-boating on the lake, ice-skating, and horseback riding. Most of the time I feel like CG is my sister instead of my grandmother.

In describing a person, you of course do not have to use the person's real name if doing so makes you uncomfortable. You can change the name somewhat, as this writer has done, or you can use an entirely different name. Indeed, if you happen to be describing someone who you think doesn't "look like" his or her name, your description might be more effective if you rename the person. But beware of overly cute names; they can stick out and take over your description.

Description is often used in other kinds of writing. Like the paragraph about CG, examples that support a point will frequently be descriptive. Vivid descriptive details may be needed to drive home an argument, and description sometimes occurs in a narrative, as you will see in the next chapter.

· ·
Exercise 1 For class discussion
· ·

Below are several pieces of descriptive writing by students. Be ready to discuss in class why each is effective and what devices have been used to make it so.

1. My childhood home, a large white Cape Cod cottage with a red roof and dormered windows, stands at the end of a long, straight driveway. My room is behind one of those dormer windows. As a child I spent long hours on the window seat, reading and daydreaming. From that window I could see apple trees, sweet-scented in spring, heavy with red fruit in summer, gay with yellow leaves in fall, and etched in snow during the winter. Returning home now all I see is concrete and asphalt. I miss my apple trees.

2. You can smell the pier before you can see it. Walking up the narrow oyster-shell road bordered with high marsh grass and cattails, you pick up the odor of old wood, fish, and creosote tar. The crunch of the oyster shells underfoot gives way to a hollow sound at your first step onto the plankings which form ragged vertical lines between the pilings. Here and there a new board of bright tan breaks the seemingly endless rows of older boards, brown and rough from years of wear. The old timber creaks and sways as the rushing tide pushes against the pilings driven deep into the bottom of the bay.

3. In the early sixties, Framingham, Massachusetts, was a small town with bicycle paths worn into the grass wherever the sidewalk didn't go. Sometimes in my dreams I ride back over those trails, feeling the bumps, the jars, and the tree roots just as they were under the wheels of my new English racer. I can even recall some of the places where if I didn't duck I'd get a mouthful of clothesline.

4. Small groups of people huddle under umbrellas to protect themselves from the burning sun, waiting for some sound, some movement. Then it happens. The street dancers, so beloved in Trinidad, round the corner ahead. Suddenly you feel a surge of energy, like an explosion throughout your body, as each nerve comes alive. Everyone rises and starts to dance, throwing up their arms and shouting for the favors being tossed by the official dancers. You forget the heat and the wait as you are caught up in the excitement—and you know it is worth everything to be here.

5. We're on our way down the Hudson on the Manhattan Excursion Line. When the motor revs up, the band revs up, and the excitement begins. As the boat slowly pulls away from the dock, it is already vibrating with rock music. The buildings and people behind us look smaller and soon disappear as though they were never there. Our boat rides so smoothly through the water that the city seems to be moving instead of us. The skyline is like a Rembrandt, as the setting sun casts an orange glow along the shore.

Exercise 2   For class discussion

The following descriptions are less effective than those in the preceding exercise. Based on what you have learned in this chapter, try to determine how each description got off the track.

1. Picture the sunrise over the bay. You are standing on the beach. Bulky waves bounce between the ancient towering rocks with a deafening crash, while the undersized ripples wash the miniature boulders of earth from beneath your feet. Suddenly the dark, peaceful, moonlit sky is filled with a kaleidoscope of light and color. Now you can see a colossal, fiery, luminous sphere rising from the hidden depths of the ocean. As you look up into the endless space, morning brings you a multitude of seagulls who seem to be gazing back down at you in the early morning light.

2. The most interesting city I know is Jacksonville, Florida. I made my first trip there when I was fourteen years old. We have relatives there and went there for our summer vacation. I was amazed to see how crowded the beaches were, because I was so used to seeing Bayside's beaches. Also, in Jacksonville there is no boardwalk with all the side stores and pizza parlors. Another interesting thing is that the cars drive right up to the beach to the edge of the water, which is rather unique compared to other beach resorts. Jacksonville is really a great city full of many wonderful sights and people, and I hope to go there again in the future.

3. The wind rushes again almost like the surf. The air feels like a rainstorm—but the sun won't let me down. I wish I were a leaf, tossing about, free and flying. Up, up, up from the ground into the blue and white sky, and then I'd float back, touching on a jeweled lake. I guess I shouldn't ask myself what it's all about so often. I feel the wind coming up stronger now. It's almost dark—I'll have to work tomorrow.

4. Like a multicolored centipede inching its way, the jammed traffic crawls through the choked, rain-drenched streets. Furiously dancing rain ricochets off everything in sight. The dark and menacing sky, seen through blurred windshields, rests on the tops of buildings like a filthy layer of gauze. Swirling wisps of gray, shaved off the billowing clouds by the buildings' granite edges, spill over into the deep concrete canyon. In the floor of the canyon, amber taillights ignite brilliantly all along the curving spine of the centipede. A line of hazy headlights hangs in the air like shimmering disks suspended from an invisible wire, reflected in water-spotted mirrors. Blaring horns add a shuddering wail of protest to the already clamorous language of the city. Undaunted, the wet, sluggish mechanical creature continues its methodical journey home.

Exercise 3 Written

Make up word pictures for eight to ten of the following sensory situations, using similes, metaphors, and personification. Observe carefully first. Be as creative as possible; don't let yourself resort to clichés. Bring your word pictures to class to share with your classmates.

1. chewing taffy
2. stroking a long-haired dog or cat
3. listening to *little* waves as they reach the shore
4. watching a fire burn down
5. feeling polished marble, bronze, or aluminum
6. smelling ripe peaches, watermelon, or bananas
7. feeling fine rain hit your face
8. smelling charcoaled hamburgers
9. tasting curry, spinach, bittersweet chocolate, or cinnamon
10. hearing rock music
11. seeing tulips, lilacs, or dogwood
12. walking barefoot on packed wet sand
13. walking barefoot on dry sand
14. motorcycling on a bumpy road
15. seeing a horizon of trees of five different shades of green, or seeing the same horizon in autumn

Exercise 4 Written

Write a descriptive paragraph on one of the following topics. Be sure to observe your material carefully before you begin to write. Use the devices you have learned about in this chapter to make your description as vivid as possible. And beware of the traps in descriptive writing you have been warned about.

1. an unusual piece of furniture
2. a walk down a city street
3. an animal or a bird
4. some physical feature of your college you especially like

5. a holiday celebration
6. a geographical scene
7. something you have made
8. a garden
9. some family treasure
10. a striking building

. . . .
Exercise 5   Written
. . . .

Turn to the long list of topics in part VII and select one that would require you to write a description of several paragraphs. Decide how much to include in your description by carefully focusing it first. Make a list from which to write your paper, and hand in your list with your paper.

. . . .
Exercise 6   For class discussion
. . . .

Read the student papers that follow this chapter and come to class prepared to discuss how well they succeed as descriptive writing.

Sample student papers: describing

11. Goat Woman

Twenty-five years ago, at the age of thirteen, while hiking in the mountains near my hometown of Vancouver, Washington, I came face to face with the legendary Goat Woman of Livingston Mountain. When the Goat Woman invited me to her home for a bite to eat, I learned that her real name was Gladys Fulton and that she had been born in Switzerland. We hit it off and have been friends ever since. Gladys left a very deep impression on me; to this day I would have to say she is the most remarkable person I have ever met.

In 1936 a doctor advised Gladys that goat's milk would help alleviate or possibly cure an arthritic condition she had. One week later she bought 300 acres of mountain land (at $1 an acre) and 150 goats. She then built a barn, which she shared with the goats until she had completed her house. The original barn and house are still being used by Gladys today.

Gladys's house is small, consisting of two rooms. One room has a small table with one chair and a wood stove, which is used for both heating and cooking. The other room holds a bed and a piano. Both rooms contain stacks and stacks of newspapers, magazines, and books. A kerosene lamp hangs over the bed and on the bed lies a Bible. Oliver, the parrot, is housed on top of the piano. In the winter, baby chicks and geese sometimes share the house with Gladys. There are no toilet facilities, no running water, no electricity. Gladys does have two luxury items though, a 1940 vacuum-tube radio and a recently acquired CB radio, both of which are powered by car batteries.

Gladys is seventy-six years old now and in addition to raising 150 goats, she has chickens, geese, a cow, a horse, five dogs, two cats, a pet raccoon, and a parrot. A typical day for Gladys starts at four in the morning. She walks to the barn to milk about 125 goats. After milking she releases the goats to the countryside, chasing them to a particular area that she wants them to feed on. She then cleans the barn, shovels manure, and spreads clean hay around the milking stalls. Afterward she feeds the remaining animals and retrieves eggs from the hens. In between all these chores, people are arriving to pick up their allotted share of goat's milk, with the local hospital receiving the biggest share. If time permits, Gladys slaughters a few male goats. Most of the dead goats are drenched in arsenic and left in the fields for the coyotes to feed on. The remainder of the meat is consumed by Gladys and her dogs. Just before dark she rounds up the goats, locks them in the barn, and calls it a day.

Gladys has a simple meal of cheese, goat's milk, bread, and fresh vegetables. While eating she listens to classical music from the radio. She spends the remainder of the evening reading a newspaper or magazine and she finishes the day with the Bible. On weekends the local CB'ers are treated to conversing with Gladys, or should I say "Goat Lady One," which is her call sign. About once a month Gladys and her retired forest ranger friend get together and indulge in a bit of merriment—drinking blackberry wine, playing the piano, and singing.

This remarkable woman is going on seventy-seven now and her way of life hasn't changed a bit. She is healthy, hard-working, self-supporting, and completely independent. I don't believe there's anyone who leads a fuller, happier, or richer life than Gladys Fulton, the Goat Woman of Livingston Mountain.

12. Charlie's Carry-out

Located on Nine Points Road, just outside the District of Columbia, is a small carry-out that, while offering substandard seafood fare to the public, does a booming business: Charlie's Carry-Out—an all-night stop for the hungry and the lonely. I recall my last late-hour attempt to beat my own hunger at Charlie's.

As I pulled into Charlie's parking lot, my car caught one of the cardboard boxes lying around and dragged it while I circled looking for a space where I could see my car from inside. The noise made several drunks turn and stare. Off to one side were three kids about sixteen years old teasing an old man. One of them had grabbed a ragged glove from the man, and a game of keep-away was going well for the kids. I parked next to the trash cans where I saw an old woman digging through the trash, occasionally stopping to polish off a leftover piece of fish.

Reaching the front door, I stepped over several people who were either sleeping or passed out. One of them was spitting blood so I stopped briefly at the pay phone to call an ambulance for him. Hanging up the greasy receiver, I called to the fat man in the dirty T-shirt to make mine a fish sandwich with extra hot sauce. Without a word Charlie picked up another piece of fish and tossed it into the grease, from several feet away.

Before my sandwich was done, the ambulance had come and gone, the guy outside had gotten his ragged glove back, and someone's angry wife had thrown a brick through the windshield of their new Oldsmobile. Dirty Charlie handed me my sandwich in exchange for $1.05, in advance, and out the door I headed. As I drove off, I looked back and saw one customer throw his sandwich across the counter at Charlie. The sandwich dropped to the floor and I remember wondering how Charlie was going to tell the difference between that sandwich and the rest of the scraps on the floor. I wished I had ordered the crabcakes instead.

13. The Eastern Shore

"Don't give a damn 'bout the whole state of Maryland. I'm from the Eastern Shore." This bumper sticker, which can be seen frequently around my old neighborhood, was really quite a joke. I could hardly share the enthusiasm of it. After spending seventeen years in the rural surroundings of Ridgely (pop. 1000), I was ready to leave. I was going to school on the western shore. Only now that I am away can I see the true values of Ridgely—values that many other places lack.

One of the many features that is unique to the area is the noisy quietness of the night. The noises begin in the spring, after the winter thaws and as the plowing begins. Birds call from blooming trees, frogs croak in rising swamps, crickets chirp in dampening corners, and otters splash in flooding streams. As June approaches, life settles down. Then the quiet nights of June are unequaled anywhere.

On a clear, cloudless night (frequent in June), one can see millions of bright stars. The stars have a pure, unadulterated luster. They are not fogged over by smog or smokestacks or high-rise buildings. The fireflies flit about, spotlighting themselves for a millisecond with their fiery tails. The sweetgrass in the fields smells almost edible. A drive down any of the area's back roads can provide quite a treat for any traveler.

Usually the evening hours are great for just such a drive. As you drive, surrounded by fields of corn and acres of wooded land, you can probably spot a family of deer feeding in a field or squirrels scampering from tree to tree or groundhogs scavenging for food. And further down the road is Tuckahoe State Park.

The park is typical of the surrounding community. Thirty-five hundred acres sprawling in two counties, Caroline and Queen Anne, Tuckahoe is unsurpassed in beauty. Although it has camping facilities, a twenty-one-acre manmade lake, a large playground, and a national champion oak tree, the rustic park is rural in tone. Hunting, the ultimate local idea of a good time, is allowed in designated areas, and fishing is permitted in the lake. An arboretum is being planned for a portion of the land.

All of these qualities—the noisy quietness, the clear nights, the beautiful area, and the sites and sports—by themselves would make for a satisfying place to live, but there is one last quality that makes Ridgely an unforgettable place to live. The most unique aspect of the area is a delicate something called solitude. Solitude? Another way to say it is peace of mind. In how many places can you take a stroll without a car in sight, or drive without being cut off or passed or caught in a traffic jam? There is no distrust between neighbors because everyone knows everybody else.

Sure, Ridgely doesn't have many of the "modern conveniences." There are no shopping centers or discos or major-league ball teams or apartment complexes. And, sure, Ridgely is changing. A second housing development is beginning, much to the disgust of the local yokels, as we are often called. It's a square town, with very little "action" at night. There isn't even a pool hall. Even so, Ridgely is a refreshing place to live.

So the next time any of you city slickers start heading for Ocean City or Rehoboth, remember, people live on the Eastern Shore all year long. It isn't a summer playground and we're no more backward than people on the western shore. We have running water, too.

14. Memories of Parochial School

How do I feel about parochial schools? Wow! The feelings are flying all over the place, and with the feelings come the memories.

I remember a bell clanging in the large schoolyard filled with squealing, laughing, busy children. With the ringing of the bell came instant silence. The children would stop in their tracks, as if playing Statues. Then *click-click*, a large wooden clicker sounded, and in unison the children moved in silent drill-like choreography. Bodies formed perfect rows, two by two. *Click-click*, every voice was heard saying the Apostles' Creed, then silence again. I always wondered how the wind could dare tickle and tease the huge friendly oak which stood in the cobblestoned yard. How could it shake and crackle its leaves, even after Mother Superior had rung the bell and sounded the clicker? *Click-click*, the columns of children marched slowly and silently into the red brick school building and down the gray halls. The discipline was absolute.

At St. Stephens School you learned and you followed rules—school rules and the Golden Rule. At St. Stephens I learned many things, so many things, too many things. I learned fear and guilt. Fear when I learned that the more I sinned, the more my soul became stained, and that those stains or scars from sin would remain on my soul until they were burned off in the fires of purgatory. I was taught that no one could escape these fires if they wanted to get to heaven. It was either purgatory fires or hell fires; the former if we were good, the latter if bad. Guilt came when I learned I was bad because I put Jesus on the cross, and that I came into the world with sin and would leave with sin. Each time I forgot and committed some terrible sin, like talking in line, the fear and guilt increased.

I also remember that I learned. I learned to read, write, add, subtract, and multiply in my first two years of school. I learned all the building blocks of a good education, even though I was absent for days, weeks, even months. In those first two years of school I had mumps, chicken pox, flu, colds, pneumonia, strep throat, scarlet fever, Russian measles resulting in undiagnosed total loss of hearing in one ear, mild polio resulting in the use of corrective walking shoes for ten years, and an undiagnosed vision problem. The doctor who finally discovered the vision problem thought it a small miracle that I had ever learned to read. I could have gotten lost and left behind in a world of undiagnosed minor handicaps. But I didn't, because of the superior teaching skills of a dedicated group of nuns.

I remember a large airy classroom with forty-five fellow students who also learned the basics and a little more. We learned how to behave like ladies and gentlemen. We were taught to be polite by always remembering our manners and being aware of other people's feelings.

I have such conflicting feelings about parochial school. I feel gratitude for being taught so well, yet I feel anger for being taught fear. I ask myself how I can question the method when the results were so good, but I do. I learned so many things so well; I had to—my everlasting soul was at stake.

15. A House of Cards

At first glance, I thought the room was unoccupied. It was dark, still, with none of the usual clutter that hospital patients tend to surround themselves with. Only the steady beeping of the heart monitor betrayed the presence of the fragile woman in the bed just a few feet away.

Lying there, unmoving, she looked like a picture that somebody forgot to paint. The soft lines around her eyes, the silvery gray hair that framed her face, were the rewards of a life well spent. She used to joke that people who didn't look their age had never learned to live, only to exist, because Time would never leave his signature on an incomplete work of art. Then she would laugh a laugh that would tickle the spirit of everyone around her. Her eyes would sparkle like a child's at Christmas, with a combination of vitality and mischievousness that was envied by women half her age.

Now her body was frozen, her face empty of expression, as it had been since the stroke a few days before. Looking at her, I felt as if an injustice had been committed, a mistake had been made. She had been a companion throughout my childhood, a confidante during my teenage years, and a treasured friend in adulthood. She was my grandmother, who always had the right words for me. My grandmother, who could do anything she set her mind to. So why was she just lying there?

I waited for her to get up and tell me it was only a joke, that she was rehearsing a part for the theater group she was so active in. I waited for her to get up, so we could both have a good laugh and stop for lunch on the way home and she could fill me in on everything she had been doing since I saw her the week before. I waited for her to get up. She didn't.

When I looked into her eyes, I could see that her mind was as alive as it had always been. The twinkle was still there, and slowly it diluted some of the bitterness I felt.

We shared many memories that day. We didn't talk; her condition wouldn't allow it, and neither would mine. But words had been nothing more than a formality with us, anyway, since we always seemed to know what was on the other's mind.

I recalled the story she told me after I had my first nightmare. She said that the angels would come and watch over me while I slept if I would build them a house of cards to keep them warm. So every night I built a house of cards, and felt quite safe from the monsters and goblins that haunted other children's bedrooms in the dark.

I could almost hear her laugh when we thought about the dozens of banana peels and orange seeds we planted in her garden. It was years before I realized that some people ate fruit because they actually liked the taste, and that planting the leftovers was not necessarily their main objective.

I thanked her for finding an excuse for me to spend the weekend with her when that Elvis Presley movie was playing around the corner from her house. And for sitting through it with me four times, because she used to feel the same way about Rudy Vallee.

I told her how hurt I had felt when she did nothing about the abuse she knew I had been growing up with, and she told me of the pain she had felt in not having the courage to do anything about it.

We had a long conversation that day; somehow we knew it would be our last. After the funeral, I went home and built her a house of cards.

16. Journey Out of My Body

I have experienced something that let me know more about death than a lifetime of reading and theorizing could. One morning, quite unintentionally, I became dissociated from my body. It happened shortly after I had finished reading Robert Monroe's *Journeys Out of the Body*.

I woke up to a gentle rain on a gray morning. It was nine-thirty. I glanced at my clock and then drifted back into what seemed to be very peaceful but light sleep. The next thing I knew, my body was vibrating slightly, as if an electric current was flowing through my veins. This slight sensation grew to an unpleasant surge of electricity-like energy which set my legs convulsing beneath the sheets. It felt as though I was running in a race, kicking and sweating profusely, but when I looked to the foot of the bed, I was astonished to see that my legs were very still. The sheets had not moved.

At this point I began to experience fear, and in hopes that some light would help bring me to my senses, I groped for the switch on my reading lamp. My hand could not turn the switch. It seemed as if my hand had gone right through the lamp. This frightened me even more. I inspected the switch, hoping that it was broken to account for my inability to make it work, but it wasn't. I looked at the switch from the top, then from the bottom, then from the inside of the lamp. When all this failed to explain why the light didn't click on, I followed the cord to the wall socket. The cord was securely plugged in. I saw the plug from the front, then from *inside* the wall socket.

By this time I was so shaken that I gave up the struggle, and surrendered to whatever was to happen. In one timeless instant, I found myself back in my body, sitting up in bed and staring at my hands. There was no sweat on my body, nor any sign of a struggle. The wall socket that I had inspected so thoroughly was still hidden behind a large trunk—where it had been for years.

This journeying out of my body has happened to me twice since the first time, and each time was just as frightening as the first. It is a very real state of being, as certain as walking down the street or conversing with a friend. I know it's not dreaming. I know I'm not dreaming right now, and I am no less certain while I am experiencing separation from my body. I have told very few people about all this, but since it last occurred well over a year ago, it's much easier for me to talk about now.

There's yet another part to this experience. That's the part that feels *good* while the whole thing is happening, a feeling of unity with all things that disappears when I come back. I don't think I've ever felt so much joy—coupled with a feeling of fear that I won't come back. Yet when I do come back, I feel as though something has been lost. Every time I have this experience, I stay longer. I may never have it again on a temporary basis. But I know I will have it again someday. And I won't be afraid, because if this is what death feels like, I'm sure I'll have no desire to hang on to this life when my time comes to die.

17. The Bowhunt

November 1st, at last. I'm finally here. I finish that last sip of coffee and climb out of the truck. A crisp coldness envelops me as I pull on that last sweater and don my camouflage jacket. I pick up my bow from the back of the truck and bravely stalk into the darkness.

Cursing the lack of a moon, I stumble through the undergrowth, shattering the eerie quiet of the woods. I finally arrive at my preselected spot on the side of a ridge overlooking several almost invisible animal trails. I settle in and huddle up against the cold.

Slowly the light increases as the sun struggles towards the horizon. The quiet is broken by a brave little bird somewhere, stirring to life. As if waiting for that cue, several more begin to chirp their morning songs, and as the shadows begin to fade more join in. A squirrel barks angrily at the dawn, as if cursing the prospect of a hard day's work ahead. Several crows fly overhead and cry the warning to the forest of the strange creature concealed in the shadows below.

As the light filters through the morning mist, the shadows begin to take form. The formidable giants of the night become stately trees, and the forest floor becomes a carpet of leaves.

Suddenly, a new sound assails me, a quiet shuffle of leaves. I tense in anticipation as I spot a grayish-brown patch in the bushes that just doesn't seem to belong. The spot shifts and begins to grow, and suddenly that spot materializes into a deer. He moves forward a few timid steps and cautiously surveys the area, as if searching for that sinister creature the crows warned of. His eyes fall on me, but quietly pass. The deer steps forward a few more steps and discovers something more interesting on the ground. I take advantage of this lapse in security and cautiously raise my bow. The deadly missile is pulled back to its tautest and the razor-sharp warhead seems to settle on the deer's shoulder as if by its own will. He looks up, as if some sixth sense has warned him of danger. His eyes seek me out again, but there is still no recognition.

I slowly release the tension of the bow string and lower the bow. The deer zooms in on me again, and finally realizes his danger. He bounds off, fading swiftly into the forest.

It was enough. I'll be able to face the world a little longer, and tell tales of "the one that got away."

15 Narrating

I was trying to write . . . and I found the greatest difficulty . . . was to put down what really happened in action; what the actual things were which produced the emotion that you experienced.   Ernest Hemingway

Your daughter is away with the Peace Corps, and you want to send her a full report of her younger brother's first high-school band parade. Or you are involved in helping to expose police corruption in your town, and you plan to relate what happened during a raid on a music store that was fronting for a drug supply source. Or you have been invited to speak to a civic group that may be interested in sponsoring a scholarship for your college, and you have decided to begin with a funny anecdote.

You are interested in becoming a sports announcer, and the local station where you are training has asked you to prepare a five-minute account of the Little League playoffs. Or you are planning to argue before your city council for a stoplight at a street corner in your neighborhood, and as part of your evidence you want to highlight a fatal accident that occurred there last month.

Each of these situations will involve you in narrative writing. You do narrative writing whenever you tell about something that happened within a defined time span. Narrative writing, then, relates an event, usually in simple chronological order. In some instances, it might be said to tell a story.

Some ground rules

You can apply a few ground rules to most narrative writing: 1) Put your readers on the scene immediately and clearly, and then get on with your story. 2) As you narrate, select details for the specific effect you want your narrative to achieve. 3) Keep your narrative moving. These ground rules can be diagrammed like this:

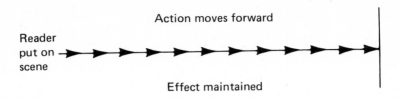

This brief narrative follows these ground rules very well:

> It happened at the dinner table at the Greenbrier Hotel, a fancy resort where I, a young bride from the country, felt even less sophisticated and more awkward than usual. My new husband and I were on our honeymoon, and the social manager of the hotel had invited us and three other honeymooning couples to a celebration dinner in the main dining room. For my dinner I ordered beef burgundy with noodles.
>
> After a while, the very French waiter returned from the kitchen and said to me, in rather breathless Parisian English, "The beef, it is strucken off."
>
> "Oh," I responded, "that's okay. I'll have ham in pineapple sauce, then."
>
> "Oh, no, Madame, the beef is all right, but it is strucken off!"
>
> "Ham is fine," I said again.
>
> "No, no, no, Madame! Beef, beef—but is *strucken off!*"
>
> This dialogue continued for longer than I care to remember—until finally another, more sophisticated new bride "translated" for me, in a tactfully quiet voice, "I believe he is saying the beef dish is beef Stroganov, rather than beef burgundy with noodles."
>
> "Oh-h-h." My eyes must have been as wide open as my mouth, in my surprise.
>
> So I had beef Stroganov for that celebration dinner, instead of either beef burgundy with noodles *or* ham in pineapple sauce, but you can be sure that I have never eaten it since without remembering with a chuckle the Greenbrier beef Struckenoff.

Here is the working list the writer of this paper made up as she prepared to write:

Desired specific effect: My relative lack of
sophistication in a setting
that assumed a certain
amount of sophistication

where event happened ⎫
when event happened ⎬ background
the circumstances/ ⎭
    situation

~~why we chose the Greenbrier~~
~~what I wore~~
~~describe other couples~~—no, keep focus
    on me and my funny story
what I ordered originally
~~what others ordered~~
conversation between waiter and me
    —ham as alternate dinner
~~my new husband's discomfort~~
another bride, from St. Louis,
    "rescues" me
my reaction when I realized what was
    going on
~~how beef dish tasted~~

characterize waiter—briefly—to add
    humor

. . . .

You the reader learn right away that this narrative is going to occur at the dinner table at an exclusive hotel during the honeymoon of an unsophisticated young woman. You are on the scene immediately and ready to get on with the story. If the writer had told you why she and her husband had chosen the Greenbrier or what she was wearing at dinner, you might have felt impatient, bogged down in needless, boring background information.

Now note what else our writer decided to delete before she began to write. As her specific effect, she wants to emphasize her relative lack of sophistication in a setting that assumed a certain amount of sophistication. So she gets rid of such details as what the others ordered, her new husband's discomfort as the situation got more and more out of hand, and where her "rescuer" was from. The spotlight needs to stay on the action between herself and the waiter. Details about her dinner partners are irrelevant. They would blur her intended effect and distract you as you read.

The deletion of irrelevant details is one reason this piece of writing keeps moving. Another is the use of dialogue, a device that helps to give a reader the you-are-there effect. The paper moves rapidly enough that you want to keep on reading to see what happens next.

You will probably choose to write narratives in chronological order most of the time. But occasionally you may decide to begin in the middle or near the end, then flash back to an earlier part of your story. The student writer of the following football narrative opens his story at its climax, as an overtime field goal is being placed at the end of a tied game. Then he pauses to take his readers back through some of the semi-climaxes of the game, to build up to whether the field goal wins the game.

> The game is tied. The date is December 14, 1975. The place is Baltimore's Memorial Stadium. Everyone in the stands is on their feet for the overtime play. Down below, Toni Linhart, behind a wall of Colts, is set to kick the field goal.
>
> For a moment before Linhart's snap, I see the game so far in my mind's eye. At one point, my team, the Baltimore Colts, is behind 7—0. Then, late in the fourth quarter, the Colts seem to hear the pleas of the shouting crowd and start to move. Like a machine, Bert Jones marches the Colts over a determined Miami defense. Then, from the six-yard line, Lydell Mitchell bursts into the end zone. Touchdown! Linhart adds the extra point and the game is tied. The gun sounds, ending regulation time.
>
> In sudden-death overtime, the young Colt defense freezes Miami's offense and the Colts take over on their own four-yard line. Once again the Colts seem to grow stronger from the crowd's screams. Jones throws to Chester, then to Mitchell, and completes a third pass to Carr. As the Colts get nearer to the goal line, the noise becomes almost deafening.
>
> And now a strange silence falls over the stadium. I realize that Linhart is ready to try to win the game. The ball is snapped and an unbelievable roar pours out of the crowd. The stadium seems to rock and then explodes with screams of joy and excitement. The referee's raised hands only confirm what 60,000 frenzied fans already know. The field goal is good. The Colts have won.

Finding a lively opener

It's a good idea to involve your reader in your narrative right away with a lively opener. In her narrative about the honeymoon incident, our writer catches readers at once with her opening words: "It happened at the dinner table. . . ." To what does "It" refer? she wants readers to ask. A student writer about to narrate his wife's delivery of their first child began with this dramatic opener: "I was awakened suddenly one morning at four A.M. by my wife."

Generally, it is wise to avoid beginning a narrative with something like "I am going to tell you a story about. . . ." unless what follows "about" is so intriguing that a reader could hardly resist it. The original opening sentence of the honeymoon dinner narrative read: "One of my favorite funny stories on myself has to do with my lack of sophistication in a very sophisticated setting." Pretty flat, isn't it?

Here are some more lively openers taken from student narratives:

While I was running an EEG (electroencephalogram) one day, the pens started clacking and throwing ink around the room.

It was a warm day of about 80 degrees as we sped along into some part of the Pacific unknown to me.

Damn, I wish Bill hadn't gone and done that, gotten his head blown open like that.

Standing in the early morning light of October in Ohiopyle National Park, I studied the swollen river below me. The water level was higher than usual from heavy rainfall. And this was to be the day of my first white-water rapids trip.

We would guess that you would want to hear each of these narratives once you had read their opening sentences.

Building suspense

Once you have caught your reader's attention with a lively opener, you want to hold it throughout your narrative. You achieve that by building suspense. Think for a moment about a recent TV segment that totally involved you. Suspense no doubt helped to keep you in front of that TV screen.

In building suspense, you involve readers through their emotions. As Ernest Hemingway suggested in the quotation that opens this chapter, you want your readers to share the emotions *you* experienced while your narrative was actually happening. Recall again that TV segment that totally involved you. It doubtless featured a great deal of action—but action that *mattered* to you, for one reason or another. You were there, your emotions were involved, you were identifying with the characters participating in the action because you were *feeling* with them. As a writer of narrative, try to get this high sense of drama into your writing. Involve your readers' emotions by building suspense.

One way to tell whether your narrative is dramatic or suspenseful enough is to test it out on a listener before you write it down. As you tell it, you can also check for how well you have observed the ground rules we discussed earlier in this chapter. Watch your listener's face as you speak. Does he or she seem puzzled as you begin to get into your story? Do you hold his or her close attention throughout? Do you see any evidence that your listener is "wandering off" at any point? The answers to these questions should tell you whether you located your listener clearly enough as you began, whether you included anything in your narrative that would be better left out, and whether you built in enough suspense.

After telling your narrative, don't forget to tighten up your expression when you begin to write. Conversational storytelling does not equal narrative writing.

We think you will agree that the student who wrote the following narrative about a barracuda chase builds suspense skillfully. You might like to know, though, that the first version of her paper had much more background information on learning how to scuba dive. Also, at the end of the third paragraph she had included several anatomical details about barracuda, which were distracting. With the deletion of these two chunks of material, her narrative moves much more dramatically.

> After completeing all the difficult tests involved in learning to scuba dive, my father and I thought we were ready for almost anything. Little did we know what an adventure we were headed for.
>
> For three days we had been taking trips into the sea to gaze at the beautiful sights the ocean holds. Swimming with a school of fish and squeezing through jagged-edged caves of pink and purple coral had provided considerable excitement. We decided we were ready to sign up for the barracuda chase.
>
> On the day of the chase we left shore just as the sun was coming up, our equipment and weapons having been double-checked for air leaks, pressure, and maneuverability. Five miles away from the Florida coast we plunged into the choppy water. Sticking together, we quietly cruised the ocean bottom searching for our target. My father motioned toward a huge field of ocean grass. A large barracuda was lurking in the waving strands of seaweed. He must have seen us first, since he was already glaring at us.
>
> As we slowly approached, the narrow body darted from the weeds into open space. Instinctively I felt the intense danger. Since I had no weapons I immediately slinked to a coral enclosure and watched my father join the group in surrounding the huge fish. I was terrified as they closed in for the catch, since all I could see were air bubbles from the divers' air tanks.
>
> Suddenly it was over. The barracuda was trapped in the iron cage brought along for his capture. A surge of joy rushed through me as I helped escort the awesome fish to our boat.
>
> Now when I go to Key Largo Aquarium House I can visit Spike—the barracuda I—or rather my father—helped to chase and capture.

Making it happen now

As you think about ways in which to involve your readers in your narrative, you might decide to cast your writing in the present or to use dialogue, or both. If your narrative is written in the present tense, your readers will feel as if it is happening while they are reading, so it will be easier for them to identify with what is going on. You can also make readers feel as if your narrative is happening in the here and now by using dialogue. If you do decide to use dialogue, you will want to be sure it rings true; otherwise it may distract readers instead of further involving them. Skillfully done dialogue often makes a narrative seem more real; it will surely liven one up.

The student writer of the following narrative both casts it in the present and lets us hear his characters conversing so that we feel a part of the action.

"Breaker one nine . . . breaker one nine!" It's two o'clock in the morning on Route 50 and I am heading toward the beach.

"Go, breaker one nine," comes the welcome response, a female voice that is crisp and clear.

"You got the Wild Turkey here," I offer. "What's your 20?"

"Hey, Wild Turkey, I'm eastbound on 50 just past the bridge, come back!" she replies.

"You must be on my back bumper. What are you driving?"

"I'm in a Ford van . . . blue and yellow. Is that you in the bronze Dodge just ahead?"

"That's me," I answer, "in the number two lane. What's your handle there?"

"You got the Eight Ball here. Where are you heading?"

"Ocean City, by the sea. And I got a problem. My speedometer isn't working and I'm worried about the smokies, come back."

"You say your speedometer went bad?" Eight Ball comes back. "Well, let me cruise past you and you can hitchhike on me all the way."

"That's a big 10-4," I reply as I sign off.

The handsome Ford van roars by me in a blink and I barely make out a quick wave from the woman behind the wheel. The next thing I know, I am staring at her rear bumper and the fatigue I was starting to feel is gone. In the next twenty miles we change lanes three times to chatter about a variety of subjects. All I have to do is steer and throttle and talk. What I forget to do is think. When the flashing lights go on behind me, I suddenly realize that Eight Ball and I have forgotten about the "double nickels" speed limit.

"Hey, Eight Ball, there's a smokey on my butt," I let her know. "How fast were we going?"

"Sorry about that, Wild Turkey, for sure. Catch you on the flip-flop."

I pull the Dodge van over on the shoulder and play that old familiar scene again. I fumble for my license and registration. I smile weakly. My mind races for all the right things to say.

"What's the trouble, officer?"

"I just clocked you at 68," replies the Maryland state patrolman, pleasantly but firmly.

While he writes my ticket, I decide to save the story about the broken speedometer and the woman in the Ford van I was trailing. It wouldn't matter anyway, I'm sure, I tell myself.

As I sign the ticket, I can't resist the pun. "I guess this is what it means to be behind the eight ball," I say, smiling.

"I guess," he answers. "Take it easy now."

I start my engine, turn off my CB, and head off—slowly—toward my destination once more.

Pacing your narrative: sentence choices

Your narrative writing will be more dramatic if the form in which you write it reflects the content about which you are writing. You can achieve this happy combination by being aware of the pace of different kinds of phrasing.

For example, note how this student's choice of expression reinforces the event she is narrating—the escape of a horse from her uncle's corral:

The horse races away in exultation. He runs as if the world is his, his head trying to touch the sky, his body strong with spirit and muscles, his mane and tail flying as if to tell the wind which way to go. His skin glistens in the sun, his feet hit the ground in perfect rhythm, never missing a beat, never slowing down, but going faster and faster until the forest stops him.

The following sentence, with which Edgar Allan Poe opens his short story "The Fall of the House of Usher," demonstrates the pacing effect you can achieve with a long sentence piling detail on detail:

During the whole of a dull, dark, and soundless day in the autumn of the year, when the clouds hung oppressively low in the heavens, I had been passing alone, on horseback, through a singularly dreary tract of country; and at length found myself, as the shades of the evening drew on, within view of that melancholy house.

This long, heavy, slow-moving sentence is exactly right to establish the despairing mood into which Poe wants to plunge his readers.

This paragraph, on the other hand, immediately establishes for the reader the detached attitude of the central character who will narrate Albert Camus's novel *The Stranger:*

> Mother died today, or maybe yesterday; I can't be sure. The telegram from the Home says: YOUR MOTHER PASSED AWAY. FUNERAL TOMORROW. DEEP SYMPATHY.

We are not surprised, as we read on, by the uninvolved quality of a hero who begins his story with such short, stark sentences.

One of our student writers uses short sentences in another way to pace a narrative. Here is her account of the final inning of a softball game for which she was catcher:

> Here comes the first pitch. It's outside. Ball one. The ball goes back to the pitcher. I return to my position behind the plate. My mind is racing. Relax. Keep your glove out there. Don't take your eyes off the ball. Here's the second pitch. It looks good. It's coming right over the plate. Smack! She hit it. I can't see it. I'm up off my knees in a split second. My glove is open. It seems like an eternity and then suddenly it's all over. The ball falls right on target into my glove. The game is over and we have won.

The student writer of the following paragraph invites readers to ride with him in a fantasy about the Grand Prix. He maintains the movement of that heady race through the steady, almost rhythmical pace of parallel structure, as he begins three successive sentences: "To feel . . ."; "To go flat out . . ."; "To know. . . ."

> To feel the wind in your face and hear the tires scream as you slide through the S-curves at Monza. To go flat out through the streets of Monaco, hearing the roar of that mighty engine and accelerating till you think you are going to be pushed through the seat. To know you are one of only twenty-four men in all the world who drive the giant V-12 Formula-1 cars in the Grand Prix International Circuit.

You can use sentences of different kinds and different lengths to vary the pace of a narrative, reflecting what is happening at a particular moment. The following paragraphs from a student narrative about a cross-country marathon use pacing in this way. Listen to how the sound of the writing echoes exactly what is happening as the race progresses:

> The runners are already at the line-up, pawing the ground like horses at a derby. The starter readies his pistol. He fires. Adrenalin surges through the runner's body, exciting every muscle into spontaneous movement. Dirt and gravel fly in faces as the human steeds head toward home.
>
> The first mile removes some of the competitive element of the race, as some runners overheat and retire to barking coaches and sympathetic parents. Others fall victim to injury and lack of stamina. But some persevere. They run —like they have never run before.

The next turn marks halfway. The runners quicken their pace as the thundering hooves round the bend. The mind recognizes the hill ahead and instinctively shifts to a traction mode. Arms pump and spikes dig in while the words "work that hill" echo through the mind.

As we mentioned at the end of the last chapter, you will sometimes need to combine narrative and descriptive writing. For example, if you were writing about a trip you took with a learning-impaired relative, you might want to describe your companion; doing so would help you show how his or her handicap made the trip unique.

By the same token, narration often appears in other kinds of writing. One student who wanted to explain why her gospel choir broke up began her paper with a startling story about the infighting between two of its members. Another student writer was concerned about why crime among youth is on the increase. Her paper included an account of a teenage break-in at her apartment and the indifference of the police officers who answered her emergency call.

- -
Exercise 1 Classroom activity
- -

Jot down some notes for a narrative you would be interested in writing and use them to tell your narrative to a classmate, to test it out. Watch to see if your narrative holds your listener's attention throughout. If it does not, talk with your partner about how you can improve it.

- -
Exercise 2 Written
- -

Below are several possible topics for narratives. Write lively, dramatic openers for at least three.

1. Christmas Day in a big house where seven cousins between two and twelve years of age, along with their parents, are spending the holiday with their grandparents.

2. The morning before the final swim meet, scheduled for noon, at a camp for young teens.

3. A human rights rally being cosponsored by American Indians, gay rights activists, Chicanos, union organizers, and ex-prisoners.

4. A dog show about to begin in a fine rain.

5. A noisy party, the fifth in a month, that is disturbing your quiet neighborhood.

6. The opening of a county fair, complete with agricultural exhibits, livestock competitions, sideshows with hawkers, daring rides, and the like.

7. A sailboat race about to get under way in unpredictable winds.

8. The day before your best friend is to go into the hospital for open-heart surgery.

. . . .

Exercise 3   For class discussion
. . . .

Read the following student paper, then go back and analyze how its writer builds suspense.

> My five children, ranging in age from two to ten, and I were vacationing on Brigantine, a rather secluded little island off New Jersey. We had all walked to the end of the island looking for shells, and had strolled leisurely back to our spot on the beach. I bent down to straighten our blanket and then counted noses—1, 2, 3, 5, no #4. My four-year-old, Danny, wasn't with us, although I knew he had returned from our walk. We searched the sand dunes and looked in the water. No Danny. About five minutes had passed when I approached the lifeguard stand, trying to appear calm. The lifeguard was talking to three young women. After several attempts, I finally got his attention.
>
> "My four-year-old son is lost—he's gone."
>
> Reluctantly he looked toward me. "He's probably around here somewhere; maybe he's playing in the dunes," he said, and immediately resumed his conversation with the young women.
>
> "No, he's not around here," I insisted. "He may have gone into the water."
>
> "Oh, no, we watch the little ones closely."
>
> I could see who he watched closely. I realized that I was no competition for his attention. I was trying not to become hysterical when I saw a beach patrolman in his jeep. I flagged him down and explained. He radioed all the beach stations. A little boy had been found 30 blocks farther down the beach and was waiting at one of the stations. Is it Danny? raced through my mind.
>
> I told the other four kids to sit on the blanket without moving, and added the threat "The next one that gets lost is staying lost!" Then the beach patrolman and I took off down the beach, dodging sunbathers as we went. The question echoed and re-echoed through my head during the interminable wild ride.
>
> When we were within ten feet of the station, I saw a very short lifeguard wearing a long droopy sweatshirt and a long droopy face, sitting high up on the lifeguard stand and eating a hotdog. Was it—yes, it was—Danny.

. . . .

Exercise 4 Written

. . . .

Write a narrative about one of the following. Pace your narrative by deliberately constructing various kinds of sentences to reflect what is happening from moment to moment.

   1. A motorcycle race over a bumpy course which includes several obstacles

   2. A five- or ten-minute segment of a three-ring circus

   3. The final minutes of a Little League softball game, with a top pitcher on the mound and a star batter at home plate; the score is nearly tied

   4. Some frightening encounter you have had—with an animal, an authority figure, a machine, or the like

   5. A trip in a canoe or a rowboat down a river with changing currents and small rapids

   6. Giving birth

   7. Being with someone else who was giving birth

   8. Skiing down a challenging slope

   9. A hurricane or other natural disaster you have lived through

10. Some exciting moments in an adult sports event you attended

11. The death of someone who died gracefully

. . . .

Exercise 5 For class discussion

. . . .

Read the student papers that follow this chapter and come to class prepared to discuss how well they succeed as narrative writing.

Sample student papers: narrating

18. It Was Halloween Night

It was Halloween night. My husband was out for the evening, and all the kids were accounted for. I had distributed the ritual goodies to the ghosts and goblins who rang the bell, put the baby to bed, and settled down to read *Ragtime*. From the rec room downstairs came the booming beat of hard rock played at full volume, courtesy of my son, Pat, and his friends. At about ten o'clock, the stereo was mercifully quiet and they trooped out. Pat stopped to ask if he could go to Jack's house, two blocks away. "Okay," I said, "but don't be too late." Less than an hour later he was dead.

At around midnight in the police station, two detectives tried to piece together for his father and me what had happened. A carful of teenagers . . . a curve on a wet road . . . a blowout . . . perhaps some beer . . . ambulance . . . helicopter . . . trauma center . . . . I listened without really hearing. I drank hot coffee, but it could not warm the icy numbness within me.

He was our second child. Born in the Indian summer of our fourth year of marriage, it was his impending arrival that made us decide to take the plunge and buy a house. I had hoped during that pregnancy that the baby would be a girl, but we were delighted with a healthy and beautiful second son. We named him for his grandfathers and took him home to meet his toddling older brother.

He grew up tall and straight, a bright student who did well in his sophomore classes. He loved the sea, and talked of becoming an oceanographer. He liked basketball, boats, biology, and peanut butter, not necessarily in that order. He was at once very ordinary and very special. Now, incredibly, he was gone.

Death came like a thief in the night. He was so much a part of us; then, with no warning, he was snatched away, and with him all the hopes, the dreams, the plans. I wanted to cry, but could not. I felt nothing but that awful, empty coldness.

As the days and months passed, I tried to put his death into some kind of perspective. I searched for answers and found none. I wanted an explanation, but none was forthcoming. I accepted, with eternal gratitude, the love and support of family and friends, and through them I found a measure of peace.

I came to the realization that all any of us really has that is enduring is what we give to each other. Patrick gave us love and joy and hope, and these we still have. My only wish is that he knows, somehow, how very much we loved him, and how glad we are to have shared his life.

19. A Dangerous State of Mind

I once served as an aide to one of our most powerful senators. That senator made me more aware than I had ever been before that some of our white leaders are still the victims of an early-nineteenth-century mentality: they're still stereotyping black people.

I don't think I will ever forget one time when I was in the senator's presence. I had been assigned to drive him from his senate office to Washington National Airport. As soon as he got into the car, I could feel his apprehension. He couldn't decide what to say to me or how to say it. He shook my hand and said, "Good afternoon, young man." Then he sat silently for a few seconds. Finally, he began by asking me my age, my educational background, and my place of birth. I wondered if he was going to ask me if I liked girls; he didn't, and I breathed a sigh of relief.

For approximately two miles we drove in total silence. Then the senator began telling me about a friendship he and his wife had with a "colored girl" who had been a classmate of his daughter at a prestigious university. According to the senator, whenever he and his wife visited their daughter, they would always request the presence of the "colored girl." She would play the piano and sing while he and his family had a merry time. I sat there behind the steering wheel, listening but not hearing. When we finally reached our destination, I breathed another sigh of relief.

My drive back to my office was not a pleasant one. I wondered to myself: What was the senator telling me? Was he saying that all black people had musical talent? Was he saying that his only exposure to black people had been on a master-servant level? I finally concluded that the senator was still living in the early nineteenth century when black slaves would sing and dance while their masters drank whiskey and clapped their hands. A dangerous state of mind for a modern-day senator, I thought to myself.

20. Intercultural Dating

May 10th
Dear Diary,
Carol, Laura, and I set out this morning for the air show at Andrews Air Force Base. There we were, stalking the flight hangars, ready to pounce like hungry wolves on any eligible bachelor we might chance upon. After several unsuccessful tries, the three of us decided to head for home. As we were walking down the flight line, I happened to glance over at a group of Army paratroopers who had earlier dazzled us with their spectacular mass parachute descent. Noticing my glance, they waved. I waved back.

Before I could blink twice, we were surrounded by six of Uncle Sam's young men, clad in green paratrooper uniforms. Their dark-complexioned faces were darkened even more with camouflaging face paint. Introductions were made and immediately I recognized a distinctive foreign accent. Imagine their surprise when I answered their greeting in their own tongue, Spanish. (Thank goodness for those six years of high-school Spanish!) Quickly conversations began to flow among the group and I turned to the young man on my left. His name was Orlando Mercado Gonzales and he was originally from Cayey, Puerto Rico.

After a lengthy conversation with Orlando, during which time we each downed a Mexican taco and a large coke, I felt that this fellow and I shared many of the same interests. But our delightful chat was cut short when one of Orlando's buddies sauntered over and hastily reminded him that the bus scheduled to return them to their duty station at Fort Bragg, North Carolina, would be leaving in approximately ten minutes. Upon hearing this, Orlando, with all the genteel ways characteristic of a Southern gentleman, requested permission to see me again. I stifled a laugh when I heard the serious tone of his voice. This certainly was a change, I thought, as I mentally recalled previous dates and the uncouthness of some of my escorts. I then considered the feasibility of a future meeting with Orlando, but made no mention of my doubtful thoughts as I hurriedly scribbled my name, address, and phone number on the back of a greasy napkin. We each said our goodbyes, and as he was leaving Orlando turned and, grasping my hand, brought it up to meet his lips. For a split second I pictured myself as a Southern belle bidding adieu to her Confederate soldier.

On the way home, after I had related my story to my two eagerly awaiting friends, Carol, Laura, and I debated the question of whether or not Orlando would even call me as he had promised. As I drove on, I pondered the implications of actually going out with him.

May 18th
Dear Diary,

Well, Orlando and his two friends, Carlos and Arnaldo, just left to return to Fort Bragg. They stayed the weekend in the military quarters at Andrews Air Force Base, only a few short miles from my home.

Orlando called earlier on Sunday evening to ask if he could visit me this weekend. Somehow I still did not believe the reality of the situation until the three of them showed up Friday afternoon.

The weekend went very well, I thought. We enjoyed many different activities. Carol, Laura, and I, escorted by Arnaldo, Carlos, and Orlando respectively, went roller-skating, sightseeing, and dining out, and we all attended church services Sunday morning.

July 6th
Dear Diary,

What has me worried right now is my parents. After Orlando had visited me for several weekends, I realized that I still had not heard an opinion from Mom and Dad. This struck me as odd because in the past after only one date with a fellow I would receive their candid opinion of the unsuspecting young man. Finally I got up my courage and came right out and asked Mom for her opinion of Orlando and our present dating relationship. In return I was met with an openmouthed expression of surprise, as if my question had been extremely unreasonable. After a few moments of silence, she replied that she considered Orlando to be a very nice young man. She praised his manners. She praised his personality. Finally, after attempting to assure me that my welfare was their main concern, she informed me that Dad did not at all like the idea of the dating relationship. Mom admitted that she did not see anything wrong with dating someone from a different culture, but she added that a girl should not even consider marrying such a person.

July 7th
Dear Diary,

Would I openly defy my father's wish and continue to date Orlando? I decided to do some real down-to-earth soul-searching of my own feelings on the subject of intercultural dating and marriage. Would I mind being married to someone from another culture? I told myself "no." Would the future of our offspring be affected by our "mixed marriage"? Hold everything! Why am I doing this to myself? Was I actually becoming as narrow-minded as I considered my parents to be? I reached for the telephone and carefully dialed the long distance number that would connect me with Orlando. I tactfully explained the predicament. Orlando quietly suggested that it might be better if we limited our weekend dates. I had to agree. Our conversation ended on a sad note.

August 10th
Dear Diary,

It has been over a month since I have seen Orlando. His letters come less frequently. My parents believe that it is better this way. Somehow I cannot bring myself to agree with them.

21. Brains vs. Brawn

Brains can sometimes be used to defeat brawn, as my seven-year-old son, Mark, recently discovered firsthand.

Mark and his classmate, John, had been reprimanded by their teacher for fighting. Mark is a small, scrawny guy and the class clown. He doesn't like fighting but he didn't know how to persuade John otherwise. He asked my advice.

I suggested that since the other boy was fifteen pounds heavier and a head taller, Mark should use his brain rather than muscle (of which he had little). He had to make it clear to the teacher which of the boys was being abused. I told him that using loud, confusing behavior would be effective.

The next day the teacher left the room and Mark's tormentor was upon him. They fought until Mark heard the teacher returning, when he collapsed on the floor and allowed John to jump on him. Mark took a few of the boy's punches and then let out several ear-piercing screams. The teacher saw what Mark had arranged for her to see and she staunchly rebuked the bully.

A few days later Mark again outsmarted his hard-fisted classmate. In front of the schoolroom stood a large green storage cabinet with the door open. The teacher was called out of the room and the tough guy saw a perfect opportunity for mischief. He threw Mark into the open cabinet. Here was the big moment Mark had waited for. He grabbed the handle from the inside, pulled the door shut with a bang and threw the lock. The bully was stunned. He tried desperately to open the cabinet as he heard the teacher returning. Right then Mark started to wail loudly.

The teacher became hysterical and she was beside herself with anger. She picked up the ruffian bodily and threw him out of the room. Mark's vengeance was complete. She knew, of course, that the one who had been inside the cabinet was the good guy.

22. Escaped Prisoner

One busy Friday evening the police department had me assigned to the Bureau of Patrol at Woodland Grove. There weren't even enough seats to go around for all the prisoners. I was working the desk, and another shoplifter had just come in. With a recent directive requiring him to be handcuffed and with no space left on the bench, I was at a real loss. So I went into a nearby office and came out with a chair. Setting the chair next to the coatrack, I handcuffed the shoplifter to the rack until I could get to him. After all, I thought, he's only a shoplifter and the rack stands nearly six feet high. Where's he going to go?

It hadn't been ten minutes until someone went to get his coat. All the coats and jackets were on the floor and both rack and man were gone. The ultimate embarrassment had befallen me—an escaped prisoner. We searched the neighborhood for the rack-laden shoplifter, and after an hour I would have settled for almost anyone who happened to be handcuffed to any six-foot coatrack. Then the call came. A lady near Central Avenue had seen a man climbing backyard fences carrying what looked like a coatrack. A quick run to her house—but the man and the rack were gone. How could anyone move so fast with such a cross?

I rode around for about another hour or so and then pulled into an empty lot to sit a while. I looked down Central Avenue and suddenly there he was. Coatrack and all. The tired shoplifter was cautiously making his way up the street. I was in a dark spot so I decided to sit it out and watch him for a few minutes. I couldn't believe it. He stopped at the Metro bus stop, and with his own jacket covering the handcuffs, pretended to be leaning against the coatrack waiting for the bus.

Almost immediately a bus showed up, and there he was—a 160-pound, five-foot-four man trying to maneuver a six-foot coatrack onto the bus and trying to be cool about the whole thing. After he had made several unsuccessful attempts at boarding, one of which knocked the driver's hat off, I pulled up next to the bus. The exhausted shoplifter was almost relieved to see me. His burden had been too much, even for the search for freedom.

Once back at the station, the shoplifter found himself facing charges of escape, but even that didn't keep him from rolling with laughter as he recounted his trials at crossing all those backyard fences with his special companion. With my own embarrassment gone, I could laugh too.

23. Orphaned at Five

Celery sticks served as slugger bats; olives substituted for baseballs to be smashed across the kitchen. Cousins Sonny and Guido were pitcher and catcher, and my sister Dorrie was a combination of infield and outfield. I came up to bat for the first time just as Gramps called for us to come into the living room.

A policeman stood in the doorway. Nonnie and Aunt Sandy were crying. All morning we had been told to stop touching the Thanksgiving dinner or we would be punished. Who expected to go to jail because of olives!

Gramps pulled Dorrie and me onto his lap and hugged us close. "Your momma and daddy were going to get Uncle Vince and a truck hit their car. God took them to heaven." He started to cry. I wished he would let us down. His picky sweater smelled of tobacco and his mouth was purple from wine.

Dorrie and I went home with Aunt Sandy. My stomach was hurting and making tiger noises, but everyone was crying so I was afraid to say I was hungry.

In the morning we went to a dark room where Mother and Daddy were lying in coffins. It smelled so sweet in that room, and the red-glassed candles burning everywhere made it sticky hot. Mother wore a lacy pink dress. A pink satin blanket covered her feet. Daddy looked so white, as if he wore makeup like Mother. Folded newspapers were hidden inside his trouser legs.

At night we all knelt down on the blue carpet and prayed a long, long time with Father Minnorra from Our Lady of the Angels Church. My knees were sore and I shifted my weight from one leg to the other. Aunt Sandy touched my shoulder and said, "Marie, stop that rocking. Kneel up."

The morning of the funeral was very bright. The curtains were opened in the coffin room. Aunt Sandy held my hand. She wore a black hat with a big black feather. Her eyes were red-circled from tears. With her bright red lipstick she reminded me of the clown in my circus coloring book.

Aunt Sandy kissed Daddy and lifted me to do the same. I touched his cheek. His skin was stiff. I kissed his forehead. We moved to Mother. Aunt Sandy lifted me again. I kissed Mother, then stood on the kneeler. I moved down and lifted the pink satin cover. Mother's shoes were pink. I moved back toward her head. Touching, touching as I went. Her hair was soft. Her lips were not soft. I pressed her mouth. It was tight. I pushed my fingers into her mouth. I saw and felt cotton. Aunt Sandy pulled me away.

A man in striped pants pulled down the backs of the coffins. Nonnie was crying. Gramps was blowing his nose. Someone took Dorrie and me to a big car. We sat on two little pull-down seats behind the driver.

At the cemetery everyone was crying and praying. Aunt Sandy fainted when the two men with ropes lowered the coffins into the graves. Father Minnorra gave Dorrie and me each a white flower. Mine was turning brown and its petals were falling. I gave the flower to Gramps so I could put my cold hands into my coat pockets.

24. On a Japanese Freighter

The year was 1962. The decision had been made that I would go to Japan to marry my Air Force fiancé. Choosing the most economical way, I purchased a third-class, one-way ticket on a Japanese freighter. It was the opposite of Love Boat. During the three weeks' voyage, I learned to survive in an unfamiliar culture.

To begin, I did not know a word of Japanese and discovered that my shipmates could not speak English. At the expense of the Japanese government, the 350 Japanese people on the ship were returning to Japan from the Dominican Republic, penniless after a farming project started many years before had failed. These people, unlike many of the people in Japan, were not "westernized." I found I was quite a curiosity because they had had very little exposure to Americans.

About two hours after I had come aboard, my first difficulty in communicating occurred. A bell rang and everybody went scurrying below the main deck. Sitting there fighting tears of loneliness, I was approached by a boy in a waiter-type uniform. After saying the same word several times, he realized I didn't understand, so he made eating motions and signaled me to follow him. He led me below to a large, noisy room filled with picnic tables fastened to the floor. It was dinnertime. After finding me a place to sit, he brought me two bowls of food and a pair of chopsticks. One bowl obviously contained rice; the other bowl had a square piece of something unrecognizable in it. I looked around, trying to duplicate the method of using chopsticks, but I couldn't coordinate them and kept dropping them. The people sitting around me were amused and laughed. When I laughed with them, they seemed to relax and patiently tried to show me how to place the chopsticks in my hand. After several attempts, I managed to get some rice in my mouth. This earned me instant applause. When I lifted the bowl with the unfamiliar object in it, my nose immediately told me it was raw fish! As much as I wanted to be like the others, I couldn't bear the thought of eating raw fish, so I offered it to one of the children at my table and made an immediate friend.

As days passed, the people, young and old, tried to teach me Japanese. They would point to an object, say the word in Japanese, and I would repeat it. After they laughed at how I pronounced it, the word would be repeated for me. When I would finally say it correctly, they would clap. Then I would say the same word in English and the process was reversed.

I quickly accepted the fact that I was literally in third-class quarters. Besides seeing rats periodically, one of the things that bothered me was that my sheets were never changed. My bunk was located in a small room filled with bunks, side by side. I had to crawl over several bunks to get to my own. I did manage to solve the problem of the sheets. One night, while exploring the ship, I discovered a clothesline with clean wet sheets hanging out to dry. I figured that they must have belonged to the officers of the ship. I ran back to my bunk, quickly removed my sheets, and swapped them with the wet ones on the line. It didn't bother me that they were wet because my bunk was near a leaking porthole, and every time the ship tilted one way, water rushed in, so my bed was damp most of the time anyway.

Because there was only a community bath, my most traumatic experience involved bathing. I went as long as I possibly could without taking a bath, but I knew that I couldn't hold off for three weeks without one. So I watched the traffic heading into the bath. When I figured the smallest number of people would be present, I decided to brave it. I picked up my towel and bar of Ivory soap and headed to the bath. It was a large tiled tub filled with steaming hot water. The tub had a ledge around three sides and a few women were just sitting on the ledge chatting with each other. I closed my mind to the fact that the bath was beginning to get awfully crowded (the American was *finally* going to bathe), removed my clothes, climbed into the tub, and started to soap up. All of a sudden, the friendly faces became enraged, and angry voices started to echo in the room. I was so startled I dropped my soap. I felt the pain of humiliation; I didn't know what was wrong, but I knew it was me because they were *all* looking directly at me. Again universal sign language was used. I quickly learned that you do not enter a Japanese bath before bathing with soap and water *outside* of the tub at a faucet located on the side of the room, and, most important, you never use soap in the bath. The bath is a means of relaxation. After retrieving my floating soap, we were ushered out and the tub had to be drained. Whenever I see a bar of Ivory soap, I have mental reruns of that incident.

After a couple of weeks on the ship, I had acquired a good basic vocabulary and could actually carry on a brief conversation at a slow pace. However, it wasn't enough. One night, sitting at a table learning to play Go, a Japanese marble game, I felt relaxed and content. I had grown very close to many of the people and considered them my friends. Suddenly a barrage of Japanese came through the loudspeaker and everyone jumped up from the table excitedly and ran up to the main deck. People seemed to run from everywhere—the bunkrooms, the kitchen, the dining room. I remember thinking, "Oh God, this rusty, creaking ship is sinking and they don't even care about me!" I didn't know how to swim. I ran to the bunkroom and grabbed as many of my valuables as I could carry—my passport, the box with my wedding dress in it, my fiancé's picture, my purse, and one suitcase. Panic-stricken, I stumbled up the stairs. The contentment I had felt earlier had changed to a deep disappointment and resentment that these people really didn't care about Americans. They were going to let me drown. Dropping some things, I awkwardly made it to the main deck. The deck was crowded and everyone was looking up. With all the noise I was making, I was a distraction. Several people turned, and seeing me breathless and ashen-looking, with all my belongings, their puzzled expressions turned to hysterical laughter. What I thought was a warning that the ship was sinking turned out to be an announcement that a satellite could be seen in the sky!

Toward the end of the journey, one of the houseboys said that if my fiancé changed his mind and didn't meet me at the ship, he would marry me so I could stay in Japan—even though he didn't like American women because of their independence.

By the time we neared Yokohama, I felt an intense affection for the group of people who had "adopted" me and helped me to overcome language and cultural differences. The three weeks of raw fish and rice, dirty sheets, rats, community bathing, and learning a foreign language had taught me that I can survive. Most of all, I learned that there is a universal sign language and that cultural barriers can be broken down.

Never underestimate your readers' intelligence or overestimate their information.   An old newspaper saying

A friend of yours wants directions for making wreaths of nuts, cones, and other natural materials to sell at a Christmas bazaar. Or you need to write to your insurance company to claim compensation for several expensive items missing from your car. Or you have just discovered a new bluegrass musician, and you want to tell your friend on a submarine—a bluegrass fan—about the unique banjo-picking style of your find.

Your art history instructor believes in comprehensive exam questions; you expect one something like this on your final: Tell me everything you know about Chagall, or Rembrandt, or Georgia O'Keeffe. Or the owner of the summer camp where you serve as a counselor has asked for a report on all the special activities you designed for your campers this summer, to help her determine who to hire next year. Or your sister, who has a partially deaf ten-year-old, knows that a family on your block also has a youngster with hearing problems, and she has written to ask you about a hearing device that child wears.

To meet the needs of these situations, you will write to inform. That is, you will be passing on information to someone else. Informative writing explains, and often it instructs. It is intended to be useful and practical. And you, the writer, may know a great deal more about your subject than your readers do. That's why you're writing in the first place: to send information from someone who does know to those who don't know.

Complete, accurate, and clear

Because your readers do not already know the information you are sending them, you'll need to take special care to be complete, accurate, and clear. To help you understand the importance of these three guidelines, we would like to show you a sample informative paper on a subject you probably know very little about.

Our writer's purpose in this paper is to inform readers about hypoglycemia, a rather common metabolic condition that can radically affect the everyday lives of its unsuspecting victims. She wants to explain what hypoglycemia is, what symptoms might indicate it, why diagnosis is important, how to find out whether one has it, and what diet to follow if the tests are positive. The paper's focus is determined for her by what she wants to explain and how much information she chooses to convey.

> Facing the fact that you have hypoglycemia is somewhat like an alcoholic's facing the fact that he or she is an alcoholic. From that day forward, if you want to feel good and to function well, you know that you must generally avoid sugary foods—just as the alcoholic must avoid alcohol. And just as with alcoholism, hypoglycemia is much more prevalent than many people realize.
>
> "Hypoglycemia" (*high-po-gly-seé-mee-uh*) means, to put it simply, that you suffer from low blood sugar. What actually happens is that pure sugar in your bloodstream makes your pancreas overproduce insulin, which in turn burns sugar very rapidly. This explains why the "pick-up" candy bar so popular with the unaware, tired hypoglycemic provides the desired sudden spurt of energy—but at the price of a new low as soon as insulin gets to the sugar in the candy bar.
>
> The hypoglycemic person—depending on the rate at which he or she burns sugar—may have functioned fairly well for years prior to suspecting hypoglycemia. But even with a reasonable level of functioning, having yourself tested if you have certain symptoms—irritability, depression, fatigue, lassitude, blurring of vision, difficulty in concentrating—is very important. For hypoglycemia sometimes precedes diabetes, a much more serious condition.
>
> It may not be easy to talk your doctor into the blood sugar test used to discover hypoglycemia; for some reason, many doctors refuse to acknowledge hypoglycemia. If your regular doctor won't cooperate with you, go to another physician, probably an internist. If your sugar test does indicate hypoglycemia, then you will need to attend carefully to what you put into your body—if you want to be a healthy hypoglycemic.

The paper continues with a discussion of foods and beverages the hypoglycemic should include in his or her diet and those to be avoided. These are listed under appropriate headings:

Include: *Avoid:*   *May be used sometimes:*

Next she mentions the effect of both alcoholic beverages and drugs. Finally, the writer explains that the hypoglycemic will probably need to eat more frequently and in smaller portions than formerly, to slow down the insulin overreaction.

Let's look at this paper in terms of our three standards for informative writing: completeness, accuracy, and clarity.

The paper seems complete enough. It defines hypoglycemia, mentions some of the common symptoms, points out its relation to the more serious diabetes, talks about the sugar test used for diagnosis and tells how to get one, and details both an approved food and beverage diet and recommended eating habits for the hypoglycemic. It even notes that hypoglycemics are likely to be more susceptible to drugs than other people are.

How accurate is this writer's information? We, her readers, are not really in a position to know. The writer certainly sounds as if she knows what she's talking about. Though she doesn't overwhelm us with medical terminology, she does give us enough technical information about blood sugar, insulin, the pancreas, and so on, to inspire our confidence in her discussion of hypoglycemia.

The paper is clear enough so that most readers could follow it and use the information if they needed to. Several specific factors contribute to its clarity. First, the writer has used everyday language rather than a lot of technical words that many readers might not understand. Second, she has been careful to define *hypoglycemia* early in the paper. She does not assume that her readers are familiar with the word. She has even taken the trouble to show the reader how to pronounce this big, rather strange-looking word—a minor tactic that can be more important than you might think. Letting readers in on how to say possibly intimidating words can make them feel more in command of what they are reading.

By referring to the "pick-up" candy bar so popular with hypo-glycemics, our writer gives her readers a common hypoglycemic situation that they can identify with. This real-life situation helps to clarify early in the paper how hypoglycemia affects human metabolism. Finally, the information about what a person with hypoglycemia should and should not eat and drink is presented in list form for easy readability and quick reference.

You might want to try out your informative writing on a test reader before you write your final draft. In fact, you might want to use *two* test readers—one to check your rough draft for accuracy, another to test it for completeness and clarity. Choose an expert on your subject to test read for accuracy. For instance, our writer might have enlisted someone in either medicine or nutrition—perhaps a nurse, a medical student, a lab technician, or a dietitian—to test read for accuracy of her paper on hypoglycemia. But to check for completeness and clarity, she would need to ask an average, uninformed reader to help her out. Only an uninformed reader—her real audience, remember—could help her see where to fill in the information gaps and where to clarify. It is probably more important to test your paper on an uninformed reader than on an expert. Why? Because it is too easy to assume that your readers know more than they do.

Opening devices: analogies and rhetorical questions

The writer of our sample informative paper opens the paper with a device that often works well in informative writing: an analogy. In an analogy, an unfamiliar subject (in this case, hypoglycemia) is made clearer by being compared with a more familiar one (alcoholism). In addition to clarifying unfamiliar content, an analogy helps to make readers feel at home with new material. Many readers of this paper may never have heard of hypoglycemia before; however, the chances are good that they know at least something about alcoholism.

Using an analogy can be tricky, though, especially if you try to push it too far. Notice how our writer qualifies her comparison of hypoglycemia and alcoholism:

> Facing the fact that you have hypoglycemia is somewhat like an alcoholic's facing the fact that he or she is an alcoholic. From that day forward, if you want to feel good and to function well, you know that you must generally avoid sugary foods—just as the alcoholic must avoid alcohol.

She says that facing hypoglycemia is *somewhat* like facing alcoholism, and that hypoglycemics must *generally* avoid sugary foods in the same way that alcoholics must avoid alcohol. Both *somewhat* and *generally* are qualifying words; that is, they keep the sentences they appear in honest.

Our writer does not try to extend her analogy too far. No analogy will validly compare every point about an unfamiliar subject with a familiar one. For that to be true, the two things would have to be identical. Actually, this particular analogy could be applied at certain other points in this paper. However, it has served its purpose once it has made the reader feel at home with the unfamiliar subject it has been used to introduce. If you try to extend an analogy too far, it can take over your material, so that you risk losing the focus on your main points as you—and in turn your reader—get caught up in the fascination of the analogy.

Analogies are fun to experiment with. Try one out the next time you need to explain unfamiliar material to someone. But don't push your analogy so far that it either becomes dishonest or overwhelms what you wanted to explain in the first place.

There is another opening device you can use in informative writing to whet the curiosity of your readers and make them want to read on: the rhetorical question. This device poses a question that will be answered by what follows. A reader begins to wonder about the answer as soon as the question is asked—and right away you have an involved reader, one who is in the right frame of mind to absorb your information.

The student writer of an informative paper about some problems in owning an aquarium of live-bearing fish began her paper with two rhetorical questions:

> You wish to start an aquarium of live-bearing fish? Are you aware of how prolific certain live-bearing fish can be?

Here are some other rhetorical questions calculated to engage readers:

1. Does extraterrestrial life exist?

2. Looking for a movie that will keep you laughing all the way home?

3. How can you locate a doctor who believes in "treating the whole person"?

4. How—if at all—should pornography be controlled?

5. What is cloning, and how near is science to being able to clone humans?

Before we leave our discussion of general informative writing, we want to share with you a student's informative paper intended to help a Western host or hostess give a Japanese dinner party. This student has been to Japan, so he knows his subject matter well.

> Traditional Japanese architecture and furnishings are so different from those of the West that it is virtually impossible to reproduce the style of a formal Japanese dinner party outside Japan. Nevertheless, I would like to venture a simple account of certain essentials which a Western hostess can adapt.
>
> In a traditional Japanese room there are no chairs and the guests kneel— or, in the case of men, sit cross-legged—on zabuton (large flat cushions). The zabuton are placed directly on the tatami mats which form the floor. The Japanese table is about the height of a coffee table but has a larger top. This table is usually used for dinner, but for very formal occasions each guest will have his or her own small lacquered table. The place of honor in a Japanese room is in front of the tokonoma, or alcove, which usually has a hanging scroll or a flower arrangement placed in it. The hostess usually occupies the place in front of the door or the one on the opposite side of the table. With the exception of a large wooden paddle used for serving rice, chopsticks are the only utensils in sight.

Prior to the meal each guest is presented with a tightly rolled hand towel which has been dampened with very hot, sometimes scented, water. It is not improper to bury one's face in the oshibori—as this towel is called—for a few seconds, in addition to using it to wipe one's hands.

The food at a Japanese dinner party is always served in individual lacquered or china bowls carefully chosen for shape and color to complement the food that goes in them. Bowls are lifted in the hand for eating from them. Since there are no spoons, soup is drunk from the bowl, and chopsticks are used to eat the fish or vegetables often found in the soup.

The basic Japanese dinner consists of clear soup with a few pieces of meat or vegetables floating in it or a thick soup containing miso (bean paste). The soup is followed by a main course, which ends with plain boiled rice and pickles. Sake (Japanese rice wine) or ochai (green tea) is the beverage. It is rare to have dessert. If dessert is served it is usually fresh fruit in season—or out of season if the hostess is trying to impress some of her guests.

Explaining a process

When you explain to someone in writing how to do something—how to repair a guitar, execute the backstroke, groom a dog, carve a totem pole—you are doing a special kind of informative writing known as process writing. For process writing we would add three more standards to our original three of completeness, accuracy, and clarity: Be direct, concise, and orderly. By *direct*, we mean you should be straightforward and to the point; by *concise*, not waste words; and by *orderly*, put the steps of the process in proper sequence. After all, we usually explain a process so that someone else can do exactly the same thing in exactly the same way.

In the following paper, a student gives directions for constructing a piñata. Notice the clear list of all needed materials early in the paper. Using this list, anyone making a piñata would find it easy to assemble all the supplies ahead of time.

To set the theme for a "south of the border" fiesta, you might make a colorful piñata, a figure filled with edibles and/or party favors, borrowed from Mexico. You will need to start your piñata several days ahead of time, since it contains paste that must dry.

To make a piñata, you will need:

a large balloon (shape depends on figure you want to create)
paste
newspaper (cut into many strips 1½" x 20")
paint (any kind that will stick to newspaper)
decorative materials, such as crepe paper, ribbons, sequins

assorted treats: candy, nuts, miniature party favors, etc.
a sheet of colored paper to match paint
transparent tape

Inflate the balloon. Then dip the newspaper strips in the paste and apply them one at a time to the balloon, leaving a small space clear to put in the party treats later. Continue this procedure until you have four or five layers of newspaper strips on the balloon. Set the balloon aside to dry for a day or two.

When the paste has dried completely, paint your creation any color you want. If you like, you can add such materials as crepe paper, ribbons, sequins, and so on, to make the balloon resemble some figure—perhaps a donkey, or a drum, or a football. To finish off the piñata, fill it with assorted treats and patch up the hole with colored paper and tape. Your piñata is now ready to be hung from the ceiling for your fiesta—and to be smashed to bits for all the goodies to fall out, as the high point of your party.

Illustrations of various kinds—diagrams, charts, graphs, and the like—can often help to clarify process writing. We encourage using this kind of visual reinforcement. However, don't assume that your illustration will explain itself. For a reader unfamiliar with your subject matter, it won't.

Remember that a process paper must enable its readers to perform the activity it explains. There are ways you can test your process paper to insure this. One way is to go through the process yourself, step by step, following your own directions. With this method you must not let yourself take for granted any essential step that you have not actually included in your paper. Don't just fill in the gaps and move ahead; your reader won't be able to do that. Because filling in the gaps can occur so readily when you read your own writing, you may want to ask someone else to test your directions. Then if what you have written needs clarification, you can attend to that before you write your final draft.

If you are assigned a process paper for a college class, you will want to put some thought into choosing your process. Certain processes are almost impossible to explain in words; how to tie a shoe is an example. Furthermore, some process topics almost inevitably produce dull papers. Shoe-tying no doubt would, and tire-changing often does. One of our students decided to write his process paper about building a doghouse and came to class the following week muttering, "I never thought a doghouse could be so boring!" So it will pay you to try to think about what your process is likely to involve before you settle on your topic.

Informing with humor

Sometimes students complain—and with reason—that informative writing is boring to do. And sometimes instructors grow weary of reading relatively dull, flat informative papers. The student paper that follows will prove to you that informative papers can be cleverly written and pleasant to read and still achieve their purpose of conveying information. It is the paper on live-bearing fish whose two opening sentences you read earlier in the chapter.

> You wish to start an aquarium of live-bearing fish? Are you aware of how prolific certain live-bearing fish can be? Black mollies, guppies, sunsets, and swordtails, for example. You may return from the pet shop with a pair of these fish only to wake up the next morning and find thirty new arrivals squirming through the filter's air bubbles—as happened to me. Soon these newcomers grow and contribute to the mass production of live-bearing fish that knows no forty-hour work week. They will fill your bathtub and your kitchen sink; and the sewers of this country must know plenty of their cousins.
>
> You may answer with, "I'll just buy one, or all the same sex." That logical solution is struck down when your single, but once impregnated, female mollie has three broods of fifty fish each without a father in sight; she left him back at the pet shop. Once a live-bearer is pregnant, she may seem to be so continuously. If you do find a group of nonpregnant females, don't be surprised if within a week a few have changed their sex. This common little trick is accomplished only by the females. The fact that males never achieve this feat poses the question, why not have all male fish? Because they will chase each other in dizzying circles, getting so confused that they will eventually commit the ultimate in aquatic suicide—and jump out of the tank!
>
> But don't despair, red velvet swordtail fans, because I have found the solution to the underwater population explosion. Supply your tank with two or three large angel fish, who will delight in a feast of newborn delicacies of swordtails. If you do decide to raise some live-bearing offspring in this same tank, plop a few plants on the surface for their protection from the angel fish. Or if you become a really serious breeder, set up separate maternity tanks for the expectant mothers. There will be plenty of future occupants waiting in line. Plenty!

We should warn you that humor is not always appropriate in informative writing. Although you may want to use it to liven up your freshman English papers, it of course has no place in business reports, records of important meetings, or statements of company policy. Your purpose and your audience will help you determine whether humor belongs in your informative writing.

Informing and other kinds of writing

Since people often need to explain on paper, you might expect to find information in various kinds of writing. And indeed you will. For example, here is a paper in which a student informs her readers about Easter in Sweden by comparing and contrasting it with three American holidays—Easter, Christmas, and Halloween.

One country where the children don't look for the Easter bunny is Sweden. Maybe the reason is that Swedish children have too much to do at that time of year.

Around Eastertime, Swedish boys and girls color eggs, just the way we do. They give each other presents on the Saturday night before Easter, presents of candy and toys and little surprises. These presents are given in egg-shaped boxes, carefully decorated with pretty beads and ribbons and bits of colored paper to look like beautiful Easter eggs. Some Swedish families have Easter trees that are almost as exciting as our Christmas trees. Made out of strong birch branches, they are decorated with blue, green, lavender, red and yellow chicken feathers. They also use other ornaments, like little chickens and paper flowers, to show that spring is coming after the long winter. Swedish fathers often build bonfires on Easter Eve, while the children watch. Swedish mothers make a special feast on the night before Easter, a dinner of special fish, cakes, and good, thick eggnog to drink.

The most exciting part of Swedish Easter for children comes when they dress up in funny costumes and knock on neighbors' doors for goodies, just like our Halloween. The children wear red paint on their faces and carry broomsticks and coffee kettles. They go to each door and say "Glod Pask," which in Swedish means "Happy Easter." Then they rattle their coffee kettles until the neighbors fill them with sweets or pennies or cakes.

You can see that Swedish families have a lot to do to prepare for Easter. They are busy coloring eggs, making boxes and presents, getting their costumes together, decorating their Easter trees, and making ornaments for their Easter tables. Many people in Sweden have never heard of the Easter bunny who hops to American homes to bring presents on Easter.

. . . .
Exercise 1 For class discussion
. . . .

Below are two informative papers on the same subject. Compare them according to the standards for informative writing discussed in this chapter.

1. Anyone can learn to play pinball. All you need is a good eye, a controlled arm, perseverance in practicing, a pocketful of loose change—and a lot of luck.

You should approach the magic machine with respect; after all, it does contain all the answers to the riddles posed by its buttons, bumpers, and bells. After you have bowed before it with proper courtesy, pull back the arm—and say a prayer for luck. If you're lucky, your ball will stay in play and away from the flippers for a long time.

You are bound to score points when you play pinball. But to be really good at it, you will have to "pop" the machine. To learn how to pop, stand and watch what several experienced players do in order to increase their scores; it never hurts to learn from the competition! If you pop regularly enough, you will soon feel that the money you have fed into the maw of this mechanical monster was well spent.

2. Although it looks rather easy, playing pinball well is an art few can master. Not many players can be termed "Pinball Wizards"*—although many lay claim to the title. On the way to becoming a wizard, first you need to understand how to play the game.

After placing your quarter in the machine, gently pull back on the spring-loaded knob which sends the little steel ball into the playing area. The object is simple enough: to keep the ball in the playing area while scoring as many points as you can by hitting buttons, bumpers, bells, even moving targets. To help keep the ball in play, there are two button-controlled flippers, which flip the ball back into the playing area if it should near one of three or four exit holes. You do not want to let the ball get past a flipper and out of play.

Scoring points in pinball isn't hard. You will always score at least 1000 points per ball played, and there are five balls to a game. But to become a great player, a master, you will have to consistently "pop" the pinball machine. Popping the machine means scoring beyond the point total needed to get a free game. This range is usually between 64,000 and 151,000 total points, depending on the machine. While even a good player may score 12,000 to 15,000 points per ball, to pop the more popular machines you would need at least 20,000 to 25,000 points per ball. Only one player out of 1000 can accomplish this with regularity. And only that one can proclaim himself or herself a Pinball Wizard.

* Pinball Wizard: the greatest player of all; the movie *Tommy* was about him.

. . . .

Exercise 2 Written

. . . .

Here are ten possible topics for informative papers. Write out an analogy or a rhetorical question that you could use to begin a paper on at least three of these topics.

1. Keeping a guinea pig or a hamster or some other small animal as a pet in a two- or three-room apartment

2. What to do if you are the first person to arrive at the scene of an automobile accident in which three persons have been injured

3. A job you have held or now hold

4. A new musical group you have heard recently and like

5. A hobby you pursue in which you would like to interest others

6. How to conduct a study of your family's history from colonial times forward

7. Tennis as a mental game as well as a physical one

8. Directions for making something unusual

9. How a person could discover the most appropriate occupation for himself or herself

10. Seals as playful creatures, or big cats as restless ones, or pandas as shy ones, or some other such topic—if you can get to a zoo to gather your information

Exercise 3   Classroom activity

Write an informative paper (not one explaining a process) about something that probably at least one person in your class does not know about. Bring your rough draft in for uninformed persons to read. Is the rough draft complete and clear enough to satisfy your test readers? Is it accurate enough to satisfy you? If the answer to either of these questions is no, do whatever additional background work you need to before writing the final version of your paper.

Exercise 4   Written

Write a process paper on one of the following topics. Assume that someone will use your directions to do whatever activity you write about.

1. training an animal

2. decorating a cake for a special occasion

3. repairing a fence, or a lamp, or a bicycle

4. learning to play a simple musical instrument

5. creating decoupage

6. building a fire outdoors

7. making a clay or ceramic pot

8. creating a flower arrangement

9. carving or sculpting some object

10. explaining how to use a small electronic device
11. teaching a youngster to swim
12. planting a vegetable garden
13. making a quilt
14. creating a needlework design
15. teaching a friend to sail

. . . .

Exercise 5 For class discussion
. . . .

Read the student papers that follow this chapter and come to class prepared to discuss how well they succeed as informative writing.

Sample student papers: informing

25. "Popsicle"

It makes me laugh to hear you say that we "spoil" Chris because she's handicapped—that we give her whatever she wants. Let me tell you what the procedure is in teaching a three-year-old deaf child one word.

One of the tools you need is a small table and chairs set so that the child can get up and down easily. Children generally are unable to sit still for long periods of time and get frustrated if they have difficulty climbing up and down when they need a break. Deaf children have a particular problem here since they do not expend the energy the rest of us do in talking.

Another necessary tool is a set of 3 × 5 cards that contain pictures of the words that Chris has already mastered; i.e., pictures of her mom, dad, and sister, and pictures of a cat and a dog. The other tools you will need are a lot of patience and a ready smile. Since deaf children cannot hear the tone of your voice, they "listen" to your expression and depend on your pleased response for reinforcement.

Okay, you're ready to start the warm-up exercises. Sit in one of the little chairs across from Chris. Show her each picture whose word she has already mastered; praise her when she says the word.

Now you're ready for the new word—"popsicle."

1) Show her the picture of a popsicle.

2) Say "popsicle," slowly and distinctly.

3) Hold the palm of her hand in front of your mouth and say "pah, pah, pah" (so she can feel the puff of air coming from your mouth).

4) Repeat step 3 until she's mastered "pop."

5) Again hold her hand in front of your mouth while you make an exaggerated "s" sound. She must see how your teeth are positioned and feel that the "sssss" produces air from your mouth.

6) For the "c" sound, place one of her hands in front of your mouth so she can feel the air. Place her other hand on your throat so she can feel the sound you make. Show her how to place her tongue on the roof of her mouth to get the hard "c" effect.

7) Repeat step 6 until she's mastered "kah."

8) Now practice the "s-c" sounds together, "sica," using the same methods as in steps 5 and 6.

9) For the "l" sound, show Chris how you roll your tongue to get the "la" sound. Hold her hand against your throat so that she feels the sound.

10) Now you're ready to put it all together. Show her the picture of

the popsicle, place her hand on your throat and say "pop-si-cul," exaggerating every syllable.

You may not get through all ten steps in one day. If she gets tired, push her further than she wants to go, but not to the point where she's frustrated. Or to the point where you're frustrated either. For if you aren't happy and smiling, you'll lose her for sure.

When at last she masters the word "popsicle," give her a popsicle. After you've both gone through "popsicle" every day for two or three weeks, every time Chris says "popsicle" you will both want to celebrate the victory. What better way to let her know she's got the idea than by giving her a popsicle?

Imagine this process with every word Chris learns, and maybe you'll understand why we tend to give her everything she asks for. Everything she asks for is to be celebrated.

26. Phillips Gallery

Washington is a unique city for art lovers. There is something for everyone, and it is all free. On the Mall, the Freer offers its Oriental treasures, the pristine marble of the National Gallery houses the old masters of the Kress and Mellon collections, and the dynamic new Hirshhorn contains the work of artists of this century. Not far away, one can browse in the National Portrait Gallery or experience the Corcoran where something new is always happening. Georgetown and Capitol Hill boast clusters of small commercial galleries abounding with contemporary efforts for those of more adventurous tastes. My favorite Washington gallery, however, is located in the once elegant and still interesting neighborhood surrounding Dupont Circle. There, on 21st Street, just above Massachusetts Avenue, you will find the Phillips Collection.

Duncan Phillips was an art collector extraordinaire. He and his wife, Marjorie, loved the Impressionists, Post-impressionists, and modern masters. Fortunately for us, they acquired their works by the score and hung them with care and pride in their red brick townhouse on 21st Street. When in 1918 Duncan Phillips decided to turn his hobby into a public institution, the house was included. To me, this is the great charm of the Phillips Collection. Many of the paintings today still hang in that original residence.

As you stroll up 21st Street, the townhouse façades conjure up a feeling of a bygone era—an era of teas and debutante parties and glittering balls. Enter the door at 1612, and you find yourself not in a museum but in a gracious home whose owners have been kind enough to ask you in to view their treasures.

Wander at will through the rooms. Bask in the beauty of the Van Goghs, the Degas, the Cézannes. On a quiet day—and it usually is quiet and uncrowded there—you will swear you can hear the tinkle of crystal and the music and laughter of an elegant long-ago party.

Suddenly, in the midst of your musings, you find yourself in a room ablaze with light, color, and life. There on the wall is Renoir's "Luncheon of the Boating Party." Take a seat and treat yourself to a longer look. Settle back and feel the joy and warmth of the painting. Smell the early summer breeze off the Seine. Hear the rustle of the leaves and the hum of the conversation. Stay as long as you like, but remember, there is more.

As the collection grew, it became evident that the Georgian town-house could not adequately display the new acquisitions. So in 1960 a new wing was opened adjoining the Phillips home. It too is beautiful in a different way, and houses the more nearly contemporary part of the collection.

As you enter the new wing, you will feel a quickening, a transition from yesterday to today. Gone are the lovely mantelpieces and views of the charming walled garden. Here all is clean and uncluttered to display to best advantage the blazing colors and stark lines of the modern masters. You will find Picasso and Pollock and Dali and Braque in profusion.

Don't miss the Rothko room. Here, against a black background, are hung Mark Rothko's huge color paintings. As you sit there, you find yourself surrounded by pure, pulsating, sensuous color. Relax. Clear your thoughts and allow yourself to absorb the impact of the blazing reds and yellows, the soothing tranquillity of the blues and greens. The results are unforgettable.

Assuming that you now can't wait to visit the Phillips Collection and claim it for your own, I must warn you that getting there is not half the fun. The neighborhood, while interesting and charming, is a maze of narrow one-way streets totally devoid of parking spaces. However, there are parking lots within two or three blocks, and I promise you the walk will be interesting.

In any event, go and see the Phillips Collection. On Sunday after-noons at five, there is the added bonus of a free concert by talented young musicians. If you are an art lover, you can't miss. If you are not an art lover, you just might become one.

27. Water-skiing to Signals

One of the most important factors in water-skiing is the communication link between the boat and the skier. To ensure that both skier and driver know what is going to happen, a series of signals have been developed. They are as follows:

In gear and hit it: When the skier is in the water ready to go up on the skis, he or she shouts "In gear" to the driver, who puts the engine in gear. As the boat moves away, the slack rope is drawn tight. The skier then yells "Hit it" and the driver throttles forward, pulling the skier out of the water. Use of these commands provides for a safe start without any sudden jerks and without tow ropes tangling around the skier's arms or legs.

Okay signal: After a fall, the skier slaps both hands over his or her head as soon as it's clear there is no injury. The use of two arms is important, as a one-arm wave could be misinterpreted as a wave for help, or it might be thought that the other arm is injured and cannot be raised.

Take me home: When the skier pats the top of his or her head, it means "That's enough and let's return to the dock."

Turn: When either the skier or the driver circles an arm above his or her head in either direction, the need for a turn is being indicated.

Speed okay: An "O" made with the thumb and index finger is a sign that the skier is satisfied with the speed of the boat.

Speed up: The thumbs-up gesture is used by the skier to indicate a need or a desire for more speed.

Slow down: The thumbs-down gesture is used by the skier to indicate that less speed is needed.

Cut the engine: A "slit the throat" motion with the arm indicates that the boat is to be stopped. This signal can be used by driver, skier, or observer. At the time of this signal the skier assumes a position directly behind the boat between the two wakes.

Some skiers develop additional signals for even more effective communication between the skier and the boat. For instance, the observer may hold his or her arms extended to signal the skier to straighten his or her arms. If additional signals are developed, all those involved with the skier should be familiar with them. In any case, the signals listed above should be retained, as they are universal in the water-skiing world and can be correctly interpreted just about anywhere.

28. Growing Orchids

For a long time I had wanted an orchid—not the corsage type you pin on, but the plant. Since I didn't know many people who had orchid plants, I thought growing one would be interesting. If you have always heard that it is impossible to grow orchids in this area without a greenhouse, don't believe it. With a little extra care, it is possible to grow an orchid in your home.

About two months ago I finally got my orchid, a *Dendrobium pierardii*. When I bought it in Florida, where orchids are much cheaper than they are here, I was told that I would not be able to keep it alive in Maryland and that it certainly would not make the long ride home. Well, it made it. My *Dendrobium pierardii* was alive and well upon arrival. As a matter of fact, it was even blooming.

A *Dendrobium pierardii* is not my idea of a typical orchid. The plant grows upside down and is attached to a piece of bark. It consists of ten to fifteen stems up to three feet long, which are covered with dozens of two-inch rose-lavender flowers as the plant blooms. It blooms only once a year, with the blossoms lasting about ten days. Unfortunately, after the flowers have gone, you are left with a lot of sticks growing from a clump of roots. But if you watch the plant carefully, you will soon see a few purple-green nubs appearing on some of the sticks. These are the new stems starting so that next year you will have even more blooms.

Orchids grow best in areas with high humidity. In a very dry house the plant needs to be misted often (two or three times a day)—but never watered. An atomizer or plant mister should be used so that the orchid gets a fine spray. While there are blooms, don't allow much water to get on the flowers. If you would like to give the plant a treat, try hanging it in the bathroom when people are taking showers. It can then soak up all the moisture it wants. Dendrobiums need to be misted heavily during their growing season, from June to October. During that time they should also be fertilized every week or two with a diluted solution of well-balanced plant food. The temperature in the room where they are kept should not go below 55 or 60 degrees.

After October, when the new stems are fully grown, the dendrobium needs to be dried into dormancy. The leaves will dry and fall off. If the stems begin to shrivel, the plant must be given water, but only a little. Around February buds will begin forming, and by middle to late March there will be dozens of tiny orchids. Somewhere near that time, the plant can be watered again.

Now if you think that you might like to have orchids blooming in your home, try a *Dendrobium pierardii*, or maybe some other orchid that likes basically the same environment. And don't believe those who tell you that you won't be able to keep it alive. My dendrobium is alive and quite happy in its new home.

29. Children's Hospital

The little children in their gowns dart in and out of the playhouse. Laughing and shrieking, they scurry from one plaything to another, overwhelmed by the abundance of toys, books, and games. Except for the nervous parents sitting quietly among the toys, this room could be any well-stocked playroom. But it is a very special playroom. It is exceptional simply because it is here—in the operating suite of a large hospital. And it is only one of the ways in which Children's Hospital strives to alleviate the fears of its young patients.

I imagine that most parents dread taking their child to the hospital for surgery. Perhaps this dread is due to our own vague recollections of childhood surgery. Do you recall being confined to bed and rolling down the hall toward the operating room, as you looked back at concerned, nervous parents and wondered if Mom would be there when you got back? You may even have wondered if you would be coming back. The people who work at Children's Hospital endeavor to change this frightening experience.

To effect this change, they invite the future patients and their families to a guided tour of the hospital on the Sunday before the scheduled surgery. The first stop on the tour is a semiprivate room in a surgical unit. Here the guide demonstrates the use of the call button and the bed controls. She carefully points out the two extra beds that are provided for the mothers and assures the future patients that Mom will be allowed to remain with them. Next the guide shows the children the bathroom and warns them they may not feel capable of walking immediately after surgery. Then she shows the bedpans and kidney basins to the children, as she explains how they are used.

The guide then leads the group to an examining room. Here, with the assistance of some of the future patients, she demonstrates the use of the digital thermometer, blood pressure cuff, stethoscope, ophthalmoscope, and auriscope. The volunteers in these demonstrations assure the other children that these instruments are completely painless. All the children are then encouraged to try these items on each other. They peer into each other's ears and eyes, listen to their hearts beat, and wrap the blood pressure cuff around each other's arms. By the time the children leave the examining room, they are all certain that these instruments will not inflict any pain.

The next stop on the tour is the O.R. playroom. This is the playroom in the operating suite, where, on the morning of their surgery, the children will play until the anesthetist is ready for them. The guide explains that the anesthetist will help the children go to sleep and make sure they do not wake up until the surgery is completed. During the tour the children are not allowed to play in this enticing room, but they are promised that they will be permitted to play here on the day of their surgery.

Then the guide escorts the group next door to the parents' waiting room. She tells the children that Mom and Dad will be with them until they are asleep, but the parents will wait here while they are in surgery and recovery, which she calls the wake-up room. Next the guide helps the children dress in surgical gowns, hats, masks, and shoe covers, as she explains that the doctors and nurses will be wearing these strange garments in the operating and recovery rooms. The black mask, she informs the children, is to help them go to sleep. As the future patients try on the ether mask, she asks each child what he or she thinks the mask smells like.

The group is then escorted to the cafeteria and served cookies and punch. The guide now circulates among the tables, answering questions and giving any further reassurance that may be needed. After the children have finished their cookies and punch, they are taken to see a puppet show about a little girl who has her tonsils removed.

When the day of surgery arrives, only Mom and Dad appear to be nervous. The patient—in this instance, our son Jon—seems perfectly at ease as he joins the other patients in the O.R. playroom. When the anesthetist comes for him, the patient is accompanied by his parents into the induction room, where he is gently anesthetized while holding hands with Mom and Dad. After the child is asleep, the anesthetist collects any pacifier, security blanket, or favorite stuffed cuddle-buddy that the patient has brought with him. These comforting objects are sent to the recovery room to help soothe the child as he wakes up.

Instead of being confined to bed following the surgery, the patient is encouraged to visit the unit's playroom. A child may be up and playing within two or three hours of his operation. If he feels like it, he is even allowed to accompany his parents to the cafeteria for meals.

From the pre-surgical tour to the postoperative care, the people who work at Children's Hospital strive to comfort, inform, and reassure their young patients. As a result of these innovative procedures, surgery is no longer a frightening and bewildering experience at Children's Hospital.

30. Dogs, Cats, And Beethoven

Pets may not know much about music, but they know what they like. Just try turning up your favorite record of Stravinsky or Hindemith and watch how Fido or Felix reacts. Chances are good that they will tell you plainly you're insulting their eardrums; taste has nothing to do with it.

I happen to be fond of classical music and have a modest library of recordings from Elizabethan lute music to composers like Lukas Foss. Whenever I play anything dissonant or atonal, my dog J.J. disappears under the bed or runs out of the room. If our other dog, Ginger, is awake, her ears twitch as though she were suddenly afflicted with mites, but if she is upside down on the rug asleep, she doesn't move a muscle. She is blessed with that kind of imperturbability that allows her to go through life with her nerves virtually intact. On the other hand, she displays real pleasure if I put on Schubert's "Trout" Quintet or a Bach Brandenburg Concerto. She faces the record player and hunkers down as though to concentrate. Coloratura sopranos and solo violins drive both dogs into a frenzy. Mozart is received happily no matter what the selection; popular music is ignored.

Since the hearing range for both dogs and cats is much wider than for humans (my neighbor swears her cat comes running from half a block away whenever she slams the refrigerator door), it is not surprising that they are sensitive to music. Both dogs and cats can distinguish between two notes separated by as little as one-fourth the range between two notes on the piano. But though they may be able to distinguish quarter-tones and halftones, they seem to prefer harmony.

Moppet, a white Persian who lives in New York, has a passion for strings: chamber orchestras, quartets, trios, whatever. I have seen her stretched out on an ottoman in front of the record player, eyes shut, the expression on her face nothing short of ecstatic, listening to the famous "Canon in D Major" by Pachelbel. At Haydn's "Trumpet Concerto" she yawned and walked out.

A beagle I knew used to throw his head back and bay at the ceiling every time he heard a violin playing solo. The cello, however, didn't bother him at all. Something to do with pitch, no doubt. A miniature poodle of my acquaintance barks frantically at both violins and flutes but seems to enjoy, of all things, ragtime.

I have known pets who paid no attention whatever to music coming out of a box: radio, television, or tape recorder. Other animals, however, respond as well to canned music as to the real thing. Many years ago a friend told me her cat positioned itself in front of the radio every Sunday afternoon in time to hear the concert from the New York Philharmonic. The cat never missed a season. An owner of three collies told me that two of them sit up at attention whenever they hear band music on the radio or television, especially "Stars and Stripes Forever," while the third dog ignores it completely. "I think she's tone deaf," her owner says.

In the evening paper recently I read about Muff, a stray cat adopted by a Pasadena, California, gentleman who plays the organ. One evening the man said to his wife, "Here's a tune for Muff," and dashed off a song he remembered from his childhood: "Kitty, my pretty gray kitty, why do you scamper away? I've finished my work and my lessons, and now I am ready for play." Immediately Muff came over and jumped onto the bench beside him. From that day on, every time he plays that song Muff comes over to sit beside him. She knows her theme song.

PART FIVE

Research writing

Research writing

What is research but a blind date with knowledge?   Anonymous

Many composition courses devote a section to research writing, which is designed to teach you both how to find information and how to document the sources of the information in your papers. Finding such information and documenting it may seem at first an awkward and bewildering process, but a sincere attempt at preparing the paper your instructor assigns should begin to convince you otherwise. You will learn that information on almost any subject is readily available, that within ten minutes you can find a dozen articles on everything from commercial use of musk-ox fur to New Wave rock music. You will also learn that incorporating information from sources in a paper does not need to be any more difficult than repeating a story your grandfather once told you. Basically, the statement, "When I was ten my grandfather told me . . ." is replaced by something like "According to the *Statistical Abstract of the United States*. . . ." In formal research papers, you add a footnote to indicate exactly where in that volume you found the information.

Through the years standard rules for using and identifying sources of information have evolved. These rules, which will be discussed in this chapter, are designed to assure accuracy, to give the reader confidence in your information, and to give credit to the individuals whose ideas and facts you are drawing on. Following these rules takes patience and discipline, but will in the long run save you time and improve your grade.

Although students tend to exaggerate the difficulties in writing research papers, some of the protests instructors hear are understandable. It does take time to write a research paper, and almost everyone has at some time cursed the awkwardness of taking notes from that necessary modern monster, the microfilm machine.

One protest, however, is less and less valid: the protest that "I will not have to do research in my job." It may have been true in the past that work involving formal research techniques was not demanded of most people, even college-educated people; but that day, for better or worse, has passed. Because society is so complex today, because new information is accumulated so fast, and because the firms or government agencies for which we work are so large, the more casual approach of the past is less and less possible. Nurses may have to participate in studies that compare their pay scales to the pay scales of nurses in other area hospitals. Police may be called upon to evaluate the accuracy of various kinds of lie detector machines. Even so seemingly simple a decision as the brand of electric typewriter a firm should buy may today involve the expenditure of thousands and thousands of dollars, and the budget-minded executive may well demand a thorough study of the long-term costs of upkeep and of ribbons for a particular brand.

Even if in your job you are never asked to submit a report on the safety of recreational equipment or on advances in computer technology, learning your way around a library will give you a sense of confidence, an assurance that you will know how to find information when you need it. And, unlike writing the report on typewriter brands, writing the college research paper can be enjoyable if you choose your subject carefully, for it gives you an ego-boosting sense of expertise on a particular subject.

Retaining your voice

Students who otherwise write clearly often lose their voices when they write research papers. They turn in papers that resemble patchwork quilts or scrapbooks, papers that are merely collections of other people's ideas. Do not let yourself be intimidated by your sources. Unless your paper is a simple factual report, it will, like all your other essays, revolve around an idea or opinion or conclusion that is your own. Your contribution may seem small and may consist primarily of a thesis statement and topic sentences, but the thesis statement and topic sentences are *your* conclusions, even if all your supporting evidence comes from sources.

For instance, three students in one class each decided to write a paper on Laetrile, a controversial cancer drug that is legal in Mexico but illegal in most American states. All three students read approximately the same articles, but came to somewhat different conclusions.

> Although individual cancer patients claim to have been helped by Laetrile, scientific study after scientific study has found no evidence that its use stops or slows down the spread of cancer.

> No scientific evidence exists that Laetrile retards the growth of cancer, and therefore the United States government should continue to ban its use. Its

legalization would only encourage people with cancer to avoid legitimate treatment and to put money into the hands of unethical physicians.

Although no scientific evidence exists that Laetrile stops or slows down the spread of cancer, neither does sure scientific evidence exist that its use is harmful. Until evidence that it is harmful does exist, the government should allow its use, for Laetrile at least provides victims of cancer a hope, a hope that could give them strength.

The three students seem to agree that there is no scientific evidence (at least in 1980) that Laetrile is effective in fighting cancer, and each goes on to establish that through reference to books and articles. The second student, however, has decided also to argue that the ban on its use in the United States should continue—a position he will probably bolster with the arguments of government officials and physicians and with his own observations about human nature. The third student apparently agrees with the other two about the scientific evidence, but has decided that legalizing the drug will do no harm and might even help patients psychologically. This student had an uncle who went to Mexico for cancer treatment in the last year of his life. What she knows about her uncle's treatment and death adds little to our scientific knowledge about Laetrile, but is very relevant to her decision as to whether Laetrile should be banned.

All three of these theses are legitimate, and they are the students' own. Each student decided after reading a number of sources what he or she wanted to say, and organized the thesis and paper accordingly. Each decided how seriously to take personal testimonials on the effectiveness of Laetrile and how conclusive the scientific research had been. And each grouped the various opinions in ways that fit into his or her paper.

The research-paper thesis

For most of the papers you have been writing this semester, you probably began with a thesis and then found evidence (usually from personal experience) to prove it. For the research paper you will need to reverse the process: you'll look at the evidence first (primarily in books and magazines) and then come to a conclusion. That conclusion will be your thesis.

For instance, let's say that you have chosen to write your research paper on the controversy over grizzly bears in the national parks. You will find as you read that attacks on people by grizzly bears have increased dramatically in Yellowstone and Glacier National Parks in recent years, mostly because more people are in the parks and the bears are becoming aware that they can find food where humans camp. Some individuals have even advocated removing the bears from areas where they might come in contact with tourists or campers. Others argue that if the national parks are to preserve what is left of wild America, visitors to the parks must accept the possibility of danger—that to remove all dangers would turn Yellowstone and Glacier into Disneylands.

Unless you have encountered a grizzly bear yourself, you will probably take all your information on attacks from sources. You will read different opinions about what should be done. But in the end it is you who must formulate the thesis, which will depend on how you feel about dangerous wildlife. Don't make the mistake of accepting the first written opinion you find and trying to compose a paper to back up that writer's opinion; other writers may think differently, or you may change your mind. And accepting the first opinion you read violates a basic principle of research, that you choose from and use a number of sources.

When finally you arrive at a thesis, you will put it into an introductory paragraph in pretty much the way you have been doing for your other papers. The research-paper thesis may differ from the theses you have been writing in two ways, however: 1) Because the subject may be more complex, the thesis may be more than one sentence long; and 2) because the research paper may be longer than papers you have been writing, the thesis is more likely to set up the major divisions of the paper, as an aid to both you and the reader. (For an example of a research-paper thesis, you can turn to the sample paper following this chapter.)

Finding sources and limiting your subject

An instructor will usually assign a general subject for the research paper or suggest specific subjects of current interest. Your first task, therefore, is to trek to the college library and begin making a list of sources. This list is called a *preliminary bibliography.*

As you locate a source, write down all the necessary information for finding the source and for footnoting later. For books you will need 1) the author or editor; 2) the title of the book; 3) the place of publication; 4) the publisher; 5) the date of publication; and 6) the call number. For magazine articles you will need 1) the author; 2) the title of the article; 3) the name of the magazine or newspaper; 4) the volume number; 5) the date of the issue; and 6) the page numbers.

Most writers find it handy to keep the information for each source on a file card like the sample that follows.

QL
696
S8
M23
1966A

Faith Mc Nulty
The Whooping Crane
New York
E. P. Dutton + Co.
1966

What sort of material you are going to locate and read will depend on the subject you have chosen or been assigned and how much you already know about the subject. You may at times feel like the foreign student in a physical education class who is assigned a paper on American football: he not only does not know the rules but has seen no football game other than the tag game running continually outside his dormitory window. If he cannot persuade his instructor to allow him to write on soccer, this student is obviously going to have to begin with general reading about football, which many American students would find unnecessary.

Don't despair if you find yourself in a similar situation. The sample research paper that follows this chapter is from a class in which students were asked to investigate the status of an endangered species. Many knew nothing about the species they chose before writing the paper, but still produced good research papers.

Step one: *General reading*
Many students make the mistake of reading material on a particular aspect of a subject before they have a clear overall view of the subject itself. If you know very little about a subject or need to brush up on what you once knew, go first to an encyclopedia or other general reference work. (These, which cannot be checked out, are usually kept in a separate section of the library.) With the background obtained from this general reading, you will better understand more specialized material you will read later, and you may find that other aspects of a general subject interest you more than the one that interested you initially. For instance, a student who was going to write a paper on the relationship between oil

companies and the Ute Indians of Colorado and Utah decided after reading a general article that he preferred to write on the use of the drug peyote in Ute religious worship.

The encyclopedia most widely used by college students is the *Encyclopaedia Britannica,* which is now divided into a ten-volume micropedia (with brief articles on tens of thousands of subjects) and a twenty-volume macropedia (with longer, more detailed articles on thousands of subjects). The micropedia will indicate where in the macropedia you will find more detailed discussions of your subject. Probably handier but briefer will be the articles in the one-volume *Columbia Encyclopedia.* For illustrated articles, you may want to try *The Random House Encyclopedia.*

Almost all areas of study have encyclopedias and reference works that go into more detail than even such a large reference work as the *Encyclopaedia Britannica* can. There are hundreds of these, and while there is no reason for you to learn the names of them all, you might want to know the names of some of those in your major field. For instance, if you are a biology major, you might find it handy to know of the *Encyclopedia of the Biological Sciences;* or if you are an engineering major, of *The McGraw-Hill Encyclopedia of Science and Technology;* or if you are in any technical field and like lots of illustrations, of *The Way Things Work: An Illustrated Encyclopedia of Technology.* Music majors should certainly know of the twenty-volume *Grove Dictionary of Music and Musicians,* which in 1980 appeared in its sixth edition, or of a number of even more specialized music encyclopedias, such as the *Encyclopedia of Pop, Rock, and Soul,* the source you might go to to find out how many top-ten hits Dinah Washington had in the 1960s, or when Diana Ross parted from the Supremes.

The sample research paper following this chapter is on the whooping crane, a bird the student first read about in two reference works on endangered species, *Wildlife in Danger* and *Extinct and Vanishing Birds of the World.* (A more up-to-date source would have been the new *Audubon Encyclopedia of American Birds.*) Such reference works can be located in one of four ways: 1) by consulting the card catalogue; 2) by going to the reference shelves directly (reference works are usually arranged by subject); 3) by consulting a reference work on reference works (there actually are such books); or 4) by consulting the reference librarian, whose job is to help you find source material.

Step two: **Locating magazine articles**
Most students choose topics of current interest when writing a research paper, and material on such subjects is most readily found in magazine articles. It is not unusual for 90 percent of a student's source material to be from magazines.

The traditional place to look for magazine articles on your subject is the indispensable *Reader's Guide to Periodical Literature,* an annual compilation by author and subject of articles in about 160 periodicals of general interest. (Articles published in the current year may be found in paperback indexes that come out every month.) Don't give up if you don't find what you are looking for under the first heading you try; whooping cranes, for instance, are listed under "Cranes," as in this entry from the 1979–80 edition:

CRANES (birds)
    Teamwork helps the whooping crane. R.C. Drewien
        and E. Kuyt. il pors maps Nat Geog 155: 680-93
        My '79
    Whooping crane; a success story. B. Hamilton. il Sierra
        64: 56-61 My '79

The shorthand technique of the *Reader's Guide* may appear puzzling at first, but it is easy to read once you get the hang of it. First appears the title of the article, for instance, "Whooping Crane: A Success Story." Then come the initials and last name of the author or authors; for instance, B. Hamilton. Then appear abbreviations giving other information about the article. In the first of the two entries above, for example, *il* indicates that the article is illustrated; *pors* indicates that the article has portraits; and *maps* indicates that it contains maps. Next comes the name of the magazine—above, *National Geographic* and *Sierra.* (If you can't figure out the abbreviation for the magazine, turn to the list of abbreviations at the front of each *Reader's Guide.*) "155:680-93" following the first entry indicates that the article is in volume 155, begins on page 680, and runs to page 693. "My '79" gives the date, May 1979. You should write all this down, except for the information about illustrations and maps, when you are gathering your bibliography.

Although the *Reader's Guide* remains the magazine index with which instructors are most familiar, students and researchers more and more make use of handier indexes printed on microfilm, such as *The Magazine Index,* an easy-to-use machine that indexes articles in the same way as *Reader's Guide* but covers a number of years and is kept continually up-to-date by inserts of new microfilm. Unlike the individual volumes of *Reader's Guide,* which often get scattered over the reference room by students, the machine stays in the same place and is lost only when its gears fail to function properly.

For most undergraduate papers the *Reader's Guide* or a microfilm resource like *The Magazine Index* will provide sufficient material, but

periodical indexes in specific fields cover the many scholarly and technical publications that the *Reader's Guide* and *The Magazine Index* do not.
A nursing student might want to know of the *Cumulative Index to
Nursing Literature;* a sociology student, of *Sociological Abstracts.* These
specialized indexes are rarely found in public libraries, but should be on
the shelves near the *Reader's Guide* in college libraries.

Indexing today is marvelously efficient, but there is still no easy way
to find articles about an event that took place last month. In that case,
go to the magazine section of the library and start thumbing; *Time*
and *Newsweek* at least will have articles on any very recent event of
importance.

Step three: **Locating books**
With almost any subject, you will want to check the card catalog for the
library's book holdings. The student writing on the whooping crane
found one book entirely on the crane and one partly on it in the card
catalog under the subject heading "Whooping Crane." If your subject is
Thomas Jefferson, abortion, or Stoicism, you will find a great many more
books than you would on the whooping crane and will be forced to select
carefully those you are going to note. (Later in this chapter we will
discuss a process you might follow if you must work primarily from
books and there are a great many books on your subject.)

Here is a sample of a card catalog entry under the subject "Whooping
Crane":

QL
696.
G8
M23
1966a
	WHOOPING CRANE
	
	McNulty, Faith.
	    The whooping crane; the bird that defies extinction. In-
	trod. by Stewart L. Udall. [1st ed.,] New York, Dutton,
	1966.
	      190 p. illus. 25 cm.
	
	    1. Whooping crane.
	
	   QL696.G8M23 1966a 598.3 66–11544
	
	  Library of Congress [3]

The catalog card gives a great deal of information, including the size of
the book and its total number of pages, but you will need to copy down

only the author's name, the title, the place of publication, the publisher, the date of publication, and the call number, which appears in the upper left corner.

Step four: **Locating news stories**

If you need for your paper up-to-date information or an account of a recent event of importance, the newspaper is probably your best bet, as it was for the student writing on the whooping crane. Although several American newspapers—the *Washington Post,* for example—are now publishing indexes, the *New York Times Index* is the oldest (going back to 1851) and still the most thorough. Like the *Reader's Guide,* the *New York Times Index* is an annual compilation with biweekly compilations for the current year. As can be seen in the sample below, the index also includes a handy one- or two-sentence summary of the story's content. Don't despair if there is nothing under the first subject heading you try; whooping cranes, for instance, are listed here under "Birds" and the subheading "Cranes."

> Coots. See also Hunting, F 24
> Cranes
>   Wildlife biologists reptdly are hopeful that 4 young whooping cranes that were born in Idaho during summer of '75 and recently migrated into wildlife refuge near Monte Vista (Colo), will form nucleus of new flock of endangered species (S), Mr 6,50:2; birdwatcher John Savage describes visit to Bosque del Apache Natl Wildlife Refuge (Sorocco, NM); notes 2 young whooping cranes raised by 'foster parent' sandhill cranes during '75 in Canada are wintering in area; says they are 1st whoopers to visit NM since 1850s; Tom Smylie notes there are only 48 wild whooping cranes in existence, excluding '75 hatch; illus (L), Mr 7,X, p9; Patuxent Wildlife Research Center head Dr Cameron Kepler says whooping crane chick was hatched May 5; birth expands whoopers' world population to 85; if chick survives, it will be 1st whooper successfully hatched and grown from parents raised in captivity (S), My 6,23:1
>   Fed Appeals Ct, New Orleans, refuses to consider decision

A shorthand entry like "Mr 6,50:2" gives first the date, then the page number, then the column; this one would be translated as March 6, page 50, column 2. Note that titles and authors are not usually given; those you will have to take down when you read the story.

Step five: **Finding other information**

Most if not all the source material you need may be found in the card catalog and in newspaper and periodical indexes, but if at some point you need further information, you almost certainly can find it in the library. There are, for instance, a number of sources for statistics. The United States Bureau of the Census each year publishes the *Statistical Abstract of the United States,* a compilation of the principal statistical information produced by the federal government. Statistics for the past may be found in *Historical Statistics of the United States, Colonial Times to 1957. Statistics Sources* will show you where to find data on industrial and business matters.

Just ask the librarian!

A review of the process

Let's move through the research process with a student who has not been assigned a specific topic like "The Status of an Endangered Species" and who has a subject that requires using more books than the whooping crane paper would.

Let's say that you are assigned a paper on some aspect of American history from 1776 to 1865. The professor obviously does not want a summary of George Washington's life or the sequence of events at Bull Run, but rather wants a paper that develops a fairly precise thesis. You obviously do not want a subject like "The Causes of the Civil War," which would involve vast amounts of reading and to which you could contribute few comments of your own. What you should do is find a subject that has caught your interest—for instance, Thomas Jefferson— and then find a topic about Jefferson that is limited enough (his interest in music, his theories of architecture, his relationship with Lafayette) for you to emerge from the paper with a reasonable expertise. You are best off if you also find a topic about which you can make some observations of your own, such as comparing Jefferson's views on states' rights to those prevalent today.

If you are interested in Jefferson but know little about him, you might first go to an article on him in either the *Encyclopaedia Britannica* or the *Dictionary of American Biography,* a standard reference work with articles on most notable Americans of the past. While reading one of these reference works, you might become interested in the fact that Jefferson frequently condemned slavery and yet owned slaves until the end of his life. (In all probability he even had several children by one slave, Sally Hemmings.) You decide at this point that your specific subject will be "Thomas Jefferson and Slavery."

The best approach now is probably to go to the card catalog or to the shelves where the books on Jefferson are kept. You will certainly not have time to read many of these books, but by using their indexes you may be able to read parts of what a number of authors say about Jefferson and slavery. These books will probably also lead you to those places in Jefferson's writing where he commented on slavery. This is not the most thorough approach, of course, but as an undergraduate you work under great time limitations, and your instructor knows that.

With a subject like Jefferson and slavery, most of the material will be in books, but you will also want to consult the *Reader's Guide* for recent years to see if writers are still commenting on the paradoxes of Jefferson's attitudes toward slavery.

Taking notes

You will not be far into your reading before your thesis will begin to take shape, however much it may later have to be modified. At this point you should begin taking notes. The best method of taking notes is to put each quotation, piece of information, or observation of your own on an individual note card, giving that card a label that will correspond to one of the sections of the paper.

The student writing on the whooping crane realized early in his reading, for example, that his thesis would be a generally optimistic statement about the crane's chances for survival. He also realized what the major sections of his paper would probably be about and labeled his cards accordingly. He soon could even see subheadings developing—for instance "Texas–Canada Flock—Hunting Dangers."

The most important thing to remember in taking notes is to be accurate. Be sure your summaries reflect what the text actually says; be sure when you quote that you quote *exactly;* be sure that you will be able to tell later what is *directly* quoted and what is not; be sure you note the *exact* page or pages on which the information appears. Such care will help avoid later trips to the library for checking—and burns from your instructor's red pen.

There are three general ways of noting a passage. The first is to summarize part of the article, as on the following card. Be certain that when you summarize, you do not "half-copy"—that is, rely too much on the wording of the text. Obviously you will be repeating some of the words in the text in your summary; but in general, when a series of words on your note card is exactly the same as a series of words in the text, you should put the words in quotation marks. To prevent half-copying, you may find it best to summarize without looking at the article and *then* check for accuracy. (See the later section on "Writing the Paper" for examples of the form of plagiarism known as half-copying.)

Texas-Canada flock — Hunting Dangers
Pressure to open up more access to
swan and sandhill crane hunting
could endanger whooper because of
its similarity to these birds.
Author thinks, however, that
fear of public wrath if a whooper shot
will prevent this. North Dakota,
e.g., will not allow sandhill crane
hunting until certain all whoopers
gone for year.
— Sherwood, 84

The second method of noting is to quote directly. This method is most frequently used with statements of opinion, for it is very important that someone's opinion not be distorted by your rewording. The following directly quoted passage could have been summarized, for it is not opinion but observation, but the student was impressed by the quality of the author's description.

Life - Cycle - Aransas

"It appears that the presence of the youngster stimulates a quicker temper and a fiercer attachment to home. Thus parents will defend their territory with greater determination than a childless couple, and usually triumph in dispute. A mated pair, though childless, in turn makes stronger territorial claims than do either the lonely 'singles'—who may be widowed or adolescent birds—or 'companions,' birds whose relationship is purely platonic. Singles or companions surrender their territory to the first challenger. They then wander, living hand to mouth as it were, chivied by the lords of whatever territories they chance to invade." [19]

McNulty, pp. 69-70

The third method, probably the most useful, is to summarize, but to quote key words and phrases, especially those that are skillfully used.

Life - Cycle — Mating Dances

    Mating dances begin in late December — but only become intense 2-3 months later. In dances birds leap, bow, posture. Because of crane's "immense size," this is "one of the great dances of the bird world." By March dances are "an almost daily occurrence."

                        Allen, pp. 68-70

Since the development of duplicating machines, students are using other methods of note-taking more and more. Particularly if you are working from magazine or newspaper articles, you can duplicate some or all of your source material inexpensively, which allows you to work from it at home rather than take notes in the library. One Soviet researcher now living in the United States calls our duplicating machines "the best thing about working in the United States." In the Soviet Union, he says, "I spent 50 percent of my time sitting in the library copying notes out of books."

Duplication, however, does not make the traditional methods of taking notes completely obsolete. With a large number of duplicated pages, you will still need to locate specific information in articles quickly. In recent years, some students have developed ingenious methods of avoiding the laborious task of note-taking. One student, writing on Stanley Kubrick's film *2001: A Space Odyssey,* decided what the divisions of her paper would be and bought eight different colored pencils, with which she marked the duplicated articles as she read.

Most likely, however, even if you are going to duplicate articles, you are best off sticking to some variation of the traditional method of note-taking, as the student writing on the whooping crane did in the note on p. 265. He described part of an article briefly and indicated exactly to the column where the discussion may be found. If your articles are long, you may even want to note the paragraph in which the information appears (for instance, "Green, p. 67, col. 1, para. 3").

Although duplication may enhance accuracy because you can check the sources quickly, it may encourage the rushed student to rely too

> *Life - Cycle — Summer*
> *Describes in detail nesting,*
> *hatching, rearing process.*
>
> *— Guthery, p. 19,*
> *col. 2*

heavily on the wording of the source, sometimes unintentionally. *Don't*—both because this is plagiarism (copying someone else's work without giving proper credit to the source) and because such heavy reliance on someone else's wording will interrupt the smooth flow of your own style through the paper.

As you approach your final thesis, you may tend to note only those opinions or that information that will support it. But remember also to note information and opinions that may weaken or oppose your position, to be fair and to make your argument most impressive by facing up to the strength of its opposition.

Writing the paper

After you have finished taking notes and have some rough idea of your thesis, you will want to polish the thesis and sketch an outline before beginning your rough draft. By this time you will know a great deal about your subject, probably more than you realize. It is therefore best to set aside your notes and work on your thesis and rough outline without them. With so many facts, figures, and opinions in front of you, it is sometimes difficult to see the forest for the trees. A good way to start— and to prove to yourself how much you know—might be to take a friend aside and tell him or her what you plan to say about your subject in the paper. If you feel you have presented a reasonably well-organized oral argument, that presentation probably can become the basis for the first draft of your outline.

Once you have polished the outline and again referred to your notes, you should be ready to begin writing. As you write you will for the most part simply back up the statements in your outline with your own observations and material from your notes.

It is extremely important in both taking notes and writing your paper not to rely too closely on the wording or organization of paragraphs in your sources. Such reliance is a form of plagiarism known as "half-copying," one of the most frequent problems an instructor meets in undergraduate papers.

Following are a passage from an article in *Smithsonian* magazine and a paragraph in which a student relied too heavily on the wording and organization of the *Smithsonian* original.

> *Original:* Allowing the entire wild population to remain concentrated at Aransas in winter, and Wood Buffalo in summer, also seemed imprudent. They were—and are—vulnerable to a wide variety of disasters. Epidemic illness is one. At Aransas, a late-season hurricane could decimate the band. So might an oil spill, or a toxic chemical that leaked from one of the many barges that pass through the refuge on the intracoastal waterway.

> *Student version* (too close to the original): It seemed unwise to allow the entire wild population to remain concentrated in one place in winter and one place in summer. There are many disasters that could strike. Epidemic illness could eliminate the flock. A late-season hurricane could wipe out the band. An oil spill might occur, or chemicals could leak from one of the barges that pass through the refuge on the intracoastal waterway.[8]

Notice that the student has borrowed too many phrases from her source and that she has modeled the organization of her paragraphs too closely on that of the original. Such borrowing, even though it ends with a footnote, is theft—perhaps unintentional, but theft nonetheless.

To protect yourself from the charge of academic dishonesty, you need to present your source material in one of two ways. Either quote the material word for word and end it with a footnote or present the material in your own words, as this student has done:

> When the entire wild population of whooping cranes is concentrated in one area, it is vulnerable to disasters that might wipe out the entire flock. *Smithsonian* cites the possibility of epidemic illness, hurricanes, oil spills, and chemical leaks from passing barges.[8]

Obviously some repetition of words and phrases from your sources will occur in your paper (there are only so many ways of saying, for instance, that Gray's Lake is in southeastern Idaho at an elevation of 6400 feet), but if your paragraph follows the organization of a source paragraph very closely and repeats a large number of words and phrases, it needs to be rewritten. Try reading your notes or the original passage, then setting the original aside and writing your paragraph without reference to it, except to check for accuracy.

What to footnote

Except for common factual knowledge (of which there is a great deal), all information taken from a source, whether it is quoted directly or put in your own words, must be followed by a footnote—all quotations, all ideas and opinions, all precise factual information such as statistics. (In some cases you yourself may know statistical information, but in such a case it is usually wise to check on your own memory by finding a source for the information.)

Much that you have read, however, is common knowledge and does not need to be footnoted, whether you knew the information before your reading or not. No absolute distinction exists between what is common knowledge and what is not (if you aren't sure, footnote), but information can usually be called common knowledge if it passes two tests: 1) if such information (that whooping cranes mate for life, that William Faulkner won the Nobel Prize for literature) appears in general reference works and is mentioned without footnotes in more than one article you have read; 2) if you can honestly say, "I know this." Thus, what you tell your friends in the cafeteria about a subject (for instance, the grizzly bear) is in all likelihood common knowledge. But you wouldn't claim as common knowledge the thirty-some uses that the Plains Indians made of the buffalo.

At times you may wish to footnote even common knowledge. For instance, it is common knowledge that no verifiable evidence exists that a wild wolf has ever attacked a human on the North American continent, but there are so many myths to the contrary that writers may wish to protect themselves by citing a source. Remember, however, that even if something is common knowledge, you *must* footnote if you are using someone else's actual wording of this information.

Incorporating source material into your paper

When incorporating source material into a paper, be sure that you make clear to the reader what is from a source and what is not. As a general rule, quotations, opinions, and ideas that appear in your paper are preceded by a signal phrase, such as "According to Carl Jung" or "As Mario Pei has observed"; the quotation, opinion, or idea is then followed by a footnote number, indicating to the reader that everything between the signal and the footnote number is from the source, whether directly quoted or put in your own words.

Here are two examples of the proper form for introducing direct quotations.

> In June of 1977, Keith M. Schreiner, associate director of the Fish and Wildlife Service, said of the whooping crane's future, "The outlook has never been brighter."[2]

> So successful have hunting regulations and educational campaigns been that *Wildlife in Danger* could say in 1969 that "the losses on migration by uncontrolled and ignorant shooting have certainly become small."[12]

Notice that the writer of these sentences was careful to let his readers know in the text itself the source of the quoted material. The reader understands immediately that the first quotation is from Schreiner and the second is from *Wildlife in Danger*. In addition, the reader learns who Schreiner is. (If Schreiner is referred to later, his position does not need to be mentioned again, just as it was not necessary to identify *Wildlife in Danger* as an important reference work, for this had been done earlier in the paper.)

Factual material is also usually preceded by a signal phrase and followed by a footnote number, but it is often put in one's own words, as in the following example.

> According to Faith McNulty, by 1938 there was only one migratory flock of twenty-two birds left.[6]

Except for numbers, the writer is not borrowing wording from his source and doesn't need to use quotation marks. The footnote exists to let the reader know just where the writer obtained the information.

On occasion you may omit the signal phrase and include factual information in the text, followed only by a footnote number. You may do this especially if you have a cluster of brief bits of information from different sources (population figures, for instance); but if you omit the signal phrase, make certain that the context clarifies what is from a source and what is not. If this is your first research paper, you are probably best off never omitting the signal phrase.

To keep from sounding like a stuck record repeating over and over "Faith McNulty says," you will want to have at hand a variety of signal phrases and to learn to place them at various points in the sentence. In the following sentence, for instance, the student has cited the author in the middle of the quotation: "If chimpanzees have consciousness, if they are capable of abstractions," Carl Sagan asks, "do they not have what until now has been described as 'human rights'?"

Incorporating the wording of others into your own writing may be a bit awkward at first, but you will quickly learn how to work such material into the texture of your paper. Following is a quotation about human hatred of wolves and three examples of ways you could use the quotation in a paper.

Wolf Hatred

"How can one hate the wolf and love the dog as his best friend at the same time? Without the wolf on the evolutionary ladder, there would be no dog. Yet there are people in Minnesota and Alaska who would lay down their lives for their huskies and German shepherds and forgetting the origin of things, go gladly into the great void still ungrateful to the wolf."

Mitchell, 20

---

1. Many people feel very differently about the wolf and its descendant, the dog. John Mitchell points out that "there are people in Minnesota and Alaska who would lay down their lives for their huskies and German shepherds," yet die "still ungrateful to the wolf."[3]

2. A puzzled John Mitchell asks, "How can one hate the wolf and love the dog as his best friend at the same time?" As he observes, the dogs for which humans even risk their lives are descended from wolves.[2]

3. Since dogs are descended from wolves, this human hatred of wolves seems inconsistent and irrational. John Mitchell points out that the same Minnesoteans and Alaskans who hate wolves would risk death for their huskies and German shepherds.[1]

Once you have learned how to use signal phrases, you will find it fairly simple to incorporate material from several sources into one paragraph and yet always make clear to the reader which information is from what source, as in the following passage from the sample research paper on the whooping crane. Any material between the signal phrase and the footnote number, whether quoted directly or put in the student's own words, is from the specific source indicated.

> This bird [the whooping crane] of which so few remain has a long history. *Wildlife in Danger* describes it as a "Pleistocene relict": bones found in Idaho are 3,500,000 years old by potassium-argon dating and "are not distinguishable from modern bones of the species."[4] According to Fred Guthery, when glacial ice was receding from North America 10,000 years ago, whooping crane numbers were high, "perhaps at their strongest point in history," and the bird was distributed over all of North America except eastern Canada and New England. The receding ice, however, meant the replacement of marshes by forest and grasslands, so that the whooping crane population had greatly declined even before humans began further to diminish its numbers.[5]

Footnote form

The nearest thing to a standard guide to footnote form for students is the *MLA Handbook for Writers of Research Papers, Theses, and Dissertations,* which is probably on sale at your college bookstore.* This guide or any of the others on the market will tackle such tough problems as how to footnote unpublished letters, radio and television programs, and telephone interviews. Most of your footnotes, however, will follow the basic format for a book, a magazine article, and a newspaper article given below. Learn these and worry about the other forms only as you need them.

1. A book:

[7] Lillian Feder, *Ancient Myth in Modern Poetry* (Princeton: Princeton University Press, 1971), p. 51.

2. A magazine article:

[8] Edward Abbey, "The Crooked Wood," *Audubon,* November 1975, p. 26.

Note that the title of the magazine article is put in quotes and that the name of the magazine is italicized (or underlined).

3. A newspaper article:

[9] Alan M. Kriegsman, "ABT Fires Two Stars," *The Washington Post,* 10 December 1980, Sec. D., p. 1.

Note that many newspaper articles will not cite the writer's name. In that case the entry begins with the title of the article. Note also that some

---

*Certain disciplines, anthropology, for instance, have developed different documentation techniques.

newspapers will be divided into sections, as is *The Washington Post,* but other newspapers paginate consecutively through the entire issue.

Following are examples of some less frequently used footnote forms.

4. A book by more than one author:

[10] Daniel Berrigan and Lee Lockwood, *Absurd Convictions, Modest Hopes* (New York: Random House, 1973), p. 18.

5. An edition other than the first:

[11] John Hope Franklin, *From Slavery to Freedom,* 3rd ed. (New York: Alfred A. Knopf, 1967), p. 348.

6. A book with more than one volume:

[12] Robert Graves, *The Greek Myths* (New York: George Braziller, 1967), II, 69.

7. A book with an editor:

[13] *The Letters of Virginia Woolf,* ed. Nigel Nicholson and Joanne Trautmann (New York: Harcourt Brace Jovanovich, 1975), I, 413.

8. A work in a collection of pieces by different authors:

[14] Richard Wright, "Bright and Morning Star," in *Short Stories: A Critical Anthology,* ed. Ensaf Thune and Ruth Prigozy (New York: Macmillan, 1973), pp. 387–88.

9. Articles in reference works:

[15] "Minerva," *The Oxford Classical Dictionary,* 1970 ed.
Rules for citing reference works vary greatly. For well-known alphabetized entries (like "Minerva"), no other information is necessary, but in other instances you may wish to give further information.

10. Personal and telephone interviews:

[16] Personal interview with O. J. Simpson, 18 April 1979.

Once you have given the complete information about a source, you don't ever need to give that information again. However, you will more than likely be citing a source several times, and in that case your later footnotes will consist only of the author's last name and the page numbers (for instance, McNulty, p. 88). If there is no author, you repeat the name of the article to identify the source.

In the past a good many Latin terms were used in footnotes, but today most of these have been dropped. Some writers still prefer to use the term *ibid.,* followed by the page number, when they have successive footnotes from the same source, but we suggest always using the author's last name, however delightful *ibid.* may sound to you.

Bibliography form

In addition to footnotes, you may be asked to submit a bibliography—an alphabetized list of your sources. Type the bibliography, which should list all the works that appear in your footnotes, on a separate page at the end of your paper. You should also include in it any other works that influenced your thinking, even if you have not referred to any of these works in the paper.

Bibliographic form is slightly different from footnote form. The entries are listed alphabetically by the name of the author, with the last name appearing first. If there is more than one author, only the first author's name is inverted. If a work has no author, it is alphabetized by the first word in the title other than *a, an,* or *the.* Each individual entry is single-spaced, with double spacing between entries. The first line of an entry is not indented (unlike the first line of a footnote). Subsequent lines in an entry are indented approximately five spaces.

Bibliographical entries for books differ from footnote entries in three ways: 1) the author's name is inverted; 2) periods rather than commas and parentheses separate the main units of the entry; and 3) no page numbers are given.

Footnote entry for a book:

[6] Robert Porter Allen, *On the Trail of the Vanishing Birds* (New York: McGraw-Hill, 1957), p. 44.

Bibliographic entry for a book:

Allen, Robert Porter. *On the Trail of the Vanishing Birds.* New York: McGraw-Hill, 1957.

Bibliographic entries for magazine and newspaper articles also differ from footnote entries in three ways: 1) the author's name is inverted; 2) periods rather than commas separate the main units of the entry; and 3) the page numbers for the entire article are listed.

Footnote entry for an article:

[9] Fred S. Guthery, "Whoopers in Idaho," *National Parks and Conservation Magazine,* October 1976, p. 20.

Bibliographic entry for an article:

Guthery, Fred S. "Whoopers in Idaho." *National Parks and Conservation Magazine.* October 1976, pp. 18–21.

Following are examples of less frequently encountered bibliographic entries.

1. A book by more than one author:

Berrigan, Daniel, and Lee Lockwood. *Absurd Convictions, Modest Hopes*. New York: Random House, 1973.

2. An edition other than the first:

Franklin, John Hope. *From Slavery to Freedom*. 3rd ed. New York: Alfred A. Knopf, 1967.

3. A book with more than one volume:

Graves, Robert. *The Greek Myths*. 2 vols. New York: George Braziller, 1967.

4. A book with an editor:

Bell, Bernard W., ed. *Modern and Contemporary Afro-American Poetry*. Boston: Allyn and Bacon, 1972.

5. A work in a collection of pieces by different authors:

Wright, Richard. "Bright and Morning Star." *Short Stories: A Critical Anthology*, ed. Ensaf Thune and Ruth Prigozy. New York: Macmillan, 1973.

6. Articles in reference works:

"Minerva." *The Oxford Classical Dictionary*. 1970 ed.

7. Personal and telephone interviews:

LaBruda, Steve. Telephone interview. 17 December 1980.

Sample research paper

On the following pages is a sample research paper, written for a class in which the students were asked to investigate the current status of an endangered North American animal species. This paper is approximately 3000 words in length—not an unusual length for an undergraduate research paper, though good papers can be written with far fewer words. If you feel your paper is going to require more pages than you want to write, it is usually possible to narrow the topic further. This student, for instance, could have written his entire paper on the controversy over the captive breeding of whooping cranes.

In order to write this paper, the student read one entire book on the whooping crane and sections of another book on endangered bird species, two fairly short articles in reference works, three short news articles, and eight magazine articles. This is not an unreasonable amount of reading for a research paper. Your topic may demand more reading or less.

Unless your instructor specifies otherwise, submit the following material with the research paper:

1. *A title page.* The title page should include the title of the paper, your name, the name of the course and the instructor, the name of the college, and the date of submission.

2. *An outline.* The outline is discussed on the page facing the sample paper's outline.

3. *The text of the paper.* Most instructors require that the research paper be typed. It should be typed with fairly large margins on all sides of the paper. The footnotes usually appear at the bottom of the page, although some instructors will allow you to type the footnotes on separate pages at the end of the text. The text itself is double-spaced; footnotes are single-spaced.

4. *A bibliography.* Follow the paper with an alphabetized list of your sources, the form of which is discussed on the page opposite the sample paper's bibliography.

A Miracle Almost Achieved:
The Status of the Whooping Crane in 1980

by

Nick Culver

English 101, Mr. Shaw
Prince George's Community College
December 1980

The thesis appears first in an outline, although in the paper it may be preceded by introductory material. The major headings of the outline are logical divisions supporting that thesis. In this outline, the three divisions are the three major reasons for the new optimism about the whooping crane's survival.

Introductions (or, in this case, background material) and conclusions are best set aside from the numbering system of the outline, for neither is a clear division of the thesis.

The logical division of this paper is ideal, but frankly, not all subjects can be divided so neatly, at least not without a great deal of manipulation of words. A danger exists that in trying to satisfy the instructor's demands for a logically divided outline, the student will oversimplify or distort the truth about his or her subject. If you are having difficulty in developing a logically divided outline, you may want to ask for suggestions from your instructor.

Outlines may be done either in sentence form, as this one is, or in topic form, which does not use complete sentences. If a paper is expressing opinions or drawing conclusions from material, a sentence outline is best; it forces you to decide exactly what you are going to say before writing the paper. If a paper is primarily a report on clearly factual material, a topic outline may be adequate.

A Miracle Almost Achieved:
The Status of the Whooping Crane in 1980

Thesis: Although the whooping crane's survival in the wild is far from absolutely assured, no one any longer sees extinction as inevitable, and many are optimistic about the crane's future. Developments in three locations provide the reasons for this optimism.

Background: The background material briefly describes the whooping crane's life cycle and briefly summarizes its history until its numerical low point in 1938.

I. The Texas–Canada flock has grown, and its protection is assured.

 A. The flock has steadily increased in number, especially in the last fifteen years.

 B. The protection of the flock is relatively assured.

 1. The nesting and wintering territories are now on government protected land.

 2. Public protests would greet any threat to the whooping crane.

 3. Hunting losses have become very small.

II. Despite controversy, problems, and failure to meet proposed goals, the captive breeding program at Patuxent, Maryland, now appears to be a success.

 A. After long years of partial failure, the captive whooping cranes are now producing eggs.

 B. Some of the fears about the captive breeding program have been allayed.

III. Although it is too soon to know if the birds will successfully breed, there have been initial successes in establishing a second migratory flock in Idaho and New Mexico.

 A. Whooping cranes have been hatched by foster parents and have successfully participated in migration.

 B. Evidence exists that the whooping cranes will eventually bond with their own kind and establish a stable flock.

Conclusion: The conclusion briefly argues that humans should continue to protect the whooping crane.

The thesis of the paper usually appears in the first paragraph, though sometimes it is preceded by an interest-catching introductory paragraph. The wording of the thesis in the text of the paper need not be exactly like the wording in the outline, though it should closely parallel that wording. In this paper the student has expanded the two-sentence statement in the outline to two paragraphs, the second of which sets up the major divisions of his paper. The longer your paper is, the more important it is that you announce to the reader what the divisions of the paper will be.

Be sure to word your thesis carefully, and don't hesitate to change the thesis if while writing the paper you decide that it is not quite what you want to say. In the process of his research, this student twice reworded his thesis. He reworded it first when he became more pessimistic about the whooping crane's survival than he had been after initial reading. Later he returned to something of his original optimism, when he read the most recent news reports on the successes of the 1980 breeding season.

Notice that though the opening paragraph contains quotations from two sources, our writer, Nick Culver, has not lost his voice. The quotations, which are quite short, are carefully integrated into the paragraph so that readers are hearing Nick Culver primarily and the quoted authors (James Greenway, Jr. and Keith Schreiner) only secondarily.

Both of the footnotes on this page are to directly quoted material, which is enclosed in quotation marks so readers will know it has been taken word for word from the source. The footnote numerals appear at the end of the quotations, and they are typed slightly above the line. The corresponding footnotes at the bottom of the page supply readers with information about the sources so that if they are interested, they can track down the material in a library. Notice that the footnotes are numbered consecutively through the paper.

Because this is a fairly long paper, the student has decided to help the reader follow his organization by inserting a subtitle before each of the paper's main sections. He has done so here with the background section, which describes the whooping crane's life cycle and history.

Although personal experience and the *I* appear less frequently in papers making use of sources than in more subjective writing, there is no reason that they should not be used if relevant. Indeed, you will probably enjoy writing a paper more if you can make personal comments on the subject.

A Miracle Almost Achieved:
The Status of the Whooping Crane in 1980

In the 1930s the whooping crane seemed almost certainly doomed to extinction. As late as 1967, James C. Greenway, Jr., in Extinct and Vanishing Birds of the World, said that even with protection, "the survival of the species would be a miracle."[1] Today, however, though the bird's survival in the wild is far from absolutely assured, no one sees extinction as inevitable and many are optimistic. In June of 1977, Keith M. Schreiner, associate director of the Fish and Wildlife Service, said of the whooping crane's future, "The outlook has never been brighter."[2]

Three developments have led to this optimism: (1) the numerical increase and the more assured protection of the wild whooping crane flock that nests and winters in Texas; (2) the successes of the captive breeding program at Patuxent Wildlife Research Center in Maryland; and (3) the initial successes in establishing a second migratory flock in Idaho and New Mexico.

Background

On the Texas gulf coast in mid-March 1980, I boarded a converted deep-sea fishing boat with two or three hundred other tourists, most of them carrying binoculars and cameras. Our objective was to sight whooping cranes from the last remaining established wild flock, a flock the people on the boat far outnumbered. On that day we saw 25 of the 76 whooping cranes that were wintering at the Aransas National Wildlife Refuge.

We did not hear the distinctive call audible for miles that gave the bird its name (it was once called "bugle crane"), but we did see this tallest American bird in hunting stance and did see the size of its black-tipped snow-white wings as it glided over the Texas salt flats.

---

[1] James C. Greenway, Jr., Extinct and Vanishing Birds of the World, 2nd ed. (New York: Dover Publications, 1967), p. 208.

[2] "A Spectacular Year for Whooping Crane," New York Times, 23 June 1977, p. 14.

The information on the whooping crane in these paragraphs is common knowledge and thus does not have to be footnoted. The student has seen the information repeatedly during his reading and can honestly say that he knows it. If the student had presented a more detailed description of the incubation process, it might have become necessary to footnote.

Notice how the writer tells the reader through the use of signal phrases and footnote numbers where the use of material from a particular source begins and ends. The general rule is that the information between the signal phrase and the footnote number is from the source indicated in the footnote. Therefore the reader can assume that all information from the signal phrase "According to Fred Guthery" to footnote number 5 is from Guthery, page 18. The reader can also assume that except for the part of a sentence put in quotation marks, this information is being reported in Nick Culver's own words. *None of it* has been half-copied.

Footnote number 3 is an information footnote rather than a source footnote. The student has placed further information about the whooping crane in the footnote. He thought this information was interesting, but felt it might clutter the text of the paper itself. This sort of footnote is frequently used when the writer feels that a term or an allusion will not be understood by all readers and needs explanation.

If your instructor allows you to type the footnotes on separate pages at the end of the paper, you should still type an information footnote on the page itself. In this case the footnote is indicated by an asterisk (*) rather than a number. If there is more than one information footnote on a page, indicate the second with a double asterisk.

The whooping cranes arrive in Texas in late October, some singly, others in pairs,

and others—the most eagerly anticipated— in pairs with a youngster. Each pair or group

establishes a territory of around 400 acres, which it will defend against intruders and rarely

leave.[3]

In April the whooping cranes migrate over 2000 miles to Wood Buffalo Park in northern

Canada. There the pairs, which mate for life, establish a nesting territory, usually the same one

year after year. Two eggs are usually laid, and the parents alternate in incubating.

This bird of which so few remain has a long history. Wildlife in Danger describes it as a

"Pleistocene relict": bones found in Idaho are 3,500,000 years old by potassium-argon dating

and "are not distinguishable from modern bones of the species."[4] According to Fred Guthery,

when glacial ice was receding from North America 10,000 years ago, whooping crane numbers

were high, "perhaps at their strongest point in history," and the bird was distributed over all of

North America except eastern Canada and New England. The receding ice, however, meant the

replacement of marshes by forest and grasslands, so that the whooping crane population had

greatly declined even before humans began further to diminish its numbers.[5]

In the nineteenth and twentieth centuries, destruction of habitat and hunting radically

sped up the decline. According to Faith McNulty, by 1938 there was only one migrating flock

---

[3]According to Faith McNulty, whooping cranes are among the few birds in which the family does not fully break up at the end of the breeding season. If a pair returns to Aransas with a youngster, they will "defend their territory with greater determination than a childless couple." A mated pair, though childless, will in turn defend their territory more fiercely than single birds. Faith McNulty, The Whooping Crane: The Bird That Defies Extinction (New York: E. P. Dutton & Co., 1966), pp. 69-70.

[4]James Fisher, Noel Simon, and Jack Vincent, Wildlife in Danger (New York: The Viking Press, 1969), p. 223.

[5]Fred S. Guthery, "Whoopers in Idaho," National Parks and Conservation Magazine, October 1976, p. 18.

The subtitle "The Texas-Canada Flock" tells readers that the background section is over and the main body of the paper is beginning. The first sentence of this section reminds readers of the organization of the whole paper: We are about to hear the first of the three reasons for optimism about the whooping crane's chances of survival.

Readers need these reminders, especially since the background section was fairly long. Usually it is best not to include a long background section, but our writer decided that he needed to give us a fair amount of material here both to attract our interest and to familiarize us with a bird about which we may know very little. How much background material you need depends on your subject and your audience. In a paper on changes in the rules of football, for instance, you would normally not need to explain in detail the history of the game. However, if you were writing about American converts to Eastern religions in the 1970s, you might find it necessary to give some background on these religions.

of 22 birds left.[6] The only other flock, a nonmigratory group in Louisiana, had even fewer birds and would be almost entirely destroyed by a storm in 1940, never to recover.

Today the whooping crane is well on the way to recovery. The total in the wild and in captivity is far greater than in 1938. Despite the persisting threats of oil spills, hurricanes, disease, and even the potential mistakes of well-intentioned biologists trying to replenish the whooping crane stock, the whooping crane is surviving.

The Texas-Canada Flock

The first reason for the new optimism about the whooping crane's future is the increase in the number of the Texas-Canada flock and the greater protection given it. Despite small declines in individual years, the Texas-Canada flock has steadily increased in number, especially in the last decade. In December of 1980, according to a staff biologist at Aransas, the flock numbered 78, with the possibility that one or two more, which had been spotted in central west Texas, would still come in to winter.[7] A growth from 22 cranes in 1938 to around 80 in 1980 may seem small, but it is greater than experts anticipated fifteen years ago.

For several reasons this increasingly large flock will be much safer than its ancestors in the 1930s were. First, although much of the bird's former habitat can of course never be recovered, the preservation of its wintering and nesting territories now seems "reasonably well-assured," to use the words of Wildlife in Danger, an internationally sponsored survey of the world's endangered species.[8] In 1937 the United States government purchased the approximately 50,000 acres on the Blackjack Peninsula near Corpus Christi, Texas, where the bird

---

[6]McNulty, p. 15.

[7]Telephone interview with Steve LaBuda, 17 December, 1980.

[8]Fisher, Simon, and Vincent, p. 244.

If a quotation is a complete sentence, as with the Allen quotation that concludes this paragraph, it is preceded either by a comma (Allen pointed out, "The welfare . . .") or by *that* (Allen pointed out that "the welfare . . ."). The period at the end of the sentence goes inside the quotation marks, and the footnote number outside.

It may be helpful to remember that the period and the comma *always* occur inside the quotation marks. Some other marks of punctuation may occur either inside or outside the quotation marks (see the "Punctuation" section of the handbook).

If the quotation is more than one sentence in length, as with the Allen quotation on hunting in this paragraph, it is usually introduced by a colon rather than a comma.

If phrases are being quoted, no punctuation mark precedes the quotation marks unless that mark would occur there in a sentence without quotation marks.

wintered. When the nesting grounds of the whooping crane were finally found in 1954, they were in an established Canadian national park, Wood Buffalo, on the Alberta-Mackenzie border. So swampy and isolated is this area that danger from human interference is minimal.

Not only are these areas government protected, but today any threat to the crane's territory in either Canada or the United States would be greeted by a public outcry, as it was, for instance, when United States Air Force bombing ranges were activated near Aransas. As Robert Porter Allen pointed out, "The welfare of the whooping crane has become front-page news."[9]

Conservation groups, however, must continue to push for legislation protecting the Aransas refuge from such dangers as oil spills and legislation protecting the flock's migratory route. As this report was being prepared in December of 1980, a battle was being waged over the building of Grayrocks Dam in Wyoming, which wildlife managers fear will endanger the water supply on whooping crane migratory feeding grounds along the Platte River.[10]

Hunting, particularly during migration, was also a major cause of the whooping crane's decline in the last century. Allen says: "They were shot on the breeding grounds as they sat on their eggs, and they were shot on migration as they came to earth to feed and rest. On the wintering grounds they were shot when they raided sweet-potato fields in Louisiana, and for sport along the Texas coast."[11]

Severe penalties now exist for shooting whooping cranes, and public and private groups conduct intensive campaigns to educate hunters along the migration route in bird identification.

---

[9]Robert Porter Allen, On the Trail of the Vanishing Birds of the World (New York: McGraw-Hill, 1957), p. 30.

[10]For a discussion of the issues involved in the Grayrocks Dam controversy, see Bruce Hamilton, "The Whooping Crane: A Success Story," Sierra, May/June 1979, pp. 60–61.

[11]Allen, p. 38.

The student remembers the phrase "any large white bird" from an illustration in one of the articles he read. There is no need to footnote this particular kind of quotation.

When you use quotations of three or more sentences, you usually set them apart from the text of the paper, as this one has been set apart. Introduce the quotation with a colon, then double-space, then indent three spaces from the lefthand margin and single-space the quotation.

It is generally not good practice to include a large number of extended quotations such as this one in your paper. The student decided to do so in this case because he wished to stress in some way that all people are not as concerned about the whooping crane as he is.

Frequently you will want to omit something that appears in the middle of a quotation you are using. If the omission is a group of words, it is marked by an ellipsis [. . .] If the omission occurs at the end of a sentence or consists of an entire sentence, add an extra dot for the period. In the long quotation from Allen, the student omitted an entire sentence.

Frequently in quoting you will need to explain or identify a word or reference for the reader. So as not to confuse the reader as to who is saying what, your insertion in the middle of someone else's quotation is enclosed with brackets, as "the whooping crane" is here. If your typewriter has no brackets on its keyboard, put them in with ink.

When you are quoting material that is quoted in another source, indicate this by using first quotation marks, then an apostrophe. Note in footnote 14 that the source is preceded by the phrase "quoted in."

When the source material is taken from more than one page, the abbreviation *pp.* (for "pages") replaces the abbreviation *p.*

One National Audubon Society poster exhorts hunters not to shoot "any large white bird." So successful have the hunting regulations and educational campaigns been that <u>Wildlife</u> <u>in</u> <u>Danger</u> could say in 1969 that "the losses on migration by uncontrolled and ignorant shooting have certainly become small."[12]

Strange as it may seem in the conservation-conscious 1980s, the attempts to bring about this protection did not always go unopposed. Robert Porter Allen describes a time of despair in 1949:

> It seems unbelievable, but in spite of the great amount of public good will that had been generated during the first years of our campaign, there were still many people who took an entirely different view. It is not often that we see or hear an outright expression of this other attitude, but several incredible samples have been sent to me. One was a letter from a distraught farmer in Saskatchewan. He told of certain of his neighbors who were outspoken in their opinion that all this fuss about the whooping crane was a lot of nonsense. They proposed that the best way to put a stop to it would be to kill the few birds that remain and then forget the whole thing, thus saving the taxpayers a lot of money . . . . They likewise announced their intention of using their guns at every opportunity to promote such results.[13]

One writer to a "leading newspaper" said, " 'From what I have observed and heard he [the whooping crane] is a dim-witted gawk of a bird whose pate has become more or less addled in the course of time until now he is not quite sharp enough mentally to be up to the fundamentals of procreation.' "[14]

I hope to give my children a view of an even stronger flock than my parents showed me, and therefore do not begrudge the relatively small amount of tax money spent on protecting the Texas–Canada flock.

---

[12]Fisher, Simon, and Vincent, p. 225.

[13]Allen, pp. 74-75.

[14]Quoted in Allen, p. 75

This paragraph may be used as another illustration of what is common knowledge and what is not. The information in this paragraph is not, for two reasons, and is thus footnoted. First, unlike the fact that the whooping cranes migrate over 2000 miles, the figures here are very specific ("15,000 of the 140,000 waterfowl"). Second, although the student now knows about this near-disaster, he read about the incident only in the article in *Science News*.

Captive Breeding at Patuxent

Despite controversy, problems, and failures to meet proposed goals, the second reason for the growing optimism about the whooping crane has been the captive breeding program at Patuxent Wildlife Research Center in Maryland. By March 1980, the Patuxent captive flock numbered 24, and a number of eggs produced through artificial insemination of captive females had been transferred to Grays Lake National Wildlife Refuge in Idaho to be hatched by sandhill cranes as part of a project to establish a second migratory flock.[15] The Patuxent flock now generally produces more eggs per year than the wild flock—21 in 1979, for instance.[16]

The captive flock was established because biologists and conservationists were aware of the Texas-Canada flock's fragility even with maximum government protection. For example, Science News reports that in the spring of 1975, just before the whooping cranes flew north from Aransas, a severe epidemic of avian cholera broke out among waterfowl at Nebraska wildlife refuges where the whoopers customarily stop to feed and rest. The disease had already killed 15,000 of the 140,000 waterfowl at Sacramento Game Refuge. Only by scaring the whooping cranes away with airplanes was contact with the contaminated birds in Nebraska avoided.[17]

Because of such threats of disaster, proposals were made to maintain in captivity a reserve flock whose young or eggs might replenish the wild stock. The plan, which began in 1966, was to retrieve one of the two eggs usually laid by whooping cranes at Wood Buffalo and to transport them with great care to Patuxent for hatching. Dr. Ray Erickson, who heads the Patuxent program, anticipated that the taking of eggs would not diminish the number of

---

[15]"The Long, Thin Track of the Whooping Crane," United States Fish and Wildlife Service news release, 7 March 1980.

[16]"Creatures," Audubon, July 1979, p. 18.

[17]"Whooping Cranes Survive Disease Threat," Science News, April 26, 1975, p. 27.

wild birds. He maintained that only one chick usually survives anyway because "newborn whooping cranes are so hostile and aggressive toward each other that when there are two, one often kills the other."[18]

These proposals were further supported by research that seemed to show that if the eggs of captive birds were removed soon after they were laid, the birds could be stimulated to produce more eggs. This has proved to be the case. In 1978, for instance, according to Smithsonian, one captive female laid ten eggs, and a second nine.[19]

The successes at Patuxent in 1977 have allayed some, though not all, of the fears about captive breeding, a very controversial subject. In a 1974 Natural History article, D. R. Zimmerman (a writer who has misgivings about captive breeding) describes the bitter debate that ensued when the Patuxent program was proposed, a debate between the "protectionists" and the "propagationists." "Protectionists," according to Zimmerman, felt there was too little proof of success in captive breeding to warrant removing eggs from the wild. They saw risks in releasing captive-bred birds or their eggs into the wild flocks, for these birds might be unable to adjust to the wild and might carry disease. "Propagationists," on the other hand, argued that the cranes were "too close to extinction not to try captive breeding to increase their numbers, particularly as a hedge against a natural or manmade disaster that could kill many or all of the wild population in a single blow."[20]

---

[18]D. R. Zimmerman, "Captive Breeding: Boon or Boondoggle," Natural History, December 1974, p. 8.

[19]David Zimmerman, "A Technique Called Cross-Fostering May Help Save the Whooping Crane," Smithsonian, September 1978, p. 62.

[20]Zimmerman, "Captive Breeding," pp. 7–8.

Initial Successes in Idaho and New Mexico

The third reason for the new optimism about the whooping cranes is the initial success of biologists in establishing a second migratory flock. This flock, which summers in Grays Lake Wildlife Refuge in Idaho and winters at Bosque del Apache National Wildlife Refuge in New Mexico, has been beset by difficulties such as coyotes, drought, infertile eggs, and barbed-wire fences,[21] but in the fall of 1979 fifteen whooping cranes at least began the migration route from Idaho to New Mexico.[22] In December 1980 the U.S. Fish and Wildlife Service estimated that five to eleven were wintering at Bosque del Apache, and others were thought to be elsewhere in the Southwest.[23]

The development of this second wild flock began in 1974 when Canada and the United States approved what has been called "the biggest gamble ever in the . . . 40-year effort to save the whooping crane from extinction."[24] The plan was to move eggs from Wood Buffalo and Patuxent to Grays Lake, where the eggs would be hatched by sandhill cranes acting as foster parents. It was hoped that the flock would follow the sandhill cranes to wintering grounds in New Mexico, and in later years fly the route independently.

In a 1977 Natural History article, Rodney Barker cites four major reasons for the gamble. First, in 1974 Patuxent did not seem to be meeting its goals. Second, many subadult whoopers were disappearing in the Canadian wilderness for unexplained reasons. Third, cranes summering

---

[21]Roderick Drewien, "Teamwork Helps the Whooping Crane," National Geographic, May 1979, pp. 680–692.

[22]"The Long, Thin Track of the Whooping Crane."

[23]"Avian Cholera Kills Geese at Bosque del Apache National Wildlife Refuge," United States Fish and Wildlife Service news release, 2 December 1980.

[24]Linda Scarbrough, "The Ugly Duckling Updated," New York Times Magazine, Nov. 30, 1975, p. 88.

in Idaho and surrounding areas would have a much shorter—and thus less dangerous—migration route to wintering grounds. Fourth, and perhaps most important, new developments in biology suggested that such a plan might succeed. After a long study of sandhill cranes, the nearest American relative of the whooping crane, biologists Rod Drewien and Elwood Bizeau had come to the conclusion that crane behavior was primarily learned through early experience rather than being innate and that therefore young whooping cranes could learn to survive and to migrate from sandhill crane foster parents.[25]

Thus, in May 1975, fourteen eggs were taken from Canadian nests and flown to Idaho— flown with many questions. Would the whooping cranes, if they hatched, survive in a new environment? Would the chicks be rejected by their foster parents? Would the whooping cranes take on the traits of sandhill cranes to such a degree that they might even interbreed, producing sterile hybrids? Would the whooping cranes learn and adopt on their own the sandhill crane migration route?

None of these questions will be answered until the birds reach sexual maturity at the age of 5 or 6, but between 1975 and 1980 many chicks survived and were not rejected by their foster parents; a number have continued on the migration route learned from their foster parents. According to Rod Drewien, there is already strong evidence that they "may be able to recognize each other even after a long separation" and prefer association with their own kind.[26]

Buoyed by these positive results, the state of Florida announced in August 1980, according to the Washington Post, that it would attempt to establish a nonmigratory flock of whooping

---

[25]Rodney Barker, "A Whooper Rally," Natural History, March 1977, pp. 24, 26.

[26]Drewien, pp. 690–692

cranes by "planting baby whoopers with sedentary foster parents and hoping they learn to stay put."[27]

Conclusion

Because whooping crane numbers were low before human interference, there may be some question as to whether the decline of the whooping crane, unlike that of the bald eagle, stems more from humans or from natural selection. However, humans have certainly sped up the decline and should be <u>humane</u> enough to try to abate it. As an editorial in the <u>Christian Science Monitor</u> once asked, " 'Can society, whether through sheer wantonness or callous neglect, permit the extinction of something beautiful or grand in nature without risking extermination of something beautiful and grand in its own character?' "[28] The contributions of Americans and Canadians to whooping crane survival indicate that society is not risking such extermination.

---

[27]Ed Bruske, "Florida Hopes to Trick Baby Whooping Cranes into a Stay-at-Home Life," The <u>Washington Post</u>, 13 August 1980, Sec. A, p. 2.

[28]Quoted in Allen, p. 31.

The bibliography is typed on a separate page at the end of your paper. It should list all the works that appear in your footnotes. You should also include in the bibliography any other works that influenced your thinking, even if there are no references to these works in the paper.

The entries are listed alphabetically by the name of the author, with the surname appearing first. If there is more than one author, only the first author's name is inverted. If a work has no author, it is alphabetized by the first word in the title other than *a, an,* or *the.*

Each individual entry is single-spaced, with double spacing between entries. The first line of an entry is not indented (unlike the first line of a footnote). Subsequent lines in an entry are indented approximately five spaces.

Bibliographical entries for books differ from footnote entries in three ways: 1) the author's name is inverted; 2) periods rather than commas and parentheses separate the main units of the entry; and 3) no page numbers are given.

Footnote entry:

[6] Robert Porter Allen, *On The Trail of Vanishing Birds* (New York: McGraw-Hill, 1957), p. 44.

Bibliography entry:

Allen, Robert Porter. *On The Trail of Vanishing Birds.* New York: McGraw-Hill, 1957.

Bibliographical entries for magazines and newspaper articles differ from footnote entries in three ways: 1) the author's name is inverted; 2) periods rather than commas separate the main units of the entry; and 3) the page numbers for the entire article are listed.

Footnote entry:

[9] Fred S. Guthery, "Whoopers in Idaho," *National Parks and Conservation Magazine,* October 1976, p. 20.

Bibliography entry:

Guthery, Fred S. "Whoopers in Idaho." *National Parks and Conservation Magazine.* October 1976, pp. 18–21.

BIBLIOGRAPHY

Allen, Robert Porter. On the Trail of Vanishing Birds. New York: McGraw-Hill, 1957.

Barker, Rodney. "A Whooper Rally." Natural History. March 1977, pp. 22-30.

Bruske, Ed. "Florida Hopes to Trick Baby Whooping Cranes into a Stay-at-Home Life." The Washington Post. 13 August 1980, Sec. A, p. 2.

"Creatures." Audubon. Juiy 1979, pp. 18-20.

Drewien, Roderick. "Teamwork Helps the Whooping Crane." National Geographic. May 1979, pp. 680-692.

Fisher, James, Noel Simon, and Jack Vincent. Wildlife in Danger. New York: The Viking Press, 1969.

Greenway, James C., Jr. Extinct and Vanishing Birds of the World. 2nd ed. New York: Dover Publications, 1967.

Guthery, Fred S. "Whoopers in Idaho." National Parks and Conservation Magazine. October 1976, pp. 18-21.

Hamilton, Bruce. "The Whooping Crane: A Success Story." Sierra. May/June 1979, pp. 56-61.

LaBruda, Steve. Telephone interview. 17 December 1980.

McNulty, Faith. The Whooping Crane: The Bird That Defies Extinction. New York: E. P. Dutton & Co., 1966.

Scarbrough, Linda. "The Ugly Duckling Updated." New York Times Magazine. 30 November 1975, pp. 88-93.

"A Spectacular Year for Whooping Crane." New York Times. 23 June 1977, p. 14.

United States Fish and Wildlife Service. "Avian Cholera Kills Geese at Bosque del Apache National Wildlife Refuge." News release, 2 December 1980.

United States Fish and Wildlife Service. "The Long, Thin Track of the Whooping Crane." News release, 7 March 1980.

"Whooping Cranes Survive Disease Threat." Science News. 26 April 1975, p. 27.

Zimmerman, D. R. "Captive Breeding: Boon or Boondoggle." Natural History. December 1974, pp. 6-8, 10-16, 19.

Zimmerman, David. "A Technique Called Cross-Fostering May Help Save the Whooping Crane." Smithsonian. September 1978, pp. 52-62.

Some endangered species topics

If you would like to investigate the status of an endangered species, these are good subjects for research papers:

1. bowhead whale
2. Kirtland's warbler
3. California condor
4. grizzly bear
5. bald eagle
6. peregrine falcon
7. timber wolf
8. red wolf
9. alligator
10. porpoise
11. mountain lion

PART SIX

A writer's handbook

Punctuation, capitalization, and spelling

PUNCTUATION

Read this paragraph about a comedienne:

during the weekend we went to see the comedienne judith grant at club ninety-five have you seen her perform she does remarkably believable impersonations of several well known movie stars bette davis tallulah bankhead katharine hepburn and greta garbo among others the performance took us all young and old alike back into the early days of the silver screen i had heard that the glories of individual stardom had passed that the big movie companies do not invest so heavily in one actress these days however i had not realized before how much moviegoers of today may be missing my evening with bette and tallulah and katharine and greta was indeed a revelation to me and my companions the time passed so quickly that it was one o clock in the morning before we even thought about going home

Did you have a hard time getting through what you just read? If so, you appreciate already how much punctuation helps you when you read.

Punctuation divides what you write into logical units so that your writing will be clearer to your readers. When punctuation is inappropriately handled, readers become distracted and confused. They may miss your meaning while they are struggling with your punctuation.

Careful proofreading for punctuation, then, is important. Reading your work through aloud just for punctuation will probably be a good idea if this is a problem for you. As you read, listen for pauses; a pause usually indicates a need for a break, which punctuation provides. When writing is read aloud, you hear the same kinds of inflections that you hear in speech. That is, the voice falls markedly and stops at the end of a sentence, and a minimal pause occurs where a comma is needed.

Read the following sentences aloud, listening for when and how long you pause and for falls in your voice.

1. We stayed home yesterday to plant tulips.

2. We stayed home yesterday to plant tulips, even though a light rain was falling.

3. We stayed home yesterday, planting tulips and other bulbs, and later we rewarded ourselves by going to the movies.

4. We stayed home yesterday to plant tulips. Although a light rain began to fall soon after we started, we finished the task.

Some pauses do *not* indicate punctuation. The best advice we can give you for deciding at these points is to ask yourself whether the words on either side of the pause depend so heavily on each other that the link between them should not be broken. Remember: Every punctuation mark is a *break.*

As you proofread aloud, if you hear a pause where you have failed to provide a needed punctuation break, or if you have punctuated where the writing should continue to flow without stopping, go back and correct at those points. You may want to ask someone else to read aloud to you, so that you do not have to concentrate on both reading and listening. Whoever reads must be sure to "read in" the punctuation marks exactly as they appear—or do not appear—on the page, or the reading aloud won't tell you what you need to know.

With a careful reading aloud, you will hear where you have overpunctuated—where the writing needs to continue to flow without a break. If you hear an awkward punctuation pause around a word that should be helping to hold a sentence together (*that* and *than* often serve in this way), or between a verb and its subject, or between an adjective and the noun right behind it, you will know at once that you have overpunctuated.

Once you have decided which kind of punctuation mark—how long a pause—is needed where, you may want to experiment some with your punctuation. Perhaps you will want to use a semicolon instead of a period between two closely related complete thoughts, or a dash instead of a comma for a special effect of emphasis.

1. The period

The period is the most common mark of *terminal* punctuation. Use it to end sentences that make a statement or convey a request.

a. Jeannie was lonely at first, but she soon came to like having the house to herself.

b. After dealing with four children, a full-time job, the care of a home, and meal preparation, I am just too tired to sit down and read before I go to bed.

c. Lucy arrived breathless.

d. Please arrive fifteen minutes before curtain time.

? 2. The question mark

The question mark is used as terminal punctuation for questions.

a. Did you know that yogurt originated in Turkey?

b. See that large bird with iridescent green feathers?

! 3. The exclamation point

The exclamation point follows expressions of exclamation.

a. Leave that poor terrapin alone!

b. Don't tell me you're still waiting for the parade!

c. We watched the sun set over the Grand Canyon—an awesome spectacle!

Caution

Do not overuse the exclamation point. It is intended to make a statement emphatic; if you use it too freely, the emphasis is lost.

We went to the swamp early to observe the alligators before they awoke. As we stood on the bank, they began to move slowly—exactly at the moment the sun came up! What strange creatures they are! We felt as if we had stumbled backward in time into a prehistoric era!

Deleting the first and third exclamation points would increase the effect of the second one.

; 4. The semicolon

4a. The semicolon may be used instead of a period between two complete statements that are so closely related that you want them to be read together as a single sentence.

a. My old country school is no longer standing; it has been replaced by a ten-room elementary school and a modern regional high school.

b. Rosie and Verna, our zoologist friends, are coming into town next week to visit the Bronx Zoo; neither has ever seen a white tiger, so we are excited about showing them one.

c. Joseph wants a job like the one in India, I know; however, he does not want to leave this country.

Caution

Be sure to use a semicolon, not a comma, to fasten together the two halves of sentences like these. Using a comma in these instances would create a *comma splice*. For more on how to avoid comma splices, see #23 in "Revising Problem Sentences."

4b. The semicolon is also used to separate sets of items in a series when the items themselves are punctuated by commas. Such semicolons make a sentence easier to read.

> There are three major divisions in the new college: humanities, which includes English, art, speech, philosophy, and drama; social sciences, which includes history, psychology, sociology, and political science; and science, which includes biology, chemistry, geology, physics, and astronomy.

You will find an exercise on semicolons and commas at the end of the "Punctuation" section.

 ## 5. The comma

The comma, the punctuation mark that provides most of the punctuation *inside* sentences, has many uses. A relatively weak mark, it punctuates sentence content that needs minimal separation and indicates a brief pause to readers.

5a. In a sentence composed of two complete statements joined by a connector word, use a comma before the connector word.

> **a.** We were tired and hungry after hiking, *but* we stopped to pick wildflowers before we returned to our car.

> **b.** The tall man in the shiny red top hat and the rainbow-striped boots led the parade, *and* all of us cheered as he marched by.

Some common connector words: *and, but, or, nor, yet, so.*

Note

You may omit the comma before the connector word if the two statements are short and misreading cannot occur.

> Charles left early *but* Mary stayed till midnight.

Caution

Do not put a comma before a connector word unless there is a complete statement on either side of it:

> After seeing the flying saucer, he ran frantically for a telephone *but* accidentally dialed his mother.

5b. Use a comma between items in a series.

a. We made a fruit salad of oranges, apples, raisins, bananas, and figs. Then we ate, sang, danced, and talked.

b. Gen teaches dancing in a private school in the city daily, at a dance club in the suburbs weekly, and out on Long Island during the summer.

c. Jennifer played the flute, William picked his guitar, and the rest of us tried to sing along.

5c. Use a comma to separate most adjectives in a series.

The awkward, velvety-eyed, shy giraffe entertained us for a long time.

Some adjectives are not separated by commas; such adjectives often designate one of the following characteristics: number, size, age, color, material, or substance:

Polly's mother made six large new green canvas tote bags for Polly's classmates.

If you cannot decide whether to use commas with a series of adjectives, you can test the situation by:

a. putting *and* between the adjectives to see whether they sound logical that way:

the awkward and velvety-eyed and shy giraffe

but not: six and large and new and green and canvas tote bags

b. reversing the adjectives, to see whether they sound all right in a different order:

the shy, velvety-eyed, awkward giraffe

but not: canvas green new large six tote bags

Caution
Do not put a comma between a final adjective and the noun:

In the Rothko room of the art gallery, you find yourself surrounded by pure, pulsating, sensuous, color. (incorrect)

5d. Use a comma after an introductory construction.

a. *Although most mice are not very strong,* we found our refrigerator had been moved three feet from the wall during the night.

b. *To get to know more people,* you need to become involved in more activities.

c. *After drinking the vanilla by mistake,* I had a peculiar hangover.

d. *Fighting for her sense of dignity,* she refused to open her mouth for the force-feeding tube to be inserted.

Note
Short introductory constructions do not have to be set off by a comma.

Before we swam we lay in the sun and talked quietly.

But
Be alert to possible misreading. The following short introductory constructions need commas to prevent misreading.

a. Soon after Nicole was well and happy again.

b. When the helicopter hit the gas tank broke loose and exploded.

c. While I watched my father changed the back tire.

d. If you can afford to go to St. Thomas for Christmas.

e. By the way things are going very well for me this year.

5e. Use a comma before a concluding construction when the added material is not essential to the basic meaning of the sentence.

a. Three of the dancers decided to skip the afternoon rehearsal, *although they knew they might lose their positions in the new production.*

b. Let's sing all the verses, *since the program time assigned to us is longer than we had anticipated.*

c. Ellen was rude to the visiting actor, *who did not know how to explain her behavior to their hostess.*

But
Do not use commas in such sentences as the following, where the added material is essential to the basic meaning of the sentence.

a. The five sisters left the room while their aunt was still trying to argue with them.

b. We have not seen our pet pigeon since she escaped from the enclosure a week ago.

c. Beverly called her sister's attention to the lame fawn that was standing beside its mother.

Caution
Be sure to use the comma before a concluding construction if misreading might occur without it.

Charles left early, *for the boat would not wait.* ("Charles left early for the boat . . ." could create a misreading.)

5f. Use a comma to set off parenthetical insertions: transitional words and phrases, opinion indicators, and other miscellaneous inserted material.

    a. Maple syrup, *I believe,* is a major native product of Vermont.

    b. Eating raw limpets, *I found out,* is like trying to eat art gum erasers.

    c. Many minority groups, *especially blacks and Hispanics,* encounter racial prejudice and language barriers when they try to obtain health-care services.

    d. The elephants, *according to their trainer,* look forward to their bath in the big pool in their enclosure.

5g. Use a comma to set off appositives (words that rename what they follow) and inserted modifiers when these are not essential to the basic meaning of the sentence.

    a. Jack Lucas, *who made those brownies,* lives over by the river.

    b. The vinegar, *which has begun to cloud,* is still usable.

    c. One of Adrienne Rich's poems, "Orion," has a special appeal for me. (appositive)

Caution
Be sure to use *two* commas for such insertions; do not forget the second one.

But
Do not use commas in sentences like the following, where the appositive or inserted modifier changes the basic content of the sentence.

    a. The man *who made those brownies* lives over by the river.

    b. Vinegar *that has begun to cloud* is still usable.

    c. Adrienne Rich's poem "Song" apeals to readers of many ages. (appositive)

5h. Use commas to set off quoted material from the rest of a sentence.

    a. In *Working It Out,* Alice Walker comments, "What . . . are we to make of Phillis Wheatley, a slave (and a poet), who owned not even herself?"

    b. "That tree looks like a good hiding place for the treasure," Terry said to himself.

    c. "When Tom's train arrives," said Ruth, "let's greet him with balloons and streamers."

5i. Use commas to set off nouns of direct address.

   a. *Jim,* come here.

   b. You, *sir,* will have to come in later.

   c. Hurry up, *Mary.*

5j. Use commas to set off mild exclamations, such as *yes* or *no,* and similar words.

   Oh, yes, I will join you for dinner.

5k. Use commas in dates and addresses.

   a. My mother left for Russia on October 13, 1977.

   b. June 19, 1979, is the last date you may apply for that grant.

   c. My best friend lives in Silver Spring, Maryland.

   d. Send the letter to Redding Thompson, 93 N. Prospect Street, Burlington, Vermont 05401.

5l. Use commas between contrasted elements in a sentence.

   a. She found on the shore only colored pebbles, not the exotic shells she was looking for.

   b. As a stranger in the African desert, I felt not only deaf, but also blind whenever I encountered a native tribe.

5m. Do not overuse the comma.

a. Do not put a comma between a subject and its verb:

   Eating pizza and drinking beer, are her favorite pastimes. (incorrect)

b. Do not put a comma between a verb and its object:

   After months away from the farm, Michael found, digging potatoes and turnips hard on his back. (second comma is incorrect)

c. Do not put a comma between a final adjective and the noun:

   The soft, silky, cape flowed gracefully. (incorrect)

d. Do not put a comma after connector words:

   Yet, he cares enough for me to pick me up when I'm financially down and out. (incorrect)

e. Do not put a comma after *such as, like,* and similar terms:

   Some countries, such as, Brazil, Mexico, and Chile, schedule their school years quite differently from ours. (incorrect)

f. Do not put a comma before a bridge word that connects the parts of a sentence:

> He works full-time and is such a determined guy, that he pays all his own tuition. (incorrect)
> She is both more talented and more disciplined, than most of the other ballerinas in the company. (incorrect)

g. Do not put a comma before a parenthesis; place it after the parentheses, if the sentence requires a comma:

> In *Kind and Usual Punishment,* (an exposé of the American penal system) Jessica Mitford describes the disturbing day and night she spent in D.C.D.C. (District of Columbia's Detention Center for Women). (incorrect)

You will find an exercise on the comma at the end of the "Punctuation" section.

 6. The colon

The colon, a rather formal punctuation mark, has several uses:

6a. to introduce a formal series:

> The reasons for a low energy level include the following: poor diet, heavy smoking, inadequate rest, metabolic difficulties, and blood deficiencies.

6b. to direct a reader's attention to the second half of a sentence:

> The decline in the public school population is understandable: children born during the last "baby boom" have finished high school by now.

6c. to introduce quoted material:

> In an article in *New Times,* Karla Brown observes: "Living in New York is still like living at the hub of the wheel of the world."

 7. The dash

The dash, a rather informal mark of punctuation, is used in two major ways.

7a. A single dash helps to emphasize whatever follows it.

> I have but one goal on this trip to Ireland—to kiss the Blarney Stone.

7b. A pair of dashes may be used to set off the material between them from the rest of the sentence.

In the 1920's, liberals argued that the opposite of repression—sex education, freedom of talking, feeling, and expressing—would have healthy effects.

Caution
Do not overuse dashes. Doing so may suggest that you have not constructed your sentences very carefully.

Note
In typing, distinguish dashes from hyphens by typing two hyphens to form a dash.

 8. The parentheses

Parentheses (singular: *parenthesis*) are sometimes used around explanatory or other added material.

   a. The two leading female gymnasts of the world (one Russian, the other German) moved with flawless timing on the double bars.

   b. The hypothalamus (our bodily temperature regulator) sometimes functions less adequately with ageing.

   c. May Sarton (1912—), author of *The House by the Sea,* lives on the Maine seacoast.

Caution
Don't overuse parentheses. If you tend to put much sentence content inside parentheses, restructure your sentences. When you do so, you may find your parenthetical details are not important enough to include.

Note
Generally, surrounding inserted material with dashes will make it stand out more; with parentheses, it stands out less.

9. The apostrophe

The apostrophe has three functions: 1) to form the possessive of nouns and of some pronouns; 2) to indicate contraction of words and omission of letters; and 3) to make plurals of numbers, letters, and words used as themselves.

9a. To form the possessive:

a. Add the apostrophe plus "s" to singular nouns:

   That cat's game with the barn mice is hilarious.
   Smokers should respect the nonsmoker's right to a smoke-free environment.

Form the possessive of singular nouns ending in "s" in one of two ways: hostess's, hostess'; Frances's, Frances'

b. Add *only* the apostrophe to plural nouns ending in "s":

> Those cats' games with the barn mice are hilarious.
> Have you seen the Schultzes' new speedboat?

But
Add the apostrophe plus "s" to plural nouns not ending in "s": women's, children's.

c. Add the apostrophe plus "s" to certain pronouns: everybody's, other's, someone else's, no one's, and so on.

But
Omit the apostrophe with the possessive of *personal* pronouns: ours, yours, his, hers, its (*it's* means "it is"), theirs.

Note
You hear a few common expressions so often that you may forget that they require an apostrophe. Be alert to them: "a day's work," "your money's worth," "a week's rest" are some examples.

9b. The apostrophe substitutes for deleted letters or words in contractions and omissions.

a. contractions: it's (it is); don't (do not); you've (you have); that's (that is); we'll (we will); can't (cannot); let's (let us); and so on.

b. omissions: seven o'clock (seven of the clock); the radical '60's (1960's).

9c. Add the apostrophe plus "s" to make the plurals of numbers, letters, and words used as themselves.

> The two "A's," five "9's," and three "of's" on the poster are all printed in ink that glows under black light.

Caution
Sometimes the apostrophe plus "s" will create a sentence that is hard to read. Watch out for such awkward constructions and recast sentences in which they occur.

> **a.** Our local newspaper's editorial page's make-up is confusing.
> The make-up of the editorial page of our local newspaper is confusing.
>
> **b.** Our barn mice's favorite game is hide and seek with the cat.
> The favorite game of our barn mice is hide and seek with the cat.

c. I borrowed my father's sister's friend's suitcase.

I borrowed a suitcase that belongs to my aunt's friend.

Caution

Do not drop in apostrophes where they don't belong.

a. in the simple (nonpossessive) plurals of nouns:

Soap opera's are absurd. Corrected: Soap operas . . . .

b. in the present singular of verbs:

Janet want's to ride the carousel. Corrected: Janet wants . . . .

You will find an exercise on the apostrophe at the end of the "Punctuation" section.

 ## 10. The hyphen

The hyphen has three major uses:

10a. to divide a word at the end of a line:

Scarves can be used to achieve many different fashionable effects.

10b. to connect the parts of compound words:

double-header, self-reliance, half-moon

10c. to connect two or more words forming a single adjective before a noun:

the long-awaited costume ball, the Nielsen-rated program, the two-year-old child, the well-known acrobat

But

When a compound adjective completes a sentence instead of coming before its noun, no hyphen is used: That acrobat is well known in gymnastic circles.

Note

For more about how to handle compound words, see "Spelling."

 ## 11. Underlining (italics)

Underlining in either handwriting or typing equals italics (slanted type) in print.

11a. Underlining is used for titles of major publications and of long literary and musical works.

   a. books: <u>Poetic Celebrations</u>, <u>The Web and the Rock</u>, <u>Exploring Canada</u>

   b. magazines: <u>Psychology Today</u>, <u>Rolling Stone</u>

   c. newspapers: <u>Washington Post</u>, <u>Christian Science Monitor</u>

   d. plays and musicals: <u>Hedda Gabler</u>, <u>The Sound of Music</u>

   e. full-length films: <u>Kramer vs. Kramer</u>, <u>The Black Stallion</u>

   f. long poems: <u>The Love Song of J. Alfred Prufrock</u>

   g. long musical compositions: <u>Mozart's Little Night Music</u>, <u>Schubert's Trout Quintet</u>.

11b. Underlining sets off terms used as themselves inside a sentence.

   a. The word <u>pajama</u> originated in the Hindi language.

   b. It is easy to confuse the letter <u>s</u> and the number <u>5</u> if they are not formed carefully.

Note

Quotation marks may be used instead of underlining to set off terms used as themselves.

11c. Underlining is sometimes used to give added emphasis to a word or words in a sentence.

   While they were hiking, she said to him, "Don't you <u>dare</u> drop that rock on my lunch!"

Caution

You should not often need to use underlining for emphasis in your writing. Strong sentences can stand on their own. Excessive underlining usually suggests hasty, lazy writing; avoid it.

 12. Quotation marks

Quotation marks are used in three ways: 1) to punctuate minor titles; 2) to set off direct quotations; and 3) around dialogue, either spoken or internal.

12a. Minor titles:

a. essays, articles, chapter or section headings:

   Thoreau's "Civil Disobedience"; Beth Thompson's column "Getting There"; "People and Places" in *Holiday* magazine; "Five Ways to Stop Smoking" in Dr. Jennie Albertson's book *Improving Your Health*

b. short stories:
    ''A Worn Path''

c. short poems:
    ''Whose Lips I've Kissed''

d. short musical compositions:
    Neil Diamond's ''Stargazer''

e. paintings:
    Helen Frankenthaler's ''Red Slash''

12b. Direct quotations:

a. Janet told Theodore, ''My introductory physics class is full of practical information about everyday life.''

b. In *A Room of One's Own,* Virginia Woolf says that ''a woman must have money and a room of her own if she is to write fiction.''

c. ''I swing out over the earth over and over again,'' from Audre Lorde's ''Love Poem,'' is one of my favorite lines of poetry.

d. When we talk about meeting child-care needs in the United States, our first question is too often ''How much is it going to cost?''

e. In her fantasy stories about the future in *The Wanderground,* Sally Gearhart defines what she calls ''grace-making'' as ''the creation of extra attention and love'' toward one or more persons who may be suffering.

12c. Dialogue:

a. Spoken:
    ''Do you like the Alvin Ailey dancers?'' John asked Sam.
    ''I don't know. I've never seen them perform,'' replied Sam.
    ''Then, let's go! You'll like their exciting choreography, I know,'' John urged.

Notice that a new paragraph begins whenever the speaker changes.

b. Internal:
    ''What will my family think if I take up truck-driving?'' wondered Alice.

12d. Single quotation marks:
Single quotation marks are used when a title or quoted material appears inside a quotation.

Laurie asked her father, ''Do you know anything about T.S. Eliot's poem 'Macavity: The Mystery Cat'?''

12e. Quotation marks with other punctuation marks:

Periods and commas go inside quotation marks.

> **a.** One of my favorite folksingers is Joni Mitchell; I especially like her "Both Sides Now."

> **b.** I also like Olivia Newton-John's "Country Girl," Jim Croce's "Time in a Bottle," and John Denver's "Country Roads."

Semicolons and colons are placed outside quotation marks.

> **a.** One of Emily Dickinson's riddle poems is "A Narrow Fellow in the Grass"; by the time you finish reading the poem, you can see the snake that is the answer to the riddle.

> **b.** Ernest Hemingway achieves highly dramatic conflict among the characters in his short story "The Short Happy Life of Francis Macomber": Francis, the weak male; Margot, the strong female; and Robert, the strong male.

Question marks and exclamation points go outside quotation marks, unless the question or the exclamation itself is being quoted, in which case they go inside.

> **a.** Did you hear her say, "All aboard"?

> **b.** Stop smiling and saying, "Yes, yes"!

> **c.** I wondered aloud, "What shall I do next?"

> **d.** Thomas kept saying to the hungry bear, "No, stop that!"

Caution
Do not use quotation marks around questionable words in a sentence, or to try to achieve a humorous effect.

> Nancy pointed out to her parents that smoking marijuana was no more harmful than getting "bombed" on alcohol.

Using quotation marks in this way has the unfortunate effect of calling attention to what they surround. If you are tempted to write this kind of sentence, you probably need to look for more precise language.

 13. Brackets

Brackets are used when you need to insert a word or words into a quotation.

> In a book about Dr. Mary Walker, I was amazed to read the following statement: "The medal awarded her for service in the [Civil] War was taken back by the United States government."

14. Ellipsis dots

Ellipsis dots (three spaced periods) are substituted for deletions from quoted material.

Original:

"When my sons grow up, then, Gentlemen, I ask you to punish them, you hurting them the same as I hurt you, if they seem to you to care for money, or aught else, more than they care for virtue." (Plato, *The Apology of Socrates*)

With ellipsis:

Near the end of *The Apology,* Socrates askes the court: "When my sons grow up . . . I ask you to punish them . . . if they seem to care for money, or aught else, more than they care for virtue."

If deleted material is at the end of a sentence, then add one more dot to the three, to indicate a period.

Exercise 1 Punctuation

To discover how well you understand punctuation after studying this section, punctuate the following sentences.

1. Harry please bring pecans walnuts and chestnuts when you come for the weekend we need those I think for between meal snacks

2. One of my favorite short stories is Shirley Jacksons The Lottery which has been filmed for classroom use

3. Its too early to take a taxi to the theater but lets think about going by Johns fathers horsedrawn carriage

4. Have you seen Natalie Smorgavich in Shaws play Major Barbara

5. My aunt Katharine Jones is in line for a diplomatic appointment but she is reluctant to leave Washington

6. Look at that dancer leap

7. Any person who wishes to apply for work at that record store must take a lie detector test

8. My neighbors cat will climb any tree in sight however that habit creates a problem when she cant get back down without a firefighters assistance

9. Whether you like it or not Im going to include the quotation To thine own self be true from Shakespeare in my psychology paper asserted Tom

10. Ruth asked the little girl How old are you

Exercise 2 Punctuation

Now punctuate the unpunctuated student paper below, dividing it into paragraphs as you work. Be sure to capitalize letters that begin new sentences. You will have to make some punctuation choices. You may want to compare your punctuated version with those of your classmates, discussing the various effects achieved by different punctuation choices.

i was suddenly awakened at four o'clock one morning by my wife its time to go she exclaimed gazing across the room and seeing her standing with suitcase in hand it dawned on me that this was the moment for which we had been waiting nine months i sprang out of bed grabbed whatever clothes were available and started dressing while simultaneously calling the doctor ill meet you at the hospital in forty-five minutes was the doctors reply to a very nervous father-to-be on the way to the hospital i tried to remain as calm as i tried to remember the training we had received in prepared childbirth classes and the reading we had done in having your baby naturally inhale exhale breathe deeply and slowly i repeated to my wife over and over again as we drove into the city arriving at the hospital i drove right up to the front door and carefully ushered my wife to the admitting office after rushing through much paperwork not really knowing what we were signing we finally made it to the labor room then it began the timing of contractions the breathing in unison and the waiting three long hours later when my wife was fully dilated the doctor sent me out to dress in the delivery room garb a green cap mask gown and shoes once in the delivery room i held my wifes hand and assisted whenever possible twenty short minutes later a beautiful six-pound twelve-ounce girl was born one does not realize how much pain a woman can tolerate or the strength she possesses until he can witness a childbirth i shall always treasure having shared my daughters birth with my wife it was an event i shall not forget

Exercise 3 Semicolons and commas

Here are some practice sentences to help you if the use of semicolons and commas sometimes confuses you. Some of the sentences are punctuated correctly; some need to be corrected. On a separate sheet write C if the sentence is correct; if it is incorrect, punctuate it correctly as you copy it. Sometimes you may prefer to use a period rather than a semicolon; feel free to do so. Reading the sentences aloud to hear the length of pauses and the falls in your voice may help you make the punctuation decisions.

1. Last summer I participated in our college's New England Literary Tour; which was sponsored by Dr. Fry of the English Division.

2. Dr. Fry reserved two large buses for the tour, later he had to locate a third bus to accommodate additional travelers.

3. The tour included visiting Emily Dickinson's home in Amherst, Massachusetts, the House of Seven Gables, featured in Hawthorne's novel, Walden Pond, made famous by Thoreau, and many other sites, such as famous churches, a one-room schoolhouse, and a silversmith shop like Paul Revere's.

4. Most of our sleeping accommodations during the tour were very comfortable, however one night I rolled off a hard bed while having a nightmare about Washington Irving's headless horseman.

5. One night we stayed at an old-fashioned country inn built in the mid-1800's, where I was tempted to leave a sign saying "G.K. slept here."

6. The food on the trip was so plentiful that I could never finish a meal although some people asked for seconds on desserts almost every night.

7. A pleasant feature of the trip was the long afternoon rides through a rolling New England countryside; during which some passengers napped, some read, and the rest of us laughed joked and exclaimed over the scenery.

8. We reached one church just in time for a candlelight service it was a peaceful way to end a long day.

9. We were on the tour for college credit and therefore we had to spend some of our evening hours writing in our travel journals.

10. I recommend Dr. Fry's Literary Tour of New England to you; but only if you have stamina and a sense of humor, you'll need both if you go!

. . . .

Exercise 4 The comma
. . . .

If you want some practice in using commas, these sentences will help you. Copy them on a separate sheet, inserting commas where they are needed. Reading the sentences aloud may help you to make your comma decisions.

1. Scott and Helen Nearing who are now an elderly couple have been living off the land for many years.

2. I first read about the Nearings in the book *Ways Americans Live* a collection of essays on life-styles by Andrew Greene.

3. The Nearings the pioneers of the back-to-the-land movement left city life long before the return to rural life became fashionable.

4. They have developed their plot of land into a reasonably comfortable pleasant attractive place to live; however there is always work to be done.

5. When people who are interested in their way of life come to visit the Nearings they are put to work building planting harvesting or otherwise using whatever skills they bring with them.

6. For many years the Nearings have been building their house using stones which as you might expect have become too heavy for them to carry.

7. Therefore one of the jobs that visitors are sometimes assigned is hauling stones for the Nearings continue to add buildings to their property.

8. According to recent visitors both the Nearings although they are aging still fiercely support their choice to live as they do.

9. A friend of mine who visited the Nearings last year commented to me on her return "It made me wish I had the courage or whatever it takes to live that way."

10. "Not me" I replied "no indeed; I'm a person who likes comfort too much!"

Exercise 5 The apostrophe

Use of the apostrophe plagues some writers. If it plagues you, these practice sentences should help you master this punctuation mark. Although sometimes the apostrophe is used correctly, each sentence contains at least one error. Copy the sentences on a separate sheet, correcting as you write.

1. Our countys fair is a highlight of every autumn for me and my three brothers, Terry, David, and Michael.

2. We dont ever go to the fair on weekends because its too crowded then; we've found that the best time to go is about two oclock on a weekday.

3. The fair is better these days than it was in the 70s because more handicraft's are shown.

4. One of the most beautiful items Ive ever seen was the Blue Ridge Mountain quilt exhibited last year by our preacher's wife's best friend.

5. Another feature of the fair my brothers and I especially like is the livestock area; one year we saw some oxen's yoke's get entangled and those oxen nearly went crazy.

6. Another time there was a great rattling over at the monkey's cages, where one monkey had wrapped it's tail around a long stick somebody had poked into the cage and wouldnt let go.

7. Anyone who enjoy's watching roosters strut and pigeon's pout surely wouldnt want to miss the area of the fair marked "Fowl's and Poultry."

8. One of the best parts of any fair is the food, and our's is no exception.

9. Our fair feature's Tonys pizza, Christopher the Greeks baklava, Macks Scottish barley soup, and Johnnys American subs, among other mouth-watering culinary attractions.

10. After a visit to the fair, my brother's and I definitely need a days rest to recuperate, because weve walked and gawked and stuffed ourselve's nearly out of existence by the end of the day.

You will find answers to these punctuation exercises in the appendix.

CAPITALIZATION

Usually you know what to capitalize without thinking much about it. But when you're not quite sure, these rules will help you.

15. In general, capitalize the names or titles of *specific* places, persons, organizations, historical events, or educational courses.

15a. Capitalize the complete names of specific geographic places.

Spring Street   the *Illinois River*
Grand Island, Nebraska   the *West*
Lake Superior

Also capitalize words that derive from names of specific geographic places.

a *New Yorker*   *Indian* food
French blue jeans   the *English* language

But

Do not capitalize the points of the compass or geographic terms that do not name a specific region.

drive *west* on route 66   a beautiful *river*
the *plains*   the *suburbs*
downtown

15b. Capitalize titles of persons if they are used with the person's name or as the person's name.

Although she had been poor all her life, *Mother* always kept her dignity.

Professor Stevens   *Uncle* Jake
Mayor Baldwin

But

Do not capitalize titles of persons when the title is not used as a name or part of a name.

Jim's *uncle*   Stevens is a *professor.*
my *mother*   Joe Baldwin, the *mayor*

15c. Capitalize all significant words in the names of specific organizations and insitutions.

Girl Scouts of *America*   *Department* of *Commerce*
American Cancer Society   *Largo High School*

But

Do not capitalize words that refer generally to groups or institutions.

steelworkers   the *unemployed*
pacifists   *high school*

15d. Capitalize names of specific historical events and names of historical eras.

the *Civil War*   the *Middle Ages*
the *Age* of *Reason*   the *Nuremberg Trials*

But

Do not capitalize words that refer generally to historical happenings or developments.

war crimes   *industrialism*
ancient *democracy*   the rise of *capitalism*

15e. Capitalize the names of specific educational courses.

Math 285   *English* 102
Philosophy 101

But

Do not capitalize names of subjects in general, except languages.

Have you thought of taking *philosophy* this semester?
Have you completed your *math* requirement?
Will you take *French* along with *English* next semester?

16. Capitalize the days of the week, months of the year, and holidays.

Friday   *Thanksgiving*
September

17. Capitalize all the words in titles except for short and unimportant ones. Capitalize even these if they are the first words of a title.

Soul on Ice   *On Death and Dying*
Reader's Digest   ''The Lottery''
The World of Zen   ''All in the Family''
Sex and Power in History   *A Time to Remember*

18. Capitalize religious names and terms of especially sacred significance.

God   the *Annunciation*
Buddha   the *Koran*
Mosaic law   the *Bible*

But

Do not capitalize the word *god* when you use it generally.

the Greek *gods*
belief in a *god*

19. Capitalize the first word of a full sentence quoted inside another sentence.

a. Corrine said to Marie, ''*That* shrub beside your pond is very rare.''

b. Don't forget to include on the announcement about the holiday tour of historical sites: ''*No* smoking is allowed in the restored homes.''

Caution

Do not use a capital letter after a semicolon.

All the audience left the play early; *they* had seen enough of poor acting.

....

Exercise Capitalization

....

Correct the following paragraph for capitalization. Write your corrected copy on a separate sheet of paper. You can check your version against the corrected paragraph in the appendix.

> I think everyone these days should take a course in Economics. People often think that the Law of Supply and Demand is about all that is taught in economics. But I can assure you that you will learn far more if you enroll in Professor Susan Brown's course entitled the American economy. There you will learn about the Rise and Fall of Revolutions—such as the agricultural revolution and the industrial revolution—as well as how the Technological/Electronic Revolution has influenced Economic Development in America. You will also learn why the Columbia River is so important to the economy of the Pacific northwest and how economic vibrations have moved from there eastward. You will even study how the german economy has affected the economy of the World in the Twentieth Century. Furthermore, you will come to realize that charitable and social service groups like the united way and Big Brothers have more of an effect on our National economy than might be expected. You may be wondering how a single Professor could pack so much material into one Economics course. Why not take The American Economy with Professor Brown and find out?

SPELLING

"Anybody who can think of only one way to spell a word is a damn fool." We have heard that remark credited to at least three persons: Mark Twain, Will Rogers, and Andrew Jackson. We would not be surprised to hear it from anyone who has ever tried to write in the English language. Because the spelling of our language is so unpredictable, you should not allow yourself to feel like a blockhead if you "can't spell." Spelling ability is *not* an index to intelligence; some of the smartest people we know can't spell! However, it is true that spelling errors make writing hard to read. So you will want to look carefully for misspellings as you proofread your writing.
Read the following paragraph.

> Most of us know at least one women who is begining colledge in her fourties. Her family may find this new arangement dificult to acommodate to. However, once they become acustomed to it, they frequently speak proudly of her. She, on the other hand, may have to struggle to overcome certian guilt feelings; somehow, the principal of self-development for her own being is hard for her to except, despite the advise of her freinds who have allready traveled the

same path. Gradualy, though, she realizes that she truely is a whole person, seperate from her husband and her childern, and she learns to function outside the wife-mother role. Then she can relax, let down her gaurd some, and finaly begin to recomend "comming back to school" to her neighbors. The growth observeable in such women is exciteing to watch; its one of the real pleasures of being in the collage enviroment today.

How many misspelled words did you spot? There are twenty-seven. (You will find a corrected version of the paragraph in the appendix.) If you as a reader found the misspellings in this paragraph distracting, you'll appreciate the importance of proofreading for spelling.

As we pointed out in the chapter on writing and rewriting, stopping to worry about spelling while you are writing can do more harm than good, because it can hinder the flow of your writing. Ignore spelling as you write; attend to it later.

If you often misspell you may want to do a separate proofreading just for spelling. To do so, read your writing aloud, making yourself say *exactly* what you wrote down, not merely what you *intended* to write, which no doubt will still be lingering in your head. In proofreading for spelling you must train your eye to pay equal attention to each individual letter of a word, rather than reading groups of words in the usual way.

One way in which to make yourself concentrate on single words as you proofread for spelling is to read your paper backwards. Start at the bottom righthand corner and read each line from left to right. If you meant to write "preserve" but you wrote "perserve," this method should force you to *see* "*per*serve." And you will realize that *unusal* cannot spell *unusual,* that *quite* cannot be *quiet,* that *conscience* cannot mean *conscious.*

If you handwrite your papers, be sure every letter of a word looks like what you meant it to be; otherwise, illegibility can be taken for misspelling. If you type your work, be especially alert to typographical errors, which can be read as spelling errors.

20. Improving your spelling

Once you learn to spot your errors, you will begin to recognize your "spelling demons"—words that consistently trip you up. Make a list of these on a 3 × 5 card—or a 4 × 6 or a 6 × 8, if you are tormented by a horde of demons—and keep it handy when you write. In this way you will save yourself the time and trouble of looking up these words. Almost everybody has some spelling demons. One of us, for example, never can remember how to spell *guarantee, obsession,* and *license.*

If you misspell many words in addition to your demons, we urge you to buy a spelling dictionary. Spelling dictionaries give just the spelling and the division of words, without any definitions, so that it is easy to locate words in them. Most spelling dictionaries will also distinguish between sound-alike words such as *affect/effect* and *advise/advice.*

Your regular dictionary can help you with spelling in a way you may not be aware of. Most hardbound dictionaries and some paperback ones feature a section on spelling rules. Look there if you need help with such spelling dilemmas as how to form irregular plurals (*children, mice*), how to form the plurals of words ending in *-y* and *-ey* (*ferry, ferries; donkey, donkeys*), how to add prefixes and suffixes (*renegotiate, finally*), and so on.

How to handle compound words (new words composed of two or more old words) is also clarified in your regular dictionary. If a compound word should be written as a single unbroken word, it will be divided by only the syllable-division marker, a dot in the middle of the line: *fel·low·ship.* If the word is hyphenated, a tiny hyphen will appear between the two older words: *self-con·fi·dence.* If the compound word remains two separate words, an empty space appears between the original words: *cross sec·tion.*

Because our language changes, you may find compound words treated differently in different dictionaries. Don't fret about that. We do suggest, though, that you should avoid spelling a compound word in such a way that deciphering it creates a problem for your reader. *Cross section* may be *cross-section* in some dictionaries. Just don't write it *crosssection;* all those *s*'s in a row are hard to read!

Over the years people with spelling problems have devised various mnemonics (pronounced *knee-mahn'-icks*) to help them remember how to spell certain confusing words. *Mnemonic,* from Greek, means "a memory aid." Probably the most common of these is the one that goes "*i* before *e,* except after *c*"—to help us remember how to spell *believe, sieve, receive,* and so on. Perhaps you know of some others you could share with the class.

You can make up mnemonics to help you remember how to spell your demon words, as we have done for one of ours:

> *obsession:* Oscar banned Sally's elephants seven Saturdays in Owen's neighborhood.

Mnemonics are often easier to remember if they are funny, so play around as you devise yours.

Some words in our language are demons for so many people that over the years, lists of frequently misspelled words have been compiled. Here is such a list to help you. You will not find sound-alike words here; those are handled separately in the section that follows.

LIST OF FREQUENTLY MISSPELLED WORDS

absence
abundance
accessible
accidentally
accommodate
accomplish
accumulate
accurately
accustomed
achievement
acknowledgment
acquaintance
acquire
adequate
adolescence
advantageous
advertisement
aggravate
aggressive
allotted
amateur
among
analysis
analyze
anticipate
anxiety
apology
apparatus
apparent
appearance
appreciate
appropriate
approximately
area
arguing
argument
arising
arrangement
article
athlete
athletic

attendance
audience
authority
balance
basically
beautiful
becoming
before
beginning
belief
believe
beneficial
benefited
boundaries
breath
brilliant
Britain
business
calendar
candidate
career
careless
carrying
category
ceiling
cemetery
challenge
character
characteristic
chief
column
comfortable
comfortably
coming
commission
committed
committee
companies
competition
competitive
completely

comprehension
conceivable
conceive
concentrate
condemn
confident
confidential
conscientious
considerably
consistent
continually
continuous
convenience
convenient
coolly
courageous
courteous
criticism
criticize
cruelty
curiosity
curriculum
dealt
deceit
deceive
decision
definite
definitely
definition
dependent
description
despair
desperate
devastate
development
difference
different
difficult
dilemma
dining
disappear

disappoint
disastrous
discipline
disease
dissatisfied
doesn't
dominant
during
ecstasy
efficiency
efficient
eighth
eliminate
embarrass
embarrassment
emphasize
endeavor
enough
entertain
environment
equipped
erroneous
especially
exaggerate
excellent
exceptionally
exercise
exhilarate
existence
experience
explanation
extraordinary
extremely
familiar
fascinate
finally
financial
foreign
friend
fulfill
fundamentally

generally	loneliness	perceive	schedule
genius	losing	perform	seize
government	magnificence	performance	separate
grammar	maintenance	permanent	sergeant
guaranteed	manageable	persistent	shining
guidance	manufacturer	persuade	significance
happily	marriage	pertain	similar
height	mathematics	phenomenon	sincerely
heroes	meant	philosophy	sophomore
hindrance	medieval	physical	sponsor
humorous	merely	possess	strength
hundred	mileage	possession	stretch
hypocrisy	miniature	practical	strictly
hypocrite	mischievous	prejudice	studying
ignorant	muscle	prevalent	subtle
imaginary	mysterious	privilege	succeed
imagination	naive	probably	successful
immediately	necessarily	procedure	surprise
immensely	necessary	professor	temperament
incidentally	ninety	prominent	tendency
indefinite	noticeable	propaganda	therefore
independent	obstacle	psychology	thorough
indispensable	occasion	pursue	tragedy
influence	occasionally	quantity	transferred
ingenious	occurred	recommend	undoubtedly
intellectual	occurrence	relief	unnecessary
intelligence	opinion	relieve	useful
interest	opponent	religion	using
interpret	opportunity	repetition	various
interrupt	optimism	representative	vengeance
irrelevant	original	resource	villain
knowledge	parallel	rhythm	weird
laboratory	paralysis	ridiculous	writing
leisure	paralyze	roommate	
likelihood	particularly	safety	
literature	peculiar	satisfactorily	

21. Sound-alike words

We want to give you some special help with one kind of spelling problem: words that sound either exactly or approximately alike but that have different meanings. It is easy to confuse such words; some "meaning aids"

may help you to keep them straight. So we are providing a list of some of these troublemakers, with sample sentences.

1. accept (verb)

Will you *accept* the offer?

except (preposition)

Put all *except* the spoiled ones into the basket.

2. advice (noun)

Give me some *advice*.

advise (verb)

I'll be glad to *advise* you.

3. affect (verb)

Will it *affect* my promotion possibilities?

effect (noun)

The *effect* of the collision was slight.

4. already (adverb)

They have *already* come.

all ready

I am *all ready* to go. (means "completely ready")

5. altogether (adverb)

Carolyn was *altogether* wrong.

all together

They are *all together* at the station already. (means "everyone gathered")

6. capital

What is the *capital* of Brazil? (place)

capital

Marie has a large amount of *capital* invested in that office building. (money)

capitol

Maryland's State House, in Annapolis, is the oldest *capitol* in the United States. (building)

7. choose (present tense)

Be sure to *choose* the best.

chose (past tense)

Yesterday she *chose* a desk for her study.

8. cloths

Those silk *cloths* come from Taiwan.

clothes

Put the *clothes* in the dryer.

9. coarse (adjective

The texture of those rugs is too *coarse*.

course (noun)

Is that *course* required for your degree?

10. conscience (noun)

His *conscience* troubled him because he had lied.

conscious (adjective)

I was still *conscious* when the dentist began to drill.

11. desert (noun)

The sands of the *desert* sparkled in the sun.

desert (verb)

Did you *desert* your friends at the party?

dessert (noun)

We had grasshopper pie for *dessert*.

12. effect

See *affect*.

13. except

See *accept*.

14. fair (noun)

Let's go to the county *fair* this fall.

fair (adjective)

She is a very *fair* executive.

fare (noun)

The bus *fare* has gone up.

15. formally

We dressed *formally* for the costume ball.

formerly

Formerly he worked as a firefighter.

16. forth (adverb)

Step *forth* and assert yourself.

fourth (adjective)

Beth sat in the *fourth* row. (from *four*)

17. hear (verb)

Did you *hear* Frank play ''Tally Ho'' on his horn?

here (adverb)

The parade should begin *here*.

18. its (possessive pronoun)

Its head is small for its body.

it's (*it is*)

It's perfect weather for skiing.

19. know (verb)

I *know* everybody in the class.

no

His answer was ''*no*''—in *no* uncertain terms.

20. later (adverb)

We will follow you *later*.

latter (adjective)

The *latter* third of the concert was too modern for my taste.

21. lead (noun)

That basket is as heavy as *lead*.

lead (verb, present tense)

Thomas will *lead* the way.

led (verb, past tense)

It's Thomas' turn, because Kate *led* yesterday.

22. lose (verb)

"Did you *lose* my turtle?" asked Jimmy.

loose (adjective)

The name of the bar is The *Loose* Goose.

23. no

See *know*.

24. passed (verb)

James *passed* the long, difficult test.

past (noun)

That happened so far in the *past* I wish we could forget it.

past (adjective)

The *past* few days have been hectic.

25. peace

That group works hard for world *peace*.

piece

Give me a *piece* of cheesecake.

26. personal (adjective)

Linda considers that her *personal* business.

personnel (noun)

Isn't it strange that all the *personnel* in that company have red hair?

27. precede

Let Richard *precede* you in the line. (go before)

proceed

Please *proceed* to the end of the block. (go forward)

28. principal (noun)

The *principal* was in his office. (person)

principal (noun)

The *principal* was $12,000. (money)

principal (adjective)

Their *principal* food was rice. (meaning "major")

principle (noun)

The *principles* Esther lives by are honesty and dependability. (rule, code of behavior)

29. quiet (adjective)

It was *quiet* in the house.

quite (adverb)

It was *quite* dark outside.

30. right (adjective)

You were quite *right* to tell John the truth.

right (noun)

All members have a *right* to their own opinions.

write (verb)

Louie is going to *write* his paper on computers in the home.

31. role

Sam will play the *role* of Helmer in "A Doll's House."

roll

He called the *roll* quickly.

32. sense (noun)

Most dogs have a *sense* of smell.

sense (verb)

Did you *sense* some hostility on Jenny's part?

since (conjunction)

Since your pet iguana will be on the train, Jake won't go.

since (preposition)

I have not talked with Betsy *since* yesterday.

33. stationery (noun)

Eleanor wrote on lavender *stationery*.

stationary (adjective)

Her desk is *stationary* in that corner.

34. than (used to compare)

Charlotte is more reflective *than* I.

then (adverb of time)

Jasper turned red and *then* left the room.

35. there (introductory word and adverb of place)
their (possessive)
they're (*they are*)

There are young people who, as soon as *they're* old enough to drive, think they should have a car of *their* own. Many want to keep *their* cars on the school grounds, over *there* near the playing field.

36. through (preposition)
threw (verb)

Timing her jump precisely, Sandy *threw* the ball *through* the hoop.

37. to (preposition and part of verb)

Is Ellen planning *to* go *to* the ballet?

too (adverb)

I want some frozen raspberry yogurt *too*. (means *also*)
It is *too* late to worry about whether your costume is *too* loose.

two (number)

Ed has *two* valuable comic books I want.

38. weather (noun)

The clear *weather* makes today just right for exploring the valley.

whether (conjunction)	David didn't know *whether* to laugh or cry.
39. where (adverb of place) were (verb)	*Where were* you when the rest of us left for the art gallery?
40. whose	Whose pocket is housing a croaking frog?
who's (who is, who has)	*Who's* coming scuba-diving with us?
41. woman (singular)	Harriet Tubman, a somewhat fragile *woman,* was nevertheless a major figure in the Underground Railway during the Civil War.
women (plural)	Are you taking the course *Women* in Art?
42. your (possessive pronoun) you're (*you are*)	*You're* likely to lose *your* coat if you take it off in this trolley car.

. . . .

Exercise Spelling

. . . .

If spelling is a problem for you, apply what you have learned in this section to the paragraph with twenty-seven misspelled words at the beginning of the section. Use the lists of commonly misspelled words and sound-alike words as you work. Write your corrected words on a separate sheet of paper. Then turn to the appendix to check your spelling against the corrected paragraph you will find there.

Revising problem sentences

frag   **22. Write complete sentences.**

Don't treat fragments (pieces) of sentences as if they were complete sentences. That is, don't begin a series of words that is not a sentence with a capital letter and end it with a period. Such incomplete series of words need to be connected to another sentence nearby, usually with a comma. In the first line of each example below, the second series of words is a fragment.

a. There is a great need for female doctors. Especially in obstetrics and gynecology.

There is a great need for female doctors, especially in obstetrics and gynecology.

b. Jim's gaily wrapped package sat waiting in the closet. Safely hidden from inquisitive little fingers.

Jim's gaily wrapped package sat waiting in the closet, safely hidden from inquisitive little fingers.

c. Europe's rail system is quick, cheap, and efficient. While European roads are primitive.

Europe's rail system is quick, cheap, and efficient, while European roads are primitive.

d. The school has been dubbed SERE. An acronym for survival, evasion, resistance, and escape.

The school has been dubbed SERE, an acronym for survival, evasion, resistance, and escape.

Exception
Sentence fragments are permissible when you use them deliberately, for emphasis.

The plane takes off with a mighty roar. Off toward Vietnam.

I sometimes think as I look at my child: "I love you, but you remind me of my mistakes and I can't bear to look at you. Or talk to you. Or think about you."

Johnson felt he could release his frustrations on his wife because he felt at home with her. Ordinarily they got along well, and talking with her about his unhappiness with his job and with life in general was a source of release for him. But not that day.

run-on/cs 23. Avoid run-on sentences and comma splices.

Do not run two complete statements together. Do not splice (fasten) two complete statements together with a comma. Two complete statements can be joined together in one sentence in *only* two ways:

1. with a connector word (*and, but, or, nor, for, so, yet*)

2. with a semicolon.

There are four possible ways to correct run-on sentences or comma splices.

1. Split the two statements into two separate sentences.

a. The worst thing about hell is that there will be no one to turn to you will be all alone.

The worst thing about hell is that there will be no one to turn to. You will be all alone.

b. I don't mind cooking, in fact I enjoy it.

I don't mind cooking. In fact, I enjoy it.

2. Put a connector word (*and, but, or, nor, for, so, yet*) between the two statements.

a. I have thirty more years before retirement by then I should have reached my goal.

I have thirty more years before retirement, and by then I should have reached my goal.

b. Jim said it looked snug around the waist, I thought it looked perfect.

Jim said it looked snug around the waist, but I thought it looked perfect.

3. Insert a semicolon between the two statements.

a. He could not respond it seemed hopeless.

He could not respond; It seemed hopeless.

b. Water conditions of the soil can be a real source of trouble when camping, however, your camp should be located close to a spring of running water.

Water conditions of the soil can be a real source of trouble when camping; however, your camp should be located close to a spring of running water.

4. Restructure the sentence.

a. This is why there are so many robberies, murders, and rapes people are just bored.

Many robberies, murders, and rapes are committed out of boredom.

b. The plains Indians were a trusting people, many of the tribes didn't even have a word for *lie*.

The plains Indians were so trusting that many of the tribes didn't even have a word for *lie*.

You will find an exercise on fragments, run-on sentences, and comma splices at the end of this section.

mix **24. Rewrite mixed-up sentences.**

Mixed-up sentences are ones that got out of control as you were writing them. They began in one way, then ended in a way that didn't quite fit the beginning. You can think of them as having the head of one sentence and the tail of another. Here is an example:

If I can help out just by listening to a child's small but pressing problems gives me satisfaction.

The "head" of this sentence is "If I can help out just by listening to a child's small but pressing problems." The "tail" is "gives me satisfaction." The problem is that the head and tail don't go together.

To revise a mixed-up sentence you can change the tail to fit the head:

If I can help out just by listening to a child's small but pressing problems, I am satisfied.

Or you can change the head to fit the tail:

Just listening to a child's small but pressing problems gives me satisfaction.

Sometimes, though, a sentence will be so badly mixed up that you can't even find its head and its tail. What should you do then? Just throw it out, then try again to express your idea—this time in a clear, straightforward sentence.

a. I found that getting involved in working with students on their reading problems a new and enlightening experience.

Helping students with their reading problems was a new and enlightening experience for me

b. I think that would be the most important thing about a job is satisfaction.

The most important thing about a job, for me, is the satisfaction I receive from it.

c. Not being able to go to her mother and talk to her the way she once did and the love for her husband not being returned, made her feel very depressed.

Her husband no longer loved her, and she could no longer talk over personal problems with her mother. Her isolation made her feel very depressed.

d. At one point I gave up completely deciding whether or not to commit suicide, to end my life at the age of twenty.

At the age of twenty, I decided to end my life.

An occasional mixed-up sentence is nothing to worry about. Just rewrite it when you discover it. But if many of your sentences get out of control, you have a problem that needs to be tackled head on.

Either by yourself or with the help of your instructor, try to discover *why* you are writing so many mixed-up sentences. If you can find the causes of your problem, you'll be that much closer to a solution. Here is a list of some common causes, each of which suggests its own cure:

Cause: You're trying to write in a style that is more formal and complex than you can handle.

Cure: Write in a simpler, more direct style.

Cause: Your only purpose for writing is that you have to complete an assignment. Attempting to spin something out of nothing, you wind up in a tangle of words and phrases.

Cure: Choose writing topics that are more "real" for you—on subjects you know something about. And as you write, focus on writing for readers who want to hear what you have to say.

Cause: You treat writing as a one-step process. Once you start writing, you just plunge forward, even when you can feel sentences escaping from your control.

Cure: Change your writing habits. Practice writing the way professionals do—use a several-step process involving false starts and lots of crossing-out and rephrasing. Control your sentences instead of letting them go off on their own.

Cause: You're not sure which sentence structures are acceptable in written English. You know that certain "loose" sentence structures are all right in spoken English, but you're not sure which ones will work in written English.

Cure: This cure will take time—a whole semester at least. Purchase a workbook or work through programmed materials on the basic sentence patterns of written English. Your instructor can advise you on books and materials available at your school.

shift 25. Avoid confusing shifts.

If you begin writing in the present tense, don't make a confusing shift to the past. If you are using one pronoun, such as *I*, don't shift to another, such as *you*. If you begin writing in the active voice, don't shift to the passive voice.

a. We left early to go to the circus. Once there, we wander around, eat popcorn, and some of us get lost.

We left early to go to the circus. Once there, we wandered around, ate popcorn, and some of us got lost.

b. The other members of the team must accept all decisions made by the leader, even if that means they won't make it to the top. You must be willing to trust the leader without question.

The other members of the team must accept all decisions made by the leader, even if that means they won't make it to the top. They must be willing to trust the leader without question.

c. The teacher focuses on main events. Trivia is included only when it helps the student understand the material.

The teacher focuses on main events. She includes trivia only when it helps the student understand the material.

Note
For more about confusing shifts, see chapters 4 and 11.

om 26. Do not omit words that are needed.

Sometimes, especially when you are trying to avoid repetition, you may be tempted to omit words that are necessary for grammatical completeness. Resist the temptation. Your readers need to understand how the parts of your sentence fit together.

a. I knew then that everything would be all right, but there would be other patients just like her.

I knew then that everything would be all right, but that there would be other patients just like her.

b. In my opinion her dependence on tranquilizers is no healthier than the alcoholic or the addict.

In my opinion her dependence on tranquilizers is no healthier than the alcoholic's dependence on alcohol or the addict's need for a fix.

c. If your hair is long, don't be surprised when the Japanese barber wraps a few curlers here and there and a good dousing with hair spray.

If your hair is long, don't be surprised when the Japanese barber wraps a few curlers here and there and gives you a good dousing with hair spray.

d. Dave saw his four-year-old brother was moving too close to the cliff.

Dave saw that his four-year-old brother was moving too close to the cliff.

e. Having grown up in the ghetto, Teresa was both delighted and uneasy about her scholarship to Harvard.

Having grown up in the ghetto, Teresa was both delighted with and uneasy about her scholarship to Harvard.

Note
If you frequently omit words, turn to the handbook section on "Dialect Interference: Problems with Omitted Words" (38).

mod 27. Place modifiers close to the words they modify.

A modifier is a word or group of words that gives readers additional information about some other word in the sentence. In general, keep your modifiers close to the words they modify.

a. Our dog Gregory nipped the blind man on the leg who was delivering light bulbs.

Our dog Gregory nipped the leg of the blind man who was delivering light bulbs.

b. Angela made apple turnovers for her sisters spiced with cinnamon and nutmeg.

Angela made apple turnovers spiced with cinnamon and nutmeg for her sisters.

c. Marlboro ads often depict a man on a horse smoking a cigarette.

Marlboro ads often depict a man on horseback smoking a cigarette.

d. Our next-door neighbor has a black Corvette whose reputation for driving wildly down the block is notorious.

Our next-door neighbor has a notorious reputation for driving wildly down the block in his black Corvette.

e. Lloyd decided on his way to the office to buy flowers.

On his way to the office, Lloyd decided to buy flowers.

dng 28. Avoid dangling modifiers.

A modifier is a word or group of words that gives readers additional information about some other word in the sentence. A modifier is said to

dangle when the writer forgets to include the word that it modifies. When a modifier dangles, readers are tempted to attach it to some other word that does appear in the sentence. The result is confusing and sometimes humorous. Notice, for example, how you are tempted to misread this sentence: "Twisting around the mast, the cook had difficulty grabbing its tail."

a. Already failing one test, my spirits were low.

Since I had already failed one test, my spirits were low.

b. While running an EEG one day, the pens started clacking and throwing ink about the room.

While I was running an EEG one day, the pens started clacking and throwing ink about the room.

c. Gazing from the hillside, the early morning fog blanketed the slough like a damp overcoat.

Gazing from the hillside, I watched as the early morning fog blanketed the slough like a damp overcoat.

d. Seeing her standing with suitcase in hand, it dawned on me that this was the moment for which we had been waiting nine months.

When I saw her standing with suitcase in hand, it dawned on me that this was the moment for which we had been waiting nine months.

e. To swim properly, each stroke should be timed.

To swim properly, you should time each stroke.

f. When playing tennis, concentration is important.

Concentration is important in playing tennis.

You will find an exercise on misplaced and dangling modifiers at the end of this section.

 29. Match your subjects and verbs.

Subjects and their verbs should agree in number. If the subject is singular, the verb should be singular. If the subject is plural, the verb should be plural.

This sounds like a simple enough rule, and for the most part you have probably mastered it. But you may sometimes have trouble with it. When you do, here are the most likely sources of your problem:

1. You're not sure what the subject of the sentence is.

2. You're not sure whether the subject is singular or plural.

3. You speak a dialect that differs slightly from standard English.

We will treat these different sources of the problem one at a time.

29a. You're not sure what the subject of the sentence is.

a. If several words come between the subject and the verb, you may mistake a noun close to the verb for the subject.

1. The large boxes of mixed candy was on sale.

The large *boxes* of mixed candy were on sale.

2. The role of the police officer in these shows seem stereotyped.

The *role* of the police officer in these shows seems stereotyped.

b. If the subject follows the verb (reversing the usual order), you may mistake a noun that comes before the verb for the subject of the sentence.

1. Behind the defensive line is several young linebackers.

Behind the defensive line are several young *linebackers*.

2. Hiding in the corner behind the plants are the long-sought-after runaway child.

Hiding in the corner behind the plants is the long-sought-after runaway *child*.

c. Sentences beginning with "There is" or "There are" present a special problem because they seem to have no subject. Actually the subject follows the "There is" or "There are" construction.

1. There is not many people on Assateague Island.

There are not many *people* on Assateague Island.

2. There wasn't even enough chairs to go around.

There weren't even enough *chairs* to go around.

29b. You're not sure whether the subject is singular or plural.

a. When the subject of the sentence is a collective noun like *committee* or *team* or *jury*, do you treat the noun as singular or plural? The answer depends on the meaning you intend. Usually you will want readers to view the group as one unit, so you will treat the noun as singular.

The committee was more successful than we had hoped.

Our team is expected to win.

But occasionally you may want readers to view the group as a number of individuals. Then you'll treat the noun as plural.

Unable so far to agree on a verdict, the jury continue to debate the case.

b. Are pronouns like *each, one, none, either, neither, any, every, whoever,* and *somebody* singular or plural? In casual speech many people treat them as plurals. But in writing, especially in formal writing, these words have traditionally been treated as singular. There is some evidence that the traditional rule may be changing, but in the meantime you should probably play it safe. Even if you would usually say "each of them were," you will find it safer to write "each of them was."

1. Whoever are going should be ready by six o'clock.

Whoever *is* going should be ready by six o'clock.

2. Each of the twelve stamps are worth fifty dollars.

Each of the twelve stamps *is* worth fifty dollars.

3. Everybody in the local jail were released.

Everybody in the local jail *was* released.

c. If the subject of the sentence is compound (two subjects connected by *and, or,* or *nor*), do you treat the compound subject as singular or plural? The answer is fairly complicated. Let's begin with the easy rule: When the two parts of the compound subject are connected with *and,* you always treat the subject as plural.

My mother's natural ability and her desire to help others *have* led to a career as a psychic medium.

And now the more complex rule: When the two parts of the compound subject are connected with *or* or *nor*, you match the verb with the part of the subject that's closest to it. If that part of the subject is singular, your verb should be singular.

Neither the students nor their instructor *was* able to find the classroom.

If that part of the subject is plural, the verb should be plural.

Neither the instructor nor her students *were* able to find the classroom.

29c. You speak a dialect that differs slightly from mainstream (standard) English.

If you make a great many errors in subject-verb agreement, dialect interference is almost certainly the source of most of your problem. For advice, turn to the handbook section on "Dialect Interference: Problems with *-s* Endings." (37)

You will find an exercise on subject-verb agreement at the end of this section.

n-p   **30. Match your nouns and pronouns.**

Pronouns are words that substitute for nouns. Each pronoun should agree in number with its antecedent (the noun it refers to). Use singular pronouns to refer to singular nouns, plural pronouns to refer to plural nouns.

> The sermon reminded us that even though temptations to be unkind are great, we must learn to resist it.

> The sermon reminded us that even though temptations to be unkind are great, we must learn to resist *them*.

For the most part you probably follow this rule quite easily, without even thinking about it. But in certain situations you may run into problems. Let's talk about those situations one at a time.

30a. Many of your problems with pronoun-antecedent agreement may arise because you do not want to discriminate against women.

Traditionally it has been acceptable to write "The average student is worried about *his* grades"; but this sort of sentence, which ignores half the human race, is becoming less and less acceptable. In an effort to avoid such sentences, you may be tempted to use a plural pronoun: "The average student is concerned about *their* grades." But this sentence is not acceptable in formal writing, because the plural *their* doesn't agree with the singular *student*.

The correct form is "The average student is concerned about *his* or *her* grades." This sentence is socially acceptable because it includes both men and women, and it is grammatically acceptable because the singular *his or her* agrees with the singular *student*.

However, too many repetitions of *his* or *her* can begin to sound awkward. To avoid such awkwardness, you can recast your sentences. You can write "The average student is worried about grades" or "Students are usually worried about grades."

Problem sentences:

If an individual on approved leave wishes to continue hospitalization coverage, they must pay the full premium.

Acceptable revised versions:

If an individual on approved leave wishes to continue hospitalization coverage, he or she must pay the full premium.

Persons on approved leave who wish to continue hospitalization coverage must pay the full premium.

When a person goes to the hospital, they are put on a schedule that is convenient for the hospital staff.

When a person goes to the hospital, he or she is put on a schedule that is convenient for the hospital staff.

Patients are put on schedules that are convenient for the hospital staff.

30b. You may be uncertain whether words such as *anyone, somebody, each, either,* and *everybody* should be treated as singular or plural.

Should you write "Everyone must cast his or her vote in person" or "Everyone must cast their vote in person"? Many people treat these words as plural, especially in informal speech and writing. In formal writing, however, these words have been traditionally viewed as singular. Although informal practice seems to be changing the formal rule, you'll find it safer to follow the formal rule for now. Write "Everyone must cast his or her vote in person."

If "his or her" begins to sound awkward to you, you might write "Voters must cast their votes in person" or "You must vote in person" or "All votes must be cast in person."

Problem sentences:

Everyone was told to make sure they attended class on Friday.

Acceptable revised versions:

Everyone was told to make sure he or she attended class on Friday.

All the students were told to make sure they attended class on Friday.

Has anyone lost their glove?

Has anyone lost his or her glove?

Has anyone lost a glove?

Each of us wanted their fair share.

Each of us wanted his or her fair share.

All of us wanted our fair share.

30c. If the noun you're referring to is a collective one such as committee, jury, or audience, do you treat the noun as singular or plural?

Your meaning will determine which way you will treat it. If you are speaking of the group as a single unit, write "The committee announced its decision." But if you want to focus on the group as a collection of individuals, write "The committee argued over their decision all afternoon."

ref. 31. Make pronoun references clear.

Pronouns are words that substitute for nouns. They are a kind of short-hand. In a sentence like "When the queen issued the order, she assumed everyone would obey it," the pronouns *she* and *it* are simply shorthand for the nouns *queen* and *order*.

Make sure that your readers will understand which noun each pronoun refers to. Most of the time your pronoun references will be clear, but occasionally you may slip up. When you do, here are the most likely sources of your problem:

1. Your pronoun does not have a noun to refer to.

2. Your pronoun could possibly refer to two different nouns.

3. Your pronoun is too far away from the noun to which it refers.

We will treat these different sources of the problem one at a time.

31a. Your pronoun does not have a noun to refer to.

a. The course consists of seven weekly sessions, each two hours long. *They* guarantee that you will increase your reading speed and comprehension.
The course consists of seven weekly sessions, each two hours long. The instructors guarantee that you will increase your reading speed and comprehension.

b. Many people watch soap operas as a form of relaxation. Like watching Monday night football games, *this* provides viewers with a relaxing escape from everyday problems.
Many people watch soap operas as a form of relaxation. Like watching Monday night football games, watching soap operas provides viewers with a relaxing escape from everyday concerns.

c. In the encyclopedia *it* states that only eight out of one hundred snakes are poisonous.
The encyclopedia states that only eight out of one hundred snakes are poisonous.

d. "Like a Winding Sheet" is about a black man who feels victimized by white people; the story shows how much friction *it* causes between him and his wife.
"Like a Winding Sheet" is about a black man who feels victimized by white people; the story shows how much friction these feelings cause between him and his wife.

31b. Your pronoun could possibly refer to two different nouns.

a. When Jack put the sculpture on the table, *it* broke.

The table broke when Jack put the sculpture on it.

Or

The sculpture broke when Jack put it on the table.

b. Mary Ellen said to Pamela that *she* was wrong to have repeated the rumor.

Mary Ellen apologized to Pamela for having repeated the rumor.

Or

Mary Ellen reprimanded Pamela for having repeated the rumor.

31c. Your pronoun is too far away from the noun to which it refers.

a. Her two teenaged girls and her eight-year-old son were causing problems. Sometimes all three children would refuse to go to school, and they frequently stayed out late at night. *He* had become the leader of a street gang.

Her two teenaged girls and her eight-year-old son were causing problems. Sometimes all three children would refuse to go to school, and they frequently stayed out late at night. The boy had become the leader of a street gang.

b. Though they are presented as keepers of justice, the police on many television programs are cold-hearted killers. In one episode last week I saw a person choked, another run down by a squad car, and four people shot to death. Instead of trying to solve a situation, *they* seem to shoot first and ask questions later.

Though they are presented as keepers of justice, the police on many television programs are cold-hearted killers. In one episode last week I saw a person choked, another run down by a squad car, and four people shot to death. Instead of trying to solve a situation, the police on these programs seem to shoot first and ask questions later.

You will find an exercise on noun-pronoun agreement and pronoun reference at the end of this section.

 ## 32. Put parallel content in parallel form.

Sentence parts that have parallel (similar) functions should be expressed in parallel (similar) structures. When you put parallel sentence parts in unparallel form, the form fights the meaning. Readers will be grateful when the form of your sentences supports their meaning.

a. This summer I plan to work a little, go to school, see some old friends, as well as just sitting around.

This summer I plan to work a little, go to school, see some old friends, and just sit around.

b. I have been accused of being rough, hardheaded, and a thoughtless individual.

I have been accused of being rough, hardheaded, and thoughtless.

c. A person may pursue a goal at college, at a trade school, a military career, or in industry.

A person may pursue a goal at college, at a trade school, in the military, or in industry.

Note

For more about parallel sentence structure, see chapters 11, 12, and 15.

p-a 33. Write in the active voice.

When a sentence is written in the active voice, the subject performs the action; in passive-voice sentences, the subject receives the action. "Carlos read the novel" is written in the active voice. "The novel was read by Carlos" is written in the passive voice. So is "The novel was read thoroughly."

In general, prefer the active voice to the passive; it is more direct and forceful.

a. The skills I need to master will be worked on.

I will work on the skills I need to master.

b. Finally, after two hours of bumbling, the pie was completed by Harriet.

Finally, after two hours of bumbling, Harriet completed the pie.

c. *I'm OK, You're OK* is a book worth reading. Time should be taken to read it thoroughly. Much self-confidence may be gained.

I'm OK, You're OK is a book worth reading. Those who take time to read it thoroughly may gain much self-confidence.

Exceptions

Though you should usually write in the active voice, you might sensibly choose to write in the passive voice when:

a. You do not know the actor of the sentence.

It was determined that her brain cells were slowly being destroyed.

b. You wish to focus on the action, not the actor.

You are shown how to pace through a book at a rate two or more times your normal reading speed.

c. The receiver of the action is more important than the actor.

Roots, according to the paper, has been seen by approximately 30 million people.

wordy 34. Tighten wordy sentences.

A wordy sentence is one that can be trimmed *without losing any meaning*. Sometimes you can tighten wordy sentences simply by deleting excess words; other times you'll need to restructure the sentence.

a. Some of the mentally retarded can be taught to lead productive lives through training.

Some of the mentally retarded can be trained to lead productive lives.

b. A choice I made that seemed to surprise almost everyone I knew was when I separated from my husband and filed for divorce.

When I separated from my husband and filed for divorce, I surprised almost everyone.

c. The basic principle of a parochial school mainly involves that of receiving a good education along with discipline.

Parochial schools provide a good education and a healthy dose of discipline.

d. The males are classically known as being dumb jocks.

The males are stereotyped as dumb jocks.

e. Having a physical education major involves taking many science courses.

Physical education majors must take many science courses.

Note
For more about wordiness, see chapter 13.

ob 35. Avoid overburdened sentences.

a. This paper is a salute to all black women all over the nation who have suffered through almost unendurable hardships trying to keep their families together as a strong and united group in the face of a relentless oppression that confronted them in their day-to-day lives.

This paper is a salute to all the black women of America who have suffered deeply as they tried to keep their families together in the face of relentless day-to-day oppression.

b. As I walked through the front door, after nearly breaking my neck on what I thought were steps, only to find that they were rotten and infested with small white termites, I was stunned by the smell of death.

As I walked through the front door, after stumbling on the rotten, terminte-infested steps, I was stunned by the smell of death.

Overburdened sentences are usually long, but long sentences aren't necessarily overburdened. When a sentence is overburdened, readers have trouble seeing how the parts relate to one another. When a long sentence is well structured, the relationships among its parts are immediately clear to readers.

Every afternoon that I am at home and not otherwise occupied, I sneak down into the basement at one-thirty and hide there in the semidarkness until three o'clock doing something that I don't really like to talk about.

Note

If you often write overburdened sentences, turn to the section on double-speak in chapter 13.

. . . .
Exercise 1 Fragments, run-on sentences, and comma splices
. . . .

Each of the following items contains one of the errors mentioned above. Correct the error as you copy the sentences on a separate sheet.

1. Before the snows come, I would like to go to the Appalachian Mountains. Where I hear you can still find some authentic banjo-picking.

2. I think I'll ask some friends, like Chip, Joan, and Martha, to go along, we could take turns driving those mountain roads.

3. Charlotte Blackman, who's in my art class, grew up in those hills, let's ask her to come.

4. Keep in mind that we need to find people who really want to listen to bluegrass it will be an unhappy outing if we ask the wrong folks.

5. Tom O'Hare says that comparing the bluegrass of different regions is one of his hobbies. Although I've never seen him at a local festival.

6. I'd vote for taking a chance on Tom, he's good company no matter where he is.

7. Let's leave early on a Saturday morning everybody should be free then, and we can stop for brunch instead of eating breakfast before we leave.

8. The trip should take about three hours if we don't run into problems driving in the mountains. Which could surely happen.

9. We should take some cheese and bread and wine for lunch you tell Charlotte to bring a treat the mountain people would appreciate.

10. Maybe we could take our own instruments and play some with the mountain people, that could be the best part of our trip.

Exercise 2 Misplaced modifiers and dangling modifiers

The following sentences contain misplaced and/or dangling modifiers. Clarify the sentences as you write them on a separate sheet of paper.

1. Balcony gardening is becoming more and more popular to grow both flowers and vegetables.

2. Gardening in pots of several sizes, plants grow especially well for the couple living just opposite me.

3. This year they have tomatoes, roses, and geraniums, as well as old-fashioned blue morning glories, which add a pleasing touch of red to their balcony.

4. Watching my neighbors enjoy their balcony garden, it occurred to me that I should try my hand at planting something.

5. Having planted petunias without much success last summer, this year's garden on my balcony will be all vegetables.

6. To pot-garden successfully, the pots must not be crowded with plants, which should be of clay or wood.

7. The orange tree is an attractive small tree for balcony gardens that bears both fragrant blossoms and colorful miniature fruit.

8. To outdo their neighbors, small rock gardens are set up by some people on their balconies.

9. Insects are beginning to invade some of our balcony gardens, which could get to be a real nuisance if they find our houseplants.

10. Maybe I'll just give up on pot-gardening and make a terrarium (a small indoor garden under glass), which is beginning to take up too much of my time.

Exercise 3 Subject-verb agreement

Some of the following sentences contain errors in subject-verb agreement. If a sentence is correct, put a C beside its number on a separate sheet of paper. Correct the incorrect sentences as you copy them.

1. Import stores, where you can find a jeweled bracelet or an inlaid card-holder or pieces of Asian pottery, all reasonably priced, is a good place to shop for presents.

2. My sister, who can afford to buy very expensive gifts, shops at such stores every Christmas.

3. A group of women I know go to the import store in a nearby town every fall; once there the group break up so that everybody is on her own to circulate and look for treasures.

4. Everyone who rummages around in import stores are almost sure to come up with unexpected treasures.

5. Last year, tucked away in a poorly lighted far corner, was some beautiful bookcovers of Moroccan leather, which Jane Tucker unearthed.

6. Unfortunately, neither Jane nor any of her friends were interested in Moroccan leather bookcovers.

7. Also in that corner were a collection of hand-painted wooden canes from Switzerland.

8. One of my best import store finds were a large, heavy, ornate marble-topped washstand from England—which I would have bought if I had been driving a truck!

9. Once when I was at an import store, there was some excellent buys still crated in their shipping boxes.

10. Long lines of adults, and now and then a restless child, stands in line waiting for import stores to open each Saturday.

. . . .
Exercise 4   Noun-pronoun agreement and pronoun reference
. . . .

The following items contain errors in noun-pronoun agreement and in pronoun reference. Correct the errors as you copy the sentences on a separate sheet of paper.

1. According to some instructors, anybody can learn to swim if they try hard enough.

2. Learning to swim is one of the best ways to make sure all the body gets enough exercise; this is easy to do at the health clubs found in many towns.

3. A person just beginning to swim regularly should not push himself beyond a comfortable endurance point; otherwise, it might discourage continuing this beneficial exercise.

4. A comfortable suit is a must for swimming, and a cap is required at some clubs; it must not restrict the swimmer's breathing.

5. Those who swim regularly often join a health club team. My team won their most satisfying trophy when we all swam in unison during a meet that excluded individual competition. In this, each of the swimmers have to coordinate their movements precisely in order not to interfere with each other's strokes.

··

Exercise 5 For proofreading

··

Here is the draft of a paper that needs to be proofread for punctuation, capitalization, spelling, and sentence problems. Look over the draft carefully. Number from 1 to 53 on a sheet of paper, and beside each number note down corrections for the line corresponding to that number. If a line in the draft is correct, put a C by the line number.

1   Shortly after leaving High School I enlisted in the Navy during the
2 Korean War. Even if I didn't want to die on a battlefield, I felt enough
3 patriotism to want to serve my country. By this I entered on the first of
4 many paths that have shaped my career and my life.
5   My choice of fire control school after basic training, was not a
6 carefully considered decision. Fire control simply sounded like an intrest-
7 ing school and besides it was the longest in the enlisted man's Navy, it
8 would last for fifty-two weeks of my four year enlistment. Learning fire
9 control did not mean putting out fires abroad ship. Instead it meant to
10 know and control the radar system by which the guns aboard the ships
11 were being fired.
12   During this long period of learning, I fell in love with and married a
13 local high .school girl. We settled down in her Hometown. After my
14 enlistment was over, I enrolled in college, feeling that would be a good
15 way for you to get ahead. I had the G. I. bill to help me through college
16 and I knew I would be expected to be the breadwinner in family in the
17 furture. Meanwhile, my wife worked—for a small salery.
18   I was lead onto a path filled with Mathematics and weapons, by the
19 courses I selected in college; as well as by my background. However,
20 going to college on the money from the G. I. bill, and liveing on my wife's
21 small income, ment we had to live frugally. As we set up housekeeping
22 on our meager means. A previously hidden talent in me for building
23 began to emerge.
24   This discovery sparked an interest totally diffrent from the one I was
25 pursuing in my education. So I left the path of mathematics and
26 weapons, young and full of dreams, for a new path to construction and
27 being independent. Unfortunatly, at the same time I started down this
28 path the country went into a deep recesion, putting many young hope-
29 fuls like out of business and into debt.
30   By now my wife had stopped working to have a family, and I became
31 our familys sole support. Fortunately my background was good; and I had
32 a freind who helped me get a job in the Defense business. My college
33 degree had to be postponed, although I never stopped working toward
34 it.

35   I never forgot the time spent in the building industry. Even though my
36   natural abilities training and later my college degree helped me advance
37   in my new career. For me hammering, sawing, nailing and sweating
38   during the creation of a building held much satisfaction then solving the
39   critcal problems related to my job in defense.
40   A chance to go back to construction never came along, so I put my
41   energy into my career as a Math Analyst. A career filled with details
42   responsibilities and at times a great deal of mental stress. Having time to
43   think on the job, the times when I could be building constantly occupied
44   my mind. Building was a rest, an escape and a pleasure. Although I felt I
45   could know longer begin a new career in construction; I became dissatis-
46   fied even with my acheivements in my prospering career.
47   Always thinking of the future and at the same time recalling the
48   passed insecurity of my parents, I maintained my position for it's retire-
49   ment benefits as a math analyst, instead of venturing out once more into
50   construction. But like a sailor who counts the days till his enlistment ends I
51   count the time until I can gain enough independence to try to re-enter my
52   dream occupation. On that final path I expect to be a contented
53   person—but not until I am on that path once again.

You will find answers to the five exercises above in the appendix.

Note

If you need practice beyond these exercises in any area covered in the handbook, consult your instructor. Several kinds of resources, including workbooks, a learning lab, and writing tutors, may be available at your school.

Dialect interference

This chapter is intended to help writers whose spoken dialect is interfering with their written English. A dialect, as you may already know, is a variety of spoken language typical of a regional or social group. For example, if you are from Appalachia, you may speak Appalachian English, or if you're black, you may speak a dialect known as Black English.

Writing, as you know, is nearly always done in standard English, a language accessible to the vast majority of English-speaking people. Dialects differ from standard English in two important ways, both of which can cause interference when a dialect speaker writes. First, a dialect has a system of pronunciation slightly different from that of standard English. Second, a dialect also has its own system of grammar that differs in small but noticeable ways from the grammar of standard English.

If you speak a dialect, your pronunciation may sometimes interfere with your writing. For example, if your dialect allows you to drop -ed from the ends of words in speech, you may tend to omit -ed's when you write. Grammatical differences between a dialect and standard English can also interfere with your writing. The grammar of your dialect may allow a sentence like "We on time for once" or "Harry type fifty words a minute," when standard written English requires "We *are* on time for once" or "Harry *types* fifty words a minute."

This chapter details common differences between some spoken dialects and standard written English. If you speak a dialect, you're probably already aware of some of these differences. Most dialect speakers are able to shift back and forth, depending on the situation, between dialect speech and standard speech. In very formal situations, or when speaking to people who don't speak the dialect, they have a tendency to shift to a more standard English. You can take advantage of whatever ability you already have to shift into standard English as you work to clear up writing problems caused by dialect interference. And you can use this chapter to increase that ability even further.

As you read this chapter you will notice that we assume that dialect English is "different from," not "inferior to" standard English. Years ago nearly everyone thought that dialect speech was just sloppy—that it differed from spoken standard English in totally unpredictable ways. But within the last twenty years linguists (scientists who study the ways people actually speak) have been steadily proving that the language of dialect speakers has a high degree of regularity. One linguist, William Labov, sums up these discoveries in a thought-provoking essay, "The Logic of Nonstandard English."* There he argues that nonstandard English is not illogical; it is just different from standard English. Nearly all linguists and a growing number of English professors agree with Labov.

As you work to conquer writing problems caused by dialect interference, don't allow yourself to lose confidence. The fact that you have these problems is *not* evidence that your mind works in illogical ways. It is merely evidence that your spoken dialect is interfering with your written English.

36. Problems with *-ed* endings

Some writers have a problem with *-ed* endings of past-tense verbs. They write "Lurleen *walk* home from school yesterday" instead of "Lurleen *walked* home." Or they write "As a supervisor, I am *charge* with the responsibility of evaluating my subordinates" or "After school the children were *suppose* to go straight home," when they should have written *"charged with"* and *"were supposed."* Occasionally a writer with this problem will add an *-ed* ending when it's not needed. One student, for example, wrote "A traffic violator was *founded* hung in his cell." The past tense of the verb *find* is *found,* not *founded,* but this student was so used to being corrected for leaving off *-ed*'s that he threw in an extra one just to be safe.

The *-ed* problem is caused by an important difference between speaking and writing. Linguists have discovered that nearly all speakers of English fail to pronounce *-ed* endings at least some of the time, and that some speakers drop their *-ed*'s more often than others. Most speakers don't even notice that they have done this. The context of their sentences usually makes the past tense clear, so dropping *-ed*'s in speech really doesn't matter much. But in written English those *-ed*'s become conspicuous by their absence; a reader, unlike a listener, consciously misses them. If you tend to omit *-ed* endings in your writing, you need to become more aware of this difference between spoken and written English.

Just being aware of the difference will help you some, and more experience in both reading and writing will reinforce your awareness. But luckily there is a faster way to attack the problem. The same linguists who

---

* William Labov, "The Logic of Nonstandard English," *Georgetown Monographs on Language and Linguistics,* vol. 22, 1969, pp 1-22, 26-31.

discovered that everyone drops at least some -*ed* endings in speech also discovered that people tend to drop these endings less frequently when they are speaking in formal situations.* The most formal situation of all, they discovered, was reading out loud. Even if you drop many -*ed* endings in casual speech, you will tend to pronounce them when you read aloud. A possible solution to your problem, then, is to read your rough draft *out loud,* using a formal reading voice.

For practice, try reading these sentences out loud in a formal-sounding voice. *Don't* be careful to read exactly what's on the page, as you ordinarily would when proofreading. Read the sentences the way you would say them in a very formal voice.

> The child is begging for attention and love which is deny her or him.

> The agency assists the batter wife or husband with temporary housing and counseling.

> She was scare out of her wits.

> My grandmother use to run a hotel in Denver.

> Last week I ask if he could get tickets for the Super Bowl.

Did a formal reading voice help you to catch one -*ed* problem in each sentence? Did you read *denied* instead of *deny; battered wife* instead of *batter wife; scared* instead of *scare; used* instead of *use;* and *asked* instead of *ask*? If you read in the missing -*ed*'s, fine. A formal, out-loud reading of your rough drafts should help to correct your problem.

It's possible that you found some of the missing -*ed*'s but overlooked others. Linguists tell us that we're more likely to pronounce these word endings in some situations than in others. If the word following the -*ed* begins with a vowel (*a, e, i, o, u*), for example, we are more likely to pronounce the -*ed* than if the following word begins with a consonant. This matter is too technical for us to go into, but we mention it so you will understand why it is possible to catch some -*ed* problems and yet miss others.

If you have the -*ed* problem, don't let it bother you as you write your rough drafts. Just focus on what you have to say and keep your words flowing. There will be time enough later to fill in those missing -*ed*'s.

37. Problems with -*s* endings

If you have a problem with -*s* endings, it may be caused by dialect interference. Actually there are three distinct ways in which a spoken

---

* W. Labov. *The Social Stratification of English in New York City* (Washington, D.C.: Center for Applied Linguistics, 1966); Walt Wolfram and Ralph Fasold, *The Study of Social Dialects in American English* (Englewood Cliffs, N.J.: Prentice-Hall, 1974).

dialect can lead to -*s* problems in written English. Let's treat them one at a time.

We'll begin with verbs. Two linguists, Ralph Fasold and Walt Wolfram, tell us that dialect speakers omit the -*s* endings from some verbs for grammatical reasons.* When a dialect speaker says "He talk too much for his own good" instead of "He talks too much for his own good," the -*s* has been omitted because the grammar of the dialect doesn't require it. It's not that the dialect speaker fails to pronounce the -*s*. The -*s* is not there to be pronounced.

Let us show you how present-tense verbs of one dialect differ from those of standard English. In the following chart we show on the left how the present tense of *to work* is marked in the dialect; on the right is the standard English marking of the same verb.

The dialect		Standard English	
I work	we work	I work	we work
you work	you work	you work	you work
he/she work	they work	he/she works	they work

Notice that in the dialect the forms of the verb have been regularized: the verb is *work* throughout. But in standard English, the third person singular (*he/she/it*) is irregular: *works* instead of *work.*

In another dialect, the markings of present-tense verbs differ from the standard English markings in this way:

The dialect		Standard English	
I work	we work	I work	we work
you work	you work	you work	you work
he/she works	the men works	he/she works	the men work
	the women works		the women work

This dialect has extended the rule of standard English. In standard English, only the third-person singular (*he/she/it*) verb is marked with an -*s*; in the dialect, the third-person singular *and* plural verbs are sometimes marked with an -*s*.

Occasionally a writer who is conscious of leaving -*s* endings off verbs may supply them where they don't belong, as in "I goes to the movies at least once a week." This may be "hypercorrection"—overcorrecting the dialect in an effort to be safe. Standard English requires the -*s* ending for present-tense verbs in the third person singular *only*.

I go	we go
you go	you go
he/she/it goes	they go

* Wolfram and Fasold, *The Study of Social Dialects in American English*, p. 154.

Though most -*s* problems have to do with verbs, two other kinds of dialect interference may also create a problem. In at least one dialect, possession is not shown by *s* plus an apostrophe: "She welcomed her husband death." Standard written English requires both the apostrophe and the *s* to indicate possession: "She welcomed her husband's death." If you find yourself omitting the apostrophe and the *s,* as in "Harry car" or "Richard Wright story" or "Alice friend," make the corrections as you proofread: "Harry's car," "Richard Wright's story," "Alice's friend."

Some dialect speakers occasionally omit the -*s* ending from plural nouns, as in "He bought six book" or "They were my friend" or "I had to work two job to support my family." Standard English requires an -*s* to mark most plural nouns: "six books," "my friends," "two jobs." Certain exceptions, however, can cause problems for dialect speakers, since the exceptions may lead to hypercorrection. Speakers who are conscious of leaving the -*s* endings off nouns sometimes add them unnecessarily, as in *childrens, womens, peoples, feets.* The standard English plurals of these irregular nouns are not marked with -*s: children, women, people, feet.*

In spite of all this talk about -*s* endings, we would like to caution you not to worry about -*s*'s as you write your rough draft. Save your concern for the proofreading stage of the writing process. If you are plagued with the problem, you might do one last proofreading just to catch those slippery -*s*'s.

38. Problems with omitted words

Most writers carelessly omit a word every once in a while, like this:

> It would be far more pleasant for if I could be accepted on the same basis as Charlie.

The writer meant to write "pleasant for *me*" but forgot to write the *me*. Perhaps this was just a slip of the pen, or maybe the writer's thoughts were racing ahead of his pen. But whatever the cause, careless omissions like these are easy enough to catch with careful proofreading.

Other omissions, however, are not quite so easy to catch. These are omissions that can be traced to dialect interference. In some dialects certain helping verbs required by standard English may be omitted. For example, standard English requires "I have gone there" or "I've gone there," but some dialects allow the *have* or the *'ve* to be omitted: "I gone there." Linguists Ralph Fasold and Walt Wolfram have an interesting explanation for this difference between the dialect and standard English.[*]

[*] Wolfram and Fasold, *The Study of Social Dialects in American English,* p. 158.

It turns out that if standard English allows a contraction (for example, *I've* for *I have,* *he'll* for *he will,* or *they're* for *they are*), then the dialect sometimes omits the helping verb altogether. It's as if the dialect had "contracted" the contraction down to nothing.

Below we list several sentences with omissions that resulted from dialect interference. For each sentence, we then list two versions that are acceptable in standard written English.

Dialect	Standard English
I gone there lots of times.	I've gone there lots of times.
	I have gone there lots of times.
He go there tomorrow.	He'll go there tomorrow.
	He will go there tomorrow.
They over there all the time.	They're over there all the time.
	They are over there all the time.
He good.	He's good.
	He is good.
She be promoted next month.	She'll be promoted next month.
	She will be promoted next month.

39. Miscellaneous problems

39a. Standard English requires the use of the word *an* before nouns that begin with vowels (*a, e, i, o, u*). Some spoken dialects do not.

Dialect	Standard English
a orange, a apple	*an* orange, *an* apple

39b. Standard English does not allow the repetition of the subject of the sentence, as some dialects do.

Dialect	Standard English
That teacher, she likes me.	*That teacher* likes me.
My father, he works in Detroit.	*My father* works in Detroit.

39c. Standard English requires the word *there* instead of *it* in sentences like this one, which are acceptable in some dialects: "It's a man in my class that I like very much."

Dialect	Standard English
It's a supermarket at the end of the street.	*There's* a supermarket at the end of the street.
Is it a Methodist church in this town?	*Is* there a Methodist church in this town?

39d. Standard English does not allow the use of *they* to indicate possession, as do some dialects. Standard English uses *their*.

Dialect	Standard English
Mary and Mike brought *they* stereo to our house.	Mary and Mike brought *their* stereo to our house.
The three little kittens lost *they* mittens.	The three little kittens lost *their* mittens.

39e. Standard English requires the words *whether* and *if* in sentences like the following.

Dialect	Standard English
I wonder is he going.	I wonder *if* he is going.
Ask him can you do it.	Ask him *whether* you can do it.

39f. Standard English does not permit the double negatives that are allowed in some dialects.

Note

In standard English the word *hardly* counts as a negative.

Dialect	Standard English
They don't know nothing about it.	They don't know anything about it.
I can't hardly believe it.	I can hardly believe it.

39g. Standard English does not recognize a use of the verb *be* that occurs in at least one dialect.

In this dialect *be* can be used to refer to an action stretched out in time. A simple translation into standard English is not possible, as can be seen from the following examples.

Dialect	**Standard English**
He be working hard.	Does *not* mean "He is working hard." Means "He works hard habitually."
She be sick.	Does *not* mean "She is sick." Means "She has been sick for some time and continues to be sick."
They be waiting for me to make a mistake.	Does *not* mean "They are waiting for me to make a mistake." Means "Habitually, they have been waiting and continue to wait for me to make a mistake."

Note

This use of the verb *be* should not be confused wtih the dialect rule that allows you to drop contractions in a sentence such as "They be here soon," which means "They'll be here soon." See the section on "Problems with Omitted Words" (38) for further information.

. . . .

Exercise 1

. . . .

Proofread the following sentences for any -*ed* problems. Remember to use a formal, out-loud reading voice as you proofread.

1. Some of the children could be consider undernourished.

2. It was mention to me during the intermission.

3. Most of the characters have die by the end of the play.

4. I was surprise at the way he responded.

5. He beated her up so badly that he was thrown in jail.

6. Everything about the place has change since last year.

7. I already explain it.

8. The cost of bread has increase because of the increase cost of flour.

9. Though it was below freezing, I walk three miles to the hospital.

10. It's suppose to last for a lifetime, but it broke after a week.

11. He looked like a scare rabbit.

12. It happen to her when she was only eight years old.

13. Jack talk about the situation and then try to clear up the problem.

14. The story capture my imagination.

15. The police follow him until he stop and pull over to the side of the road.

. . . .

Exercise 2
. . . .

Proofread the following sentences for problems with -s endings.

1. The girl father was a doctor.

2. He seem to be doing well.

3. The story illustrate how one man, Howard, overcame his physical handicap.

4. In most instance the people do not pay attention to his sermons.

5. Poe stories can be read in one sitting.

6. Al travel to South Carolina once every two weeks.

7. Whenever he get a chance, he like to try to speak French.

8. Though I am forty years old, many time I am called a "girl."

9. The average farmer expenses have doubled in the past ten years.

10. The movie last only twenty minutes.

11. The film give the viewer a new way of looking at the Civil War.

12. Old people are not respected in today world.

13. Steve main problem is that he can't spell.

14. Many new career have opened up in the medical field.

15. He believe in justice for all peoples.

. . . .

Exercise 3
. . . .

Proofread the following sentences for omissions.

1. It a subject most people don't want to talk about.

2. You're nervous because you been in school only a short time.

3. I don't think it fair.

4. Do you know someone who be good for the job?

5. They can't read as well as they supposed to.

6. In the opening lines, he saying that he afraid of death.

7. He be here in a few minutes.

8. In the movie she displaying all her talents.

9. Before you know it, it full of fish.

10. She mainly a career woman.

. . . .
Exercise 4
. . . .

Proofread the following sentences for problems caused by dialect interference.

1. Some of the student work full time.

2. Jill was dress up for the party.

3. Where you been lately?

4. As far as I'm concern, he's innocent.

5. I'd like to know who stole they car.

6. Her childrens were born two year apart.

7. My job keep me very busy.

8. Did you see a ostrich at the zoo?

9. They be ready in a few minutes.

10. I worried unnecessarily because my answer prove to be correct.

11. Jack been living there since 1975.

12. Student with good grades can get tutoring jobs.

13. The carp is place on a board and cook in the oven for an hour.

14. Your sister, did she win the tennis match?

15. I feel faint. Is it a place where I can sit down?

16. There are two basic method of preparing hard-shell crabs.

17. Larry founded out too late.

18. If you give him a raise, he be happy.

19. It doesn't seem like the kind of story that Flannery O'Connor usually write.

20. Ask him is it suppose to rain tomorrow.

21. Suzanne be sick.

22. When she was young my daughter ask me all kinds of strange questions.

23. Their argument don't amount to nothing.

24. Lask week she fix up my brother room for my grandmother.

25. This story tell about a young man who destroys a house.

You will find answers to these exercises in the appendix.

PART SEVEN

A list of writing topics

A list of writing topics

A. The world of work

1. Write about the way in which a particular job has been glamorized. Contrast the job's image with the reality.

2. Describe your job to someone who is considering applying for a similar position.

3. Describe your job to a new coworker who needs to be broken in.

4. Explain what a person must do to get into the profession or vocation you've chosen. Aim the paper at readers who are considering the profession.

5. Interview someone who does work that is interesting. Describe the job to readers who might want to consider that line of work.

6. Sketch a popular stereotype of persons in your profession. Then contrast the stereotype with the reality.

7. Have you rejected a career because pursuing it seemed too demanding, with too many barriers to overcome? Write a paper warning others about the difficulties.

8. Warn readers about a job or position that is not all it is advertised to be.

9. Are there features of your job that encourage you to treat customers or clients as though they were not really people? (For example, a doctor or nurse might be tempted to look at a person as a disease or a collection of symptoms.) Make readers see why it is so easy in your job or profession to forget that clients are people.

10. Describe to a new coworker the possibilities for advancement in his or her position.

11. What effect does prolonged joblessness have on a person? Make this topic come alive by talking with someone who has been out of work for a long time.

12. If your job tends to dehumanize you, convince your employer that this is so. Include specific suggestions for improvement.

13. Show interested readers that a college education is not necessary for a person to get a job that pays well.

14. Argue that a college-educated person is much better off in the world of work than a person with only a high-school degree.

15. Describe some of the difficulties involved when a person of the other sex enters a line of work previously considered all-male or all-female. You might want to give newcomers of your sex some hints on how to avoid difficulties that are likely to arise.

16. Do you feel that you have been discriminated against—either as a member of a minority group or as a woman—in hiring, in assignments, in promotion, in firing, and so forth? If so, write a letter of protest to an appropriate audience.

17. If you feel that you have been the victim of "reverse discrimination," write a letter of protest to an appropriate audience.

18. If you are a supervisor, describe one or more of the difficulties of overseeing other workers. Your audience is people who plan to become supervisors.

19. If you work for an agency that can help people in some way, write a paper explaining how clients can obtain aid.

20. Some work places are experimenting with flexitime and/or job sharing to fit the scheduling needs of a variety of persons better. If you know of such a system, describe it to interested readers. Or write a letter in which you persuade an employer to try such a plan.

B. Education

1. Robert Frost said, "We come to college to get over our little-mindedness." Cite specific examples of ways in which college has "expanded" you. Your audience is someone who is thinking about going to college.

2. Describe something specific about your child's schooling of which you either approve or disapprove. Aim your paper at an appropriate audience, perhaps other parents in your community.

3. Choose an instructor (other than your college English instructor) from whom you are taking a course this semester. Describe in detail one actual class period in such a way as to communicate either your admiration of or your distaste for his or her teaching style. *No real names*, please.

4. If you have attended both parochial and public schools, contrast the two systems of education. Your audience might be parents trying to decide where to send their children, or it might be young people whose parents have given them a choice.

5. Write a letter to one of your instructors suggesting changes he or she might make in his or her teaching. Assume that the instructor is interested in improving. *No real names*, please.

6. Choose a course that you're enjoying (other than college English!). Convince a friend to sign up for it next semester.

7. If you feel that one of your instructors is incompetent and if talking to him or her has not led to improvements, write a letter to the head of the department explaining the situation. *No real names*, please.

8. If one of your instructors gave a lecture this week, summarize it for a friend who missed class.

9. If you have attended school in another country, contrast some aspect of that country's educational system with an aspect of ours.

10. Have you ever taken a course taught primarily with programmed (self-teaching) materials, through either machines or books? If so, how effective was the method? Your audience is people thinking of taking a similar course.

11. An ancient Greek scholar defined students as "lamps to be lighted, rather than vessels to be filled." Show readers that you agree or disagree—perhaps by contrasting two teachers with opposing philosophies.

12. Visit your child's school for at least half a day. Report on what you observe to interested parents in your community.

13. If you have attended high school recently, write a report to your county's board of education about how your high school could be improved.

14. Attempt to convince a classmate of the importance of taking some courses other than those directly related to his or her chosen career.

C. Religion

1. Retell last week's sermon for a member of your church who was away for the weekend. Comment on the sermon if you wish.

2. If you are a Jew or a Christian, describe your concept of God to someone unfamiliar with the Judeo-Christian tradition.

3. Encourage parents in your church to send their children to Sunday school.

4. What is the value of prayer, as you see it?

5. Do you disagree with your church's position on any important issue? Defend your own position. Your audience includes church members who disagree with you and those who have not yet made up their minds.

6. Should prayer be allowed in public schools?

7. Should women be ordained?

8. If you have recently converted to a religion (or to atheism), explain what led you to convert.

9. If your religious beliefs differ from those of your parents, contrast the two sets of beliefs.

10. Are the women and the men in your church expected to serve it in different ways, or are all areas of participation equalized? Argue for or against the policies that presently exist.

11. If you have firsthand experience of some non-Protestant or non-Catholic religion in America (for example, Quaker, American Indian, Black Muslim, Jewish), explain some of the basic tenets of your religion to someone who knows little about it.

12. Read about situation ethics (for example, see books on the subject by Thomas Fletcher and James Pike) and make a statement about how that approach to "living religiously" strikes you for your own life.

13. Read Hermann Hesse's *Siddhartha*, a short novel about a young Indian searching for spiritual understanding. Write a character study of Siddhartha.

14. Examine the story of Adam and Eve in *Genesis* from a feminist viewpoint. (Be sure to look at *both* accounts of the creation of man and woman, the one at the end of chapter 1 and the one at the beginning of chapter 2.)

15. Write a paper in which you compare the Judeo-Christian account of Creation in *Genesis* with that of some other religion—perhaps Hindu or American Indian. Ask a librarian to help you locate other accounts.

16. If your religious beliefs have remained generally the same since childhood, have you examined those beliefs independently? If you have not and you feel any need or desire to do so, write a paper in which you conduct such an examination.

D. Violence

1. Write about the way in which violence is glamorized in the media. Use specific television programs, advertisements, films, newspaper items, or comic strips to illustrate your insights. You will need to limit this topic.

2. If you have served in a war, write about a personal experience with violence.

3. How might a family provide harmless outlets for the aggressive impulses of children?

4. If you have seen a violent movie recently, describe it in a way that emphasizes the violence and shows how ridiculous, sordid, or painful it is.

5. There have been many complaints about violence in the news media. In your opinion, should unpleasant, disgusting, or painful pictures appear in newspapers or on television? Try to convince readers who disagree with you.

6. Write a humorous essay in which you show that certain fairy tales, or some other stories intended for children, are perversely violent.

7. Movies in which women are abused in some way have increased in recent years. Although such films are often advertised as "sexy," they may in fact have more to do with violence than with sex (or love). If you have seen any movies that might be analyzed in this way, write about one of them as an expression of violence.

8. If you have ever been the victim of police brutality, describe the incident. Your audience is a citizen's review board.

9. Write about an experience with guns, either a positive or a negative one. Make sure your paper has a purpose.

10. A number of modern phenomena are cited as possible causes of the high level of violence in contemporary society—among them noise pollution, urban density, lack of recreation facilities. Select one such possible contributing factor (preferably one you yourself have had to deal with) and show readers why violence results. Or if you know of a program that successfully counteracts one of these causes of violence, describe the program to interested readers.

11. If you are in a position to witness violence or the results of violence in your community, perhaps because you work in a hospital emergency room or for a community hotline, inform readers about what you have seen.

12. Violence between parents and children or between husband and wife

has received much attention in the media. Write about a particular incidence of such violence, making sure that you are telling your account for some purpose.

13. Write about the nonviolent philosophy behind the art of karate.

14. If you are a pacifist, explain your philosophy to readers who are skeptical of pacifists.

15. If you are concerned about unnecessary violence to animals, write about your concern. Your audience is either people who exhibit such violence or those in a position to limit it.

16. Show readers how easy it is to become hardened to violence from continued exposure to it. If possible, write from personal experience.

E. The arts and creativity

1. Take your reader on a tour of an art museum you have visited. Write the paper to encourage a visit by your reader.

2. If you are in a position to encourage creativity in other persons in any way, how do you go about doing so? Share your insights with someone else who can provide this kind of support.

3. Write about the achievements of a favorite artist, musician, or writer. Explain why the work of this particular person is especially significant.

4. Argue that your city should establish a special high school for the arts.

5. Some people do not acknowledge that photography is an art form. If you are especially interested in photography, defend it as an art.

6. Review a play (or an opera, ballet, or concert) that you have attended recently. Either encourage readers to attend the performance or discourage them from attending.

7. If you belong to a working musical group that has survived for at least a year, explain how you have managed to make it in this competitive business. Your audience is a newly formed group.

8. If you plan to enter the world of art—for example, as a painter, sculptor, musician, dancer, actor, or writer—explain the discipline required for success.

9. When schools trim their budgets during periods of recession, activities related to the arts are often among the first to be eliminated. Either support or argue against such priorities in education.

10. Contrast your expectations of a concert with the reality of it.

11. Explain to someone who is skeptical of avant-garde art, literature, or music why you feel certain works have merit.

12. If you have studied an art under a particularly effective teacher, describe the teaching techniques that helped you grow as an artist. Your audience might be either students or teachers of that particular art.

13. If you have recently worked behind the scenes during a performance, as a makeup artist, a lighting technician, or a set-builder, inform readers about your work.

14. If you have ever directed a group of performers (for a church choir, a school play, a fashion show), describe how you managed to lead your group from amateurism to professionalism.

F. Food

1. Write an article advertising a natural foods store in your community.

2. Criticize from a nutritional standpoint the food served by a particular school, hospital, or other institution.

3. Give your neighbor advice on vegetable gardening. Your neighbor has a small plot, so limit your advice to how to grow three to five vegetables.

4. Write a critique of your school cafeteria, a fast-food chain, or a local restaurant. A critique may be either positive or negative.

5. Show readers that they can save money, be better off nutritionally, or both by substituting fresh foods for canned, frozen, or ready-mix ones.

6. Describe soul food (or some other specialized kind of food) to someone completely unfamiliar with it. Don't let your paper become a list of recipes.

7. Write a critique of your local supermarket.

8. Excess weight is a problem for many Americans. If you have found a diet that works for you, share your discovery. If there are any medical precautions about the diet, be sure to note them.

9. Certain conditions (such as hypertension and hypoglycemia) can be treated with special diets. If you know of such a diet, describe it to someone who has just learned that he or she has the problem.

10. Inform your reader about some particular nutritional issue he or she is unlikely to know about, such as the dangers of nitrites or the need for fiber in the diet.

11. Suggest low-cost, nutritious menus to a family on a tight budget.

G. Death and dying

1. Write out instructions for how your body is to be handled after your death—with a traditional funeral, a memorial service, cremation, a donation to medical research, or whatever. Your audience is your parents, spouse, or a close friend whom you trust to carry out your wishes.

2. If you have known someone who knew that he or she was dying, describe that person's resistance to and/or acceptance of the fact of death.

3. Describe a funeral you attended recently so that your readers will understand how you felt about the ceremony.

4. If you have ever had a close call with death, describe the experience. Make sure your paper has a purpose.

5. Write about the death of someone you loved, if you can do so without being sentimental. Remember that most of your readers will not have known the person.

6. Choose a religion (Judaism, Christianity, Hinduism, Buddhism, Unitarianism) and explain how that religion deals with the fact of death.

7. How would you inform a child of the death of someone he or she loves? Write from personal experience if possible, and include the age of the child you're writing about.

8. Write about the suicide of someone you knew. Focus your paper as you see fit.

9. Would you rather die in a hospital or at home? Why?

10. Read the first seven chapters of Elisabeth Kübler-Ross's well-known book, *On Death and Dying*. Summarize what she says for someone who has not read the book.

11. Have you ever known someone who was dying? Describe your own reaction to his or her impending death. What did you do and say?

12. If you have worked with terminally ill patients (as a nurse, hospital technician, or volunteer), what have you been able to do to ease their suffering? Share your insights with others who work with such patients.

13. Write your own obituary. Or write the obituary of a family member who is (or was) important to you.

14. Should parents have the right to decide whether their deformed or mentally defective child should be allowed to live?

15. Should a child be allowed to visit his or her dying parent in the hospital?

16. Should either passive or active euthanasia be legalized? Passive euthanasia involves *allowing* someone to die by withholding certain medication or by not utilizing life-sustaining machines; active euthanasia involves *helping* someone to die by administering drugs or by "pulling the tubes."

H. Justice

1. Write about some inequity in our judicial system. Use at least one true anecdote to illustrate the inequity.

2. Have you ever been in jail? If so, write about the experience, focusing your paper as you see fit.

3. Write about a time when you were the victim of a crime. Make sure your paper has a purpose.

4. Interview a police officer—or better yet, accompany the officer on his or her beat (many communities have ride-along programs). What did you learn about the officer, the job, or both?

5. Why are our prisons filled with a disproportionate number of black people?

6. If you know of a police officer who deserves special praise, write a letter of commendation to his or her supervisor. Or write a letter to the editor of a local newspaper, expressing your admiration for the officer.

7. In what areas of your life are you called upon to act as judge (for example, as a parent or as a supervisor)? Share your experiences as a judge, focusing your paper as you wish.

8. Find out what kind of vocational rehabilitation is offered to prisoners in a jail near you. Is the program realistic, in view of the employment likely to be available to such a person once he or she has been released?

9. Show that comparable behavior is unjustly labeled as "lawful" or "criminal" depending on a person's status (age, social position, sex, color, religion, professional position, and so on). Be sure to narrow this topic.

10. Write about the experience of visiting someone in jail or prison, focusing your paper as you wish.

11. Some communities have alternatives to the punishment system of committing lawbreakers to traditional "holding facilities"—local jails, state and federal prisons, and so on. Find out about one of these alternatives in your community, such as a halfway house, and report on your findings.

12. If you have a supervisor who is prejudiced against a particular group or who shows favoritism to certain persons, write a letter to an appropriate audience protesting that injustice.

I. Sports/exercise

1. If you are very good at a team sport, summarize your qualifications to impress a coach or a scholarship committee.

2. If you've coached a team, give advice to a new coach.

3. Argue against football, ice hockey, or some other team sport for its physical danger or violence. Or argue in favor of such a sport as an important training in teamwork, cooperation, how to deal with winning and losing in life, and so on.

4. Write a paper about the exaggerated language of sportscasters and sports reporters.

5. Argue that schools should emphasize sports that any individual can participate in and benefit from throughout life (for example, swimming, bowling, tennis) instead of such sports as football and basketball.

6. Title IX states that schools receiving any federal funds must provide equal sports programs for male and female students. Investigate whether your college complies with Title IX; if not, write a letter pointing out the inadequacies and submit it to your college newspaper.

7. Write about the high cost of some sport such as skiing. Or advise readers on how to cut the costs of an expensive sport.

8. Write a letter to your local TV news program suggesting any improvements you would like to see in their sports coverage. Or write a letter praising it.

9. Explain why you admire a favorite sports figure.

10. Write about the extreme discipline required for ballet or for a sport such as gymnastics.

11. Write about some program that uses sports or physical activity as therapy for persons with physical, mental, or social handicaps.

12. If you're familiar with a sport popular in another culture, such as cricket, describe it to American readers.

13. Think about whether your life includes enough physical activity at work or during your leisure time to keep you healthy. If it does not, write a paper about a plan you could follow to remedy this situation.

14. Encourage a friend to take up a particular sport such as jogging, tennis, golf, bicycling, or swimming.

J. Growing old

1. Write a paper about someone you know who has aged in a way that you admire and respect.

2. *The Coming of Age*, a book by Simone de Beauvoir, contains an interesting chapter on old age in historical societies. Read this chapter and summarize it for someone who doesn't have the time to read it.

3. We hear a great deal about the disadvantages of growing old. Talk to some older people (sixty-five or over) about some possible advantages of age, then write a paper about these advantages.

4. Be alert to how people about sixty or older are portrayed on television. Does stereotyping occur? Watch enough situation comedies and similar programs to be able to describe two or three stereotypes.

5. Find out whether your college has a continuing education program for senior citizens. If it does, try to get some retired person who seems to need new interests involved in the program.

6. If you know of some especially good community program for senior citizens, describe it to readers who might be interested in taking advantage of it.

7. Write about a close friendship you have with someone who is much older (or younger) than you are. What have you gained from this friendship that you could not have received from someone your own age?

8. Describe someone you know who is over sixty-five and who defies the commonly accepted assumption that old age is horrible.

9. Do you think about growing old? If you do, what inner resources are you developing to counteract the inevitable diminishing of your physical resources as you age?

10. What responsibilities do you think children have as their parents grow old?

11. If you are fairly familiar with either a retirement home or a nursing home, write a letter suggesting some changes that might make living there more pleasant. Try to make realistic suggestions. Or write a letter commending some feature or features of the home.

K. Race and ethnic identity

1. Describe someone you know who has lost his or her ethnic character in the attempt to become assimilated into the mainstream of American culture.

2. Write a jazzy description of "soul."

3. Write a positive description of your ethnic background—Italian, Polish, Irish, or whatever.

4. If you have experienced interracial or intercultural dating, write about that experience, focusing your paper as you wish.

5. If you experience a cultural conflict between your world of work or school and the world of your friends, describe it.

6. What picture of American Indians, black Americans, Italian-Americans, Southern whites, Chinese, or other minority group is presented in movies or television dramas? Limit this topic radically, perhaps by discussing the image of one of these groups as presented in one film or TV series.

7. It is often said that the liberation struggle of the black woman and the white woman differ. If you are a woman, talk about this question with a woman of the other race and report your findings in a paper.

8. Describe a stereotype of any ethnic group and then write a character sketch of someone you know who disproves that stereotype.

9. Have you ever been stereotyped? Describe how you felt.

10. If you are prejudiced against a particular group of people, try to recall how your prejudice originated; then write a paper in which you attempt to reason your way out of it.

L. Men and women

1. Write about the way a television series depicts male-female relationships.

2. If you have lived in another culture, describe the position of women in that culture.

3. Should prostitution be legalized?

4. Write about the extremes to which some women will go to look beautiful.

5. Argue that men will benefit as much as women from women's liberation.

6. Are you acquainted with any couples in which the woman has a career and the man maintains the home and looks after any children they have? Interview such a couple and shape your paper around your interview, using whatever focus most interests you.

7. If you are a woman who combines motherhood with a job, tell readers how you manage to cope. If you've decided that such a life-style is more than you can manage, explain why you came to such a conclusion.

8. Compare and contrast your expectations of marriage with the reality.

9. Write about the problems of being married to a person of another faith, culture, or race. Or write about how you have overcome such problems.

10. What effect does divorce have on a woman who has not worked outside the home and who has no marketable skills?

11. If you know any divorced parents who have split custody of the children, describe how well the arrangement works.

12. Under what conditions, if any, should alimony be awarded to either spouse?

13. If you know a gay person who will talk freely with you, interview him or her concerning his or her life-style. Write an article based on the interview, focusing it as you see fit.

14. If you have been married more or less "happily" for a long time, share any seasoned insights with a young couple about to marry.

M. Parents and children

1. Describe someone you know who is, in your opinion, a bad parent. Or describe someone who is an ideal (or nearly ideal) parent.

2. Write a character sketch of one of your children.

3. Contrast your expectations of motherhood or fatherhood with the reality as you have experienced it.

4. Find out about family life in another culture, preferably by talking to someone who has experienced it firsthand. Report on your findings in an interesting, readable style.

5. Write about the difficulties or satisfactions (or both) of being a single parent. Your audience includes people who have recently become single parents.

6. Write a paper based on the following statement: "If you think raising a toddler is hard, wait until your child is a teenager."

7. Write a review of a favorite children's book. Your purpose is to steer parents toward the book.

8. A problem for working parents is adequate child care. If you have discovered a good solution to this problem, such as an excellent day-care center, share your discovery with other parents in your community.

9. Warn parents about a poor child-care center.

10. Write a love letter to one of your children, showing why you are glad you had him or her. Try not to be too sentimental.

11. Describe some older person in your family whom you would like to emulate as you grow older. Or describe someone after whom you would not like to pattern yourself.

12. Explain your philosophy of discipline for a particular age group, giving real examples of the kinds of rewards and punishments you find workable.

13. Show readers that a parent can often steer a child in the right direction without resorting to rewards and punishments.

14. Write about an interracial or intercultural adoption with which you are familiar. Shape this topic as you see fit.

15. Argue that when parents divorce, women should nearly always gain custody of the children, or that men should gain custody much more often than they do at present.

N. Ecology and nature

1. Describe your neighborhood as it is. Then describe how you would improve it if you had the power to make it more beautiful and more livable. Use enough details so that your reader can visualize the changes you suggest.

2. If you are happy in your neighborhood, describe its virtues to readers looking for a place to live.

3. Select some area other than your own neighborhood and describe how you would redesign it to make it more pleasant and functional. You might work with one block, part of one street, a shopping center, or an entire residential area.

4. If you or someone you know is using solar energy in any way, describe the system to readers interested in trying it.

5. How would ordinary Americans need to change their living habits if the government were to decide seriously to combat pollution and environmental decay?

6. If you prefer country to city living, try to explain why to persons who don't seem to understand its appeal.

7. If you or anyone you know has been involved in a wilderness survival program such as Outward Bound, describe the program.

8. If you know of unusual ways to conserve energy, persuade readers to adopt them.

9. Write a letter to the editor in which you warn against the dangers of noise pollution. Or compile a set of suggestions to your city council for decreasing noise pollution.

10. Assume that the federal budget for the upkeep of national parklands is in jeopardy. Grass-roots views are being collected, and you plan to testify at a local citizens' hearing. Write up your testimony for or against budget-trimming in this area.

11. If "getting close to nature" is therapeutic for you, encourage a reader to try your method by describing how the experience helps you.

12. If you have been involved in a successful community effort to save a historic building or to preserve parkland, describe the methods that led to your group's success. Your readers are people interested in organizing a similar effort in their own community.

Appendix

Chapter 3, Exercise 5. The paper on the Hayloft Dinner Theater might be polished as follows:

One place in our community where you can enjoy a pleasant evening is the Hayloft Dinner Theater. Too few people know about this local cultural attraction on Route 450. As its name suggests, the Hayloft Dinner Theater offers both food and entertainment—for only $11.00.

The Hayloft is open every night except Monday. Beginning at 5:30, dinner is served buffet style, with a waiter coming to your table to take drink orders and menu preferences. Everybody goes to the salad bar, which features many chopped vegetables, cottage cheese, bacon bits, and a variety of salad dressings. You could make yourself a meal at the salad bar itself.

When my family and I went to the Hayloft recently, we ordered several different main dishes: chicken kiev, ham supreme with pineapple, crab imperial, stuffed veal, lasagna, and egg rolls with fried rice. The food at the Hayloft is varied enough to suit every taste. Each serving was quite adequate and everything tasted delicious. I could have been happy to leave the Hayloft right after that satisfying meal.

But of course we stayed for the show. That night the Hayloft Hayseeds were performing "Fiddler on the Roof." The Hayseeds have built a reputation for their musicals, and they certainly did an excellent job with "Fiddler." Everyone caught the spirit of the evening, and I could hardly believe it was 11:00 when we gave the cast a standing round of applause. Just then someone shouted, "Chef! Chef!" so that we got to express our appreciation for the food as well as for the play.

So gather your family or friends and head for the Hayloft. I assure you that you will find there an enjoyable yet inexpensive evening's entertainment.

Chapter 8, Exercise 2. Identifying fallacies:

1. (b) faulty cause-and-effect reasoning

2. (a) arguing in a circle

3. (f) appealing for sympathy

4. (a) arguing in a circle

5. (c) hasty generalization

6. (d) using loaded words and labels

7. (b) faulty cause-and-effect reasoning

8. (f) appealing for sympathy

9. (c) hasty generalization

10. (d) using loaded words and labels

11. (b) faulty cause-and-effect reasoning

12. (b) faulty cause-and-effect reasoning

13. (e) name-calling

14. (c) hasty generalization

15. (e) name-calling

16. (c) hasty generalization

17. (f) appealing for sympathy

Chapter 11, Exercise 4.

The sculpture of Louise Nevelson relies on her placing unlikely pieces of wood together to create interesting surfaces that emphasize light and shadow. Nevelson collects bedposts, two-by-fours, mantels, spools, dowels, and other shaped wood and then begins to experiment with these shapes in various arrangements. Once arranged, the protruding pieces of wood stand out as if highlighted and create shadows on the recessed areas. Sometimes Nevelson paints the finished sculpture—gold, silver, flat black, perhaps white; sometimes she leaves the piece in its natural state. She nearly always ends up with an exciting collection of wood that distinguishes her as a sculptor.

Chapter 11, Exercise 5. The following are *suggested* revisions; revisions may of course vary.

The first paragraph needs bridges.

One summer when I worked as a camp counselor each counselor was in charge of a cabin of ten boys. In Tahoe, my cabin of nine-year-olds, all the campers were white except one, a black youngster named Jonathan. The rest of the campers ignored Jonathan in the beginning; indeed, sometimes they outright excluded him from their activities. Since the camp master had told the counselors that each cabin should function as a unit, I worked hard to create a unit out of those nine-year-olds. And I succeeded. My most treasured object from that summer is a photograph of Jonathan hoisted on the shoulders of three new friends with six more nine-year-olds crowded around—all of them Jonathan's cabinmates from Tahoe.

The second paragraph needs to be improved for consistency.

The Chuckling Oyster at Land's End serves delicious seafood. Their specialties are crab imperial, oyster stew, fried clams, salmon steak, and stuffed flounder. The last time we were at the Chuckling Oyster I ordered salmon steak and my wife ordered crab imperial. First our waiter brought us a large salad with house dressing and salty rye bread. Another waiter served the next course—corn on the cob with plenty of butter. After that a waitress delivered lime sherbet "to cleanse the palate for the specialty." By then we were almost too full to eat our main course. When we finally finished, I left the Chuckling Oyster convinced that it must be one of the best seafood restaurants in the United States.

The third paragraph needs parallel structure.

Have you ever known a hermit? A hermit named Mr. Joe was a special part of my childhood. Mr. Joe knew about everything, or so it seemed to us children: how to catch minnows by hand, how to crack walnuts so the meat came out whole, how to tell time by the sun. Mr. Joe lived way back in the woods in a log cabin he had built himself. He had hand-tied the hammock in his yard himself. He had dug his trout-breeding pond himself. He had dug up flowers in the woods and transplanted them around his cabin himself. But the best thing about Mr. Joe was that, even being a hermit, he loved us kids and always carried treats for us—sweet, juicy oranges; shiny, crunchy apples; and always fresh, forbidden Juicy Fruit chewing gum.

Chapter 13, Exercise 2. The following are *suggested* revisions; revisions may of course vary.

1. Today, with fierce competition for too few well-paying jobs, I need to concentrate on my education if I expect to have a successful career.

2. The atheist avoided church regularly.

3. In "Raisin in the Sun," a black family decides to buy a house in an all-white neighborhood.

4. During our tour of New England in August, glasses of iced coffee were served every afternoon.

5. The student answered no to Mr. Battle's question.

6. The principal finally located the injured child's parent via telephone after 3:00 P.M.

7. In applying for a job, an educated black person confronts problems that may not affect a white person with exactly the same education.

8. An actual Chinese meal is considerably different from the meals served in many Chinese restaurants.

9. Sociologists claim that hardened criminals are rarely rehabilitated successfully.

10. American Indians are portrayed in an insulting way on TV.

Chapter 13, Exercise 6. Translations of euphemisms

Euphemism:	*Translation*:
1. adult entertainment	pornography
2. correctional facility	jail, prison, detention center
3. down-sized car	small economy car
4. encore telecast	TV rerun
5. Egyptological pornoglyphic sarcophagi	graffiti on a mummy
6. engage the enemy on all sides	to be ambushed
7. expired, passed away, left us	died
8. for motion discomfort	for travel sickness, nausea
9. grief therapist	undertaker
10. inner city	ghetto
11. nervous wetness	sweat
12. powder room	women's toilet
13. preowned automobile	used car
14. protective reaction strike	bombing
15. twilight years	old age

Punctuation

Exercise 1.

1. Harry, please bring pecans, walnuts, and chestnuts when you come for the weekend; we need those, I think, for between-meal snacks.

2. One of my favorite short stories is Shirley Jackson's "The Lottery," which has been filmed for classroom use.

3. It's too early to take a taxi to the theater, but let's think about going by John's father's horsedrawn carriage.

4. Have you seen Natalie Smorgavich in Shaw's play *Major Barbara*?

5. My aunt, Katherine Jones, is in line for a diplomatic appointment, but she is reluctant to leave Washington.

6. Look at that dancer leap!

7. Any person who wishes to apply for work at that record store must take a lie-detector test.

8. My neighbor's cat will climb any tree in sight; however, that habit creates a problem when she can't get back down without a firefighter's assistance.

9. "Whether you like it or not, I'm going to include the quotation 'To thine own self be true' from Shakespeare in my psychology paper," asserted Tom.

10. "Ruth," asked the little girl, "how old are you?" *Or:* Ruth asked the little girl, "How old are you?"

Exercise 2.

I was suddenly awakened at four o'clock one morning by my wife.

"It's time to go!" she exclaimed.

Gazing across the room and seeing her standing with suitcase in hand, it dawned on me that this was the moment for which we had been waiting nine months. I sprang out of bed, grabbed whatever clothes were available, and started dressing while simultaneously calling the doctor.

"I'll meet you at the hospital in forty-five minutes," was the doctor's reply to a very nervous father-to-be. On the way to the hospital I tried to remain calm, as I tried to remember the training we had received in prepared childbirth classes and the reading we had done in *Having Your Baby Naturally*.

"Inhale, exhale, breathe deeply and slowly," I repeated to my wife over and over again as we drove into the city.

Arriving at the hospital, I drove right up to the front door and carefully ushered my wife to the admitting office. After rushing through much paperwork (not really knowing what we were signing), we finally made it to the labor room. Then it began: the timing of contractions, the breathing in unison, and the waiting. Three long hours later, when my wife was fully dilated, the doctor sent me out to dress in the delivery room garb—a green cap, mask, gown, and shoes. Once in the delivery room, I held my wife's hand and assisted whenever possible. Twenty short minutes later a beautiful six-pound, twelve-ounce girl was born.

One does not realize how much pain a woman can tolerate or the strength she possesses—until he can witness a childbirth. I shall always treasure having shared my daughter's birth with my wife; it was an event I shall not forget.

Exercise 3. Commas and Semicolons

1. Last summer I participated in our college's New England Literary Tour, which was sponsored by Dr. Fry of the English Division.

2. Dr. Fry reserved two large buses for the tour; later he had to locate a third bus to accommodate additional travelers.

3. The tour included visiting Emily Dickinson's home in Amherst, Massachusetts; the House of Seven Gables, featured in Hawthorne's novel; Walden Pond, made famous by Thoreau; and many other sites, such as famous churches, a one-room schoolhouse, and a silversmith shop like Paul Revere's.

4. Most of our sleeping accommodations during the tour were very comfortable; however, one night I rolled off a hard bed while having a nightmare about Washington Irving's headless horseman.

5. C

6. The food on the trip was so plentiful that I could never finish a meal, although some people asked for seconds on desserts almost every night.

7. A pleasant feature of the trip was the long afternoon rides through the rolling New England countryside, during which some passengers napped, some read, and the rest of us laughed, joked, and exclaimed over the scenery.

8. We reached one church just in time for a candlelight service; it was a peaceful way to end a long day.

9. We were on the tour for college credit, and therefore we had to spend some of our evening hours writing in our travel journals.

10. I recommend Dr. Fry's Literary Tour of New England to you, but only if you have stamina and a sense of humor; you'll need both if you go!

Exercise 4. The Comma

1. Scott and Helen Nearing, who are now an elderly couple, have been living off the land for many years.

2. I first read about the Nearings in the book *Ways Americans Live*, a collection of essays on life-styles by Andrew Greene.

3. The Nearings, the pioneers of the back-to-the-land movement, left city life long before the return to rural life became fashionable.

4. They have developed their plot of land into a reasonably comfortable, pleasant, attractive place to live; however, there is always work to be done.

5. When people who are interested in their way of life come to visit the Nearings, they are put to work building, planting, harvesting, or otherwise using whatever skills they bring with them.

6. For many years the Nearings have been building their house, using stones which, as you might expect, have become too heavy for them to carry.

7. Therefore one of the jobs that visitors are sometimes assigned is hauling stones, for the Nearings continue to add buildings to their property.

8. According to recent visitors, both the Nearings, although they are aging, still fiercely support their choice to live as they do.

9. A friend of mine who visited the Nearings last year commented to me on her return, "It made me wish I had the courage, or whatever it takes, to live that way."

10. "Not me," I replied, "no, indeed; I'm a person who likes comfort too much!"

Exercise 5. The Apostrophe.

1. Our county's fair is a highlight of every autumn for me and my three brothers, Terry, David, and Michael.

2. We don't ever go to the fair on weekends because it's too crowded then; we've found that the best time to go is about two o'clock on a weekday.

3. The fair is better these days than it was in the '70's because more handicrafts are shown.

4. One of the most beautiful items I've ever seen was the Blue Ridge Mountain quilt exhibited last year by the best friend of our preacher's wife.

5. Another feature of the fair my brothers and I especially like is the livestock area; one year we saw some oxen's yokes get entangled and those oxen nearly went crazy.

6. Another time there was a great rattling over at the monkeys' cages, where one monkey had wrapped its tail around a long stick somebody had poked into the cage and wouldn't let go.

7. Anyone who enjoys watching roosters strut and pigeons pout surely wouldn't want to miss the area of the fair marked "Fowls and Poultry."

8. One of the best parts of any fair is the food, and ours is no exception.

9. Our fair features Tony's pizza, Christopher the Greek's baklava, Mack's Scottish barley soup, and Johnny's American subs, among other mouth-watering culinary attractions.

10. After a visit to the fair, my brothers and I definitely need a day's rest to recuperate, because we've walked and gawked and stuffed ourselves nearly out of existence by the end of the day.

Capitalization

I think everyone these days should take a course in economics. People often think that the law of supply and demand is about all that is taught in economics. But I can assure you that you will learn far more if you enroll in Professor Susan Brown's course entitled The American Economy. There you will learn about the rise and fall of revolutions—such as the Agricultural Revolution and the Industrial Revolution—as well as how the Technological/Electronic Revolution has influenced economic development in America. You will also learn why the Columbia River is so important to the economy of the Pacific Northwest and how economic vibrations have moved from there eastward. You will even study how the German economy has affected the economy of the world in the twentieth century. Furthermore, you will come to realize that charitable and social service groups like the United Way and Big Brothers have more of an effect on our national economy than might be expected. You may be wondering how a single professor could pack so much material into one economics course. Why not take The American Economy with Professor Brown and find out?

Spelling

Most of us know at least one woman who is beginning college in her forties. Her family may find this new arrangement difficult to accommodate to. However, once they become accustomed to it, they frequently speak proudly of her. She, on the other hand, may have to struggle to overcome certain guilt feelings; somehow, the principle of self-development for her own being is hard for her to accept, despite the advice of her friends who have already traveled the same path. Gradually, though, she realizes that she truly is a whole person, separate from her husband and her children, and she learns to function outside the wife-mother role. Then she can relax, let down her guard some, and finally begin to recommend "coming back to school" to her neighbors. The growth observable in such women is exciting to watch; it's one of the real pleasures of being in the college environment today.

Revising problem sentences

Exercise 1. Fragments, Run-on Sentences, and Comma Splices

1. Before the snows come, I would like to go to the Appalachian Mountains, where I hear you can still find some authentic banjo-picking.

2. I think I'll ask some friends, like Chip, Joan, and Martha, to go along; we could take turns driving those mountain roads.

3. Charlotte Blackman, who's in my art class, grew up in those hills; let's ask her to come.

4. Keep in mind that we need to find people who really want to listen to bluegrass; it will be an unhappy outing if we ask the wrong folks.

5. Tom O'Hare says that comparing the bluegrass of different regions is one of his hobbies, although I've never seen him at a local festival.

6. I'd vote for taking a chance on Tom; he's good company no matter where he is.

7. Let's leave early on a Saturday morning; everybody should be free then, and we can stop for brunch instead of eating breakfast before we leave.

8. The trip should take about three hours if we don't run into problems driving in the mountains, which could surely happen.

9. We should take some cheese and bread and wine for lunch; you tell Charlotte to bring a treat the mountain people would appreciate.

10. Maybe we could take our own instruments and play some with the mountain people; that could be the best part of our trip.

Exercise 2. Misplaced Modifiers and Dangling Modifiers

The following are *suggested* revisions; revisions will vary.

1. Balcony gardening, to grow both flowers and vegetables, is becoming more and more popular.

2. The couple living just opposite me gardens in pots of several sizes, and their plants grow especially well.

3. This year they have old-fashioned blue morning glories as well as tomatoes, roses, and geraniums, which add a pleasing touch of red to their balcony.

4. While watching my neighbors enjoy their balcony garden, I began to think that I should try my hand at planting something.

5. Having planted petunias without much success last summer, I will grow only vegetables on my balcony this year.

6. To pot-garden successfully, one should use clay or wood pots, which should not be crowded with plants.

7. An attractive small tree for balcony gardens is the orange tree, which bears both fragrant blossoms and colorful miniature fruit.

8. To outdo their neighbors, some people set up small rock gardens on their balconies.

9. Our balcony gardens are beginning to be invaded by insects, which could get to be a real nuisance if they find our houseplants.

10. Maybe I'll just give up on pot-gardening, which is beginning to take up too much of my time, and make a terrarium (a small indoor garden under glass).

Exercise 3. Subject-Verb Agreement

1. Import stores, where you can find a jeweled bracelet or an inlaid card holder or pieces of Asian pottery, all reasonably priced, are a good place to shop for presents.

2. C

3. A group of women I know goes to the import store in a nearby town every fall; once there the group breaks up so that everybody is on her own to circulate and look for treasures.

4. Everyone who rummages around in import stores is almost sure to come up with unexpected treasures.

5. Last year, tucked away in a poorly lighted far corner, were some beautiful bookcovers of Moroccan leather, which Jane Tucker unearthed.

6. C

7. Also in that corner was a collection of hand-painted wooden canes from Switzerland.

8. One of my best import store finds was a large, heavy, ornate marble-topped washstand from England—which I would have bought if I had been driving a truck!

9. Once when I was at an import store, there were some excellent buys still crated in their shipping boxes.

10. Long lines of adults, and now and then a restless child, stand in line waiting for import stores to open each Saturday.

Exercise 4. Noun-Pronoun Agreement and Pronoun Reference

The following are *suggested* revisions; revisions will vary.

1. According to some instructors, anybody can learn to swim if he or she tries hard enough.

2. One of the best ways to make sure all the body gets enough exercise is to learn to swim, which is easy to do at the health clubs found in many towns.

3. People just beginning to swim regularly should not push themselves beyond a comfortable endurance point; doing so might discourage continuing this beneficial exercise.

4. A comfortable suit that does not restrict the swimmer's breathing is a must for swimming, and a cap is required at some clubs.

5. Those who swim regularly often join a health club team. My team won its most satisfying trophy when we all swam in unison during a meet that excluded individual competition. In unison swimming, all the swimmers have to coordinate their movements precisely in order not to interfere with each other's strokes.

Exercise 5. For Proofreading

Shortly after leaving high school, I enlisted in the Navy during the Korean War. Even if I didn't want to die on a battlefield, I felt enough patriotism to want to serve my country. By enlisting I entered on the first of many paths that have shaped my career and my life.

My choice of fire control school after basic training was not a carefully considered decision. Fire control simply sounded like an interesting school, and besides it was the longest in the enlisted man's Navy; it would last for fifty-two weeks of my four-year enlistment. Learning fire control did not mean putting out fires aboard ship. Instead it meant knowing and controlling the radar system by which the guns aboard the ships were fired.

During this long period of learning, I fell in love with and married a local high-school girl. We settled down in her hometown. After my enlistment was over, I enrolled in college, feeling that would be a good way for me to get ahead. I had the G. I. Bill to help me through college, and I knew I would be expected to be the breadwinner in the family in the future. Meanwhile, my wife worked—for a small salary.

I was led onto a path filled with mathematics and weapons by the courses I selected in college as well as by my background. However, going to college on the money from the G. I. Bill and living on my wife's small income meant we had to live frugally. As we set up housekeeping on our meager means, a previously hidden talent in me for building began to emerge.

This discovery sparked an interest totally different from the one I was pursuing in my education. So, young and full of dreams, I left the path of mathematics and weapons for a new path to construction and being independent. Unfortunately, at the same time I started down this path the country went into a deep recession, putting many young hopefuls like me out of business and into debt.

By now my wife had stopped working to have a family, and I became our family's sole support. Fortunately, my background was good, and I had a friend who helped me get a job in the defense business. My college degree had to be postponed, although I never stopped working toward it.

I never forgot the time spent in the building industry. Even though my natural abilities, training, and later my college degree helped me advance in my new career, for me hammering, sawing, nailing, and sweating during the creation of a building held much more satisfaction than solving the critical problems related to my job in defense.

A chance to go back to construction never came along, so I put my energy into my career as a math analyst—a career filled with details, responsibilities, and at times a great deal of mental stress. Since I had time to think on the job, my mind was constantly occupied with the times when I could be building. Building was a rest, an escape, and a pleasure. Although I felt I could no longer begin a new career in construction, I became dissatisfied even with my achievements in my prospering career.

Always thinking of the future and at the same time recalling the past insecurity of my parents, I maintained my position as a math analyst for its retirement benefits instead of venturing out once more into construction. But, like a sailor who counts the days till his enlistment ends, I count the time until I can gain enough independence to try to re-enter my dream occupation. On that final path I expect to be a contented person—but not until I am on that path once again.

Dialect Interference

Exercise 1.

1. considered
2. mentioned
3. died
4. surprised
5. beat

6. changed
7. explained
8. has increased; increased cost
9. walked
10. supposed
11. scared
12. happened
13. talked; tried
14. captured
15. followed; stopped; pulled

Exercise 2.

1. girl's
2. seems
3. illustrates
4. instances
5. Poe's
6. travels
7. gets; likes
8. times
9. farmer's
10. lasts
11. gives
12. people; today's
13. Steve's
14. careers
15. believes; people

Exercise 3.

1. It's or It is
2. you've or you have
3. it's or it is
4. who'd or who would

5. they're or they are
6. he's saying or he is saying
7. He'll or He will
8. she's or she is
9. it's or it is
10. She's or She is

Exercise 4.

1. students
2. dressed
3. Where have you
4. concerned
5. their car
6. children; years
7. keeps
8. an ostrich
9. they'll be or they will be
10. proved
11. Jack's been or Jack has been
12. Students
13. placed; cooked
14. Did your sister win the tennis match?
15. Is there a place
16. methods; shelled
17. found
18. he'll be or he will be
19. writes
20. if it is supposed to rain
21. is sick or has been sick
22. asked
23. doesn't amount to anything
24. fixed; brother's
25. tells

Sources of quoted material

Page

4   James Gould Cozzens, *Time* (September 2, 1957).

4   Toni Morrison, quoted by Mel Watkins, "Talk with Toni Morrison," *New York Times Book Review* (September 11, 1977).

5   Anne Tyler, "Because I Want More Than One Life," *Washington Post* (August 15, 1976), p. G-7.

7   Carson McCullers, *Playbill* (October 28, 1957).

7   Van Wyck Brooks, source unknown.

8   Jacques Barzun, *On Writing, Editing, and Publishing* (Chicago: University of Chicago Press, 1971), p. 12.

9   Barzun, *On Writing,* p. 5.

9   Flannery O'Connor, source unknown.

9   William Carlos Williams, "How to Write," *New Directions in Prose and Poetry,* edited by James Laughlin (New York: New Directions, 1936), p. 45.

9   Virginia Woolf, source unknown.

9   P. G. Wodehouse, *Collier's* (August 31, 1956).

10 Albert van Nostrand, quoted in Edward B. Fiske, " 'Functional Writing' Course Catching On at College Level," *New York Times* (November 24, 1976), p. 59M.

10 William Faulkner, quoted in Donald M. Murray, *A Writer Teaches Writing* (Boston: Houghton Mifflin, 1968), p. 235.

10 Anne Tyler, "Because I Want More Than One Life," *Washington Post* (August 15, 1976), p. G-1.

10 Sinclair Lewis, quoted in Donald M. Murray, *A Writer Teaches Writing* (Boston: Houghton Mifflin, 1968), p. 240.

11 Lancelot Law Whyte, "Where Do Those Bright Ideas Come From?" *Harper's* (July, 1951).

11 Joan Didion, "Why I Write," *New York Times Book Review* (December 5, 1976), p. 2.

11 Henry Miller, *The Wisdom of the Heart* (New York: New Directions, 1941).

Page

11 Anne Tyler, "Because I Want More Than One Life," *Washington Post* (August 15, 1976), p. G-7.

14 Toni Morrison, interviewed by Karen De Witt, *Washington Post* (September 30, 1977), p. C-1.

15 Gene Olson, *Sweet Agony* (Grants Pass, Ore.: Windyridge Press, 1972), p. 35.

24 Ezra Pound, *ABC of Reading* (New York: New Directions, 1960), p. 62.

25 Samuel Johnson, quoted in *Bartlett's Unfamiliar Quotations,* edited by Leonard Louis Levinson (Chicago: Cowles Book Co., 1971), p. 334.

25 Bernard de Voto, source unknown.

25 Louis Brandeis, source unknown.

25 James Michener, source unknown.

25 Ernest Hemingway, quoted in Samuel Putnam, *Paris Was Our Mistress: Memoirs of a Lost and Found Generation* (Carbondale, Ill.: Southern Illinois University Press, 1970).

25 Ben Lucien Berman, quoted in Donald M. Murray, *A Writer Teaches Writing* (Boston: Houghton Mifflin, 1968), p. 232.

25 Dorothy Parker, *Writers at Work: The Paris Review Interviews (First Series),* edited by George Plimpton (New York: Viking Press, 1959), p. 79.

25 John Updike, quoted in Donald M. Murray, *A Writer Teaches Writing* (Boston: Houghton Mifflin, 1968), p. 244.

25 Raphael Hamilton, quoted in an interview by Michael V. Uschan, *Washington Post* (September 4, 1977).

28 John Steinbeck, *John Steinbeck: A Life in Letters,* edited by Elaine Steinbeck and Robert Wallsten (New York: Viking Press, 1975).

29 Jonathan Swift, *On Poetry* (1712).

42 Walker Gibson, *The Limits of Language* (New York: Hill and Wang, 1962), p. 104.

42 Gerald Levin, *Prose Models,* 3rd ed. (New York: Harcourt Brace Jovanovich, 1975), p. 161.

49 Walker Gibson, *Persona,* p. 5.

50 Mary McCarthy, *Writers at Work: The Paris Review Interviews (Second Series),* edited by George Plimpton (New York: Viking Press, 1963), p. 302.

50 Anthony Burgess, *Writers at Work: The Paris Review Interviews (Fourth Series),* edited by George Plimpton (New York: Viking Press, 1976), p. 326.

Page

50 Laurence Sterne, *Tristram Shandy*, II, 1760.

52 Wayne C. Booth, "The Rhetorical Stance," *College Composition and Communication* 14 (1963), p. 139.

53 Elizabeth Bowen, quoted in Donald M. Murray, *A Writer Teaches Writing* (Boston: Houghton Mifflin, 1968), p. 232.

57 Sojourner Truth, "Ain't I a Woman?" in Jacqueline Bernard, *Journey Toward Freedom: The Story of Sojourner Truth* (New York: Grosset & Dunlap, 1967).

57 Imamu Amiri Baraka, "Expressive Language," *Home* (New York: William Morrow, 1966), p. 171.

58 José Ángel Gutiérrez, "Mexicanos Need to Control Their Own Destinies," *Pain and Promise: The Chicano Today*, edited by Edward Simmen (New York: New American Library, 1972), pp. 252–53.

63 Kenneth Turan, "Smokey's Enduring Appeal," *Washington Post* (November 10, 1976), p. B-1.

64 B. D. Colen, "S. Bear, Fire Fighter," *Washington Post* (November 10, 1976), p. B-1.

70 Matthew Arnold, quoted in Donald M. Murray, *A Writer Teaches Writing* (Boston: Houghton Mifflin, 1968), p. 231.

70 *H.E.W. Training Manual #7:* "Getting Your Ideas Across Through Writing," p. 42.

83 Sholem Asch, *New York Herald Tribune* (November 6, 1955).

86 Stuart Chase, "Writing Nonfiction," *On Writing, by Writers*, edited by William W. West (Boston: Ginn, 1966).

90 W. Somerset Maugham, quoted in *A Treasury of Humorous Quotations*, edited by Herbert V. Prochnow and Herbert V. Prochnow, Jr. (New York: Harper and Row, 1969), p. 367.

91 E. B. White, source unknown.

91 Darcy O'Brien, source unknown.

91 Ivan Turgenev, quoted in *The Viking Book of Aphorisms*, edited by W. H. Auden and Louis Kronenberger (New York: Viking Press, 1962), p. 277.

91 Emile Chartier Alain, source unknown.

91 Georges Simenon, source unknown.

91 Henry David Thoreau, *Journals*, July 14, 1852.

91 *Zen Flesh, Zen Bones*, edited by Paul Reps (Garden City, N.Y.: Doubleday), pp. 30–31.

92 Patrick Dennis (Edward Everett Tanner), *Vogue* (February 15, 1956).

93 William James, quoted in *The Viking Book of Aphorisms*, edited

Page

     by W. H. Auden and Louis Kronenberger (New York: Viking Press, 1962), p. 277.

95   George Santayana, quoted in *The Viking Book of Aphorisms,* edited by W. H. Auden and Louis Kronenberger (New York: Viking Press, 1962), p. 332.

102 Donald M. Murray, *A Writer Teaches Writing* (Boston: Houghton Mifflin, 1968), p. 51.

109 Mortimer J. Adler and Charles Van Doren, *How to Read a Book* (New York: Simon and Schuster, 1972), p. 90.

111 Cyril H. Knoblauch, quoted in Edward B. Fiske, " 'Functional Writing' Course Catching On at College Level," *New York Times* (November 24, 1976), p. 59M.

111 Rudolf Flesch, *The Art of Readable Writing* (New York: Collier MacMillan Publishers, 1949), pp. 58–59.

111 Donald M. Murray, *A Writer Teaches Writing* (Boston: Houghton Mifflin, 1968), p. 7.

112 Rudolf Flesch, *The Art of Readable Writing* (New York: Collier MacMillan Publishers, 1949), pp. 58–59.

113 Donald Hall, *Writing Well* (Boston: Little, Brown, 1973), p. 143.

113 Hall, *Writing Well,* p. 144.

128 Anatole France, source unknown.

133 Jo Goodwin Parker, "What Is Poverty?" in *America's Other Children: Public Schools Outside Suburbia* (Norman, Okla.: University of Oklahoma Press, 1971).

143 Henry David Thoreau, "Sunday," *A Week on the Concord and Merrimac Rivers* (1849).

157 Eldridge Cleaver, *Soul on Ice* (New York: Dell, 1968), pp. 6, 18, 38.

159 Joan Didion, "Why I Write," *New York Times Book Review* (December 5, 1976), pp. 2, 98.

160 Mark Twain, source unknown.

161 George Orwell, "Politics and the English Language," *Shooting an Elephant and Other Essays* (New York: Harcourt Brace Jovanovich, 1974).

162 Wallace Stevens, "Adagia," *Opus Posthumous* (New York: Alfred A. Knopf, 1957), p. 169.

165 John O'Hayre, *Gobbledygook Has Gotta Go* (Washington, D.C.: Department of Interior, 1966).

169 Sidney Smith, quoted in *Peter's Quotations,* edited by Laurence J. Peter (New York: William Morrow and Co., Inc., 1977), p. 545.

169 Pliny the Younger, source unknown.

Page

169 William Zinsser, *On Writing Well* (New York: Harper and Row, 1976), p. 6.

170 Oscar Levant, source unknown.

170 Somerset Maugham, quoted in Donald M. Murray, *A Writer Teaches Writing* (Boston: Houghton Mifflin, 1968), p. 240.

170 Abraham Lincoln, source unknown.

170 William Zinsser, *On Writing Well* (New York: Harper and Row, 1976), p. 18.

188 Flannery O'Connor, *Mystery and Manners: Occasional Prose,* edited by Robert and Sally Fitzgerald (New York: Farrar, Straus, and Giroux, 1969), p. 67.

192 Raymond Barrio, *The Plum Plum Pickers* (New York: Harper & Row, 1971).

192 Annie Dillard, *Pilgrim at Tinker Creek* (New York: Bantam Books, 1974).

192 Frank Walters, *The Man Who Killed the Deer* (Chicago: Swallow Press, 1970).

193 *Sappho: A New Translation,* translated by Mary Barnard (Berkeley and Los Angeles: University of California Press, 1966), fragment 3.

207 Ernest Hemingway, *Death in the Afternoon* (New York: Charles Scribner's Sons, 1932), p. 2.

214 Edgar Allan Poe, "The Fall of the House of Usher," *The Rinehart Book of Short Stories,* edited by C. L. Cline (New York: Rinehart and Company, 1952), p. 1.

215 Albert Camus, *The Stranger,* translated by Stuart Gilbert (New York: Alfred A. Knopf, 1946), p. 1.

264 "Sputnik Plus 20: The U.S. on Top," *Newsweek* (October 10, 1977), p. 54.

Index